The Politics of Canadian Urban Development

The Politics of Canadian Urban Development

by David G. Bettison

This is Volume I of a 2-volume work on
Urbanization in Canada, the results of
a study undertaken by D. G. Bettison,
J. K. Kenward, and Larrie Taylor.
Volume II appears under the title
Urban Affairs in Alberta.

Published for the Human Resources
Research Council of Alberta by
The University of Alberta Press
1975

First published by
The University of Alberta Press,
Edmonton, Alberta, Canada

1975

Copyright © 1975 The University of Alberta Press

ISBN 0-88864-008-0

Printed in Canada by
Printing Services of The University of Alberta

Table of Contents

Preface

This study originated with Lorne Downey, Director of the
Human Resources Research Council (HRRC), and his staff in November,
1969, when they called together a variety of persons interested in the
urban affairs of the province of Alberta for a symposium at The
University of Alberta. This symposium explored the prospect of
developing a research capacity in urban studies in Alberta. Papers from
the symposium were edited by Gordon McIntosh, Ian Housego, and
Glenda Lamont and published in 1970 under the title *Urbanization and
Urban Life in Alberta.*

The Human Resources Research Council moved cautiously in
developing such a complex research area and requested that a year
be spent on identifying appropriate research problems before launching
a major project on the urban affairs of the province. The idea that the
most prosperous of the prairie provinces should commit resources to the
study of urban phenomena was novel. Subsequent events, such as
Premier Harry Strom's "Task Force on Urbanization and the Future,"
under Peter Boothroyd as co-ordinator, and the imminent "Urban policy
for Canada" bear witness to the foresight of the council and its staff in
this regard. We regret to note, however, that, following the change of
government in Alberta, in January, 1972, the government announced
that both the Human Resources Research Council and the Task Force
were to be phased out of existence.

An advisory committee on Urban Studies was struck in early
1970 to assist the authors. Our thanks are due to Erwin Adderley,
Executive Director of the Oldman River Regional Planning Commission,
Bruce Proudfoot, Professor of Geography at The University of Alberta,
Jack Snary, Director of Industrial Development, Department of Industry
and Tourism, and R. W. Wright, Dean of Arts and Science at The
University of Calgary for their advice and generously given time during
the study and its subsequent writing. The opinions expressed in this
study, however, are not necessarily their own either individually or
collectively.

The advisory committee agreed in early 1970 to grant limited
financial support to a study of migration and migrants to some of the
smaller towns of the province. This had been a forgotten research topic
amid the rush of migrants to the metropolitan centres of Calgary and
Edmonton in recent decades. Under the guidance of Professor
Proudfoot, Glenda Lamont undertook this study which was presented as

viii

a report to HRRC in 1972 under the title "Migration and small towns in Alberta." We would also acknowledge the assistance of Frank Jankunis of the Department of Geography at The University of Lethbridge for a tour he undertook in the summer of 1970 to gather data on a wide variety of small towns and villages in the province. This study has been made available through the Department of Geography, The University of Lethbridge.

The three authors of this study were asked to undertake a year of inquiry into appropriate research problems. The team was carefully chosen to represent a variety of perspectives. John Kenward is a political scientist with particular interests in community political processes; Larrie Taylor is an architect and town planner with experience in England, Sweden, and Canada; and David Bettison is a sociologist and anthropologist with experience of urban affairs in South Africa, Australia, and elsewhere. The three authors shared their criticism and advice over the whole book; but the task of collecting the evidence and preparing the early drafts was divided so that Larrie Taylor concentrated on Edmonton and the planning facilities of the province; John Kenward on Calgary, the Crowsnest Pass, and other small towns; and David Bettison on the more general nature of federal and provincial matters.

During the writing of this book, the assistance of Lija Bane was obtained to catalogue and put order into the array of research material procured. Throughout most of the work the secretarial and machine calculating duties were willingly performed by Jean Rigaux. Betty Dahl prepared the final draft of the report for submission to HRRC. The co-operation and constructive criticism of all members of the team are warmly acknowledged.

Through generous, continued financial support by the HRRC, it was possible to extend the time of inquiry beyond the initial year. The field work was conducted from April, 1970 to May, 1971, and the writing of this report was extended to the close of 1971. We would like to thank the council for its extended support of our efforts, and The University of Lethbridge for granting David Bettison three-fifths of his time free from teaching duties to undertake the job.

Acknowledgement of the help given us by numerous officers of the provincial administration and many local authorities of the province is little compensation to them for their assistance. Their frankness and honesty bear witness to the openness of governmental institutions in Alberta. Though we cannot say we were given everything we asked for, the co-operation we received was heartening. To many individuals of the province, from Crowsnest Pass to Grande Prairie, we express our gratitude for the many hours spent in discussion with us during field work. Without their interest and support this study would have been impossible because we aimed to discover the situation on the ground, as far as time permitted, as well as to appreciate what official statistics and reports indicated the situation might be. Whatever misinterpretation there may remain in this study is our responsibility, though sorting opinion from fact was not easy. Needless to say, however, this is precisely the situation with which Albertans themselves are concerned, particularly in the development of Alberta's urban culture.

Thanks are due finally to the Government of Alberta for supporting the publication of this book both financially and morally, to The University of Alberta Press for publishing it, and to Stuart Piddocke for editing the manuscript.

David G. Bettison
John K. Kenward
Larrie Taylor
August 1972.

The original purpose of this study was to identify useful research problems associated with urban development in Alberta in order to clear the way for more intensive research in later years. These problems could be identified, however, only if we could forecast the future of urban development in Alberta. To this end the study had to be thoroughly practical, with theory used as a predictive instrument. The research problems had to be relevant to the concerns of future policy makers. Future research could be done at any level of significance, from provincial-federal relations over urban areas to the design of suburban roadways. We decided to tackle those issues which were least likely to receive the sustained attention of the various specialized research units of local authority or provincial departments. We were also aware that the thought behind the establishment of the Human Resources Research Council included "the study of social problems and the analysis of government policies in their relation to the total socio-economic system, rather than on a limited departmentalized basis."[1] We therefore adopted an approach significantly different from the usual method of extrapolating statistics into the future.

Urban phenomena, of whatever kind one chooses, are the outcome of human decisions. People concerned with urban affairs are making decisions about what to do now in the light of their understanding of the present situation and the future they wish to bring about. People differ, however, in their power to shape these futures. A bankrupt farmer who decides to sell out and become a city worker in somebody else's factory and live in a house rented from another owner, is not in the same position to affect Alberta's urban areas as the provincial representative of a large eastern-based lending institution, or the Alberta Minister for Municipal Affairs.[2]

Because this range of power is so wide, one can identify the positions and institutions most likely to influence the future. Only a revolution would disturb this assumption. It is also possible, by analysing the constraints upon the institutions, to assess their probable effect on current and future situations. The implications for public policy may then be discerned by asking the question: if an institution continues to act in this way, or continues to fail to act in a given way, then what is likely to be the outcome?

Some examples will illustrate our approach. The population increase in Calgary and Edmonton (about 5.3 percent per annum in the

5

last decade) is likely to involve these cities in capital expenditures that increase at a faster rate than the population. This costliness, however, will not necessarily oblige councils to limit the influx of new business and employment opportunities. The provincial government may not choose to implement a policy designed to influence such a trend. The city councils may be caught up in a process which they have no power to change. The production of wealth derived from manufacturing and other activities within these cities, wealth which accrues to private companies, may be judged by responsible authorities to exceed the greater public costs of the growth of these cities. The presence of the giant cities in the United States seems proof of this possibility. Conversely, the existence of industrialized and wealthy countries such as Sweden and Switzerland which have not developed the "uncontrolled" type of metropolis, suggests that there is no necessary reason for doing so.[3] The question is therefore to identify the institutions whose management decisions contribute to the growth of the "uncontrolled" metropolis and to ask which other institutions may be used to support or to diminish the process.

The smaller towns of Alberta, whose rate of population growth or decline has not been conspicuous in recent decades, provide another example. Many small towns have built excellent public amenities from water and sewerage facilities to ice rinks, parks, and swimming pools. But this public investment does not necessarily attract extensive private investment. Private companies prefer to locate where their management and employees have pleasant surroundings and amenities only if their assessment of the relative advantages of other sites is less favorable. But when the exploitation of natural resources or the obtaining of some governmental incentive handout makes it necessary to locate in some run-down little town, or even where there is no town at all, private investment readily adapts to the problems of its location.

How, then, may well-serviced small towns attract and benefit from additional private investment? A great deal is now being done by their citizens and by the provincial government to promote interest in these towns on the assumption that "development" is a matter of local initiative and that the provincial government's continued obligation to them is to treat all on a "fair equal" basis. In many towns the public "development" has already been done; the problem is rather one of getting companies to recognize the towns in preference to following the lead of their competitors and peers into Calgary and Edmonton.

There are many adverse factors in the major cities which could change company policy — factors such as city blight, rush-hour congestion, and high taxes and costs. There are also other factors which could change company policy, such as public and governmental identification of certain small towns for deliberate stimulation and the investment of public money by establishing regional headquarters of government departments in them. Yet this is not done overtly, in part because of the outcry that would follow from the residents of other towns who had not received the apparently favored treatment, and in part because of the political hazards likely to befall any party with courage enough to announce such a policy publicly. Calgary's and Edmonton's business and city leaders would be quick to appreciate the threat such actions would represent to their interests. Yet the federal government, in so far as it is constitutionally able, has adopted a policy that would have that result. If the well-serviced small towns of Alberta are serious about their continued existence and their potential for growth, policy issues of an unpleasant kind will shortly need to be made. In the present situation, perhaps wrongly in terms of their own long-term future, Calgary and Edmonton will offer little help.

These examples should make clear the perspective adopted in this study. Our emphasis is on human decisions and behavior. We have avoided abstracting human, cultural, and social affairs into quantifiable models. Such models have to be given an artifical anthropomorphic quality and energy of their own, derived from no explicit source, which blinds the observer to the fundamentally political nature of urban affairs. These models also conveniently preserve much of the anonymity of the important decision-makers in the urban process.

We are conscious that our study may do very little to help many decision-makers to improve their decisions by providing more "hard data" to place in their computers. The 1970s are years in which immensely consequential policy decisions will be made concerning the urban affairs of Canada. The Canadian constitutional issues, Mr. Andras's "urban policy for Canada," the request of the Canadian Federation of Mayors and Municipalities for "partnership" status of the cities with provincial and federal governments, the similar requests of American cities for state status, the ever expanding influence of automated production processes on unemployment, and the struggles of government to work out a satisfactory "welfare" system for individuals, are only some of the historically significant issues of our times. We believe that this period will go down in history as the turning point of many past trends. It is not, therefore, a time for studies which merely provide additional hard data to perpetuate current trends or to perfect the status quo. It is rather a time when the impact of decisions taken both outside and inside the province should be assessed and turned to good account for the longer-term interests of Alberta. To some extent it is a time for deciding in what ways and to what extent Albertans may be prepared to swim against the tide and create for themselves a genuinely Albertan type of urban culture. This study was done with these possibilities in mind.

The Scope of the Study

Alberta has been a province of Canada since 1905. As the farthest west of the prairie provinces, it was for many decades the last frontier of settlement and development from eastern Canada. Calgary and Edmonton might be considered the newest of Canadian provincial cities, for when the lower Fraser Valley in British Columbia was attracting business from Victoria, Alberta's cities were little more than police and trading posts. Their development can only be understood as part of the overall development of Canada.

The book is therefore divided into two volumes. Volume 1, *The Politics of Canadian Urban Development*, discusses the evolution of federal government policy concerning regional economic development programs, the National Housing Acts, municipal development funds, slum clearance, urban renewal, and the question of an urban policy for Canada. Our purpose is to analyse federal urban policy since 1935, a matter strangely neglected in studies of Canadian society.[4] Even as recently as May 1971, Robert Andras, then the federal minister responsible for housing, remarked in Indianapolis:

> Two years ago even the federal government had not realized the tremendous impact that its activities had upon the cities of the nation. Our urban study documented 117 federal programs operating through 27 departments and agencies of the federal government which have a direct effect on the shape and growth of Canadian cities. And although this fact may have not been news to some in Canada, it was a startling revelation to all governments.[5]

Volume 1 attempts (1) to examine the steps taken by the federal government with regard to rural and urban development in Canada, and their implications for the provinces and their governments; and (2) to identify the trend that these federal steps appear to be taking, and thus permit the provincial governments, especially that of Alberta, to be aware of what the immediate future may hold. Chapter 1 discusses rural and regional degredation. Since there are several books of substantial merit on this subject, the topic is treated generally. Chapters 2 through 5 consider the urban centres with particular reference to housing, the lending institutions, urban renewal, and similar matters. Chapter 6 examines the new "urban policy for Canada" and the studies which led to its formulation. The final chapter attempts to identify the direction of federal measures and to offer some conclusions.

Volume II, *Urban Affairs in Alberta,* describes the relationships among the important institutions of the province which mold the way cities, towns, and villages expand or decline. The important institutions of the province can be identified as private companies and corporations with their immense investment potential; the provincial government and its agencies such as the Alberta Municipal Financing Corporation, the Alberta Housing and Urban Renewal Corporation, and the Alberta Commercial Corporation; the local governments of the metropolitan cities, towns and rural districts, and their agencies and associations such as the regional planning commissions, school boards, and the associations of urban municipalities and rural districts. Besides these organized institutions, however, there are other influences which modify the effects of governments and their agencies. The freedom of private companies and individual citizens to move across Canada with little regard for provincial or municipal boundaries is one such influence. Another is the attitude of residents whether in small or large towns to the developments in their midst. The jealousy of local authority councils towards their competitors for benefits from provincial coffers or from private investment, the strict approach of the provincial government towards local authorities as expressed in "fair and equal" treatment, and the province's reluctance to get involved in local affairs, are examples of facts and policies that strongly affect urban affairs in Alberta. Volume II of the study was intended to identify at least some of these other influences and to trace their effects on the urban development process of the province.

Volume II proceeds from the general to the particular. After examining some unique aspects of Alberta, this part considers the provincial instruments of physical and financial planning in so far as they have influenced, or failed to influence, industrialization and the growth of metropolitan and urban areas. Planning in this sense directs an existing process rather than proposing a new process for the achievement of a goal. Edmonton (Chapter 4) and Calgary (Chapter 5), the two metropolitan centres of Alberta, are studied next. Together these cities contain about 55 percent of the provincial population; their growth in the past decade has been rapid even by North American standards, and they show interesting contrasts in policy concerning their respective hinterlands. Particular attention is paid in this section to predictions, cost, and planning implications of capital expansion.

The conclusion draws together matters discussed and identifies research problems which appear to be the most useful for the years ahead.

The Relative Inconsequence of Provincial
Decisions on Urban Affairs

Decisions made by the provincial government have much less effect on urban affairs in Alberta than decisions made outside the province. This situation arises, on the one hand, from the relationships between Alberta and the other Canadian provinces to the federal government and to the internationally organized coporations or national companies; and on the other, from the relationships between the provincial government and local authorities within the province. Inevitably the provincial government's influence is greater within the province, but because local authorities are the creation of the provincial legislature, one should not assume that Alberta's cities, particularly Calgary and Edmonton, are the creation of the provincial government. The broad limits of provincial legislation, the grants and fiscal amenities of the province, do have some importance; but the city is a creature of forces that transcend all lévels of government.

The relative inconsequence of provincial decisions is not a fixed or predetermined phenomenon. It varies with the influence of Alberta on the governments and companies with which the province relates. This influence in turn depends upon changing circumstances in North America, in Canada, and in Alberta itself. Governments and company managements continually review the world with which they interact and, as part of this review, assess the resources they possess for coping with certain situations. The British North America Act of 1867, through the responsibilities it allocates to provincial and federal governments, perhaps has been one of the greatest long-term steadying influences, but the way this Act has been maneouvered by the federal government since 1935 demonstrates the flexibility of even entrenched agreements. Alberta has almost a tradition of opposition to external influences, whether financial or governmental. This opposition has been tempered since the Leduc oil strike of 1947; but since about 1964, the relation of provinces generally to the federal government appears to have turned increasingly in the provinces' favor. As metropolitan city areas accommodate more of the Canadian population, the provinces have been able to oppose or influence federal policies more strongly.

Concurrently this metropolitan pressure has become directed against provincial governments, and metropolitan governments have come to use the federal government increasingly in their struggle with the provinces. To the chagrin of local governments the Canadian constitution grants to the provinces the responsibility now sought by cities. Mr. Andras's urban policy for Canada might be interpreted as a last ditch stand to retain for the federal government the kind of influence over urban development it has enjoyed for the past thirty-five years. One of the consequences of our study might be to open up new ways for the Alberta government to influence the federal government.

Urban affairs are heavily affected by past arrangements which have entrenched certain institutions in positions that enable them to determine the future. The way the Alberta government responded to outside influences in the past has its inevitable consequence for the present; in fact, many contemporary policy decisions are responses to past events whose consequences are felt now and will be felt in the future.

A further constraint on provincial decision-making arises from the economy. If expanding industrial enterprises look for sites in which to locate, they will consider incentives offered them by the various provinces and local authorities. Inducements such as direct financial assistance, tax holidays, and cheap serviced industrial land offered by provinces other than Alberta will affect firms' decisions to locate, and Alberta will be required to step up its own inducements. This competitive situation within which the provinces of Canada are obliged to conduct their affairs produces, in part, the relative inconsequence of local decisions.

The decision-making powers of companies and corporations[6] are even more important then the incentives provided by governments in determining where firms will locate. When a management considers whether or not to invest in Alberta, it examines Alberta's facilities and opportunities. The firm's investment will be designed deliberately either to meet the Alberta situation — the demand for its products and the opportunity of sales within the province — or use that situation for other purposes that it may have in mind, such as the sale of Alberta gas and oil in the United States.

Corporations may easily transfer liquid assets and resources across national or provincial boundaries, and they increasingly do so. Their activities can be concentrated or dispersed, or totally removed as by the sale of their possessions, with an ease and indifference that a government could not contemplate.[7] While a government adopts a protective, considerate perspective towards those it governs, a corporation can be exploitive and demanding to the limits of the law. Management therefore enjoys considerable freedom to select the community in which it invests. Management regards this freedom as a right held sacred to itself; it is respected by governments which guarantee the conditions necessary to compete with other companies and corporations. This right is, as it were, a *quid pro quo* for the risk carried by a corporation. It is one of the essential attributes of what is popularly called the "competitive system." No government in Canada claims an unfettered right to decide where a company or corporation will locate, though all are able to influence that decision. That decision is the prerogative of management after considering the pros and cons of possible sites, the legislated incentives available to it, and the arrangements it may negotiate with different authorities.

The instruments used by government to influence the decisions of corporate management include, at one extreme, outright prohibitions backed by punitive sanction for offences such as failing to register as a company or contravening pollution regulations; and, at the other extreme, gifts to corporations and companies in the form of incentive grants, subsidized industrial land, tax concessions, and the like. Between these two extremes are what may be called "negotiable provisions."

These negotiable provisions in turn take many forms. Public services provided by a local authority or province, such as water supply, electricity, or road access, at given quantities and standards, are negotiated by management. A priority of their supply in terms of the corporation's needs may be arranged. These negotiable provisions tend to become formalized in legally supported procedures laid out in advance by regulation or legislation, or to be subject to the formal approval of a statutory authority. Negotiable provisions are not *ad hoc* gestures. They are regarded by local authorities as their part in the provision of an essential service. They always carry explicit social approval, formality, and an air of public consent.

The formal prohibitions, the inducements and gifts, and the negotiable provisions provide the limitations and opportunities which the company and corporate management must consider. But having considered them and having negotiated terms with a variety of places, a company or corporation reserves to itself the right of final decision on location. It decides in terms of the deals it may make with a variety of authorities and localities. These deals are carefully prepared and involve contractual agreements among the parties.

Corporations engaged in the extraction of primary resources, such as minerals, gas, and timber stands, have assumed an increasing importance in Alberta. These corporations are obliged to locate at least the extractive component of their plant at the resource site. In 1930 the federal government transferred all mineral rights, except those in National Parks and on Indian reservations, to the Alberta government, which now owns some 81 percent of the mineral rights in the province.[8]

Primary resource development requires that leases and other rights to operate and the terms of the operation must be negotiated directly with the Alberta government. These negotiations can be protracted, and the corporation moves slowly from step to step as it demonstrates by research the feasibility of the final operations. This process is undertaken through a series of options made available to the corporation by legislation or by agreements with the government that involve time limits. Though these timing restrictions act as regulators on the corporation, they also imply the right of the corporation to decline to proceed further with the project it had intended. Agreements ensure to corporate management the right to move deliberately and cautiously within prescribed but previously negotiated terms. It is a tacit understanding of all parties that the corporation is bound, in theory, to produce a product at a price it cannot itself wholly determine. Corporate management thus reserves to itself the right to flexibility of decision, even though the location of its operation is fixed. Only when the management has given up its right to a lease, or fails to continue negotiation, is the government freed from its obligation to that corporation and only then may it offer the resource to another corporation.

The sensitive nature of these negotiations is evident from the long time they take and from the secrecy which surrounds them. The agreement between the Alberta government and the Buckeye Cellulose Corporation, a division of Proctor and Gamble Co., of Cincinnati, concerning an $80 million paper plant near Grande Prairie, was announced suddenly in 1971, although it was reported that studies made by the Corporation and the government had taken more than three years.[9] Such agreements may be given social significance by being made public simultaneously or by being accompanied by some ceremonial gesture.[10]

Manufacturing enterprises have more freedom to manoeuvre. Apart from legal details such as the provincial registration of a company, the management of a manufacturing company or a commercial enterprise negotiates largely with the local authority in whose jurisdiction it may wish to locate. These negotiations can become protracted if the company or corporation is unable to procure the site it wants on land suitably zoned for the purpose and meeting all the regulations of the local authority. Most frequently, however, the decision to locate is made within six months of the decision to search for a suitable location.[11]

The flexibility of decision possessed by companies and corporations extends to managements' choice of location among the provinces of Canada, or even among countries. The consequence is that Canada, in all of its provinces and its large number of local authorities, seeks to attract business from outside local jurisdictions. Provinces and local authorities also foster the growth of already existing businesses and encourage the starting of new ones by local residents.

Since 1935 when the Dominion Housing Act was passed, the federal government has opted increasingly to work with private financial and industrial companies and corporations to solve national urban problems. This association with lending institutions has been substantially responsible for the concentration of housing in the large cities, and has contributed to the decay of vast rural regions throughout settled Canada. As recently as 1969 the federal government turned to companies and corporations to help it with industrial development in run-down regions in every province of Canada.

This collaboration of the federal government with private capital has reduced the ability of the provinces to determine their own affairs.[12] The means to circumvent the constitutional authority of the provinces of Canada was provided by the right of the federal government to contract with private companies, which in turn have always been granted the right to choose the location of their investment and to contract with individual citizens or other companies. In the case of housing, the individual citizen seeking a mortgage loan for his house would be accommodated by a lending institution only if he intended to build where, in the opinion of the lending institution, the money loaned would be secure.

In 1947 Central Mortgage and Housing Corporation (CMHC) was given powers to counter this tendency by accepting responsibility for direct loans to individual borrowers, particularly in small towns and rural areas. In the case of industrial incentives, provincial and national policies have tended to work against each other, thereby providing industry with added opportunities to negotiate.

The Alberta government struggled hard to cope with the effects of the power afforded lending institutions throughout the latter part of the 1930s. In 1939 the Honourable E. C. Manning remarked in a speech on the budget:

> every outstanding Act passed by the people's duly elected representatives in this legislature which challenged that financial monopoly and claimed for the citizens of Alberta the right to exercise some measure of control over matters so vital to their welfare, has been either disallowed by the federal government or declared *ultra vires* by the courts.[13]

More recently, the influence of the federal government in directing industrial investment in terms of its view of national and regional needs is demonstrated by the distribution-by-province of the estimated capital cost of approved industrial innovations under the 1969 Industrial Incentives Act (see Table 1.)

Nova Scotia, Quebec, and Ontario have been the chief beneficiaries of this legislation[14] which was intended to assist the degraded areas of the country and was an elaboration, with some important differences, of 1961 legislation that benefited the Maritime provinces especially.

The federal government is no longer concerned with the application of legislated measures to all parts of the country on a basis of "fair and equal" treatment. National problems, as they are identified in Ottawa, are treated by measures that discriminate in terms of need and region. As the case of the Maritimes shows, the provinces that work

TABLE 1. Distribution by province of the estimated capital cost of approved innovations under the Industrial Incentives Act, January to December, 1970*.

Nova Scotia	$110,133,385
Quebec	108,542,980
Ontario	70,707,078
New Brunswick	17,450,584
Manitoba	16,139,077
Alberta	13,342,332
Saskatchewan	5,112,993
Newfoundland	2,847,386
Prince Edward Island	2,828,328
British Columbia	1,729,064

*Compiled from the monthly reports of the Department of Regional Economic Expansion, Ottawa.

closest with Ottawa get the attention; as Quebec shows, the province that threatens Ottawa also gets the attention; and in the case of Ontario, the province that supplies most of the tax revenue is obviously not forgotten.

Ironically, this attempt to compensate for regional underdevelopment was adopted in response to the centralization inherent in the growth of the major cities. Only government, through its powers of taxation, can extract urban-generated wealth and redistribute it to impoverished regions, if private companies do not wish to pursue such a policy themselves. Private companies prior to 1969, when the federal Regional Development Incentives Act was passed, had no effective incentive to invest and operate in degraded rural regions. Local urban authorities were demanding more and more money to generate and sustain public services. Larger contracts for increasingly bigger jobs could be expected as cities grew. The concentration of population provided greater prospects for sales and turnover. The case presented by city authorities for more money rested both on increasing populations and the raising of standards of service to meet the greater expectations of private business, expectations generated by the increasing rationalisation of production and service. As resources were concentrated, jobs per unit of output declined; but the overall diversification of the urban economy and the growth of the personal service industry, best identified through education, ensured the overall growth of job opportunities in urban areas. The contrast between neglect in rural areas and opportunities in urban centres obliged country people, particularly the youth of both sexes, to give up rural assets and migrate to the metropolitan areas. This in turn strengthened the case of city governments for yet more public funds to meet population increases; increases which enlarged the pool of labor available to employers, increased the effective demand of consumers for manufactured products, and also increased the demand for loans by individuals and companies from lending institutions. The vicious circle of metropolitan and urban expansion was set in motion at an ever increasing velocity. International migration in recent decades further added to metropolitan claims. Only in the 1960s did the federal government devise a deliberate policy to cope with the relation of urban growth to regional degradation. Earlier actions were more attempts to ameliorate rural distress than counter-measures to curb a process that had been increasingly visible over many decades. The early measures taken through the National Housing Act sought only to relieve depression unemployment (with useful results in the form of new housing for Canadians) and to encourage lending institutions so that the savings of Canadians might be put into mortgages. These measures were expected to encourage city growth and amenities for manufacturing industry. They were part of a policy that assured higher total and per capita incomes from manufacturing rather than agriculture and conformed to the general worldwide industrial and urban trend. By 1961 the disparity between the circumstances of individual Canadians in metropolitan and degraded regions led the federal government to reconsider the practical consequences of its earlier measures.[15]

The aim of the federal government since the inception of the Agricultural Rehabilitation and Development Act (ARDA) in 1961 was to obtain a "parity of income" and an equalization of opportunity between the cities and the regions they impoverished. The federal government assumed that governmental help must be given to those below a defined minimum of wellbeing, while those who were well-off could continue to look after themselves. To achieve this end, the government was obliged to make grants to encourage companies and corporations to locate in the designated regions, as well as to inject billions of dollars of public money in other ways.[16]

The right to decide where to locate afforded to private companies and corporations since before Confederation, has contributed more than any other influence to the concentration of energy and resources in the major cities. The urban growth process has long been recognized, though authorities differ on the emphasis they ascribe to parts of the process and on the cause-effect chain they identify.

In a chapter entitled "The Source of the Urban Problem," N. H. Lithwick has described the process of growth as follows:

> We have argued that growth is dependent on technological change, capital formation in human and physical forms, and the development of markets. All these processes are made feasible, and indeed are optimized, in an urban environment. Where population is dense, access to markets is greatest, labour supplies are plentiful; specialization, a key source of improvement, is made possible; information flows — essential to innovation, education and efficiency in general — are highly developed. All these elements make possible a rise in productivity and *thus in income,* and the cycle is completed through consequent increased savings. As a result of this process, higher rates of capital formation are made possible. Increased spending out of higher incomes also accelerates the rate of growth of marekts, raises profits and thus savings, improves potential profitability of new investments, and introduces further technological

improvements. Cities, then, are what make modern economic systems work . . . [17]

This description makes no mention of the influence of government on the growth process. Growth is seen as if its conditions for existence were self-contained within the variables identified as contributing to it. Yet there is undeniably a relation between the growth process and the local, metro, provincial, and federal governments in whose jurisdiction it occurs.

In recent decades growth and industrialization have been characterized by an increasing concentration in particular and readily identifiable places — the very thing that makes the "modern economic system work," as Lithwick remarks. This identification of growth centres has always existed in Canada, starting with the ports. In Alberta, Calgary and Edmonton were identified as growth centres even before the railroad crossed the prairies in 1882-83. The pre-eminence and concentration associated with secondary industry since World War II has markedly affected the competitive relation of the governments.

The federal government has been concerned to maintain the economic growth of the nation in relation to what was happening outside Canada, and to devise ways of coping with impoverishment of people and the degrading of physical property whether in town or country. Other interests were left, constitutionally, to other levels of government. The provinces' prime concern was the administration of its internal affairs which included authority over local government. Provincial governments were also left the task of meeting the needs of their individual citizens by way of education, health services, and public planning of the general environment.

City municipal government, in so far as it accepts the governmental role that private investment would otherwise be obliged to perform at the location of its physical plant, is the government most closely related to private investment. Provincial governments are relatively remote, and in so far as investment is organized interprovincially, of secondary importance. Provincial governments are secondary also in the sense that it is the federal government, and not the provincial, that determines national economic policy. If a provincial government adopts policies that hurt private investment — as indeed Alberta did in the late 1930s by assuming the right to establish finance institutions and lay down the terms under which external lending institutions could operate in Alberta, such companies move elsewhere and the federal government becomes obliged to disallow such activities of a provincial government. The province, therefore, can do little more than provide the general framework within which companies and municipal governments must arrange their affairs. This framework sets limits and guidelines; but it is not an effective control over what may or may not take place within provincial boundaries.

Provincial governments maintain power to control activity in the areas they have kept under direct jurisdiction, but their control over factors that determine city growth and rural regional degradation is limited. A provincial government may decline to influence, beyond

16

the limits of its overall regulatory guidelines on such matters as physical planning, the process of city growth. It could continue to meet the needs of individual citizens without regard to the form of their employment or the extent of their spatial concentration. The Alberta government since World War II has tended to opt for such a policy, though it has undertaken to encourage the centralization of educational and specialist medical services. In distributing revenue from natural resource royalties, it has chosen to apply a per capita rule of distribution to local authorities rather than to use this money with deliberate intent either to stimulate rural regions relative to the metropolitan cities or vice versa. This rule was part of the provincial policy of "fair and equal" treatment for all. But to the extent that lending institutions preferred to concentrate investment in major cities, the provincial government's policy could not stimulate rural and small town growth. Through the 1971 Industrial Development Act, the Alberta government sought to stimulate existing and new industries in towns of under 40,000 population and where the establishment, expansion, or modernization of an industry could not be accomplished through federal measures. This Act is used more to counterbalance the advantages accruing to those towns designated by the federal government as eligible for industrial incentives under federal measures than to counter the growth tendency of Alberta's metropolitan centres. The board established under the Act, however, is given wide discretionary powers.

Slum clearance and providing the poor with housing display a similar set of circumstances up to 1964. The National Housing Act from its inception in 1938 expressed federal concern in this area and has offered a continually expanding financial service to provincial governments to encourage them to act in an area that was constitutionally theirs. Until 1970 the provincial response was negligible and many federal ministers responsible for housing explained away their difficulties by reference to provincial unwillingness to move in this obvious area of need. But provincial governments were only vicariously responsible for the municipal poor because they had delegated to local authorities the right and duty to plan and care for their local citizenry. Provincial governments could be accused of interfering in the affairs of city municipalities if they imposed sanctions on them to improve the lot of the city poor by measures costly to the ratepayers. Provincial government interest in the social welfare of individuals, beyond education and health, improved greatly when the concept of insured risk against inevitable events, such as the Canada Pension Plan, became accepted. This concept gave to the provinces a substantial annual premium for long term investment in the public facilities it wished to provide. The concept was different from the conditional grants the federal government had hitherto provided to be spent on specific public facilities.

The cost-sharing agreements that typified federal-provincial financial relations during the 1960s were aimed at providing the services required by the Canadian people on a national basis, while at the same time recognizing provincial constitutional rights. The federal government tended to set the standards of service and paid its part towards the costs. Because by this time populations were predominantly urban, a major proportion of such expenditures was made in urban areas. High standards and specialized services became increasingly typical of cities rather than of rural towns, a factor which in turn obliged rural residents increasingly to use city-based services to meet their needs. The pre-eminence of cities as centres that met the full range of human needs was reinforced by cost-sharing agreements arranged between the senior levels of government. Even national highways linked one metropolitan area to another, and in so doing they provided a valuable service to the metropolitan centres at each end, but only an improved standard of road for the rural regions in between. Though everyone benefited from cost-sharing agreements, the cities benefited more than the rural regions.

When the federal government acted decisively through the Regional Development Incentives Act of 1969 to set the pace for rural regional rejuvenation, it did so not through provincial governments but through locational incentives to private manufacturing industry. As it had already done in 1935 by using private lending institutions to finance housing and reduce unemployment through the Dominion Housing Act, the federal government turned to private investment to cope with the problem. Only in the Maritimes, apparently, had the provinces been sufficiently co-operative to be used as the effective instrument of regional rejuvenation. It may not be coincidental that, apart from the Halifax-Dartmouth region, there are no metropolitan areas in the Maritimes.[18] The large and persistent rates of growth of metropolitan areas have tended to exhaust the resources and consume the attention of provincial governments, while provincial governments have become increasingly threatened politically by the metropolitan areas they have succored. These concentrations are the wealthiest tax resource and therefore a powerful political influence.

The Department of Regional Economic Expansion (DREE) program has tended to use the same instrument, private manufacturing investment, but with a considerable public service facility to support it if required. The urban policy for Canada has thus far worked at the level of seeking public (that is, governmental) co-ordination. The role of private investment, in the data so far published at least, has scarcely been identified. The Minister of State for Urban Affairs, and Dr. Lithwick, have made only casual reference to the need for more concerted direction of private investment with public goals. This will surely be a subject of major provincial government concern in future tri-level governmental conferences, for it lies at the very heart of the relative inconsequence of provincial government decisions over urban affairs.

The Municipal-Provincial Political Threat

The Canadian Federation of Mayors and Municipalities (CFMM) presented a position paper to the Ministers of Municipal Affairs, meeting in Winnipeg in August, 1970, making a case for increased governmental powers for local authorities.[19] This paper

18

argued that Canada has become an urban society but urban governments have been denied sufficiently responsive revenue sources with which to meet the costs implicit in the role they must now play, and are dominated by the province.[20] The Joint Municipal Committee on Intergovenmental Relations, which prepared the position paper, remarked:

> The growing complexities of the modern industrial state (in the creation of which local government has had little say) have generated many interrelationships among governments and between governments and the people.[21]

Later the committee elaborated as follows:

> The situation has not been made easier by the fact that over the years, especially since the war, both national and provincial policies have acted upon the local structure directly or indirectly so that the local authorities have had at least some of the burden but only limited initiative, influence or control. Policies in health, welfare, transportation, housing and education are typical of this. At the same time the increasing pressures have resulted in the growth of local policies and activities, especially in the larger municipalities, which have had and will continue to have influences which spread far beyond their political limits. This influence can be weighed in the fact that there are municipal governments today with budgets larger than all but the wealthier provinces.[22]

The position paper argues that local authorities can no longer remain bystanders to something that in the past was a matter of provincial-federal relations. The larger municipalities through their policies and actions "can influence the trend of events in the broader area of the provincial and the national scene."[23] The committee argued:

> Under the existing rules of the game, urban centres, whether organized as such or merely the regional conglomeration of separate municipal authorities, have no recognition of their status consistent with their economic and social influence in the country. In many respects they are regarded in the same way as the township or the rural district, and in the last analysis are still dependent on the good-will or the good sense of a legislature (or perhaps more accurately, a government caucus) dominated in nearly every province by rural representation. Time, custom and the courts have altered the original federal-provincial relationship beyond recognition.[24]

The political aspect of the committee's paper is clearly demonstrated in its insistence on the domination of provincial

19

governments. In a very questionable preamble, wherein it remarks "It is difficult today to escape from the reiterated claim that the provinces are the primary and essential element in the whole fiscal, economic, political and social structure of Canada," the committee points out that the position of the local authority is demonstrated by its subordinate legislative existence:

> An examination of almost any of the provincial acts governing municipalities will indicate that the provinces apparently believe in their own infallibility where municipalities are concerned, regardless of the size or competence of the local government. The attitude, more often than not, is that of prohibition rather than of guidance and support, of domination rather than partnership.[25]

Later the same point was made:

> ... it is an inescapable fact that any successful intergovernmental relation is going to have to be achieved through partnership rather than through a process of subordination.[26]

The committee also argued that the urban rather than the rural municipalities demand urgent attention. The inevitability of "the direction of the forces of change," the increasing urban population concentration, and the relatedness of responsibility already existing among the levels of government were seen as the key factors that support the case of the urban centres. The paper said, in effect, that the urban municipalities have been caught up in a process they were not responsible for, but for which they are provided too inflexible a source of revenue.

This disavowal of responsibility for urban growth seems to neglect such facts as the subsidy on serviced industrial land offered by many local authorities or on advertising for local investment by companies, and the jealous claims of mayors about their cities and the possible deleterious consequence of regional development on them. Calgary, for example, is not slow in relating itself to Edmonton or noting the growth of meat canning in Lethbridge. Their actions, however, are not merely a mad rush for growth for its own sake, though indeed they take on that appearance. Rather it is the behavior of responsible mayors and businessmen whose public and private investments are dependent upon ever-expanding city or market growth. They have committed themselves to investment that, were it not for continued growth, the taxpayer or shareholder increasingly would have to pay. The solution municipal governments seek is the removal of their legal dependency relation to provincial governments. This is a political answer to a problem formulated in financial and status terms.

The case of the Federation of Mayors and Municipalities rests on its claim to put right a *fait accompli*, not to ask for the intercession of the provincial government in a process to which it has been secondary for so long. Their case further increases the relative inconsequence of provincial decisions. As an immediate practical step, the committee recommends:

> Until a more fully developed institutional framework can be devised, the recognition by the senior governments of the right of the municipalities to be consulted in all matters directly affecting their interests would be a great significant step forward.[27]

Representation of municipal interest is envisaged as through the provincial association of mayors and municipalities on matters of provincial concern and through the Federation of Mayors and Municipalities on national matters, with appropriate subordinate arrangements for matters of common concern to particular municipalities being dealt with by those affected. Whatever the method used it is important, in the committee's judgements, that it be understood and accepted; and thereby raise the significance of urban government from that of "an administrative tool" to governmental partnership. It recognized the benefit of retaining the provincial authorities "as a co-ordinating and guiding instrument, something entirely aside from their basic legal responsibility."[28]

The real nature of the political component is seen in two suggestions: the grant system by senior levels of government to local authorities, and a change in the Canadian constitution that would re-arrange the status of urban areas.

After admitting that "there are very real limits" to the municipal use of individual and corporate tax and sales tax, the committee identified three general types of grant that could be used to assist local authorities in their financial difficulties: conditional grants, unconditional grants, and shared revenue sources. Conditional grants, the committee notes, "are open to the objection so often made by the provinces to their restriction of authority and their influence on priorities," and it concludes that "they should not be a predominant element in intergovernmental relations."[29] The advantages of the unconditional grant are stated as follows:

> . . . they do leave the choice of alternative policies to the recipient rather than to the benefactor. However, it would not be realistic to regard them as the whole answer as they remain a mechanism of control for the senior governments in the matter of their size, the method of their distribution, and, of course, their continuing existence.[30]

The method preferred is the sharing of individual and corporate tax and sales tax according to some predetermined formula which "would be the logical approach." That this raises the issues of management of the economy in general and decision over the relative priorities of the different levels of government is admitted by the committee, but it falls back on a very questionable argument — "if an effective

21

municipal role in government as we know it is not worth preserving then perhaps we should consider alternatives."[31] No alternative is considered.[32] If by this sentence the committee means that urban municipalities do not play an important role in government it has forgotten its own evidence. On the other hand, the committee is intent on recommending a change in its role, so that urban government would be very different, and not "as we know it" at all.

The question of basic constitutional change was introduced by an assertion of its inevitability. The committee remarked:

> Changes in Canadian social, economic and political organization, stimulated by the increasing demands of urbanization will soon, we believe, make new approaches to the fundamental questions of governmental organization and structure inevitable.[33]

The committee noted that the process of urbanization, by which it meant urban concentration, was proceeding in Canada at the fastest rate of any developed country and gave the Economic Council of Canada estimates that by 1980, 81 percent of the total population will be in urban communities, with 60 percent in cities of 100,000 population or more.[34] The committee elaborated its claim for a constitutional review by reference to forecasts such as, "Some people even foresee a time when a majority of the population will be concentrated in several large metropolitan areas, with only a small minority scattered throughout the broad regions of rural Canada,"[35] though it was wisely reluctant to base its case on such hypotheses. Nevertheless, mentioning these forecasts, statistical projections of past trends, without reference to the governmental policies that have contributed to them is to use the supposition of inevitability derived from mathematical mechanics rather than from human and social dynamics. The committee's recommendations in turn, would contribute substantially to the very situation the use of mathematical mechanics predicts. The issue is without doubt the nub of major political questions now before the country.

The committee indicated its indignation at not being party to the steps already taken for consideration of the political issues. It noted that in 1967 the need for a special study of urban development was recognized in the federal Speech from the Throne, and that a three-level government study would be initiated. It continued:

> Three years later the only accomplishment of these stated intentions seems to have been an unsatisfactory federal-provincial conference on housing and the formation of the little known "Intergovernmental Committee on Urban and Regional Research" in which the municipalities are not even represented. The municipal level of government for all practical purposes is still excluded from any realistic involvement in matters in which it is inevitably concerned and from discussions of the basic issues of public policy.

We can only presume that vested provincial political interests and federal constitutional timidity have worked to preserve the existing situation.[36]

The committee concluded by expressing its belief "that a full and objective consideration of the whole question of the municipal role is fundamental to any successful examination of Canadian federalism."[37]

Premier H. E. Strom, representing the position of the Alberta government, in his written statement to the September, 1970, constitutional conference in Ottawa stated his position on the question of municipal involvement in the constitutional issue in these terms:

> The municipalities tend to see the proper solution to their problems lying in a redrafted Constitution which, presumably, would on the one hand, guarantee their existence and responsibilities, and on the other, guarantee them adequate sources of income. The Alberta government has given this suggestion careful consideration and recognizes its merit. However, we have concluded that municipal participation in redrafting the Constitution is not the best means to solve municipal problems.

First, as we have suggested elsewhere, the present process of Constitutional review is not meeting the expectations of the participants. The addition of municipal representatives to the present structures would make matters all the more difficult. It is our firm belief that the process of Constitutional review must be continued as a dialogue among present parties: the provincial and federal governments.

Second, the increasing functional interdependence of municipalities provides better reason than ever for municipalities — including the large cities — to be treated as creations of the provinces. Most municipal problems can be adequately dealt with within the present framework of provincial responsibilities.

Where, however, there is a recognized need for federal help in solving municipal problems, there should be a discussion among the municipalities, the provinces in which the municipalities are located, and the Government of Canada.[38] At this point in time the constitutional matter rests there: but the conflict underlines the potential relative inconsequence of provincial decisions if provincial governments continue their present policies.

The Recent Federal Initiative

The metropolitan local authorities, though administratively subservient to the provincial governments, have called through the organized voice of mayors and municipalities for the acceptance of the reality of their *de facto* political significance. This is the final expression of the relative inconsequence of provincial decisions within the provinces themselves. It has been brought to a head, allegedly, by the financial stringency of city government relative to the potential growth they detect in themselves. Lending institutions in particular, but also developers, retailing establishments, and many manufacturers, exert pressure to insure that city growth continues in order to provide security for their already massive investment in metropolitan areas. Opposed to this are the public's outcries against pollution, traffic congestion, and other urban inconveniences which compound the difficulties and susceptibilities of elected urban officials. Enhanced financial provision and political independence are seen as the only way out. Such answers, however, only guarantee the acceleration of the process which causes these urban difficulties. These answers also provide no remedy for rural and non-city degradation, except to denude the rural areas of all but a tiny percentage of their potential carrying-capacity of population.

The federal government's response poses a similarly direct challenge to the administrative effectiveness of provincial governments. The novel difficulties faced by the federal government since 1967 have centred around an unprecedently high interest rate on mortgage loans, which effectively prevents perhaps the majority of Canadians becoming eligible to own a dwelling, plus the need to restrict the activities of the construction industry in order to damp down a "cost-push" type of inflation. At the same time, more new dwellings are needed to meet the increasing rate of new family formations. The Hellyer Task Force of 1969 was intended to have "a hard, new look at housing and urban development in Canada."[39] Its term of reference were "to examine housing and urban development in Canada and to report on ways in which the federal government, in company with other levels of government and the private sector, can help meet the housing needs of all Canadians and contribute to the development of modern, vital cities."[40]

One of its recommendations was the establishment of a Department of Housing and Urban Affairs. This suggestion had been made frequently by government and opposition speakers in the federal House throughout most of the 1960s. The provinces since 1964-67 had been setting up provincial agencies concerned with housing and urban renewal, but these had tended to limit their interests to public housing for the poor, land assembly, and activities connected with particular financial minorities rather than the expansive, general aspect of housing in general. The federal departmental idea was changed in 1970, as part of a more general policy, to the concept of a Ministry of State. The Ministry of State for Urban Affairs will have no program delivery capability, but will emphasize by research and policy development the formulation of a co-ordinated policy for urban development in Canada. The Honourable Robert Andras, who was the Minister without Portfolio Responsible for Housing, was made the new Minister of State for Urban Affairs in June, 1971.

In a speech on February 27, 1970 to the Canadian Institute of Public Affairs, Toronto, the minister explained that in the past a speech on the federal approach to urban policy would have been

24

extremely brief: "We have none."[41] This is correct, however, only if policy is construed in the positive sense of a formulated initiative. Policy can, however, be implicit in a failure to formulate an initiative, and that was the case until very recent times. The federal policy on urban areas was precisely to let them grow under municipal and lending institution direction, federal incentives and grants, and without too much interference from the provinces at the level of policy input — though with a constitutional administrative input that could not be entirely avoided.

Since July, 1968, when the Hellyer Task Force was set up, the positive formulation of policy has become pronounced. In his February, 1970, speech the minister remarked:

> In the course of the on-going development of our low income housing strategy, several stark realities struck me. The first was that if we were to properly house this low income group in the cities, the volume of resources required was vastly greater than anyone had assumed. Second, the very same urban processes that kept this group in poverty appeared to be continually threatening a group even larger in size, namely the one immediately above it in terms of income. A policy which attempted to solve our housing problems by merely building more houses thus seemed to be destined to failure — the problem was too large, and growing larger annually.[42]

These realities gave rise to research to understand more fully "the nature of the urban processes that were leading to these results." N. H. Lithwick's study, *Urban Canada: Problems and Prospects,* is one result of this endeavor.

The position adopted by the minister, and contained also in Dr. Lithwick's report, is that the cities provide immense benefits:

> The modern urban unit is a direct product of and key contributor to modern economic development. These units provide the enormously important dimension of *scale* in terms of large accessible markets and pools of labour, skills, specialization and capital that permit modern industry to continually undergo expansion and rapid technological change. Urban growth is thus the spatial aspect of modern economic development.[43]

The intense competition for urban space is said to underlie most of the observed urban problems.[44] Very high growth rates in this limited urban space are said to make the urban process particularly "unmanageable." The size and scale of the modern metropolis engenders dilemma for those responsible for regulating it. These considerations are said to explain "why public policy in all modern nations has been unable to deal with their urban problems." It has been a matter of *ad hoc* solutions to particular problems. He remarked:

25

It should have been clear that the piecemeal approach was getting us nowhere, but apparently the lesson has not yet been learned. Debates about alternative transit modes continue as if the long term overall urban impact was irrelevant. Some side-issues enter the argument — such as the effect on the core (of the city) — but not in the context of the urban totality . . . Housing policy remains exclusively that, carried out as an end in itself despite the critical impact of housing on the whole urban structure.[45]

The problem was one of retaining the benefits of urban concentration for the productive and commercial processes while arranging urban growth through a national urban policy for Canada. Such a policy would achieve national scope through the co-ordinative, consultative, and co-operative endeavors of all three levels of government. The public and active urban associations would also be heard. An image of the future urban Canada had to be achieved before the means could be worked out.

Dr. Lithwick identified two basic alternatives for the urban future. One was derived from an "unconstrained future," where the processes of the past would be allowed to continue, and the second a "constrained future," where goals could be deliberately implemented and urban development could be a product of man's will. His prognosis of the "unconstrained future" was not entirely a happy one. He expected the urban population of Canada to increase by the year 2001 by between 10 million and 16 million. About a half of this increase was expected to take place in the major metropolitan centres of Montreal and Toronto. "Consequently, our policy must be geared primarily towards solving the problems of these centres."[46] Costs of the giant metropolis were likely to eat up all the benefits of increasing per capita production despite enormously increased productivity. He wrote:

If we select 500,000 (population) as a crude measure of maturity, we will have five mature units by 1971, all of which will be running into major urban problems. The following decade will see three more enter that range; the years 1981-1991 will see Calgary enter that range, and the final decade will see London and Windsor enter the same phase . . . The most important aspect of these findings is the immediacy of the need for an urban policy. The greatest problem areas are already almost unmanageable. By the year 2001, we can look forward to the type of intractable situations presently facing major urban centres in the United States and elsewhere.[47]

To forestall the "intractable situation" of modern United States' cities, urban policy in Canada would be directed at favoring cities over other calls on the public purse. He identified the problem of policy in these terms:

It is obvious that policy directed at the city must discriminate among other objects of public concern. Yet it is the absence of just this abstraction of urban from other policy that has been so apparent in the past. For a great number of possible reasons, the federal and provincial legislatures of this country have been beset by tension between demands for policies of selective development. The cross-pressures of political life have pushed public policy towards the middle ground, militating against specialized treatment of unique cases. Thus, the unique material needs of urban centres, they often have been treated as general categories. This approach is bound to be exacerbated and become more anomalous as urban Canada grows ... Urban policy, then, requires recognition to the unique character of cities and it must be designed to have selective impact.[48]

While this argument points to the nub of the governmental position, it fails to appreciate that federal policy in the past was deliberate. Through its own legislation and decisions the federal government was part of the structural arrangement within which the cities and population concentrations of today were built. Dr. Lithwick's study virtually ignores the inter-relation of urban population concentration and rural regional degradation, the role of lending institutions in discriminating among possible borrowers, the effects of private capital's right to decide on the location of its enterprises, the undermining of provincial authority through the federal use of lending institutions and CMHC to house an ever-expanding urban population, and so forth.

Under conditions of a "constrained future," Dr. Lithwick's study did open up a number of possibilities. The one he preferred was the building of increasingly viable virgin cities at the points of intersection of the routes connecting existing cities. By this means, some of the growth destined under conditions of an "unconstrained future" to the largest and most problem-ridden centres would be diverted to the new virgin cities whose planning would be directed from the start. It is an attractive and sensible possibility, for it recognizes the advantages of public planning to residents and the advantages of concentration and scale required by private investment. Even this, however, is only one possibility among others.

Dr. Lithwick's study tends to assume under conditions of both "unconstrained" and "constrained" futures, the inevitability of the vast proportion of Canadians living in major metropolitan centres. He does not examine the possibility of a considerable decentralization not to rural conditions but to the city or town of 50,000 or less population. His emphasis is on the improved and planned virgin city. For this reason he does not examine techniques that might save some of the billions of dollars now spent on the degraded regions of the country, and that might in addition enable the major cities to grow in a manner that relates them to their rural hinterland and to the rest of Canada in a mutually supporting capacity. The "unique character of the cities" is not just that they contribute so greatly to the economy. The unique feautre of urban concentration is its relation to the country and its people as a whole. This is not always expressed in terms of the interests of an economy associated increasingly with powerful city institutions. It is expressed more often in the concerns that politicians sense as matters of more general importance for the whole country.

In September, 1970, Mr. Andras addressed the Union of British Columbia Municipalities, and emphasized the interdependence of problems within the city itself. He remarked that "the central feature of these problems is that they are all interdependent, each contributing to the severity of the others." In so far as an urban policy is intended to sort out the currently obscure issues within the city, it can only be commended; but to ignore the corresponding interdependence of cities with the remainder of Canadian institutions perpetuates the error considered responsible for the present urban and rural problems. This error is ascribed to a lack of urban policy in the past. It is poor reasoning to argue on the one hand that a lack of policy towards the cities has created urban problems while governments have been too concerned with "policies of equalization" across the country, and on the other hand that future urban policy should, *ipso facto,* be directed specifically to intensify urban concentration and expansion because they are selected areas of need.

Ivor Dent, Mayor of Edmonton and President of the Canadian Federation of Mayors and Municipalities, in the personal preface to the Prime Minister on the submission of the federation's 1971 brief to the Government of Canada, remarked:

> We reject the view that the Federal Government does not have the right to seek the views of Local Government and we deplore the result of this view which is the reluctance of ministers to hear those views even when invited by the mayors, and the refusal of federal officials to respect the integrity, authority and boundaries of Local Government.[49]

This is much clearer than the federation's 1970 brief to the Ministers of Municipal Affairs in Winnipeg on the political aspirations of local authorities. It is forthright, as the following remark shows:

> For too long we have watched the erosion of what little authority exists at the local level. For too long have we tolerated the willful distortion of local priorities to satisfy an incomprehensible jungle of conflicting objectives at the Federal and Provincial levels. For too long have we laboured under the yoke of sharply increasing responsibility and sharply reducing resources.[50]

The point is pushed home by stating that, in terms of gross expenditure over the period 1961 to 1970, local government expenditure had risen from three billion to eight billion dollars as opposed to an increase from six billion to thirteen billion (1970) for federal responsibilities. From 1947 to 1967, furthermore, municipal employment figures increased from 4.1 to 12.0 persons per thousand, in contrast with the federal increase of from 7.5 to 11.8 persons per thousand population. These are strong figures on which to demand partnership, and the brief makes this clear:

> Many Canadian citizens claim they are the victims of economic dislocation, technological change and the kind of misallocation of resources that gravely threaten their standards of living. Local Government has no choice but to demand a co-ordination of the efforts of all levels of Government towards the attainment of economic growth and improvement in human well being.[51]

The brief is clearer also with regard to its own views on the nature of the forces creating urban concentrations and the role of the local authority. It argues that "Having acquiesced in an economic-growth-for-its-own-sake policy to date, we must now set goals for a balanced socio-economic program . . ." The shibboleth the brief adopts for this purpose is "National Strategy for Planned Community Development."

Municipal requests and recent federal policy have much in common. Both are national in terms of the scale of action suggested. The organized municipalities would relegate the provinces to "co-ordinating and guiding instruments,"[52] but no mention is made of what would remain to be co-ordinated provincially if "partnership" were obtained. The federal government is a little clearer, but appears to be hard-pressed to identify a specific function different from that played by the provinces since 1935. In his Commons speech of 28 June 1971, when the House was debating the Proclamation to establish Canada's first Ministry of State for Urban Affairs, Mr. Andras is reported to have remarked that:

> The Ministry's role will be *coordinative* between federal policies and their departments. It will be *supportive* to all relevant federal programs and projects on behalf of comprehensive urban policy. It will be *consultative* with the provinces and their municipalities in achieving an integrated approach to solving urban problems that none of the three areas of jurisdiction can solve on their own.[53]

The consultative capacity with the provinces and their municipalities had been tried often in the history of amendments to the National Housing Act. During those decades the municipalities were not the political force they are today. His speech also contained reference to a change in general attitude towards responsibility for urban development. He remarked:

> General acceptance has been given to the principle that the three levels of government, whose urban activities are so

interdependent, must find new ways of meeting together so that our *policies and programs* will become more interdependent — complementary and not contradictory in their pursuit of common objectives and priorities.[54]

The Winnipeg meeting of federal, provincial, and municipal representatives had led to the formation of a committee to create "a national forum for continued consultation." The cities were now to be party to discussions of city problems.

This organizational change may bear fruit. The provinces at least retain a seat on the new "national forum," though it appears they may well be outvoted or outmanoeuvred. Though "consultation with the provinces" has been a persistent excuse for federal manoeuvres since the National Housing Act was first legislated in 1938, Mr. Andras's policy has one important difference from earlier gestures. He remarked in the same speech:

> it has been too easy for the federal government unilaterally to develop in an *ad hoc* fashion *one* policy or *one* program and come to this House and the people of this country and suggest, now, with this one new program, urban renewal or urban transit or whatever, we will solve the complex urban problems which have accumulated over decades. Such simplistic patchwork responses may solve short term political problems. They don't solve urban problems and in fact are often perverse.[55]

Mr. Andras thought in June, 1971, that:

> cities are excellent social systems, with still more benefits than costs (at least in Canada). We know that the costs are rising rapidly. We think there is still time in our nation to maintain the opportunity gain over these costs, provided we join with other levels of government and the Canadian people in a concentrated effort to do so.[56]

This joining with "other levels of government, and the Canadian people" is a new approach only to the extent that it is overt, deliberate, and seeks a national consensus on urban goals. It is a return to the policy of co-operation with the provincial governments that opposition speakers so often recommended in the troubled times of the late 1930s and 1940s, but which the federal governments of the day rejected in favor of support for, and guarantees against loss by, the private lending institutions. It offers the chance of a wider measure of control over urban development in the nation, but not necessarily in the particular jurisdiction of any province. Therein lies the difficulty for provincial governments: it could readily lead to continued "relative inconsequence" for provincial decision. This is particularly the case because the federal government had the opportunity to concentrate within the Ministry of State for Urban Affairs some of the best analytic brains available to the country, and had three years in which to prepare its strategy.

The Implications for Alberta

If a diversification of locale and specialization of city functions can be achieved under a new national urban policy, the role of provincial governments becomes clear. They no longer will be able to turn an approving but blind eye to growth in any form and in any locality. Local city and metropolitan groups will no longer be able to challenge their authority, for this authority would be needed in the proper planning and distribution of diversified city locations and specialized city functions on at least a province wide basis, and probably inter-provincially where boundaries meet and where specialized functions serve a national purpose.

Alberta is well placed in many respects to respond to a national urban policy with this type of aim. Its metropolitan areas are still small enough to experience continued growth of a specialized functional type. They need not anticipate an absolute decline. They are also modern, with physical structures capable of many years of useful life. The province has many well serviced small cities and towns with potential for expansion. These are well placed across the developed areas of the province. The growth of new towns in resource-developing areas of the north-central region of the province is a natural focal point for expansion. Transport, communication, electricity, and natural gas are well distributed throughout the province. The public facilities required for diversification of local and specialized functions of cities are already largely present. On the other hand, the public facilities for the continued heterogeneous and rapid growth of the two metropolitan areas are not, as the predicted capital expenditure estimates of Calgary and Edmonton clearly demonstrate. The implication of such a policy for the provincial government, however, is that it must relinquish its "fair and equal" treatment for all local authorities. Such an internal policy is clearly inappropriate in the new situation, just as it has been inappropriate in the traditional situation, from both a practical and metropolitan political perspective. The federal government gave up such a policy many years ago; and the metropolitan local governments subscribed to it vocally when a proposal was detrimental to their interests, but forgot it just as conveniently.

Part II of this study attempts to discover the implications for Alberta of a national urban policy for Canada; but until the aims of national policy become clearer, and until the difficulties surrounding a new constitution for Canada have been resolved in so far as they affect urban affairs, many of the details of the course of action Alberta can take must remain undecided. In the meantime, a clearer understanding of the issues and continued research into apparently critical aspects of them, should assist those involved to formulate appropriate public policy.

1. *A White Paper on Human Resources Development,* presented to the Alberta Legislature by the Honourable E. C. Manning, March, 1967, p. 57.

2. The term "lending institution" refers to the array of companies whose activity is to finance the needs of borrowers. These include life insurance companies, trust companies, loan companies, investment companies, the commercial banks, etc. The importance of any one type of lending institution for housing and urban growth has changed over the years. For a useful discussion of these institutions and of the changes in their contribution to housing, see Royal Commission on Banking and Finance, 1964 Report (Ottawa: Queen's Printer, 1965), Chapters 6 and 14.

3. By "uncontrolled" we refer to that situation where the influence of public planning authorities has been insufficient to impose a form of city growth commensurate with deliberate, public intent. The term carries no suggestion that the form of actual city growth was uncontrolled or uncontrollable in an absolute growth process, and in that sense the growth was highly "controlled."

4. There are many studies which deal with particular programs or aspects of any given piece of legislation, but we could find none aimed at giving an overall view of federal attempts to cope with urban and regional matters over the last few decades.

5. Remarks by the Honourable Robert Andras, May 26, 1971 at the Conference on Cities, Indianapolis, Indiana, p. 11.

6. The words "company" and "corporation" will be used to refer to organizations whose principal source of finance is private shareholding, retained profits, or tax advantages. The term "company" will tend to reflect those of smaller size than the internationally organized "corporation." It is not intended to belabor the distinction, but merely to convey an impression of scale. Crown Corporations will be indicated by the use of the adjective.

7. There is a vast research area which may apply less to the provinces than to Canada as a whole, concerning the implications for urban areas of the increasing trend towards production in foreign countries by multinational giant corporations. The issues are raised in general terms in books like Myrdal, Gunnar *Rich Lands and Poor* (New York: 1957, Harper); Turner, Louis *Invisible Empires* (New York: 1971, Harcourt Brace); and Kindleberger, Charles (editor) *The International Corporation.* Such corporations can adopt a much more flexible approach to investment than a company with national allegiance only. The terms the international company may impose on a government may therefore be more stringent and demanding. The consequences of this added power on locational decisions and therefore on urban development, appear to warrant research.

8. *Report of the Public Expenditure and Revenue Study Committee, Province of Alberta* (Edmonton: March, 1966), p. 63.

9. The *Financial Post,* January 16, 1971.

10. In this case the announcement was made simultaneously by Premier Harry Strom and George Williams, President of Proctor and Gamble Company of Canada, acting for the Cincinnati principals.

11. *Decision Making in Plant Site Location,* Urban Research Group (Saskatoon: September, 1970). This survey also revealed that the decision time varies by the size of the community and by whether it is a branch plant or a new company planning to establish itself in a community.

12. The federal government is not unique among national governments in this regard. The centralization of production and the concentration of people in metropolitan areas is a world-wide phenomenon and is most pronounced in highly industrialized countries. Where the process has occurred within a provincial or state system, the tendency has been to compromise the lower level of government.

13. Published in a pamphlet entitled *Financial Tyranny and the Dawn of a New Day* and cited in MacPherson, C. B., *Democracy in Alberta: Social Credit and the Party System* (Toronto: 1962, University of Toronto Press), p. 201. The purpose for which this control was needed in Alberta was hardly that of urban planning in the modern sense. Nevertheless the principle of being master in one's own house was at stake.

14. In terms of the amount of federal money given out as incentives to industry by province, the distribution appears to be somewhat different from that shown in Table 1. Official figures do not appear to be available, but from our calculations Quebec appears to have received about double the funds given to any other province.

15. The tax sharing agreement worked out at the Federal-Provincial Conference of November, 1958 had initiated the principle of ad hoc assistance to the Maritimes. See Chapter 3.

16. The Atlantic Development Council in *A Strategy for the Economic Development of the Atlantic Region, 1971-1981* (Fredericton, 1971), p. 15, after relating investment targets to employment targets, estimated "that a total capital investment of about $25 billion in current 1970 prices will be required in the 1971-81 period. This figure includes both the direct investment requirement to meet the employment objectives, the indirect investment in infrastructure required, i.e. utilities, transportation, and communications systems, and in housing requirements." The council also indicated that a greater degree of urbanization of the population will be required.

17. Lithwick, N. H., *Urban Canada: Problems and Prospects, A Report Prepared for the Honourable R. K. Andras, Minister Responsible for Housing* (Ottawa, 1970), p. 48.

18. The Halifax region had the lowest value of new construction in 1964 of any metropolitan area in Canada. See Lithwick *Urban Canada,* p. 77.

19. *The Municipality in the Canadian Federation,* Position Paper prepared by the Joint Municipal Committee on Intergovernmental Relations, August 1970. This is a document of historic significance and deserves careful reading.

20. From 1951 to 1968 local government expenditures, except for Quebec, increased from $721 million to $3.5 billion. Although revenues increased from $614 million to $3.3 billion the direct tax source increased only three times while transfers from higher levels of government, especially provincial conditional grants, increased eight times.

21. *The Municipality in the Canadian Federation,* p. 3.

22. Ibid., p. 4.

23. Ibid., p. 1.

24. Ibid., p. 3.

25. Ibid., p. 2.

26. Ibid., p. 9.

27. Ibid., p. 19.
28. Ibid., p. 20.
29. Ibid., p. 12.
30. Ibid., p. 13.
31. Ibid.
32. An alternative not considered in the paper is for the provincial governments to assume the role of urban local government itself, or have regional rather than local system of government which modern means of communication may well make possible. If the committee's recommendation was accepted then most of the resources now being used for rejuvenating the degraded rural and non-city regions of Canada would presumably be in jeopardy.
33. *The Municipality in the Canadian Federation,* p. 21.
34. Ibid., p. 10.
35. Ibid., p. 22.
36. Ibid., pp. 13-14.
37. Ibid., p. 22.
38. Strom, the Honourable Harry E., Premier of Alberta, *A Position Paper* (September, 1970), pp. 91-92.
39. *Report of the Task Force on Housing and Urban Development* (Ottawa: 1969, Queen's Printer).
40. Ibid., p. 1.
41. Andras, Robert, *An Address to the Canadian Institute of Public Affairs,* (Toronto: February 27, 1972), p. 2.
42. Ibid., p. 4.
43. Ibid,. p. 7. The same arguments are mentioned in Lithwick's *Urban Canada,* pp. 32-35 and 48-50.
44. It may be argued that competition for space is not necessarily underlying any urban problem, though it may be a concomitant of it. To attribute a causative quality to competition for space ignores a set of social facts that may equally be attributed a causative component.
45. Andras, *Address to Canadian Institute,* p. 11.
46. Lithwick, *Urban Canada,* p. 235.
47. Ibid., p. 147.
48. Ibid., p. 172.
49. Brief of Canadian Federation of Mayors and Municipalities (Ottawa: April 26, 1971).
50. Ibid., p. 1.
51. Ibid., p. 3.
52. *The Municipality in the Canadian Federation,* p. 20.
53. Press release, 8 p.m. June 28, 1971. Remarks by the Honourable Robert Andras, Federal Minister Responsible for Housing, p. 3.
54. Ibid., p. 5.
55. Ibid., p. 4.
56. Ibid., p. 6.

Chapter I
Federal attempts to cope: regional underdevelopment,
1935-1970

For almost forty years the federal government has been coping with a doubly relative situation. On the one hand, it has separated urban from rural and on the other, the well-to-do from the impoverished or degraded.[1] By legislation and finance it has attempted to meet degradation in specific localities and in terms of conditions it felt were amenable to action.

Before 1970-71, the federal government subscribed to the principle that it should not interfere with persons, companies, or cities which have wealth and that might be considered successful. The programs of the 1969 Department of Regional Economic Expansion (DREE), for example, were to assist in the economic rehabilitation of regions of Canada with higher-than-average unemployment. They were not intended, except perhaps vicariously, to reduce or make more articulate the growth of Toronto and Montreal, despite the increasing public cost of servicing these cities. That the condition for the improved economic welfare of the degraded regions of Canada might be the imposition of a user-cost basis of taxation in the major cities apparently was not considered. The 1970-71 urban policy for Canada departed from this precedent. It proposed, albeit hesitantly, that federal initiative inject into the governmental institutions of Canada a willingness to arrange the urban situation by conscious decision. Previously, federal policy needed only to devise measures which would assist those who had "fallen by the wayside" in the general movement of the overall economy. These measures were remedial actions taken in the context of letting the successful continue in their success and bringing the unsuccessful closer, by increased opportunities and personal capacity, to where the others had got.

In every instance, to achieve its intentions, the federal government has worked primarily with companies. Only in 1970-71, when the "urban policy for Canada" was being worked out, has this trend been changed. While it could be claimed that the federal government has also worked with the provinces and the local municipal authorities[2] in such things as joint agreements, tax sharing formulae, and grants, the records of *Hansard* display a tendency to regard the Canadian constitution as a severe handicap to federal efforts. Provincial rights under the BNA Act have affected federal legislation. The fact that the federal government has relied overwhelmingly on the resources and initiative of companies corresponds to the supra-territorial characteristic of private capital.

The Prairie Farm Rehabilitation Act of 1935 was aimed at meeting some of the effects of the depression[3]. It was concerned with the rehabilitation of individual farmers and of areas of land which had suffered deleterious farming practices, drought and wind erosion. As prices fell after 1929, the farmers responded in their struggle to keep solvent by increasing production. Increases in volume were seen as a means of countering decline in per unit price. Drought made this impossible and the land suffered in consequence. The Act was specific to Prairie farming and was a response to hardship suffered there. By financial assistance to support dam and dugout construction, or to provide water for farm irrigation, stock or domestic use, the farmer was to be assisted to get himself going again.[4] Only two years later, in 1937, the measures made available under the Act were expanded by amendment. Resettlement of farmers, guidance and financial assistance towards new land utilization were provided. The administration set up to handle the Act was empowered, by agreement with the provinces, to provide financial and engineering skill to farmers at levels that varied from their individual and farm needs to that of catchment wide reservoirs and community wide irrigation. Expenditure on the program after 1945 increased many fold. In Alberta the expansion of facilities under the St. Mary's Irrigation Project of 1946 to half a million acres and the Bow River Project involving some 240,000 irrigable acres are examples of the scale of this activity.

These larger projects amended the type of farming that could be carried on — from dry land to irrigation. The instrument was substantial public investment at both the personal and community wide levels. There was some opposition from farmers at the time, though these developments assisted in later years in making Lethbridge a centre for Canada's meat packing industry. The success of irrigated land was consequent upon capital costs of construction being paid from public funds. The Meeks Commission, after examining the proposed St. Mary's Dam in Southern Alberta, in 1942, wrote:

> It is recognized by irrigation authorities and has been proven
> by the results of completed irrigation projects that, in
> general, successful operation of large projects is impossible
> if the entire cost of construction is charged against the
> irrigation spread widely through various services and
> functions for transportation, merchandizing, processing
> of farm products and in the manufacture of equipment and
> supplies utilized on the farm. These benefits accrue (1) to the
> farmer who lives on the land, (2) to local urban and
> community centres, to municipalities and the province, and
> (3) to the country at large in increased capital wealth and the
> maintenance of employment and business activity.[5]

The Prairie Farm Rehabilitation Act, with amendments, is still in force. It is now a part of a battery of enabling and administrative legislation brought down between 1960 and 1970. During this decade, to mention only the most significant, the following were passed:

> The Agricultural Rehabilitation and Development Act, 1961, (ARDA) which was renamed in 1966 amending legislation to:
> The Agricultural and Rural Development Act, 1966 (ARDA)
> The Atlantic Development Board Act, (ADBA)
> The Department of Industry Act, 1963, which in turn included provision for:
> The Area Development Agency, 1963, (ADA)
> The Fund for Rural Economic Development Act, 1966 (FRED) which was part of the amendment introduced into the 1966 ARDA Act;
> The Government Organization Act, 1969, which in turn created The Department of Regional Economic Expansion (DREE), and The Regional Development Incentives Act, 1969.

Besides these, the funds established under the various Acts were increased.

These Acts, with the possible exception of the Department of Industry Act, were introduced to meet one or another aspect of human degradation or area underdevelopment. They were a direct response to the consequences of centralizing population, employment opportunities, and manufacturing in cities, and to changes in the methods of agricultural production. The federal government was coping with rural degradation directly rather than by interfering with the processes contributing to the continued growth of cities. The steps it took may be identified by examining the circumstances surrounding, and the proposals contained in the ARDA Acts of 1960 and 1966, the FRED legislation of 1966, and the Regional Development Incentives Act of 1969.[6]

The ARDA, FRED and DREE Legislation

The Prairie Farm Rehabilitation Act of 1935 had identified a region of Western Canada as having peculiar problems. In 1956, the Prime Minister drew attention to large areas of eastern Canada that appeared unsuitable for the type of farming being practised upon them. He suggested that these areas might more usefully be returned to forestry and water conservation. The marginal farmers might be replaced and be found more rewarding occupations elsewhere. In 1958 the problem was seen as being one of small farms and land use. The answer appeared to lie in evolving better land-use methods, improving the technical capacity of farmers whether they wished to remain on the land or move to urban areas, and setting up farms large enough to be remunerative. In January, 1957, a special committee of the Senate had been struck on survey land use in Canada and to encourage the public to consider appropriate solutions to rural poverty.[7]

The small farm was identified as being in difficulties largely because of the marginal land the farmer had to use. In the early stages of thought about the problem, the land's physical properties were seen as critical. Technical solutions and rearrangements should provide an answer. This perspective was encouraged by geographers and soil scientists who were then influential in the determination of policy. According to T. N. Brewis, "They gave a slant to early policies which has since been regretted. Their emphasis on the physical properties of land distracted attention from the more fundamental causes of distress in rural areas."[8]

By 1960 the problem before the Minister of Agriculture was how to assist areas of the country apparently unable to benefit from the regular national agricultural program based on price stabilization, credit, crop insurance, and information on marketing and agricultural practices. A set of problems emerged here which were different from those that faced well-to-do farmers.[9] In December, 1960 the minister introduced a resolution in the House outlining his intentions.[10] Through agreements between the provincial and federal authorities, three kinds of projects were initiated:

(i) projects for the alternative uses of lands that are marginal or of low productivity;

(ii) projects for the development of income and employment opportunities in rural agricultural areas;

(iii) projects for the development and conservation of the soil and water resources of Canada.

The concept inherent in these projects paralleled the early ideas of the Prairie Farm Rehabilitation Act. During the Debate on the Resolution the minister made it clear that he saw the future ARDA legislation as complementing the PFRA and extending it to other parts of Canada. The problem was considered fundamentally agricultural. But the minister was already aware of underlying and more basic issues. These issues came forward in the amendment to ARDA of 1966; but during the debate of the second reading of the bill in 1961, the minister is quoted:

> While the program is focused mainly on farm people, it cannot be exclusively agricultural. Rural economies are no longer separate from town or urban economies, and the program must be one of area development embracing local centres of population as well as the farms surrounding them.[11]

The minister's aim was to build up income in the depressed regions. It was not intended to legislate for farmers to be pushed off the land.[12] Excess production of agricultural goods and a lowering of prices were fundamental problems, but the ARDA legislation was intended, in James McCrorie's words:

> ... to complement a national agricultural program designed to ensure that those engaged in the agricultural industry (and facing social and economic adjustments to technological change) would receive a reasonably fair share of the national income, or, to use the minister's words, "parity of income."[13]

ARDA was a support mechanism to depressed areas and rested on the assumptions that balances should and could be established between rich and poor, that federal aid through the provinces and local committees set up under the Act would achieve this, and that the aid had to rest on farmers helping themselves in their problems of technical adjustment to land type, machinery, and scale of farm operation.[14]

The agreements made between the federal and provincial governments under the 1961 ARDA legislation require that the provinces initiate the remedial programs and contribute towards their cost. The provinces were responsible in large measure for directing the programs and for determining the local policy implicit in them. The federal government could not act without an agreement with the province. The federal administration advised and recommended; it withheld its contribution only if it had serious objections to provincial proposals and their application in practice. Some $50 million was made available to meet the cost of the entire 1962-65 program, and it is significant that only two-thirds was used.[15]

This expectation by the federal government of the role to be played by the provinces is of fundamental significance. The provinces were to be responsible for determining how the federal initiative would be applied on the ground. Provinces were granted the use of federal funds to apply a new approach to an old but recently identified problem. They did not, in fact, construe this facility in these terms. Indeed the same issue had emerged two decades earlier with respect to the National Housing Act and the responsibility for urban planning and community development. In interpreting this evidence, the problem becomes one of deciding whether the provinces were tardy in their appreciation of what the federal facility offered, or unable to interpret the significance of the federal initiative for the solution of their particular problem, or were simply adopting the perspectives that their affairs were something different from the affairs of the federal government.

During the second reading of Bill C-77, the minister had indicated his awareness of uncertainty over the extent to which ARDA would be used by the provinces. He is quoted as saying:

> ... that the Bill does not state what the Act will do . . . This is true . . . because no one in the provinces or in farm organizations or at the federal level knows yet what the Bill will bring forth and the extent to which we are going to use the Bill.[16]

It would seem, from the evidence of both Brewis and McCrorie, that the ARDA legislation caught the provinces unprepared.

Only Alberta had passed legislation which anticipated some of the more important provisions of ARDA and the remainder, except Manitoba, subsequently passed provincial legislation to meet the federal initiative.[17] The provinces were not ready to meet the terms of the federal provisions. Buckley and Tihanyi commented, "Federal ARDA assists its generally understaffed provincial counterparts with technical experts — water engineers, economists, geographers, sociologists, and rural development officers."[18] Provincial officials recognized ARDA as a source of federal money, but it was available only on the submission of a well-prepared case that demonstrated need on a regional basis and indicated the steps proposed to meet it. ARDA required the delineation of areas characterized by serious unemployment, unsatisfactory land use, and potential for constructive change.

In his analysis of reasons why the provinces held back on the 1962-65 agreements, Professor Brewis suggests that the poorer provinces could not afford their share (usually 50 percent) of the costs, and that among the provinces who could afford it there may have existed a belief that rural poverty was not serious. The provinces were uncertain of the specific projects that should be initiated, according to Professor Brewis, and

> In many cases there seemed to be a reluctance to favor one area rather than another, and this led to a multiplicity of minor projects scattered here and there, or to none at all.[19]

The provinces made varying use of ARDA under the 1962-65 agreements. Tables 2 and 3 show the type of project initiated by the provinces and their distribution by province.

TABLE 2. Distribution of ARDA projects by type: 1962-65

Type of project	Number	Percent
Alternative land use	211	30.9
Soil and water conservation	206	30.2
Rural development	50	7.3
Federal research	120	17.5
Research	96	14.1
Total	683	100.00

Table 2 shows that some 61 percent dealt with alternative land use and soil and water conservation, or natural resources. Only 7.3 percent fell under the more general rubric of "rural development." This covered the idea of comprehensive planning for the development of rural areas. Personnel were to be located in rural areas to work with local residents in planning co-ordinated developmental activity. Plans were to include a broad variety of projects for assistance under ARDA that were not necessarily agricultural in nature. Of all the provinces involved, only Alberta and British Columbia initiated no projects under this provision.[20] Provinces already undertaking natural resource development tended to see ARDA as an entry by the federal government into financing an area

TABLE 3. Distribution of ARDA projects by province, 1962-65

Type of project	Nfld.	PEI.	NS.	NB.	Que.	Ont.	Man.	Sask.	Alta.	B.C
Alternative land use	4.1	34.3	31.6	34.1	13.1	56.8	15.2	57.9	46.2	143
Soil and water conservation	4.1	31.4	22.8	13.6	59.1	15.9	11.9	22.1	12.8	543
Rural Development	6.1	5.7	3.5	2.3	18.8	2.3	10.2	1.4		
Federal research	55.1	14.3	19.3	18.2	2.7	6.8	25.4	6.9	12.8	200
Research	30.6	14.3	22.8	31.8	6.3	18.2	37.3	11.7	28.2	114
Total percent	100.0	100.0	100.0	100.0	100.0	100.0	100.0	100.0	100.0	1000
Number	49	35	57	44	176	44	59	145	39	35

Source: The ARDA Catalogue: 1962-65, Ottawa: Department of Forestry, 1965. The total number of provincial projects involving federal cost-sharing is 683.

Both tables reproduced from J. N. McCrorie's *ARDA: An Experiment in Development Planning* with permission of the author and the Canadian Council on Rural Development.

provincial governments had long been supporting. Their applications reflected this search for additional revenue rather than the initiation of a new approach to an old problem.

In James McCrorie's view, most of the provinces missed the fundamental attribute of the ARDA intent which was to inaugurate through inter-government consultation and finances, planned and systematic programs to remove rural degradation. He writes:

> The provinces responded in terms of one consideration: money. The contrast between federal expectations and provincial responses is striking, to say the least . . . Conspicuously absent is any significant evidence of long range, comprehensive planning in respect of resource use and rural development. The emphasis, rather, was on *ad hoc* resource projects; projects that were relatively easy to design; projects that lent themselves to tapping the federal coffers with a minimum of effort and commitment.[21]

He quotes a remark by a provincial public servant to support his opinion, namely:

> There is no sense of urgency about ARDA in this province and others I have visited. In the meantime, the poor get poorer. No amount of political hogwash can obscure or diminish this tragedy.[22]

In attempting to be fair to all provinces, the federal government's allotment to each province was based on a formula that took into account the size of the rural population and the number of "low-income" farms. In the second agreements, 1966-1970, this formula was elaborated to include the number of "poor" rural non-farm families.[23] As the provinces were obliged to contribute to the cost of the project, on a one to one basis for all projects but acquisition of land for pastures, the formula burdened the poorer provinces relative to the richer. However, the richer provinces did not take up their full allotment.

The amendment of 1966 to the original ARDA provisions suggests that the federal government sensed an inadequacy in the program. The amendment was initiated within government by the Department of Justice as a result of doubts "about the legality of certain projects submitted to us (government) by some of the provinces and which, while they concerned rural areas, were not meant for a region where agriculture was possible."[24] It was not that the program was failing, but that it was too restrictive. The provinces had sought ARDA funding for purposes beyond the terms of the Act, to develop land on the settlement frontier rather than degraded but fully developed land, for example, to help with small town off-farm degradation, or to develop land where agriculture was hardly possible.

The provinces were tending to use the federal facility to pay for the developments they construed as economically marginal. Though we have been unable to collect sufficient evidence to determine the point with certainty, it does appear that the provinces in general were not submitting to Ottawa co-ordinated programs, but, rather, a number of *ad hoc,* opportunistically conceived projects.

Concurrently, thought in Ottawa about the nature of the problem ARDA was to cope with was itself changing. Five years of experience had taught the federal authorities that what had been identified as an agricultural problem was in reality a rural one. The minister in 1961 had indicated his observation that rural and urban economies were no longer separate. Low incomes generally, rather than low agricultural incomes, were now the issue.

Among the important changes introduced in the second agreement with the provinces was the provision, under the land use and farm adjustment section, for funds to assist farmers wishing to establish themselves in non-farm occupations. There was also a clear distinction drawn between Rural Development Areas (RDA) and Special Rural Development Areas (SRDA). The special category was in effect a sub-region eligible for particular assistance. Buckley and Tihanyi write:

> SRDA development programmes involve a series of physical,
> economic and social studies and the preparation of
> comprehensive plans with the participation of local residents
> through rural development committees — all culminating in a
> broad range of co-ordinated major programmes by federal
> and provincial agencies financed partly from the Fund for
> Rural Economic Development.[25]

FRED was associated with the 1966 amendments to ARDA but the fund applied only to the Special Rural Development Areas. During the debate in the House, the minister was at pains to emphasize that FRED was separate from monies allocated by parliament for ARDA. He is cited as saying:

> The Special Fund . . . will be employed to finance
> development and adjustment programs which cannot be
> financed by other public programs, whether Federal,
> Provincial, or joint programs, including the normal ARDA
> program.[26]

Thus the position at this time was that regions designated for assistance under ARDA — regions where land use, farm adjustment, soil and water conservation, training for off-farm employment, and such programs were emphasized — and special sub-regions within which FRED resources could be employed on a much wider front. A sum of $50 million was at first allocated to FRED, but in March, 1967, the aggregate amount in the fund was raised to $300 million.

There were also some important administrative changes. The 1966 amendments provided for the Governor in Council to determine the ministry under which ARDA was to be administered. It had previously oscillated between agriculture and forestry. Also, under

FRED, an Advisory Board was established to review proposals and advise the minister. It consisted of not more than ten senior officials of federal departments. It could not recommend to the minister any project that could be more appropriately carried out under any other form of assistance. FRED was to be the catch-all to meet both particularly degraded areas and the odd-men-out of the regular programs. Special areas could be designated only by agreement between the minister and the province, and there was no obligation on the part of the minister to recognize the case promoted by any province. There were careful defences prepared against an inordinate exploitation by the provinces of this special fund. The federal involvement was to be interdepartmentally co-ordinated at a senior level and made direct with the provinces in the execution of the proposals on the grounds, wherever such involvement was adjudged desirable.

In reviewing the 1965 agreements and the FRED provisions Professor Brewis notes the changes in direction federal activity had taken. He remarks:

> Some of the original emphasis on the qualities of land is still in evidence, but preoccupation with those qualities no longer dominates the scene in the way that it used to. Not only are the over-all expenditures larger, but in conjunction with the expenditures under FRED their allocation has shifted decisively in the direction of education, training, and the provision of employment in non-primary occupations.[27]

The comprehensive quality of FRED programs inevitably led to the introduction of problems associated with industry and its stimulation in rural areas.

In February, 1969 the government introduced legislation to set up the Department of Regional Economic Expansion.[28] This new department would absorb the FRED, ARDA and other programs which would in turn be dissolved. During ARDA and FRED's lifetimes some ambitious projects were initiated, involving over a billion dollars, but the machinery was considered inadequate. Jean Marchand, Minister of Forestry and Rural Development, when defending the bill in Committee, emphasized the novel nature of the government's current attempt to cope with "economic disparities which exist between different regions of Canada."[29] Again he emphasized the ideal of working towards the assurance "that Canadians have good opportunities to earn their living at roughly comparable standards wherever they live from sea to sea."[30] The new department was to get down to the roots of the problems:

> The department's goal will be to ensure that economic growth is dispersed widely enough across Canada to bring employment and earnings opportunities in the hitherto slow growth regions as close as possible to those in the rest of the country.[31]

The problem with the previous programs was their variety and the lack of co-ordination among them. "This approach has obviously not worked. It may have stopped the gaps between regions from widening, but it has not narrowed them."[32]

The new departmental machinery was to have central responsibility for federal regional development programs. The Advisory Board set up under the 1966 ARDA amendment and FRED was to be discarded. When an opposition amendment was introduced to allow for the continuation of this type of co-ordinatory machinery in the programs of the Department of Regional Economic Expansion, the minister remarked:

> . . . I am firmly opposed to this amendment. I think it [co-ordination] is really a household matter. It would be wrong, I think, to provide in such a legislation that a minister is to chair a committee composed of officials of other departments. We would then confuse things. I am sure there will be an interdepartmental committee to study these matters; so it is a matter of internal economy.[33]

Although there were good reasons, from the parliamentary perspective, to dispense with the advisory board, this action was illustrative of the greater emphasis to be given to political rather than scientific issues in the new developmental proposals. The minister's obduracy indicated the nature of the new approach to regional development. This approach was to permit the national identification of growth regions, rather than a provincial-federal identification of degraded and depressed regions. The emphasis was now on growth centres and the conditions needed for their stimulation. This approach both included the provinces, in those matters over which they had clear jurisdiction, and excluded the provinces by associating federal initiative with inducements and incentives to companies whose liberties were not restricted by territorial and jurisdictional considerations.

A further important change was the emphasis proposed for employment opportunities in industry. The federal government was already committed through the Department of Industry and Canada Manpower to industrial stimulation in Canada. The new department was to concentrate on industrial employment, and the development of the main centres, in the special areas designated for assistance through the department. This was a fundamental change in the orientation of assistance. No longer was help to be offered only to farmers and for natural resource development, or to the rural degraded areas and people with low incomes. Included now were industry and the growth centres in the designated special areas. The minister remarked:

> I will be seeking to work out with the provinces plans for the development of the main centres within the regions where economic growth has hitherto been slow . . . So far we have FRED plans for rural development, and this is important. I am

proposing to extend that approach to plans for urban
economic and social development.[34]

The small and medium sized towns were to be aided as trading centres
and locations for smaller industries. Whatever financial assistance was
needed to meet the special circumstances and difficulties of an enterpise
in the special areas was to be arranged. The new legislation made easier
the instigation of the conditions necessary to get the development of
these areas under way. The Bill, C-173, envisaged continued agreements
with the provinces, but the respective rights of each party were again
left largely to interpretation in practice.

The Regional Development Incentives Act, 1969
One of the earliest and most influential pieces of legislation
the new department brought before the House was the Regional
Development Incentives Act, 1969. When introducing the Bill, C-202, to
provide for the development of productive employment opportunities,
the Minister for Regional Economic Expansion stated its aims in these
terms:

> the primary objective of the legislation is to offer a new
> opportunity for recovery to the areas of Canada that have
> suffered so long from slow growth. The proposed incentives
> will be powerful enough to ensure industrial expansion
> wherever it is possible. I think that in this way we shall be
> able to launch a real process of economic expansion and
> that our new program associated with the other programs
> of my department, will enable us in a not too distant future to
> provide new jobs to hundreds of thousands of Canadians in
> the areas which are now the least prosperous in our country.[35]

This program, which was to launch "a real process of economic
expansion," offered monetary assistance in the form of a capital
incentive to companies and corporations. They had to be willing to
locate new plants, or expand existing plants into the manufacture of
new commodities, in certain designated areas of the country. The
Incentives Act superseded the Area Development Agency (ADA)
program, started in 1963 under the Department of Industry.
A new Department of Industry had been set up in 1963.
Concurrently, an Area Development Incentives Act was created,
granting a limited duration tax holiday (federal and provincial taxes)
to industries locating in certain high unemployment areas of the
country. The Act was administered by an Area Development Agency
(ADA) and its provisions and amendments have come to be known
collectively in terms of these initials. In 1965, the Act was amended to
provide incentives in the form of either a tax holiday or an outright
capital grant of up to 20 percent of approved cost of the plant (maximum
of $6 million). Like the ARDA legislation this incentive applied only
to designated areas of limited size and implied federal-provincial
co-operation.

46

The Regional Development Incentives Act of 1969 elaborated this earlier principle of direct monetary assistance to companies.[36] The elaboration took the form of adding what was called a "secondary development incentive" to the primary one provided originally under ADA. The concept of a tax holiday, however, was discarded and the 1965 ADA principle of a capital grant was made the sole instrument of incentives policy. The secondary development incentive was explicitly related to the number of jobs made available through the proposed plant or through modification of an existing plant, as well as the capital cost involved.

The basis of calculating the size of the incentive to be awarded an applicant company is complex. It must involve at least some ministerial discretion. In principle it is a matter of relating the job opportunities created to the capital intensiveness of the operation. The minister remarked, when introducing the Bill in the House:

> In an industry using an average amount of capital, we will be prepared to provide an incentive of up to $12,000 for each new job created. If the industry is one that uses a lot of capital, we will go as high as $30,000 per job.[37]

The formula is designed to help both the capital intensive and labor-intensive industries. It is a matter of balancing job opportunity with capital intensity so as not to preclude the high-cost, capital-intensive industry from locating in a designated region.

In describing the financial arrangements, the Act consistently uses the phrase "development incentive," rather than "grant," "award," or "subsidy." The "development incentives" are divided into two types, "primary" and "secondary." The primary incentive is based on the approved capital costs of establishing, expanding, or modernizing the structure, machinery, and other equipment of a manufacturing or processing operation up to 20 percent of the approved costs or $6 million, whichever is the lesser amount. Initial processing operations in a resource-based industry are excluded by the Act.

The amount of the secondary development incentive is based on the approved capital costs and the number of jobs created directly by the proposed operation. But the amount of the secondary incentive cannot exceed 5 percent of the costs approved as part of the secondary incentive plus $5,000 for each job that the minister determines has been created directly by the proposed operation. There is, of course, a maximum limit to the amount the minister can authorize as assistance under a secondary incentive. Section 5 (3) of the Act reads:

> A secondary development incentive in respect of any facility shall not exceed an amount that when added to the amount of the primary development incentive authorized in respect of that facility, would result in an combined development incentive that exceeds:
> (a) $30,000 for each job determined by the Minister to have been created directly in the operation,

(b) $12,000,000 or
(c) ½ of the capital to be employed in the operation, whichever is the least amount.

Thus a highly capital-intensive plant, employing only a few workers, would be limited more by the $30,000 per job created than by the $12 million ceiling or half the capital cost. Similarly, the labor-intensive operation is limited more by the 5 percent of approved secondary incentive capital costs in association with the $5,000 per job.

The legislation is not intended to assist initial processing in resource-based industry. In general terms, mining, oil refining, pulp and newsprint operations are excluded, but petrochemical processes, the production of paper and paperboard, sawmilling, and the processing of farm and fish products are included.[38] Also, where, in the minister's opinion, a facility would be established without the provision of an incentive, no incentive may be provided. The facility must also clearly contribute to economic expansion and social adjustment within a region. (Section 7 of the Act).

The theory behind the incentive is that a company is now, with the publication of the formula, in a position to calculate where its prospects will be greatest. If, by its examination, it decides to locate or expand outside the designated region, and thus receive no incentive grant, its management has presumably weighed the difficulties and costs of locating with incentives in the degraded parts of the country. It can balance higher operating costs such as transport, a limited labor pool from which to draw employees, a small town atmosphere, and the like, against the value of the incentive.

The minister remarked:

> The only thing we are trying to do with this . . . is to put the companies which accept to go into these underdeveloped regions or slow-growth regions on exactly the same footing, from a competition point of view, as companies which establish themselves in large centres such as Montreal, Toronto, Calgary, Vancouver and so forth. We·say "You are away from the markets, you have transportation problems. We are going to give you a grant so that you are on exactly the same footing."[39]

As a number of industries settle in a given town the advantages of interaction among them and the stimulation of supportive activities will generate an atmosphere of growth and development. The minister remarked:

> The difficult thing is to get the growth process started. Once it is started at the best industrial locations in the region, it gets a momentum of its own and the need for incentives gradually diminishes. That is what we are going to try to achieve.[40]

48

Government assistance is now to go directly to companies and corporations willing to put their own resources into degraded regions and thus stimulate employment. The concept is not entirely new as the ADA program shows, but the implication of the phrase "at the best industrial locations in the region" is a radical departure from all previous legislation. While previous assistance was based on shoring up the most degraded areas and those of highest unemployment, the Incentives Act envisages delineating huge areas of the country that contain a variety of circumstances. Industry then, theoretically at least, is left to make its choice within this variety. The Act is explicit in Section 3 (2) that a region may be designated only if the Governor in Council is satisfied that:

> (a) existing opportunities for productive employment in the region are exceptionally inadequate; and
> (b) the provision of development incentives under this Act for the establishment of new facilities in the region or modernization of existing facilities in the region will make a significant contribution to economic expansion and social adjustment within the region.[41]

The Act restricts the geographic application of incentives to particular areas, but widens the specific choice management has, within that restriction, to decide on a place to develop. Regional urban growth centre development is implicit in the fundamental assumption of the Act.

The designated region, shown in the accompanying map, covers the entire length of the Canadian southern boundary except for a small area in British Columbia and the Windsor-Ottawa peninsula in Ontario. The Maritime provinces and Newfoundland are included, as well as some major cities such as Winnipeg, Port Arthur, and Sault St. Marie, and the environs of Montreal. The only stipulation laid down in the Act concerning the designation of a region in any province, *apart from* degradation, is that it should not be less than 5,000 square miles in size. Approximately one third of Canada's population lives within the regions finally designated across Canada.

The question of regional size was hotly debated in the House and in the Standing Committee on Regional Development. The minister's original proposal was for an area of not less than 10,000 square miles, where, if a hypothetical region of 100 miles was set up, the central point would be about 50 miles from its boundary. With modern motor transport this was thought not to be an excessive distance for a person to travel to work.[42] The regions would not be delineated by rigid administrative boundaries, as was the case in previous programs (ADA, for example, used Canada Manpower Centre areas), but would be very broadly spread and would tend to follow natural geographic and communication areas. This was essential in that theoretically company management was involved in the decision to apply for an incentive. The factors that management would consider in this decision had to be provided for sensibly in the legislation. These were not likely

This map depicts the regions designated for assistance under the Regional Development Incentives Act of 1969. However, following revisions to the Act and amendment of boundaries, this map became inapplicable after June 30,

to follow administrative boundaries, but to follow the lines of economic opportunity.

The Incentives Act, ironically, exposed most of "developed" Canada — that is, all but the primary resource base developmental frontier of the North, the Ontario Industrial peninsula, and the southwestern part of British Columbia — to the scrutiny of companies and corporations who otherwise might consider only the major metropolitan areas.[43] They were to carry the risk of their decision to locate in relatively inopportune localities once the benefit of the initial incentive was consumed. The success or failure of this Act to influence management's locational decisions was a measure of the balance that favors or disfavors location in established cities. The minister, and many members of the House in debate, foresaw tremendous pressure from industry to benefit from grants. Some $49 million was allocated in the 1969-1970 financial year. To a great extent this prediction of demand has been verified. For the moment it is necessary to look

1974. (Map reproduced here by kind permission of the Department of Regional Economic Expansion, Ottawa.)

briefly at the aspect of this legislation which concerns federal-provincial relations.

Federal-Provincial Inter-relations under the 1969 Incentives Act
      The Department of Regional Economic Expansion was aware in 1969 of the interest of almost every province in attracting manufacturing enterprise. Many had incentive schemes of their own. When asked if the department would continue with the type of research study that had grown with the ARDA and FRED, the deputy minister said before the Standing Committee on Regional Development:

> We will certainly be prepared and be eager to make any studies that are called for for that purpose. In industrial development, though, on the whole the provinces are for the most part quite active in this field and we would expect to complement what they do, to fill in the gaps, rather than

51

to rush in and do a great deal ourselves which would be in any way duplication of effort.[44]

In the same reply the deputy minister elaborated on the expected order of priorities that the department might adopt in implementing the Act. He said:

> . . . the Minister, I think, has indicated that we would be putting a rather higher priority in the first phase on plans for some urban areas where a good response to the industrial incentive might be expected, and there would therefore be a heavy call for further urban services of all kinds and we would be prepared to make joint plans with provinces to enable those services to be provided. That is comprehensive planning in terms of all the types of services involved, but it is a good deal simpler and faster than the sort of planning studies that were conducted for the FRED plans.[45]

The Act makes specific provision under Section 6 (b) and (c) for the minister "in determining whether to authorize the provision of a development incentive in the maximum amount so provided or in any lesser amount" to take into consideration:

> (b) the probable cost to provincial, municipal or other public authorities of providing services or utilities required for or in connection with the facility;
> (c) the amount or present value of any federal, provincial or municipal assistance given or to be given, other than under this Act, in respect of the establishment, expansion or modernization of the facility.

Costs of public services incurred by an applicant may be met from development incentives, but such costs plus those of the plant cannot together exceed 20 percent of the total amount of approved capital costs involved in the facility. Thus, though the federal government will accept service costs as items to be covered by an incentive, an applicant company cannot become the instrument through which a local authority or province is able to expand its public services. The remarks of the deputy minister, suggest that the "joint plans with provinces to enable those services to be provided" may yet be forthcoming.[46] In this sense the success or failure of this Act to influence management's locational decisions is a measure of the adequacy or inadequacy of local urban public services in designated regions, or of the ability to improve them rapidly. If the necessary management is precluded from locating or expanding there, and the anticipated stimulus to employment opportunity is thwarted.[47]

The minister was asked in the Standing Committee if his department had any studies which could be made available to the committee about the concept and potential size of growth centres. The minister's reply was:

No, there is not because the growth centres are supposed to
be designated after consultation with the provinces. If we
decide what the growth centres are, this would be useless. . . .
We want to try not to exclude the natural growth centre and,
instead of excluding them from the designated region, try to
reinforce them. This is the whole idea and the whole
philosophy behind the Bill which is before us today. There
is no analysis on all the potential growth centres in Canada
because this does not exist.[48]

But the generation of growth in any centre will result largely, at least in
theory, from the company management's choice of location.[49] Differing
industries will have different locational ideals.

The federal government, in awarding incentives, is implicitly
initiating and stimulating a process that must oblige the provinces to
react. If the provinces refrain from direct involvement, preferably at
the initial points of decision in this process, they are bound to find
themselves coping *post facto* with a process initiated by companies and
the federal government together. The provinces will find themselves
obliged to provide public services in locations that industry and the
federal government together have identified for growth. They become
obliged to go along with a *fait accompli,* and thereby fail (a) to impose
their judgements on the situation and (b) to behave as the BNA Act
expected them to do, to maintain responsibility for certain
developments in terms of their own policies.[50]

The older theory of federal-provincial agreements on matters
of regional development, that expressed itself in such ways as
equalization payments, the PFRA, ARDA, FRED, and ADA, can no
longer be assumed to hold. Such agreements have been superseded by
the Incentives Act which relies on company management to make the
locational decision over vast regions of Canada. It relies, by implication,
on an attribute of companies and corporations which over the decades
has generated the contrast between centralized metropolitan areas and
degraded regions. The Act has attempted to reverse this process. The
provinces, by reason at least of their control of public services, retain
the regulative capacity over company decisions, at least in so far as
the designated regions within any province are concerned. Unless
provinces move deliberately towards directing the growth centre
process in terms of the equalization of differences between cities and
degraded regions, the outcome of the Incentives Act may be merely to
repeat on a provincial scale, within the designated regions, what has
occurred on the national scale since Confederation, namely, vast
regional degradation and intense urban concentration with no
regulative mechanism to adjust the two processes. It should also be
observed that the Act permits regulations to be made that prevent the
authorization of a development incentive if the proposed capital costs
are too small. Under the regulations an incentive will not be awarded
if the approved capital costs of the facility fall below $30,000 in the
case of a primary development incentive and $60,000 in the case of a
combined development incentive. The purpose of this restriction is to

limit the volume of applications from small family enterprises all over the designated region. Such enterprises would, in the minister's view, have little effect on employment opportunity, which was the prime purpose of the legislation.[51] Concurrently, of course, this minimum will forclose the possibility of every small town and village seeing in the Incentive Act an opportunity to assure its future. The effect of the Act will therefore be to stimulate further the concentration of production into growth centres.

In emphasizing secondary and manufacturing industry, rather than primary industry and service industry, the minister had hopes of stimulating an array of subsidiary activity. Resource and primary industry were thought not to stimulate tourism and other activity, but possibly to discourage it. Secondary industry, on the other hand, can stimulate service industries, including tourism, many of which tend to be provincially administered. It would seem that from this perspective also, the Incentives Act assumes considerable provincial initiative in the designated regions. The minister admitted in the Standing Committee that much thought had been given to including tourism in the Incentives Act. He remarked:

> With respect to the tourist industry, I agree with you that this is a real problem and I will tell you that we have given a lot of thought to the tourist industry. One of the problems we meet is that we are in the field of provincial jurisdiction, there is no doubt about that.[52]

If a province does not appreciate this potential, he felt that it would be difficult to provide an incentive in the absence of a general development plan to which both provincial and federal governments agreed. The minister further remarked:

> We can have agreements and make plans with provinces which cover roads, schools, hospitals, and all the infrastructures of the communities. We can do it. We can develop a tourist industry, but this has to be done with the provinces according to a general plan.[53]

The agreements under a general plan would fall not under the Incentives Act, but under the Industrial Research and Development Act, which was part of the legislation enacted with the establishment of the Department of Regional Economic Expansion. The two pieces of legislation were seen by the minister as complementing each other, but at the same time recognizing the prerogative of a province over the areas of its special jurisdiction. In reply to a question, the minister expressed it this way:

> Regarding those two pieces of legislation, in the first one [Industrial Research and Development Act] the emphasis is on the agreement with the provinces to develop infrastructures or activities which do not fall under the

Industrial Incentives Act. The other one [the Incentives Act] we will surely discuss with the provinces concerning, say, the regions that the province wants to develop more, the priorities of the province and so forth. However, we do not need any agreement with the provinces. We can give a grant to this company because we think it is a good thing. So we have two different pieces of legislation. . . . It is not fair to use the general law instituting or creating the department because there we are tied to the province and to an agreement with the province. . . . Of course, some regions need schools, others need roads, and still other regions need sewage systems. All this is within the jurisdiction of the province, so if we want to help, we must have an agreement with the province. This [The Incentive Act] is a very specific piece of legislation and it is administered directly by Ottawa and is aimed at giving grants to industry without any form of agreement with the provinces. So we need both.[54]

Thus, in the minister's mind, the federal government's provisions now include a complete package for rendering financial assistance to a province for both the provision of the urban infrastructure needed by secondary industry and the incentive to get this industry located there. It would seem that through the offices of the Department of Regional Economic Expansion a partly effective antidote may have been provided to company management's preference for locating in metropolitan areas.

Industry moved rapidly to investigate the new prospects. The regulations under the Act and the orders designating regions were authorized August 6, 1969. In a little over two months, to October 20, the department received 131 applications and by the close of 1969 had received 383. Of these 383 the department rejected 16, ten more were withdrawn by the company, and in one case, an offer lapsed through time. Construction had begun on 18 cases by the close of the year.

During the calendar year 1970 the department received 1,202 applications. Of these 1,202 applications the department rejected 259, and 299 applications were withdrawn. Offers were made in 428 cases, 56 offers were declined, 20 offers lapsed, and a total of 345 offers were accepted.[55]

The effect of the Act, during the twelve months January to December 1970, had been to assist companies to locate in the designated regions to the extent of $348,833,259 allocated in terms of their estimated capital cost for the innovation. These innovations were spread over the provinces as shown in Table 1.

The rate of applications received by the Department over the twelve months averaged 106.5 per month, with a peak of 134 during the month of January. There is little doubt, therefore, that this Act has been well received by manufacturing and secondary industry.

The Direction and Trend

Since the Prairie Farm Rehabilitation Act of 1935, the emphasis of the federal government's attempts at coping with regional degradation has changed from the particular to the general, from agriculture to secondary industry, from the small locality to massive regions, from partnership with the provinces to partnership with companies.

By a series of tentative steps the federal government has been obliged to move persistently towards an ever-widening scale of geographic effort across the country. It has moved concurrently towards expanding the generality of its efforts: from down-and-out prairie farmers to watershed dams; from agricultural assistance to general rural assistance; from rural job retraining and rehabilitation to the provision of a variety of jobs through assistance to industries locating in depressed areas; from industrial incentives in special areas, and from Development Areas, to growth centres extending over almost the whole southern boundary of Canada.

The federal government, tied constitutionally to co-operation with the provinces, has established a wide variety of relations with the various provinces. The general direction of this relationship, viewed from the perspective of the limited federal legislation reviewed above, appears to be from contractual agreement on the financial implications of provincially proposed action programs, through contractural agreement on the financial implications of federal and provincially proposed action programs, to programs that reflect both financial and policy implications for action direct from Ottawa. Under the Incentives Act the provinces are still involved, at the point of agreeing to the designated regions, but not at the point of agreeing to the company which will be supported in its decision to locate within a province. The federal government has retained its respect for provincial jurisdiction over the infrastructure services — roads, schools, etc. — of localities where industry locates, but has, through the Industrial Research and Development Act and the Special Areas legislation, a battery of provisions involving provincial plans and federal agreements to initiate adequacy in this area. The situation appears to be one of the provinces agreeing to, or alternatively, themselves initiating through the federal services, the actions and programs which the federal government feels obliged to instigate.

If the lessons of the past have meaning for the present, it seems safe to predict that the next stage of federal-provincial negotiation will concern their relative influence over provincial growth centres. As industry identifies centres for investment within the incentives areas the pressures to build an adequate urban infrastructure will mount. If the provinces act in concert with industry and the federal government, these pressures will be contained; but if a province does not act in this way, if it ignores the implications of federal measures on the centres in its jurisdiction, the federal government will be obliged either to withdraw federal incentive support from that province or to enact measures once again to circumvent the jurisdictional rights of the provinces.

In this situation lies the opportunity for the provinces to reduce the relative inconsequence of provincial decisions on urban affairs — but this reduction will require close and planned co-operation between the provincial and federal governments in dealing with the implications of companies' and corporations' freedom to locate as they choose.

1. The words "degraded" and "degredation" are preferred to "poor," "impoverished," and similar descriptions. "Degredation" is more appropriate in its sense of being degraded, or made different by qualitative inferiority against some supposed standard. "Poverty" tends to convey some absolute standard which becomes unreal when compared with, for example, the poverty of parts of India.
2. There is some ambiguity in Canada over the terms "local authority" and "municipality." For the purposes of this part of the study, the two terms are used synonymously to mean local governments of cities, towns, and villages which are the consequence of provincial legislation.
3. A substantial argument has been made in *The Case for Alberta* (Edmonton: 1938 Government of the Province of Alberta), pp. 51-55, that the random, speedy, and ill-considered dominion policy of the settlement of the prairies contributed as much as anything else to the plight of the southern farmers. Drought exacerbated the situation of people wrongly placed there in the first instance.
4. An account of the program is given in Buckley, Helen and Tihanyi, Eva *Canadian Policies for Rural Adjustment,* Economic Council of Canada, Special Study No. 7 (Ottawa: 1967, Queen's Printer), Chapter 3.
5. Ibid., pp. 72-73.
6. It would be possible to do approximately the same thing by using the reports and special studies of the Economic Council of Canada since its inception in 1963. The establishment of this council also represents an attempt by the federal government to cope with "levels of employment and efficient production in order that the country may enjoy a high and consistent rate of growth and that *all Canada* may share in rising living standards." Section 9 of the Act, 12 Elizabeth II, Chapter XI, 1963. (Emphasis added.)
7. Senate of Canada, *Report of the Speical Committee on Land Use in Canada* (Ottawa: 1964, Queen's Printer).
8. Brewis, T. N., *Regional Economic Policies in Canada* (Toronto: 1969, Macmillan), p. 106.
9. The regular national agricultural programs have been shorn since 1935 when the Wheat Board was established and pricing of primary commodities fixed by deliberate decision instead of "market forces." Buckley and Tihanyi, *Canadian Policies,* pp. 48 and 49, wrote: ."... particularly since the Agricultural Stabilization Act was passed in 1958 price support payments by the federal government have become a permanent feature in the production of many agricultural commodities. Some provincial governments have also been paying subsidies on various accounts ... Subsidies among farmers tend to be distributed according to their share of production, which implies benefits in rough proportion to the scale of enterprise ... "
10. *House of Commons Debates,* 1960-61, 1:819.
11. McCrorie, James N. *ARDA: An Experiment in Development Planning* Special Study No. 2, Canadian Council on Rural Development (Ottawa: 1969, Queen's Printer), p. 10.
12. House of Commons Debates, 1960-61, 5:5195.

13. McCrorie *Development Planning,* pp. 7-8.

14. Ibid., p. 15.

15. Brewis, *Regional Economic Policies,* p. 108.

16. McCrorie, *Development Planning,* p. 6.

17. The legislation in Alberta included (i) the use of Lands and Forests Acts, 1955, authorizing the appointment of a conservation and utilization committee that included representatives of the Departments of Agriculture, Lands and Forests, and Municipal Affairs, and the Power Commission; and (ii) the Agricultural Service Board Act, 1955, which made provision for local Advisory Boards to assist in the application of the Act. The Special Areas Act of the 1930s provided for the designation of areas where rehabilitation and resource development programs could be conducted. Alberta's use of ARDA before July, 1966 is outlined in Buckley and Tihanyi's *Canadian Policies,* pp. 247-54.

18. Ibid., p. 96.

19. Brewis, *Regional Economic Policies,* p. 108.

20. In the second agreement, 1965-1970, Census Division 14, North and West of Edmonton, was served by this provision.

21. McCrorie, *Development Planning,* p. 44.

22. Ibid.

23. Buckley and Tihanyi, *Canadian Policies,* pp. 96-97. The details of the formula for the second agreement are supplied in their footnote, p.97.

24. Speech by the Minister of Forestry, cited in McCrorie, *Development Planning,* p. 10.

25. Buckley and Tihanyi, *Canadian Policies,* p. 101.

26. McCrorie, *Development Planning,* p. 12.

27. Brewis, *Regional Economic Policies,* p. 128.

28. It was part of the Government Organization Act, 1969.

29. *House of Commons Debates,* March, 1969, p. 6893.

30. Ibid., p. 6894.

31. Ibid.

32. Ibid.

33. Ibid.

34. Ibid.

35. *House of Commons Debates,* 1969, 9:9844.

36. The Government Organization Act of 1969 had authorized the transfer of the ADA program from the Department of Industry to that of Regional Economic Expansion. Industry, in turn, gained Trade and Commerce.

37. *House of Commons Debates,* 1969 9:9842.

38. *Federal Services for Businessmen,* Department of Industry, Trade and Commerce (Ottawa: 1970 Queen's Printer), p. 54.

39. Standing Committee on Regional Development, *Minutes of Proceedings,* No. 16 June 16, 1969, p. 390.

40. *House of Commons Debates,* 1969, 9:9842.

41. 17-18 Elizabeth II, Chapter 56, Assented to July 9, 1969.

42. Standing Committee on Regional Development, *Minutes of Proceedings,* No. 15, June 11, 1969, p. 324.

43. The department, at least at the time the parliamentary committee dealt with the bill, did not intend to favor any particular province or region of a province or to favor any particular type of industry in any region when deciding on the merits of an application. As far as money allowed, it was to be an open deal in terms of the flow of applications. Ibid., p. 339.

44. Ibid., p. 332.

45. Ibid., pp. 332-33.

46. In reply to a further question before the Standing Committee the deputy minister indicated that the department was already in the process of discussing with several provinces plans to generate an adequate urban infra-structure, Ibid. p. 333. He was presumably referring to the Industrial Research and Development Act, 1969.

47. In practice, provisions exist in the legislation establishing the Department of Regional Economic Expansion, with the approval of the Treasury Board, to

cope with particular and difficult situations, but these provisions are outside those of the Incentives Act.

48. Standing Committee on Regional Development, *Minutes of Proceedings, No. 16.* June 16, 1969, pp. 355-56.

49. "Negotiable provisions" have played a part in the decision of management over location. Federal officials also indicate privately that location and incentive tend to be linked. This may be expected when regional growth is a matter of public and governmental policy.

50. In a recent study, T. N. Brewis and G. Paquet found themselves "close to being overwhelmed by the multitude of policies, programs, institutions and administrative arrangements introduced by the various provinces, most falling outside any conceptual framework of plannjng." Policies and programs were in a constant state of flux. *The Financial Post,* December 18, 1971, p. 10.

51. Committee on Regional Development, *Minutes of Proceedings,* p. 384.

52. Ibid., p. 370.

53. Ibid., p. 371.

54. Ibid., p. 375.

55. At time of writing, the 1971 figures were not available, but from partial evidence the rate of acceptance did not appear to be declining.

Chapter 2
Federal attempts to cope: degraded city areas,
1935-1952

The Dominion Housing Act of 1935,
The Home Improvement Plan of 1937,
and The Municipal Improvements Assistance Act of 1938.

      The Dominion Housing Act, 1935, was largely an anti-depression measure. Some 72 percent of skilled tradesmen in the construction industry were unemployed in 1934. There was also an urgent need for urban housing. At the time an estimated 27,500 new starts were needed annually, and the backlog had built up to 82,000 housing units.[1] Government measures so far, both to pull out of the depression and to cope with urban degradation, had proven ineffective. The Act was the first attempt by the federal government to legislate on housing as a national problem.[2]

      The 1935 Act is important because of what it introduced, and because of its relationship to the policy choices available to government at the time. The government had before it a variety of proposals emanating from the parties in the House and also from a parliamentary committee, chaired by A. D. Ganong, Member for Charlotte, which had reported on April 16, 1935.[3]

      The federal government was also pressed from many sources, including its own parliamentary committee of inquiry, to set up scientific and statistical instruments to measure the need for housing over different income groups and areas of the country, methods of financing housing, the extent of slums, etc. The prospects of formulating a national housing policy based on these scientific and statistical analysis seemed good.

      When moving the second reading of Bill 112 on June 24, 1935, Sir George Perley, on behalf of the Minister of Finance, advised that the government had decided to give the scientific and statistical aspect to a newly formed economic council rather than to set up a housing commission. A housing commission had been argued as an instrument both for fact gathering and for funding housing starts across the country, an administrative and applied research unit of government that could act quickly and in the right place. Sir George argued that the administrative aspect could be better handled by a branch of the Department of Finance. A fund of $10 million was to be provided in this branch.

      The most fundamental decisions concerned the kind of assistance to be given the home owner and the nature of the instrument to provide this assistance. The provision of housing grants to the provinces, to be administered by a provincial housing authority, was rejected. So also were direct grants to local authorities. The mode of assistance was to involve federal collaboration with approved private lending and finance institutions to the extent of 20 percent of construction costs which would be met by loans from the fund. The lending institutions would put up 60 percent of construction costs, and the borrower — either an individual home builder or a commercial builder — the remaining 20 percent. Land was included as part of the cost. Loans from the fund to the lending institutions were to be a 3 percent interest and they were to be passed on to the borrower by the lending institution at an average of not more than 5 percent. No doubt, though Sir George did not admit it, the difference between 3 percent and 5 percent was to be a lever to encourage private institutions to open their own resources to accommodate builders and domestic borrowers. The government and the institution were to be construed as providing a joint mortgage and any loss was to be administered by the Minister of Finance according to the details of the actual case.

The federal government's policy at that time is best described as "pump priming." Sir George saw the government's $10 million fund as having a $50 million financial stimulating effect "in order to start this very necessary program of housing particularly of the class required by the low paid man."[4] The problem faced by the government was to get lending institutions to move into the residential mortgage field. The 20 percent required of the borrower was applicable also to a building company intent upon large-scale production for renting to tenants. Rented accommodation would take care of the employed person who moved house frequently and the employed person without the means of contributing his 20 percent of construction cost.

The Ganong Committee had received evidence from lending institutions that they had plenty of funds available under appropriate conditions. A member of the Committee, G. D. Stanley, Member for East Calgary, pointed out in the debate:

> that they had $75,000,000 today which they wished to place if they could be convinced that the security was sufficient. When you have loan companies and organizations coming before the committee and saying that they have $75,000,000 which they wish to loan, you have a very splendid beginning at any rate; and all they need — so they said — is sufficient confidence in the undertaking, that their security will be assured.[5]

The uncertain part of the legislation was whether the private institutions would free their 60 percent of construction cost for low-income housing. At the time, the figure suggested for the cost of a house for low-income persons was $2,700, and the heads of large lending institutions had indicated that in Toronto, as an example, they would not lend on a house costing less than $3,500.[6] Whether the low-income person was ever likely to raise his 20 percent of the total

($500 to $600) was also an uncertainty. The opposition was quick to point out that similar legislation in the U.S.A. had proved abortive, and one reason given was that:

> Experience has unfortunately shown that many of the
> private housing projects submitted were conceived rather
> as a means of utilizing unsuccessful land subdivisions
> controlled by the applicants than as a means of meeting a
> definite need for low cost housing.[7]

The Dominion Housing Act was seen as a quick, interim measure that would not involve the expense and delay of a more thorough approach which could be considered at leisure. The government had apparently accepted the principle of a housing policy by referring to an economic council the task of finding facts on which policy could be based. The immediate task was to get houses started. The instrument was to be the private commercial lending and finance institutions stimulated by federal incentives.[8] These could be relied upon to transgress provincial boundaries, and they were not obliged to distribute their loans in proportion to the revenue they received from different provinces across Canada.

The question was raised whether local authorities would be empowered under the Act to put up the 60 percent of construction cost instead of lending institutions. The government's reply was that if they raised money by debenture and floated their own lending institution which in turn was approved by the Minister of Finance, there would be nothing to stop them.[9] In fact, most provinces prevented local authorities from incorporating companies for purposes of this kind, except by special enactment by the provincial legislature. It was clear at the time that few, if any, local authorities were in the happy position of being able to float a debenture for housing at a rate of interest less than 5 percent. As a practical matter the private lending institutions were the only source of funds likely to be applied and the federal government knew this.

The matters to be referred to the new economic council, in addition to those of statistics and inquiry, were stated by Sir George as follows:

> It is proposed that the economic council shall make an
> investigation about these various matters and among
> others, (c) as to plans or proposals that have been
> attempted elsewhere than in Canada to improve housing
> conditions and the results that have been achieved;
> (d) upon the necessity for and as to the feasibility of
> undertaking clearance and redevelopment of overcrowded
> areas in any city or town; in other words an investigation
> into the question of slum areas and what action may be
> taken to improve them, and (e) as to the factors that

enter into the cost of construction of houses and as to the feasibility by any means of securing economics and increased efficiency in such construction.[10]

The government of the day was relying on two stimulation effects to aid the lower income groups: first a "filtering down" effect of construction, for the class which could afford new housing would leave those houses they vacated to lower income groups either to rent or purchase; and second, new employment following rejuvenation of the construction industry. The government was also aware that slum clearance, as it was known in those days, was a major problem — considered, indeed, by some political critics as being a greater problem than housing — and could be tackled at the same time as the supply of housing. The government, however, was not prepared to move on such a scale. Similarly, it was unprepared to devise instruments for coping with the rental gap of the poor — the difference between what it was feasible for a family to pay for rent when food and other costs had been allowed for, and its available income.

The bill omitted measures to assist the renovation and rehabilitation of existing structures in both urban and rural areas. The parliamentary committee had recommended clearly that this aspect of housing be stimulated. They had argued that "more living units could be obtained more rapidly by repairing existing houses up to reasonable standards than by any other means."[11] Run-down urban dwellings, particularly tax-sale properties owned by local authorities, were but part of the accommodation which could be renovated to provide housing. Around the cities many smallholders had been forced off the land by land speculators or by rising taxes on land, and the houses were decaying through misuse or vacancy. Many rural properties were empty as a consequence of the migration from the land, yet other rural accommodation was grossly overcrowded as a consequence of sons, with their wives and children, returning to the parental farm after becoming unemployed in the city, and thus saving themselves the cost of rent for urban accommodation. As a purely humanitarian measure to cope with accommodation needed by people, the bill seemed to the opposition parties to be avoiding some simple and available solutions. The difficulty which government of the day saw was that of administering such small-scale and widely dispersed operations, though the provincial administration was not considered. Lending institutions also would be reluctant to support such operations as their interest was in new, long-term investment in housing if they were to support the Act at all.

For these several reasons, therefore, the Dominion Housing Act, 1935, was little more than a federal means of inducing the lending institutions to put their surplus funds into residential mortgages. Its provisions were designed to assist the class of person with income sufficient either to pay the 20 percent down payment required or the rental on accommodation built by commercial builders under the terms of the Act. It was not a measure designed effectively to meet the needs of the poor or to assist in the most direct way possible the improvement of existing accommodation in urban or rural areas.

In January, 1937, the federal government, now under Mackenzie King, introduced a bill to guarantee approved lending institutions against losses resulting from loans for home improvement, repairs, and additions to residential buildings in urban and rural areas. But a new type of guarantee was needed to get them into this activity. The liability of the federal government under such guarantees was limited to 15 percent of the aggregate amount of home improvement loans made by any single approved lending institution. The extent of the federal liability was to be $7½ million, which in turn would facilitate a total amount of $50 million of loans under guarantee. The government could announce at any time that no further loans would be guaranteed.The scheme was known as the Home Improvement Plan. It, too, had "pump-priming" characteristics. It was also the first means by which the chartered banks were brought officially into housing under federal sponsorship. The The scheme was a direct result of a report submitted by the National Employment Commission, set up in 1936, as a method of absorbing the unemployed across the country. The United States had implemented a similar scheme in 1934 under the Federal Housing Act, where it was known as the "modernization credit plan."

As with the Dominion Housing Act, 1935, the financial institutions of the country openly supported the legislation. The Minister of Finance, when introducing the Home Improvement Plan, said:

> Under date of September 28 the president of the Canadian Bankers Association, acting on behalf of all the chartered banks, wrote to me as Minister of Finance stating that the banks had agreed to co-operate fully with the dominion government in carrying out the plan, and moreover that they were willing to commence making loans on their merits without awaiting the legislation.[12]

The difficulty the banks had experienced since 1934 was to find borrowers for their accumulated assets in whom they could place faith to repay a loan. The point had been strongly made by the Leader of the Opposition, R. B. Bennett, during debate on the Employment Commission legislation in 1936.[13] Some government security seemed to be the stimulant required.

The Minister of Finance envisaged the plan operating on the basis of people's individual credit worthiness. He remarked:

> But any owner of a home, who is credit worthy and desires to make improvements, can get from a chartered bank or any of a number of other institutions . . . a loan under the terms of this home improvement plan.[14]

In reply to a question, he remarked:

> If loans have been refused for any other reason than that
> the borrower is not in the view of the lending institution credit
> worthy, or that the money is not to be used for the purpose
> contemplated by the scheme, I have not heard of it. These
> are virtually the only two valid reasons for refusal of loans.[15]
> We are not compelling the lending institutions to lend
> where they do not think a loan would be repaid; they must
> have reasonable confidence of that.[16]

As the legislation did not require any collateral or endorsement for the
loan, the lending institutions were to rely solely on credit worthiness,
though the fact that the legislation referred only to home owners
presumably allowed the banks to hold title deeds in safe keeping if
the property was not already mortgaged. Remarks in the House referring
to cases of loans already made, showed that lending institutions were in
fact asking for endorsement and other additional security. The minister
stated:

> This scheme is devised for the individual on his own credit,
> without endorsement and without collateral security. That is
> why the government is standing behind the scheme.[17]

Another member raised the question of poor localities for which
lending is discouraged:

> The bank, taking the attitude they have maintained for the
> last five years, said that the locality did not warrant a loan,
> although the man was definitely of a good type to whom
> money could be lent, and is well employed.[18]

The Leader of the Opposition summed up the issue neatly by saying:

> The government has not undertaken under this plan to
> direct that banks shall make loans. The banks must make
> their own decision, based upon the exercise of discretion.[19]

This discretion, however, was to be applied rather generously.
During the second reading the minister elaborated on the publicity its
facilities were to be given through the agency of the National
Employment Commission. Their task was to be "the organization of
the co-operative community effort" necessary to insure success.[20]
This was viewed as an all-important function. Publicity, paid for by
public-spirited citizens and business interests, was to popularize the
facilities. Committees in the various provinces, but not part of
provincial governments, were organized as well as "local advisory
committees in every community to stimulate home improvement
activity, to afford every encouragement and information to prospective
borrowers, and to interest local participating industries and business

66

groups."[21] A vital issue for these latter groups was to hold the local property assessor at bay so as to forestall the imposition of additional local taxation on home improvements and thereby thwart the scheme *ab initio* in its unemployment-reducing potential. The minister remarked:

> In all parts of Canada local committees are dealing with that phase of the matter, either with their municipalities, . . . or by making, in respect thereto appropriate representations to the provincial governments.[22]

Similarly, it was by implication the responsibility of municipalities or provincial governments to prevent the use of the legislation to renovate condemned dwellings or slum properties. The federal government did not feel it could "enter into an argument as to whether a dwelling is or is not habitable or suitable for human occupation. The determining authority in such instances would be not ourselves but the local authority."[23] The plan therefore relegated local authorities to a watch-dog role on habitability while local private enthusiasts were to stimulate the use of the legislation through financial institutions. This was possible because the plan was an instrument to repair existing property. Repair and renovation could not damage the interests of mortgage holders in the properties and the plan did not cover the construction of new properties. Local authorities might benefit later from re-assessments when the economy generally had improved to the point where local taxation would no longer be an impossible burden for many home owners.[24]

In May, 1938, the federal government in a measure to cope with unemployment legislated to assist municipalities in making self-liquidating improvements. Many local authorities during the depression had been unable to keep their income-producing utilities such as water, sewers, and transport up-to-date. The public investment market had not been available to many of them, partly because of its own financial situation. High operating and maintenance costs were suffered because money could not be procured or provided for improvements. The federal government proposed to lend money to municipalities "on easier terms than ever before," namely at 2 percent interest.[25]

The constitutional problem of provincial responsibility for local authorities was met by having the provincial governments approve each local authority's project and also guarantee to the dominion the repayment of the loan and the amortization charges of the municipality. It was recognized as a new departure for the federal government to make loans direct to municipalities for municipal purposes. The routing of municipal applications for loans was to be through the provincial governments, who would confirm the facts supporting the loan request as well as affirm their approval of the request. The maximum limit of federal loans was fixed at $30 million and the distribution among municipalities of this money was to be determined by the ratio of a municipality's 1931 census population to the population of the dominion at that date. It amounted to about $3 per head. The smaller municipalities, which in consequence of this limit would be in no position to borrow a significant sum, were to be treated as having available a maximum loan of $200,000 notwithstanding their actual population. The length of time the loans would run was uncertain as it depended on the nature of the improvement to be made and the rate of return coming from it. The governor in council was authorized to stop making loans at any time when the sum of money approved for the scheme was running out. It had no limit of duration beyond that.

The federal government was emphatic that the Municipal Improvements Assistance Act was to be construed as part of a national program to cope with unemployment. It was not a matter of entering municipal financing in a way that would pre-empt the provincial jurisdiction. The minister was very conscious of the variety of relations that existed across Canada between local authorities and their provincial governments, and hoped that provincial arrangements would be legislated if necessary to enable local authorities to borrow from the federal government with some form of provincial guarantee. This was the first occasion, in housing and urban development, on which provincial governments were expected to legislate enabling provisions for their municipalities to use federal incentives.

The Act had to be non-discriminatory concerning which local authority might benefit from it. The government did not intend to favor those municipalities where unemployment was higher than in another. Nor would a specially advantageous self-liquidating project in one municipality be preferred to any other in another municipality. The minister remarked:

> I do not desire and the government does not desire to
> be placed in a position of even appearing to discriminate
> between the thousands of municipalities in this country . . .
> if in this legislation we make it possible for one or two of our
> great cities to take larger amounts than their proportion of
> the whole population, I am afraid that we shall seriously
> lower public confidence in the scheme.[26]

The federal government was adhering to a policy of "fair and equal" treatment of the lower levels of government. It was not a matter of fair and equal treatment of the unemployed or of the needs of the local authority as evidenced by the condition of its utilities. This legislation was confused between being a measure to deal with unemployment in terms of its severity and distribution and a measure to provide a nation-wide service to local authorities. There was, however, nothing to stop a provincial government from favoring particular local authorities, within the rather minimal provisions of the legislation, by offering guarantees or support for only those it wished to favor.

The position prior to 1938 was, therefore, one of federal initiative to cope with national unemployment through the construction industry. The individual had been offered home ownership and home renovation and repair at federally subsidized rates of interest on loans made available through private, commercial lending institutions. These services had been provided without reference to the provincial governments as they used the right of individuals and the federal government to contract with lending institutions. The provincial governments had no rights to interfere in either of these contractual situations. The federal government had also offered local authorities finance at unprecedently low interest rates and had involved provincial governments in the scheme not as the primary lending source, but largely as guarantors of their local authorities' indebtedness. The provinces' right to policy formulation over their local authorities' acitivites was relegated to one of approval of the local authority's proposals.

From 1935 to May 1939, the federal government, in a time of national depression, instituted the three main provisions of its housing policy that have remained to the present time. First, through the Dominion Housing Act it established the role of lending institutions and succumbed, we assume, to their dictates of freedom to determine who should receive a loan and thereby both the income group and the location of the physical structure to which the loan referred. Secondly, by the Home Improvement Plan, it introduced the chartered banks as auxiliary contributors to housing finance when other lending institutions were unwilling or unable to assist. Also by this legislation it set up the early machinery for coping with run-down housing, and what later came to be known as urban renewal. Thirdly, by the Municipal Improvement Assistance Act, it had established the right to deal directly with the affairs of a local authority subject to some form of recognition of provincial constitutional authority. The Dominion Housing Act, the Home Improvement Plan, and the Municipal Improvements Assistance Act were therefore the beginning of the relative inconsequence of a province's decisions over its urban affairs with regard to both its individual citizens and the activities of its local authorities.

The First National Housing Act, 1938

The National Housing Act (NHA), passed in 1938, was the legislation that finally set the pattern for the federal government's approach to new housing and urban degradation. It repealed the 1935 Dominion Housing Act, though it kept several of its principles, including the use of private lending institutions as the means of accommodating the house owner. The 1935 legislation had proved too unwieldy for the federal government. Up to May 31, 1938, only 4,249 family housing units had been financed under the 1935 Act, as amended through regulation in 1936. Of the federal government's $10 million subvention, only $4.5 million had been committed, with a total aggregate expenditure on home construction under the Act of $17,350,000. Building permits of all kinds in Canada between 1935 and 1938 were running at between $140 million and $200 million. The Minister of Finance admitted in 1938 that the 1935 Act had achieved something; but the reasons for the lack of general support were stated by him to be:

First, the unwillingness of the lending institutions to make loans in many small and remote communities, and second, the reluctance of the lending institutions to make loans for small amounts in what they regard as the less desirable residential areas of the larger urban communities, despite the fact that these districts are, in many instances, the only areas in which it is possible for the people in the relatively low income groups to build houses for themselves.[27]

The federal government had also been under pressure in the House to deal with slum clearance. A resolution introduced by Denton Massey, Member for Greenwood, in February, 1937, had stimulated consciousness throughout the country of the urgent need for action. The Bruce Report on conditions in Toronto, produced by H. A. Bruce, Lieutenant-Governor of Ontario, had revealed the seriousness of human degradation in Canada's major city. Mr. Massey pointedly remarked that the country was diligent over its education for youth but was permitting "this cancerous growth of slums to eat at the very vitals of our nation."[28] Sickness was costing the country about $300 million a year, while "these diseases are being fed by the conditions under which we compel men and women to live."[29] He pointed to three major difficulties:

> The first is that the federal government cannot force municipalities and provincial governments to introduce housing schemes and slum clearance plans. Second, there is our system of realty taxation. Third, have we the funds available to underwrite such schemes if, as and when approved by the provinces or the cities?[30]

The Minister of Finance, C. A. Dunning, concurred that the major stumbling block to effective national action on slums and housing was that the BNA Act required the provinces and municipalities to institute action.

Douglas Ross, Member for St. Pauls, a slum area of Toronto, analyzed the financial difficulties in these terms:

> The trouble is that there is no provision for the replacement of low cost houses in this country. If the ability to pay rent is represented by the sum of $12 per month and the economic rent necessary to support the investment is $22 per month, how can there be any replacement except with state assistance? . . . But there is the problem — a fifty percent gap between the ability to pay and the economic rent. How can private enterprise in any form, be expected to enter a field of business which involves a loss of fifty percent of the capital before you start?
> The low cost housing field, as I have stated, is one in which the principal part that private enterprise can play is to keep

going thousands of dilapidated, obsolete, broken down old houses.[31]

The strategy of the 1938 legislation arose from studies made of housing legislation overseas. Different schemes to meet particular situations had to be created which in turn would meet the Canadian quality of the local housing problem. The three-part omnibus bill was custom-built legislation, while the 1935 Act was too simple, too uniform to have had any marked effect. Being custom-built the new legislation had to meet the needs of every item involved in house construction in urban and rural areas. It had to relate together the fears and difficulties of the poor, low-wage earner who had hitherto been reluctant to apply for loans, the fears of the private lending institutions, all levels of government, and the construction industry in every part of the country. The minister's assessment of these parties and their respective anticipated contribution under the new Act was as follows:[32]

(i) With regard to the poor man, who had (if it was not a building speculator making use of the Act) to initiate the request for a home building loan in first instance:

> to my mind it is most important to rid the mind of the man of small means of the fear which is there now of the responsibility involved in building even a low cost home for himself. Fear is very largely the cause of this depression . . . The evidences of fear on the part of people of small means who have small savings are found in the growing savings deposits in our banks and trust companies. People in many would rather put their money into the safe keeping of institutions which they deem to be safe than attain the ambition of a lifetime by the ownership of a home of their own, involving a commitment for the future, rendered uncertain in their view because of the high taxation, the uncertainty of employment, and this widespread fear of depression.
> If the government and parliament of this country can . . . stimulate the man of small means through the knowledge that his parliament and his government have faith in the future of the country, and that the people as a whole are willing to put their credit behind the small man, and are willing to give him advantages — ease of payments, ease of costs, contributing towards his load of taxation — something worth while will have been accomplished.

(ii) The minister singled out the role of life insurance companies as illustrative of the general role of lending institutions. He remarked:

> The people of Canada have displayed their faith in life insurance to a degree that is exceeded by only one other nation on the face of the earth, and the sums entrusted to

our life insurance organizations are immense . . . this
legislation is designed to cast out fear on the part of those
investment institutions also, and to encourage them, as
partners with the parliament of Canada, to make advances
for the purpose of building homes not merely in our larger
great centres where everything is easy, and where salability
of property in case of foreclosure is relatively greater,
but also in the smaller centres throughout the country. The
tendency in the last few years with respect to the financing
of homes has been to accelerate the growth of our great
communities and to retard the normal growth of those small
communities throughout Canada which are still the backbone
of our country.

(iii) With regard to the construction industry, the legislation
was designed deliberately as a challenge. Charges had been levelled at
this industry that it was laggard in advancing new techniques, in the
scale of its operations, and hence in its cost-cutting capacity — an
opinion the minister did not share, but he did say:

that there is one way in which anything this parliament may
do in connection with housing can be killed . . . [and that] is
for the building construction industry, capital and labour,
material suppliers and all the rest, to believe that they can,
be reason of it, start a steady upward trend in the price of the
commodities they have to sell.

(iv) The co-operation of governments was envisaged in the
following way:

We also require . . . the co-operation . . . of municipalities in
the setting up of the local housing authorities, providing for
adequate zoning and planning ordinances, granting the
partial tax exemption called for under Part II of the bill
relating to low rental housing, and doing real constructive
work on the planning of low rental housing objects. We desire
the co-operation of the provincial governments in providing
legislation . . . in giving leadership, we hope, and direction to
the municipalities within the province, and in giving the
provincial guarantee where low rental projects must be
carried on by a local housing authority which is municipal in
character.

The minister admitted that the provincial governments would continue
to be excluded from that part of the Act dealing with private borrowers
and commercial lending institutions as they had been in the 1935
legislation, on the grounds that the law provided for a contract between
the federal government and approved lending institutions to meet the
needs of individual borrowers.[33] With regard to the federal
government's role, which was to supply most of the money, the minister
remarked:

care has been taken to safeguard the interests of the dominion
and to surround the various parts of the program with
provisions to ensure safe and sound businesslike procedure.

As with the previous legislation, the federal government's constitutional
argument for intruding into what had previously been considered a
matter of provincial jurisdiction rested on housing being a national
solution to a national problem of unemployment.[34]

The bill had the unmistakable quality of being based on
thought whose assumptions are those of the social engineer. Such a
model of social action implicitly assumes that by the removal of or
reluctance to action and by the provision of inducements that guide
action in a particular direction, the sum of human acts supposed by the
model will lead to a given course of collective action. If only the parts
were put together in a way which insured that each part played its
anticipated role, the national housing problem would be solved.
Different parts of the society thus modelled, particularly the individual
borrower, the lending institutions, and the municipalities, had to be
offered legislative inducements in order first to act at all and then to
act according to the role anticipated for them. Much of the debate which
ensued in the House involved judgements about the kind and extent of
inducement needed. This model has been largely responsible for the
ad hoc nature, and the almost annual amendments, which have
typified the NHA over the decades.

This game of judgement over inducement has been typical of
legislation and regulation surrounding housing since 1938. The
numerous amendments to the NHA since that time and the battery of
regulative amendments reflect the attempts to cope with the changing
real situation the model had to reflect. The three parts of the Act were
but one expression of the specialized nature of the legislation, namely,
that expression which identified the types of problem which legislation
had to meet and the instruments which were appropriate to meeting
them.

Part I was intended for families wishing to own their own
homes, with particular emphasis on the low-income groups in urban
and rural communities, and the incentive needed for lending
institutions to lend to them wherever they may be located. It envisaged
what was called a "normal" case for a loan and a "special low cost
provision," with particularly easy terms for the borrower and extra
guarantees by government security to the lending institution, for the
very poor person or remote rural house. The "normal" case was one
where a housing loan could be made for from 70 to 80 percent of the
"lending value" of the new house. Of this total, whatever it might be,
the federal government would advance 25 percent and the lending
institution or local municipal authority the remaining 75 percent. The
"lending value'" was defined as the lesser of estimated cost of
construction or appraised value, as the case may be. The cost of land was
included.

The "special low cost provision" applied to a house whose
construction cost did not exceed $2,500. In this case a loan could be

made for from 50 percent up to 90 percent of the lending value, of which the federal government advanced its 25 percent. This 90 percent scheme would meet the case where the accumulation of a down payment by the home owner was difficult and also where some capital had been accumulated but only a small house was required, as for older persons. To take care of the risks lending institutions would be incurring under this 90 percent scheme, and also to cover the greater risks run by lending institutions on loans made in the degraded areas of both urban and rural regions of Canada, the federal government applied the aggregate loss guarantee that it had introduced under the earlier Home Improvement Plan legislation. The application of the principle under the new legislation was to be up to a maximum of 20 percent of the total amount of the 80 percent portion of loans made by the lending institution for properties whose lending value did not exceed $4,000. The earlier legislation provided for only a 15 percent aggregate loss guarantee.

This aggregate loss principle was to apply only to certain areas designated for the purpose by the minister. These were mainly in country districts, but it made the "special low cost provision" at least in part a geographically defined phenomenon. Even so, the minister himself was not entirely convinced that lending institutions in general would enable it to work. He stated:

> I am confident . . . that we shall be able to get the consent of at least some lending institutions to make these small high percentage loans to deserving people in certain sections of our larger cities, in the suburban and rural areas, in fishing villages, mining towns, and small urban communities generally.[35]

The application of the aggregate guarantee principle was to induce and justify the lenders

> in making loans in communities remote from the larger centres, small communities which as an ordinary business proposition do not commend themselves to lending institutions, both because of the cost of looking after a few loans involving considerable travelling expenses, and also because of the security factor involved in the low re-sale value of property situated where sales are infrequent, as is the case in rural communities as compared with our larger urban centres.[36]

The government intended to raise the amount of its guarantee in proportion to the total percentage of the loan and to the reluctance factor of lending institutions to lend in particular areas. No lending had been going on in areas the minister intended to designate.

In order yet further to induce lending institutions to lend in designated areas, the bill provided for payments to them by the federal government to defray

> special costs incurred in arranging loans, making appraisals,
> inspections and so forth in small and remote communities.
> ... This payment is not to exceed $20 for any one loan, plus
> a mileage allowance fixed by the minister for necessary
> travelling expenses based upon the distance from the nearest
> place from which the loan can be arranged and supervised
> by the lending institution.[37]

The set of assumptions implicit in Part I was that by adequate financial
support by the federal government, and by adequate security for risks
taken by institutions lending their assets to a variety of persons,
sufficient funds would be forthcoming from lending institutions to meet
the demands of individual and commercial builders. Concurrently, as
lending institutions were playing the role of administrators of loans to the
individual applicant, the federal government had to meet their unusual
costs when serving people in outlying areas and to give added security
to them in loans to these areas. It was also assumed that sufficient
control over lending institutions existed in the coercion of the
competitive market in which they operated, in the requirement that they
had to be approved by the minister, and in the legislation already
regulating their activities as finance houses.

Part II contemplated an experiment in low-rental housing
by facilitating federal loans to local housing authorities.[38] The federal
commitment was put at a maximum of $30 million under this heading.
This part of the Act was based on arguments suggested by the National
Employment Commission. These arguments concerned the supposed
relation of adequate housing to personal health and decency on the one
hand and on the other, the threat to the employability and efficiency
of the work force living under such conditions. The minister remarked:

> While the primary responsibility for decent, safe and sanitary
> housing conditions must rest, under our constitution, upon
> the province and upon the municipalities, nevertheless, the
> proposed dominion program is justified by emergency
> conditions, because it is designed to create needed
> employment, to direct attention to the importance of the
> housing problem generally, and to provide a basis of
> experience upon which the provinces and the municipalities
> may follow sound and proven policies in the future.[39]

The minister viewed Part II as an instrument for dealing with the slums
of the major cities if the municipalities took the initiative. There would
be no investment required of the tenants.[40] The "local housing
authorities" the bill recognized were of two kinds. Both were to be
concerned with the construction of houses for lease to low income
families. Local authorities themselves could operate the provisions as
a municipal matter or as a municipal housing authority with 10 percent
capital provided by the local authority (which could take the form of
land), or local authorities could enlist the co-operation of private
enterprise in working out their low rental housing scheme. In the latter

case, the local authority acted through a limited-dividend housing corporation (maximum 5 percent dividend) with capital sufficient to provide for 20 percent of the cost of the project. This capital would be supplied "by public-spirited citizens who may be expected to plan, construct and administer the enterprise on sound business lines."[41] The federal government was to put up the remainder of the capital at very low interest rates, in the case of the limited dividend scheme at 1¾ percent per annum, and in the case of the local authority types at 2 percent per annum, plus, in both cases, a 1 percent half yearly amortisation cost. The loans were to be retired in 34 to 35 years.

The provincial government was to fit into this arrangement only with respect to the two local authority types of administration. If the rental housing came under the local authority types, the province was asked to guarantee repayment — as in the Municipal Improvements Assistance Act of 1938. But no such guarantee was to be required of the province in the case of the limited dividend housing corporation. The minister noted these advantages:

> Obviously the larger equity, double the amount, renders that less desirable and from my point of view at least it has this advantage, that those municipalities which desire to undertake low rental housing projects will . . . be able to get going . . . very much more quickly if they can interest public-spirited citizens in putting up 20 percent of the cost . . . than they will be able to do, by reason of delay due to changes in law which might be required in some cases before the municipal law would be sufficiently broad to enable them to operate municipally.[42]

Though the limited dividend housing corporation was to circumvent the provincial interest entirely, it was not to be totally outside municipal responsibility. In addition to approving the project, the municipality had to agree to limit its municipal taxes on the project, while any of the loan was outstanding, to not more than 1 percent annually of the cost of the whole project. The management of such a project had also to agree to hand it over to the local authority on demand at any time, with suitable financial adjustments. If the administration of such a project involved a shortage in the amount due to the federal government on interest and principal, then the local authority had further to reduce its local taxation on the project to make up the shortage. The minister remarked:

> Not having the guarantee of the provincial government, we must there insist upon the closeness of municipal interest in the scheme and a degree of responsibility.[43]

Further, a local authority had to plan, construct, and supervise the project as well as familiarise itself with the project's accounts and daily operation. The minister expected only the larger municipalities to favor large-scale apartment-type buildings where the limited-dividend scheme might have a particular appeal to private investors and at the same time reduce the monthly rental to the tenants. Small schemes would not be economical. This step involved the fundamental matter of differential taxation within local authorities and was in consequence a highly problematic proposition.

Corresponding to these conditions imposed on local authorities, a set of conditions had to be imposed on the type of tenant that could live in the low-rental housing schemes. This subsidization brought with it an immense bureaucracy. No family could be rented accommodation whose total family income was equal to more than five times the economic rental of the unit, unless there was no demand for the unit from families of lower income. The economic rental was determined as one giving a return of 9½ percent on the cost of construction, plus the annual municipal taxes. The annual rental to be charged was not to be in excess of 20 percent of the family's total income.

A rent reduction fund, assisted by voluntary contributions from individuals, the local authority, or the province, could be established to reduce the rentals below costs if they so wished. The minister saw this rent reduction fund as the means whereby lower levels of government and particularly local authorities could build new accommodation for slum dwellers at no, or next to no, rental costs if the local authority found it cheaper to do so than to administer the high-cost slum areas already existing. He saw Part II of the Act as infinitely flexible, allowing a local authority to get to work on all aspects of slum degradation if it chose to do so.[44] On the other hand, the federal government felt the bill did not authorize it to deal with slums itself.[45]

The $30 million of federal money was to be distributed among the local authorities according to the relation of their 1931 census population to the total urban population of Canada in the same census. "That proportion," the minister remarked, "will give ample opportunity for the development of large scale experiements, particularly in our larger centres, in the direction of low rental housing projects."[46]

The assumption implicit in Part II was that the constitutional responsibilities of provincial and local authorities would coerce them into action if federal funds were made available, and that it was therefore possible for the federal government to impose a set of conditions on them concerning both the instrument they were to use — the limited dividend corporation — and their relation to the tenant. Concurrently, the possibility was left open to them to disregard this coercion, if only because they were left with the obligation to take the initiative. It is little wonder that the minister had to argue for Part II in terms of its experimental character. The control considered necessary for local authorities also contrasts with that implicit in Part I towards lending institutions, which were assumed to be inherently controlled by the competitive forces of the market and their own self-interest.

Part III contemplated an attack on what was thought to be "the major obstacle retarding the building of new houses," namely real property taxes. It contemplated a three-year tax holiday, scaled down by year, for construction started between June 1, 1938 and December 31, 1940. The federal government was to pay up to 100 percent of the municipal taxes levied on a new house for the first year in which the house was taxed, and up to 50 percent and 25 percent respectively in the two following years. It applied to houses costing up to $4,000 only, that is, to low-cost houses whether built under the provisions of Part I of the National Housing Act or not. This tax included the general municipal tax and the school tax, but excluded special and local improvement taxes. In return local authorities owning considerable numbers of lots suitable for low-cost housing had to co-operate with the federal government by making them available, at not more than $50 per lot, or the amount of tax outstanding on them, to the people who wanted to build low cost homes. The house had to be occupied by the owner. This provision of the bill had limited duration, the house had to be started before the end of 1940. It was seen as being an important way of stimulating construction, thus reducing unemployment, which in turn was expected to reduce local taxation for the ordinary property owner by decreasing the number of people on unemployment relief.

The ideas suggested by some members opposed to the principles of the NHA are not without contemporary importance. Instead of setting up this elaborate bureaucratic and administrative machinery which impinged directly on provincial jurisdication, some members suggested that part, perhaps a third, of the income taxes recieved by the federal government should be returned to the local authorities of the country. The local authorities would then have money to start their own construction and to provide public services. A member remarked:

> In Canada our municipalities have been starved; they have had no money for any public works . . . No new construction can be undertaken, and the result is that taxes on real estate are such that nobody wants to own it.[47]

Other members doubted if the lending institutions would really provide the money. Speaking of his personal experience in Edmonton under the Dominion Housing Act, a member remarked:

> Last year I tried to obtain a loan personally from different insurance companies in Edmonton for the purpose of building a home for myself . . . I even went to the mayor of the city of Edmonton and called up several insurance companies, but with the same result. They say they have not made loans for the last seven years in Alberta, and that suggested to me that it was not because of any opposition at that time to the social credit government.[48]

The member's emphasis on "at that time" referred to the reluctance of lending institutions to advance money before the steps taken by the Alberta government in 1937 to reduce the cost of mortgages and the rates of interest and to prevent foreclosure that subsequently made them reluctant to lend in Alberta at all. The Leader of the Opposition put the matter this way:

> There is in Edmonton, for instance, a life insurance company which has substantial sums loaned on mortgages. Owing to recent legislation in Alberta the solvency of that company is threatened. Therefore insurance companies have now, I think, practically concluded that it is unsafe to make any further loans in Alberta. The minute legislation was passed which took from insurance companies two percent of their mortgages, they having predicated their reserves — that is the measure of their ability to meet their responsibilities — on the expectation of life according to the mortality tables and on a three percent rate on their investments, this had the effect of reducing their capital by two percent. And the other provision does away with the payment of interest. The result is that the companies which have to maintain a reserve will not put in into mortgages in Alberta. That is the real trouble.[49]

The Leader of the Opposition extended this argument, about the reluctance of lending institutions to play their role, to a wider context. He remarked:

> One of the difficulties the minister should face fairly is the fact that the old spirit with respect to local institutions is gone. You cannot bring it back by merely invoking the spirit of the past; it will not come back . . . Our federal tax touched these [small, local] companies just as it did the great companies. A case came to me . . . a man had a small private bank, and he had all the funds he borrowed invested in real estate mortgages. Between the operation of the Farmers' Creditors Arrangement Act and other legislation he is ruined . . . it closed him up. The morgages cannot be realized upon. The minister knows that the business of life insurance companies does not permit of experiments being made in connection with these matters. They have to know that the investment of the premiums received from their policy holders will return sufficient to pay their claims on the estimated dates when they become due according to the mortality tables. If they fail to do that they come within the punitive provisions of the law . . . the local institutions can no longer be relied upon; in fact they are getting out of business just as fast as possible . . . The reason is that it is no longer possible for local business to carry on successfully.[50]

This debate raised two issues of fundamental importance to urban affairs that influenced Alberta at the same time as the province's own political decisions. The issues concerned: (a) the centralizing tendency implicit in the finance houses' own policy towards the loans they were willing to make — a policy they were obliged to follow in pursuit of profits under conditions that obliged them to safeguard the investment of their customers' deposits and provide the returns they had contracted with their depositors to pay; and (b) the pressures which finance houses had experienced under (a) above, obliging them to close their unprofitable branches — or in the case of locally registered finance companies in towns and small cities, to go out of business — and thereby impoverish the financial services available to the dwellers of towns and small cities across the country, both literally and in terms of the opportunities available to them. This process had been continuing at least since the 1920s. The consequence of linking the nation's housing policy to lending institutions, who themselves were irrevocably involved in the centralizing process of major city growth and sequentially the degradation of towns and small cities, virtually guaranteed that not only finance, but human dwellings and the necessities of life would be linked to the process of city growth. It made the growth of the cities, with all its associated phenomena, appear to be the inevitable outcome of inexorable natural law.

The lending institutions approved by government under the 1935 Act until June 1938 included 13 life insurance companies which were all national in their scale of operation, 13 trust and mortgage companies, and three other lending institutions (two in Quebec and one in Manitoba). Of the head offices of these companies, 20 were in Ontario, five in Quebec, three in Manitoba, and one in New Brunswick.[51] The distribution of loans made up to March 31, 1938 is shown in Table 4.

TABLE 4. Distribution of loans, to March 31, 1938, from lending institutions by province.

Province	Millions of dollars	Family units
Ontario	$7.91	1,959
Quebec	4.95	1,057
British Columbia	2.14	705
Nova Scotia	1.53	351
Manitoba	0.43	87
New Brunswick	0.33	78
P.E.I.	0.05	10
Saskatchewan	0.01	2
Alberta	nil	nil

House of Commons Debates, 1938, 4:3773

As with the 1935 legislation, the new legislation made no provision to oblige lending institutions to make loans. Their discretion was to remain inviolate. There were many institutions, in the minister's opinion, which did not particularly like the idea of being in partnership with the government, but he considered that by educating them in this method of co-operation the problem could be solved.[52] In a discussion of the Act during committee of supply in 1939, the minister indicated that for February, 1939 there had been a 100 percent increase in the use of Part I of the Act over the corresponding month of 1938, but the difficulty of getting the lending institutions to lend in areas they disfavored had persisted. He added:

> I may say that a very large amount of the time of one branch of the department is taken up with endeavouring to work out with companies the difficulties of, shall I say, problem areas.[53]

Taxation problems and municipal financial adjustment problems continued to affect the attitude of lenders towards both Parts I and II of the Act. The minister by this time had come to the following conclusion:

> If we are looking at it from the point of view of large scale development . . . we need the co-operation of those large estate corporations which themselves at present own land in various ways and would be able, through the medium of the housing act, to take advantage of a constructive method of employing their assets. We have some hope of getting that kind of co-operation in some quarters.[54]

As early as 1939, therefore, it had become clear that the ambitions of lending institutions were not to be limited to mortgage financing alone, nor to family residential properties alone.

The total use made of the joint loans from the federal government and lending institutions under the Dominion and the National Housing Acts from 1935 to July 31, 1944 was 21,839 joint loans, amounting to $87,388,517. Some 26,433 families had been accommodated. No lending under the NHA was taking place in Alberta up to 1944. The net loss incurred by the federal government under both these Acts had amounted to only $970.[55] The lending institutions had indeed been circumspect in the use of their discretionary powers![56]

Wartime Developments and the 1944 National Housing Act

World War II changed the situation for both unemployment and housing. The industrial cities began to boom from war contracts. The national housing program tended to slip into insignificance. In March, 1940, Part II of the NHA expired without any loans having been made for low rental construction, and some of the conditions of Part I were narrowed in the same year. In October the fund set aside to finance the Home Improvement Plan was exhausted and not refurnished. A wartime housing corporation known as Wartime Housing Limited, set up by the Department of Munitions and Supply, was working to meet urgent housing needs, particularly in temporary, prefabricated, mass production units designed to accompany new military or industrial plants. In April, 1941, the federal government sought the permission of the provincial governments to take over the corporate and personal income tax fields as a temporary war-time measure.[57] The municipalities, which had also been levying income tax up to this time, were obliged to cede this power to the federal government also. A scheme of reimbursement allowances was introduced. By 1942 all construction projects not related directly to the war effort were held over, but by 1943 thoughts were already turning to the post war problems of peace.

The Canadian Federation of Mayors and Municipalities, after analyzing the 1941 census' findings on housing, made representation to government over the shortage of housing in Canadian cities. Some 25 Canadian cities, with populations in excess of 30,000 reported that 61 percent of their people lived in rented accommodation. Some 17 percent of such accommodation had neither bath nor shower. Over 143,000 housing units would be needed in the cities if each family was to have its own unit and about 83,000 in the country districts. The position taken by the opposition in the House was that the Wartime Housing Ltd. project was not meeting any of the permanent housing needs of the country, the project was costly per unit and likely to lead to slums in the future. Toronto in particular was experiencing threateningly disorganized suburban development as a result of war industries. The municipalities had found that the allowance supplied to them by the federal government as a wartime measure to cover extraordinary public utility costs, school services, policing, etc., was too small. Although some housing under Part I of the NHA was still being constructed there was little co-ordination between the two schemes. The Minister of Finance, C. D. Howe, indicated the limitations of Wartime Housing when he said:

> Wartime Housing does not enter a community unless there is need for industrial workers in excess of those that can be housed in the community. I would also point out that the location of houses in the community is governed by the proximity to the plant which the houses are intended to serve. It is not the function of Wartime Housing to go in for elaborate schemes of improving cities.[58]

Up to March 31, 1943, Wartime Housing had spent $48 million. Some 15,802 houses had been built in 70 municipalities. Ontario had received well over half. None had been built in Alberta or Manitoba and only very small numbers in Saskatchewan.[59] The average cost per house was $2,229 with approximately $500 additional for services.[60]

On August 5, 1944, the Minister of Finance, J. L. Ilsley, introduced the resolution that produced the 1944 National Housing Act, to be carried on under the National Housing Administration of the Department of Finance. It was an ominous 6-part bill that tended to consolidate the existing variety of legislation. The only major new principle was the emphasis to be given to city and community planning as part of developmental policy.[61] Some $275 million was involved in the proposals. The bill was intended to put "a house building programme and the improvement of housing conditions well up in the forefront of the general programme of reconstruction which we are preparing for the post-war period."[62] Wartime Housing was to continue to meet the needs of military personnel in particular localities on a rental basis. The special needs of demobilised personnel were to be taken care of, if necessary, under special provisions outside of the proposed legislation.

According to Part I of the bill, the federal government was to promote the construction of houses by prospective home owners and the sharing of losses in respect of loans by joining approved lending institutions. The amount sought for this purpose from parliament was $100 million. The onus was placed on a lot owner or builder to take plans, specifications, details of location, and such to an approved lending institution to seek a loan. The institution, which was more broadly defined under this bill, would ascertain the cost, appraise the land, check the plans and specifications to determine that they conformed with the government's prescribed standards, and check the credit worthiness of the borrower, before submitting it all to the National Housing Administration for its examination and approval. The minister remarked:

> We may then approve the plans and application as
> they stand or require certain necessary modifications.
> If we approve the application, a loan is made jointly by the
> lending institution and the Minister of Finance with the
> first mortgage or hypothec running jointly to the two of us.[63]

Loans were to be repaid in monthly (not quarterly) installments and would include interest, amortization of principal, and the annual taxes on the property.

The extent of loans was also reduced to not less than 50 percent of the lending value of a house, nor more than 95 percent of the first $2,000 of lending value, plus 85 percent of the amount by which the lending value exceeded $4,000. This was an administratively improved version of the scaling principle of the 1938 Act. The new contracts would provide for an interest rate to be charged the borrower of not more than 4-1/2 percent, made possible by the government advancing its 25 percent of the joint loan on a 3 percent interest basis while the lending institution obtained a return of 5 percent on its share of the loan and for the work it had to do. The maximum term of a loan was to be 20 years, except in those cases where "there is sound community planning and adequate zoning restrictions in respect of the area in which the house is to be located, where the term will be a maximum of 30 years."

The guarantee against loss continued the aggregate amount principle of 1938, but in this Act the federal government set up "classes or categories" of loans that reflected the location in which the house was to be built. The 15 percent of aggregate amount remained the limit the government would guarantee for each lending institution's loans. This enabled the government to:

> establish a number of guarantee pools in order
> to encourage the making of the type of loan which from
> our point of view is more desirable ... we can provide a higher

pool guarantee for loans on small homes where the
percentage of loan to lending value would be very high, and
also a higher guarantee for loans made in
smaller or more remote communities or in what the lending
institutions regard as less desirable residential sections
of our larger towns and cities.[64]

Low aggregate guarantees would be given on loans in the best
residential areas. This new approach continued and elaborated on the
geographic designation that had been introduced under the 1938
legislation as part of the "special low cost provision" but by
somewhat different techniques. The federal government was still
searching for a way to influence lending institutions in the location of
their investment. In this instance it was a matter of greater guarantees,
but as the net loss incurred from 1935 to 1944 was $970, it was
hardly a realistic effort on the part of federal authorities.
        The bill also recognized in Part I the possibility of
co-operative housing projects being set up by tenant owners. A
corporation could be set up or a trustee hold title to the project. The
assumptions implicit in the model represented by Part I were little
different from those of the 1938 Act. Technique was improved, and the
lending institutions would now do all the preparatory work. Greater
latitude in the extent of the loan — from 50 percent to 95 percent
depending of the cost of the dwelling — was also introduced. The
incentives were again extended to encourage lending institutions to lend
in undesirable areas.
        According to Part II, by joining approved lending
institutions and limited-dividend housing corporations to make loans,
the federal government would assist in the construction of rental
houses and the sharing of losses. Part II of the bill elaborated
its counterpart of the 1938 Act by providing for four types of project or
activity: (a) ordinary, commercial renting housing projects would be
financed by joint federal-lending institution loans in much the same
way as under Part I of the bill; (b) low-cost rental housing could be
financed through limited-dividend housing corporations. In this case
rents might be below actual cost. The corporation would have to
subscribe 10 percent of the capital, as against 20 percent in the 1938 Act.
The federal government would raise the remaining 90 percent of the cost
at 3 percent per annum interest. The term of the loan could be 50 years.
Any lower level of government or social agency could contribute to the
rent reduction fund as in the 1938 Act. If the project were sold, the
proceeds had to be arranged in such a way that no capital gains accrued
to the corporation; (c) life insurance firms and other designated
institutions with federal jurisdiction could be authorized to invest
an amount not exceeding 50 percent of their assets in Canada to
purchase land and construct low or moderate cost rental housing projects,
and to manage them. These projects could include accommodation
for retail stores, shops, offices, and other community services
(excluding hotels) "as the company may deem proper and suitable for
the convenience of the tenants of such rental housing project."[65]

Before the minister would approve the investment, the project had to agree "with an official community plan satisfactory to the minister." There was to be a limited guarantee by the government involving 2½ percent profit per year on the cost of the project if the insurance companies met certain earnings limitations. The minister explained the reasons for this innovation in these terms:

> One of the great weaknesses in the house-building industry in Canada is the absence of a substantial number of companies with competent management and with sufficiently large resources to acquire large blocks of land, particularly in our larger cities where land values are high, and to develop such areas in a comprehensive way providing all necessary community and incidental services.[66]

This provision, and the following clause (d), were supposedly the start of a national program of urban renewal, that really came into its own only some twenty years later. (d) The federal government was to provide direct grants to municipalities for clearing slums. The conditions to be attached to such grants were that the land acquired and cleared must be developed under a master plan approved by the local municipality; that the land must be sold either to a limited dividend housing corporation or life insurance company, which had agreed to build a low or moderate cost rental housing project on it; and that the acquisition and clearing of the land had to be approved by the provincial government. The federal government's grant would be directed at the difference between the cost of the land and its resale value for rental accommodation. It had become realized that slum areas of the major cities were high value land, which, after the cost of purchase and demolition of structures on it would be too expensive to build on subsequently for low or moderate cost low density rental accommodation. The federal grant was to meet the difference and was described as an "excess acquisition cost" grant. The size of the grant was limited to 50 percent of the amount of the excess acquisition cost. The municipality, possibly in conjunction with the province, would meet the remainder. A limit of $20 million was assigned to this assistance.

The elaboration of the 1938 model, contained in the 1944 Act, was largely an extension of the range of institutions and techniques that might be used to cope with low rental accommodation and slum clearance. Lending institutions of a specific kind, namely those likely to encourage large construction projects, were given the opportunity of combining low and moderate rental high density accommodation with community and ancillary commercial services. The hitherto neglected area of rental accommodation for the poorer sections of the urban community was to be stimulated by offering the incentive of commercial and remunerative activities associated with it. By permitting the insurance companies to put up to 5 percent of their Canadian assets into land and rental accommodation, by obliging limited dividend corporations to supply only 10 percent of the equity, the federal government envisaged itself stimulating this difficult area. Construction had to be done on planned terms, obliging local authorities to move ahead with official community plans. The specific slum clearance provision of clause (d) circumvented the jurisdiction of the provinces except that their approval was required for a municipal proposal on slum clearance. But the conditions imposed on local authorities obliged them to sell federally supported slum-land acquisitions to insurance companies or limited dividend corporations for the rebuilding part of such operations. Municipalities were not to be free to reconstruct on their own initiative or with provincial assistance, if the federal excess acquisition grant under the Act was to be used.[67]

According to Part III, by providing lending institutions with special assistance the federal government would encourage them to lend in rural areas, on farms, and in small communities, and by entering into contracts with manufacturers of building and home appliance equipment, would insure the production of components for rural homes on an economic cost basis. The liability to the federal government under this part was not to exceed $5 million.

According to Part IV, the federal government would assist lending institutions by guarantee in making loans for the repair, alteration, and extension of existing homes. The aggregate amount of such loans, under guarantee, would not exceed $100 million. This was a re-enactment of the essential features of the successful 1937 Home Improvement Act.

Part V provided that the federal government promote research into technical matters of construction and design to lower costs and to promote better housing conditions and more efficient planning of communities. It gave authority to the minister to investigate housing conditions across Canada, and to fund research into building standards and the technical aspects of construction either independently or in conjunction with the provinces, local authorities, or individuals.

Part VI concerned the staffing provisions and regulations, and also provided for a borrower to take out reducing term insurance to pay the outstanding amount of a loan in the event of his death.

The 1944 debate exposed more clearly than any previous occasion the issues of policy in dispute. The pre-war legislation and the policies implicit in it had not met the situation, and the war had exacerbated it. On the question of adequacy alone the proposed $275 million was but a start in meeting the 600,000 housing unit shortage in urban and non-farm areas estimated to exist by the Curtis Committee on post-war housing and reconstruction. However, the "pump priming" quality of the bill could make a figure appoaching $950 million the possible contribution of the legislation from all sources. The issue of federal versus provincial and local authority responsibility, however, became the nub of the debate.

The urgency of unemployment, of getting the construction industry to contribute to pre-war economic rejuvenation, and of putting under secured arrangements the surplus funds of private lending institutions to public benefit, had dominated the pre-war policies of the federal government. These matters had pushed aside the constitutional responsibilities of the provinces on the ostensible grounds of national calamity and need. In his introductory remarks to the 1944 bill, the minister made his position clear. The bill

> does not adopt the views of those who believe that our municipalities should engage directly or through local housing authorities in a vast programme of state housing furnished largely by dominion government funds
> . . . under Canadian conditions we cannot believe that such a programme would be sound or necessary. Several at least of the provincial governments would, I am sure, not wish their municipalities to embark upon municipal housing projects and we as a dominion could not contemplate with equanimity the pouring out of vast sums of dominion funds to municipal authorities to be expended in the construction of municipal housing which would involve grave problems of administration.[68]

The minister was setting federal policy explicitly against the handling of housing in general by local authorities. The policies applied in Europe and elsewhere to cope with this matter were unsuitable to Canada. In effect, the minister's policy was to retain federal control of the urban growth process through lending institutions.[69] Even rental housing, to be used largely by lower-income persons, was to be retained under federal and lending institution initiative. In this regard the administrative problem foreseen by the minister was to assure that municipalities did not let tenants whose income was too high into low-rental accommodation; or that municipalities did not charge rentals in excess of 20 percent of family income for those who were eligible. He remarked:

> I do not think it would be possible in a municipal housing project to assure that such control of tenants and rentals would be administered on an efficient and independent basis.[70]

In the minister's view the bill provided an adequate alternative machinery.

Later in the debate, the minister was obliged to indicate a further difficulty of working, in this case, through the provinces. He remarked:

> I do not think the setting up of provincial authorities was considered. It must be remembered that we have had a pretty sad experience in dealing with certain of the provinces so far as recovery is concerned. There are four provinces all of which owe us large sums which apparently they have no intention of paying. When it comes to relations between the dominion government and other public authorities we naturally are getting a little bit careful. But I am not putting it entirely on this ground. There are

87

disadvantages in advancing money and putting other
public authorities in this country in debt to the dominion
government. It can lead to a very serious situation.[71]

When pressed on the delinquency as a national calamity, the minister
replied:

All the fertility of the human intellect comes right
into play in finding reasons why solemn obligations signed
by interior jurisdictions in this country will not
under certain conditions be honoured, and we are absolutely
powerless to do anything about the matter.[72]

This attitude is a far cry from the hesitant, persuasive
attitude of ministers towards provincial jurisdiction that typified the 1935
and 1938 legislation. The attitude was adopted, again, at a time of
national uncertainty and provincial government weakness. The federal
position was espoused in 1944 on grounds of administrative
incompetence and financial delinquency on the part of junior levels
of government. The difficulty was pointed out more clearly in the 1945
debate that preceded the setting up of the Central Mortgage and
Housing Commission. On that occasion the minister remarked:

The government does not, in general, believe that public
housing with dominion ownership represents a sound
approach in a country of divided jurisdiction in which
property and civil rights are the unquestioned field of the
provinces under peace-time conditions.[73]

Concurrently, the federal government was offering financial support to
lending institutions and also to the junior levels of government,
if they undertook co-operation on its terms. This may be interpreted
as national leadership, but it was a case more of wielding the big stick
than playing big brother.

This attitude is illustrated by references to the concept, then
new, of community planning. The minister, in a public statement before
the bill was introduced, had advised provinces and local authorities to
review their legislation on official community plans. He had said:

I must emphasize that it is not the dominion's function to
prepare or be responsible in any way for specific projects or
community plans. Provincial governments should see that
there is enabling authority on the statute books to allow
municipalities to take the necessary steps to develop and
enforce strict zoning ordinances and sound community
plans, but the people of each community through their
local authorities and planning boards or commissions must
be responsible for the working out of specific plans or projects
adapted to the needs and conditions of the particular
community.[74]

The minister had also appointed to his staff "one of the best known and most competent town planning engineers available in this country." Provisions of the bill, particularly on slum clearance and the length of time permitted on housing loans, were dependent on the existence of officially approved community plans. This approval was to be given by the federal government as well as by provincial and local government. In reply to a question on federal approval the minister remarked:

> It has to be approved by the federal government too. That is the very fundamental of it. The municipality, the province and the federal government have to agree.[75]

But money would be available only on obtaining federal approval.

This position led to members from Western Canada speaking very frankly about the policy of the federal government. J. H. Blackmore, Member for Lethbridge, asked, "how long is it going to take the idea to percolate into the heads of the men in the government of Canada that there are first class administrative bodies in this dominion called provincial governments" and he added that these governments stand ready to take the lead "if the dominion government will get out of their way."[76] The Member for Vancouver-Burrard, G. G. McGeer, referred to the constitutional position, by saying:

> In my opinion, of all the violations of the true spirit of our Canadian constitution we find the greatest one in the selfish attitude of the federal parliament to the junior departments of government. I find no better expression of that same weakness . . . in our national administration than in the attitude expressed in this bill in connection with slum clearance, and in the utter indifference on the part of the federal authorities to any desire to become associated with provincial and municipal governments in making conditions in the cities better for the masses of the people.[77]

He supported his contention by reference to the Sirois Commission.[78] The minister's reply was that Part II of the bill provided local authorities with a mechanism for going ahead with slum clearance if they so wished. Should the $20 million set aside to meet the "excess acquisition cost" of land prove inadequate, a further provision could be approved by parliament. With a shortage of labor and building material resulting from war activity, he doubted if even this sum would be used.

Later in the debate, the minister was obliged to clarify the point that Part II was "not a slum clearance proposal nearly so much as it is a housing proposal. Slum clearance here is merely incidental to the other provisions of the bill . . . It is not in any way an attempt to deal with the slum situation in the dominion."[79] The general question was to be worked out with the provinces and municipalities at a later date and a forthcoming federal-provincial conference would be used to initiate it.

That the slum clearance provisions of Part II were to be construed as an aspect of housing, rather than as measures in their own right, raised the age-old issue implicit in this type of legislation of government guarantee for the profits of lending institutions rather than of government action to meet the needs of people suffering urban degradation. Mr. McGeer concluded a long and penetrating criticism in these terms:

> Why should the Department of Finance become, as it is rapidly becoming, the mainstay, the main support, the helping hand, the guiding light and the guardian angel of all the debt-piling bodies in Canada? That is where we are going to on this housing legislation. All the way through it is helping the financial organizations.[80]

Similarly, other members interpreted the 2½ percent guarantee of profit to insurance companies or limited-dividend corporations — with a deliberate exclusion of municipalities — as obliging a municipality to "keep its slums, but you give a guarantee against loss to a life insurance company or to some lending institution, while you refuse to extend that privilege to a municipality."[81] Mr. McGeer had emphasized the obsolescent quality of urban slums, particularly in the old cities of eastern Canada, and argued that a good deal of the $20 million could be spent "in a young city like Vancouver . . . there are whole areas in that young city that are outmoded to-day."[82] The way to cope with city blight was no longer through housing alone. The whole environmental concept of human living, as epitomised in the community centre idea, was, in his mind, now required, but the bill had got no further than the ideas contained in the 1935 and 1938 leglislation, and those, even in their day, had proved inadequate. His case was supported further by reference to the use of city housing authorities in the major cities of the eastern American seaboard, in the United Kingdom, and in Scandinanvian.

There was also, in the case made by members from western Canada, something of a personal touch that should be provided for in legislation. The Member for Lethbridge, early in the debate, had argued that the policy was to give "the bankers a lot more business . . . The whole object of the government seems to be to turn business their way and to guarantee that business so that they will not lose anything on it."[83] This was not entirely a socialist argument, but one reflecting also the remoteness and the indifference to personal needs of finance houses based largely in eastern Canada compared with the relative warmth expected to follow from a genuine local community effort to accommodate local people. The case carried on assumption of local capacity to care for local people and their needs if only given an opportunity. It was a feature of face-to-face responsibilities and obligations, of Christian brotherhood, rather than the coercion of large-scale bureaucratic operation and the onus of contractual obligation enforced by distant, calculating operators.

The now repetitive criticism of legislation involving the discretionary powers of lending institutions — that by remaining the arbiter of who will receive a loan, in what areas of a city it will be approved, and what parts of the country might benefit, they hold the reins of developmental decision — was expanded in the 1944 debate to include the built-in waste of available rural housing now lying empty. The war industries had effectively consolidated population and manufacturing in the cities, leaving many non-farm and farm houses available. Although Part V of the bill reintroduced the 1935 concept of a research wing to national housing, and a survey of vacant accommodation was to be undertaken as part of the new proposals, this research was unlikely to influence the lending institutions' decisions towards desirable areas for lending money for housing or for the location of industry and employment. The bill seemed to guarantee the waste of vacant accommodation in small towns at the same time as it set apart the city from the countryside.

Central Mortgage and Housing Corporation, 1945

Little more than a year after the passage of the 1944 legislation, in October, 1945, parliament was considering the establishment of the Central Mortgage and Housing Corporation (CMHC). This corporation was to act in the place of the Minister of Finance in operating the National Act, except in certain issues, and to provide discounting facilities for loan and mortgage companies. The corporation was given an initial paid-up capital of $25 million.

It is no accident that CMHC was established so soon after the enactment of the politically powerful 1944 NHA. In all probability (and we could discover no evidence to the contrary), it was not seen in 1944 as a necessary consequence of that legislation. The administrative measure considered necessary in 1944 was a branch of the Finance Department, but this very quickly became inadequate. The federal government's commanding position over housing and urban affairs, resulting from the 1944 legislation, virtually necessitated an administrative instrument of the kind that CMHC was to become. Nevertheless, the corporation was not to determine housing policy in Canada. This was to remain directly with the federal minister responsible for administering the corporation.

The reason advanced for this change was that the NHA provisions involved the government in business:

> principally in the business of lending money on long term for the construction of houses. Bargaining and negotiation are involved. Risks have to be appraised . . . those responsible for the administration of the Act require a background of commercial knowledge and an intimate day to day contact with development in mortgage lending throughout the country.[84]

The proposed change was considered a part of the general policy of administering government lending activities through crown corporations, such as the Bank of Canada, the Industrial Development Bank, or the Farm Loan Board. As with other crown corporations, general policy and by-laws would require consent of the governor in council. The discount function was argued in these terms:

> to provide a supplementary source of credit for the loan and trust companies to which they can turn in time of need. In some respects, therefore, the corporation will provide for these lending institutions the kind of rediscount facilities made available by a central bank for the ordinary commercial bank.[85]

The problem of the lending institutions was seen as a limited market for mortgages. Mortgages were not as negotiable as, say, government bonds with which they competed in the investment portfolios of long-term lending institutions. The effect of the bill was "to enable the corporation to put lending institutions in funds that otherwise might run out of funds, or be out of funds, and in that way supply money for lending to the public of Canada."[86] By being empowered to buy and sell mortgages the corporation would give mortgages a liquidity not hitherto provided, which, in turn, would tend to lower the rate of interest on mortgages as it would bring them more into line with the liquidity of other types of security, such as government bonds. The minister explained that:

> it is desirable so far as possible to have loans made by local lending institutions or trust companies. They might very well run out of money, if there is a large demand. Their cash resources are limited; but if they have access to a central institution which has the power either to buy mortgages or to discount mortgages, they will be able to do more business and lend more money in that local area within which they are included than they otherwise would . . . Loan and trust companies borrow short and re-lend long, which in many cases is the reason why they are not operating under the housing act.[87]

Because of the liquid position of the lending institutions at the close of the war, the minister did not expect them to make such use of the facility "but the knowledge that they are available will give the private institutions confidence and thus enable them to meet effectively the borrowing needs of the public."[88] The government had in mind the desirability of maintaining an adequate flow of mortgage loans in all parts of the country as well as "working steadily in the direction of lower rates and suitable terms on all kinds of mortgage lending, both rural and urban."[89]

Immediately following the war the problem of completing the 50,000 housing units anticipated for 1946 was shortage of materials rather than finance — though as much as 50 percent of Canadian lumber was then being exported, mainly to the U.S.A.[90] Nevertheless, the lending institutions had already sensed a dilemma over finance. This dilemma involved, on the one hand, the possibility of using all their resources on more profitable and more negotiable operations in the general growth of cities than on the provisions of the NHA. On the other hand, they were committed to support the federal government in its now decade-long policy that favored the use of their facilities under the NHA. This remains today their basic dilemma. In the immediate post-war situation the leaders of insurance companies had negotiated with the Minister of Finance, at the latter's request, over their terms for engaging in large-scale rental housing — housing intended largely for the lower-income group. The companies had expressed their preference for projects in the moderate-rental level rather than in the low-rental level, particularly when building costs were low (due to wartime price restriction) and relative to the anticipated post-war increases in prices. They knew where greater profits lay.

As an urgency measure they proposed to set up subsidiary, limited-dividend corporations of their own. These subsidiaries, if approved by the minister, would operate under those provisions of the Act that enabled government to advance 90 percent of the loan for low rental accommodations. The subsidiary, as a limited corporation, would provide its 10 percent of the equity and run the project in terms of a maximum profit of 5 percent of the equity and a guarantee by government of a minimum profit of 2½ percent. This scheme would enable them "to spread the dollars which they were prepared to invest at once over several times as many houses."[91] As events turned out, all the life insurance companies in Canada joined together to form Housing Enterprises of Canda Ltd., which was a mutual institutional holding company. This company initially proposed a two-year program of about 10,000 units and planned to distribute them in the cities from coast to coast. (This program was reduced in 1946 to 3,400 units in view of the increased costs of building and the consequent higher rentals involved if they were to be economic.[92])

From the government's point of view this financial commitment to meet 90 percent of the loans on limited dividend corporations could be met safely since the 1944 legislation had produced an expenditure only slightly in excess of $15 million of the appropriate $275 million under the Act as a whole. This was over a fifteen month period. Also, under the provisions of the Act dealing with limited dividend corporations the government's liability for losses was limited to 15 percent of the company's aggregate losses and insurance companies had been allowed to put only up to 5 percent of their assets in Canada into this type of low-rental accommodation. No loans had been made for low-rental projects at all to date, though $1.5 million had been used moderate-rental projects. No grants under the slum clearance provision had been made. The Act since 1944 had been used mainly under Part I. The federal government was slowly being obliged to face the fact that its method of stimulating housing for low-income people was ineffective. Up to 1969 it had found no substantial solution to this problem.

The one provision of the NHA not to be handed over to the proposed CMHC was grants for slum clearance. The minister argued in this case that as it was a grant and not an investment, the corporation would do only the preliminary investigation, and the assessment of the total residential situation as an aspect of its research, leaving the minister and the governor in council the final authority to make grants for slum clearance under the NHA. During the second reading debate the minister advanced a second reason: that the need for shelter was now so great that the country could ill-afford to pull down any structure. "Slum clearance," he remarked, "must come a little later when the pressing needs of housing are met better than they are at the present time."[93]

The minor issues of the debate that followed this resolution of amendment to the NHA centred around the privileged position of Wartime Housing over scarce building materials. Private builders had been unable to get a fair share unless they contracted with Wartime Housing projects. Private builders in turn were allegedly building only expensive houses and very few for the poor or for returned veterans. A further difficulty was the inflated price of residential land.

The first major issue was the principle of setting up a crown corporation which would "consolidate the moves the government had made in going into the business of housing."[94] The government was seen as being caught in a difficult squeeze — by having committed itself to the lending institutions it was now important to invest the billion dollars over the four or five years needed to do the job itself, and at the time, by fixing 5 percent as a fair rate of return to lending institutions, it had put a floor on interest rates such that the poor could never afford the houses likely to come from the NHA provisions. The minister was reluctant to consider the possibility of direct subsidy for houses for the poor, though the discrepancy remained between average income, about $1,400 per year and the rental cost of the cheapest house.

The second major issue surrounded provincial jurisdiction relative to the bill's proposal to permit CMHC to go where it liked "and buy up and secure any mortgage in existence in Canada."[95] Solon Low, Member for Peace River, Leader of the Social Credit Party in the House and one time Provincial Treasurer of Alberta, saw in the bill the resurgence of the 1939 Central Mortgage Bank Act, that had never been proclaimed although it had been passed in the House.[96] He remarked:

> And now I see that same proposal being brought back into the House, dressed up in a very innocent-looking, indeed a very worthy dress — housing . . . I see in this bill what might be one more attempt to arrogate to the dominion government the powers and rights that were allocated to the provinces provinces under the British North America Act . . . We are determinedly set against the centralization and the arrogation of provincial rights into dominion hands.[97]

94

He envisaged the proposed CMHC coming into conflict with the provinces on the adjustment of outstanding arrears and thereby raising constitutional issues. Should the bill, he asked, not contain a mechanism to facilitate adjustment in the case of necessity? If the corporation finds itself in some time of stress in possession of a fairly substantial volume of mortgages, what would happen?"[98] Mr. Low's concern was the centralization of the mortgage business in the hands of a corporation that was extra-provincial in its jurisdication. A province had to be left in a position to prevent a "cold-blooded foresclosure" on the part of any group if its constitutional responsibility to safe-guard property and civil rights was to mean anything. He remarked:

> I am concerned about trying to preserve for the provinces a modicum of their original rights, and perhaps to reverse the whole procedure we have been following for many years and got those rights back into the hands of the provinces . . . It is not necessary to work through mortgage companies, it could be done through the existing machinery, through the provincial and municipal governments and the Bank of Canada; and we ought to be giving consideration to that sort thing, rather than to approve what I think is a corporation money-lender's charter.[99]

Mr. Low argued that he was not speaking for Alberta alone, but his argument applied equally for Saskatchewan, Manitoba, British Columbia, or even Nova Scotia or New Brunswick, for the degraded provinces of Canada, by implication. The minister replied by asking which was preferable — for the crown to keep out of the provinces with its money, or to go in and have some assurance that it will be able to collect if it is necessary to do so?[100] Mr. Low replied that it was not a matter of choosing between the two; but of seeking a workable alternative — "I contend that the minister will have to make a wholly new approach to this housing problem . . . I would be happy to try to work out something with the minister."[101]

The minister recalled "the great efforts which the government of Alberta made, their visits here and the interviews they had, to try to get us to see that the National Housing Act was applied in Alberta and that loans would be made in that province . . . It seems to me that the honourable gentleman must elect what position he wishes to take."[102] In a less personal vein, the minister argued that if it became necessary to enforce foreclosure on a mortgage, the corporation would be free to do so. He remarked:

> I do not know what the constitutional position is, but our contention has been that in a case of that kind we are not bound by debt adjustment legislation of the provinces. I have said to the provinces that we think the thing operates almost automatically; that I cannot take the taxpayers' money and put it in a province where I know it is going to be lost,

or may be lost by reason of provincial legislation. I have to stay out of that province; and that is exactly the way other people look at it. Recently the province of Alberta has taken a very sane and reasonable view, comparatively speaking, at any rate, about this, as compared with former years. Lending institutions, governments and others are lending with more confidence in Alberta; and I assume that there would be some rediscounting business done in that province.[103]

The minister felt that the setting up of the proposed CMHC would itself prevent a constitutional clash between the provinces and the dominion over the question of property rights and debt adjustment. By working through CMHC and lending institutions the mortgage was not held specifically by the crown and the dominion did not get into "the business of lending money from the Atlantic to the Pacific and all these loans are free from the trammels of debt adjustment legislation, provincial legislation generally."[104]

In one sense, CMHC could therefore be viewed as a further means of circumventing a constitutional facility of the provinces. Its advantage was to give a nation-wide administrative facility to the federal government. Regional offices were opened in 1946 in every province. Despite this, however, CMHC was also the means of getting loan approval underway in Alberta under Part I of the Act where joint CMHC and lending institution agreements were involved. Table 5 shows the loan approvals arranged under Part I by province.

TABLE 5. Loan approvals by province, Part I NHA, January to June of 1945 and 1946

Province	January to June 1945		January to June 1946		Percent increase in dollar value
	Loans	In thousands of dollars	Loans	In thousands of dollars	
P.E.I.					
Nova Scotia	17	80	75	360	450
New Brunswick	5	20	39	189	945
Quebec	200	1,026	361	1,744	170
Ontario	1,400	5,937	1,726	7,810	132
Manitoba	331	1,386	522	2,536	183
Saskatchewan	41	181	158	694	383
Alberta	116	521	425	1,925	369
British Columbia	307	1,187	623	2,596	219

House of Commons Debates, 1946, 4:3683.

The table shows that Ontario took advantage of the NHA very rapidly, but that Nova Scotia, New Brunswick, Saskatchewan, and Alberta caught up rapidly in the first half of 1946. The Leduc oil strike occurred only in 1947.

A further matter of provincial jurisdiction was raised in connection with community planning and the orderly development of urban areas. An opposition member remarked:

> under this bill the government is empowering houses to be built which may, unless safeguards are taken, become a liability to the municipality in which they are built.[105]

He then moved an amendment limiting the proposed CMHC's loans to applications where the proposed housing conformed to plans approved by the municipality and provincial government. As the law was now proposed, the tail was to wag the dog. The amendment, he argued, would insure both the appropriate activity at the lower levels and greater care being taken of the dominion's investment. Cases of the major cities preparing elaborate community plans but never coming round to implement them in the face of large-scale building proposals already financed, prepared, and ready to go, were cited as evidence. He concluded:

> under present construction, the unplanned and uncorrelated construction that we are going ahead with today, we are building up for ourselves a problem of debt and blight the like of which this country has never seen before. [106]

The minister declined the amendment for a variety of reasons: first, that the individual citizen, and not the dominion government, builds the house, or, as a contractor, undertakes to build houses; second, that the onus is on the citizen to apply for loans and build within the terms of municipal by-laws; and third, that the province and municipality already possess the power to regulate the individual's building activities. These governments had long been advised, he argued, to prepare their community plans and be ready for the post-war building boom. Proper planning would prevent the construction of houses in declining areas and thereby save the individual borrower from investing in a declining asset. From a practical perspective, the minister remarked:

> if we were to make our loans conditional upon there being a proper town plan in existence it would mean that we would be cutting off a large proportion of our loans, and there would be a great outcry from all parts of Canada at the present time. Therefore, I think the only thing we can do is to work along offering inducements and do everything we can to prevail upon the provinces to enact town planning and community planning legislation and upon the municipalities to adopt it. [107]

The NHA, unlike Wartime Housing, was not to be construed as an interim, temporary measure, but as an instrument of long-term urban development satisfactorily conceived in its community dimension and regulated in terms of the standards necessary for an individual residence.

Thus, through CMHC which was now an established social institution, the federal government saw itself as contributing not only to the solution of urban degradation, but also to general urban development on a permanent institutional basis. This institutional role of CMHC, apart from its role as a mortgage broker and facility to lending institutions, is comparable to the roles assigned to the lower levels of government. The provinces were to be approvers of municipal initiative, especially in low income rental accommodation, and were to provide enabling legislation to their local authorities to put order into and make planning provisions for urban development. Local authorities had, in effect, been prevented in 1944 from undertaking construction on their own through federal finance in any general housing program, but had been left with housing the sub-economic poor. The stage had been finally set for the concentration of urban development in limited metropolitan centres across Canada at the instigation of lending institutions and with the assistance of CMHC. The latter, within a year of its founding, was itself to be asked to care for the needs of the small towns and rural regions of Canada that the lending institutions and city governments increasingly ignored.

Amendments to the NHA were numerous in the immediate post-war years. They dealt mainly with extending the powers of CMHC or lending institutions, or with broadening CMHC's scope of operations. Examples of amendments include family-type buildings rather than bunk houses in remote lumber and mining towns; the right of CMHC to contract with builders for large numbers of family dwellings with guarantees to the builders; the right of insurance, trust and loan companies to assemble land for building purposes approved by CMHC with government guarantees against losses; and the granting of double depreciation for income tax purposes to certain projects in the rental field approved by CMHC. In 1947 CMHC was empowered to make direct loans in areas where lending institutions did not carry on a lending business. The amendments were concerned on the one hand with meeting genuinely new housing needs and on the other with changing the incentives to stimulate lending institutions to get particular jobs done. The latter amendments were, in effect, playing with different parts of the model.

The Dominion Bureau of Statistics, supported by CMHC research money, was concurrently refining its survey techniques. The need for housing, the location of that need, the type of dwelling, size of dwelling, the ability to pay for it, and the like, were steadily determined. Policy making became increasingly done within CMHC and became based upon survey data. This connection between DBS data and decisions within CMHC had a dual effect. First, it insured that the needs of some people who had responded by migrating to the ever growing and increasingly centralized cities were partly met by rational, statistically determined criteria. Secondly, through active involvement with housing, the construction industry, and lending institutions, CMHC favored the continuation of the very process it had been set up to handle, namely, the consequences of urban growth and some of the forms of degradation which have inevitably accompanied it, by providing to lending institutions the financial flexibility which guaranteed this process.

Housing and the Changing Scene

Under the conditions of rising construction costs which typified much of the postwar decade, and where there was no provision for a subsidy on rentals *per se,* it became more and more difficult to build for a significant minority, the poorest quarter perhaps, of the urban population. The cost of the lowest interest rates, amortization, and local taxation added up to more than the lowest income groups could be expected to pay. Year after year during the post-war period the federal government admitted its inability to get low-rental accommodation in adequate numbers under the NHA. Rental accommodation seemed the only answer as the costs of building and financing the smallest and simplest home by methods provided under Part I of the NHA and to standards prescribed by CMHC were prohibitive. In the immediate post-war years the problem of the poor was understood only in these terms. The immense social and political significance of relocating the poor evicted from slum-clearance areas came to be realized only about 1964 when the urban renewal programs were seriously initiated.

In 1948, the government amended the Act to permit CMHC to guarantee an annual return to investors by way of rentals on approved rental housing projects for a period up to 30 years. It also provided for loans direct to owners of rental housing construction projects if loans were not forthcoming from commercial lending institutions. But, faced with post-war inflation and rapidly-rising building and land costs, the amendment required that construction costs not exceed $6,800 per unit or carry a maximum rental of $37.50 per month. This virtually nullified the intent of the amendment.

As was so often the case in the years to follow, the supply of accommodation to the poor was to be affected not only by their relative inability to afford a new house of their own, but by the federal government's use of CMHC, the lending institutions, and the construction industry to cope with cyclical economic conditions and the threat of inflation. CMHC and its endeavors early became a party to the federal government's efforts to cope with inflation; just as the early housing acts of pre-war decades had been part of the anti-depression measures of the federal government.

Faced with the additional costs and demands on materials for defence caused by the Korean War in 1950, the housing program was reduced. In February 1951, an increase in down-payments required under the NHA contributed to a decline from $310 million to $237 million in institutional approvals of new construction loans. In October, 1951, a new impetus was given housing by raising again the loan levels available to borrowers. Housing starts rose rapidly again in 1952; but unlike the 1945-1950 period, when life insurance companies were selling off their government war bonds, a shortage of private mortgage funds emerged in 1952.

During 1952-53 parliament took stock of the NHA and the CMHC. For the first time, the Annual Report of CMHC was sent for scrutiny to the Banking and Commerce Committee of the House. David Mansur, President of CMHC, provided some measure of the housing needs of the country and the extent to which they had been met. Table 6 shows the relation of estimated net family formation in Canada to house construction from both NHA and private arrangements.

TABLE 6. Estimated net family formation and dwelling construction, 1946 to 1952.

Year	Estimated net family formation	Dwelling units constructed	Differences
1946	107,500	67,194	-40,306
1947	75,400	79,231	+ 3,831
1948	83,000	81,243	- 1,757
1949	77,100	91,655	+14,555
1950	73,500	91,754	+18,254
1951	96,500	84,810	-11,690
1952	93,000	73,087	-19,913
	606,000	568,974	-37,026

These data suggest that since the end of the war house construction had not kept abreast of estimated net family formation. There was a deficit of 37,026 houses with respect to new families alone, not to mention coping with the process of obsolescense in the cities or catching up on the backlog of unmet needs from the war years and the depression years. Looked at from another perspective, the 1951 census showed the existence in Canada of 3,387,000 families and 3,423,000 occupied dwellings. There were also 456,000 non-family households. This would suggest that about 320,000 or 9 percent of families and households shared accommodation. [108] In terms of absolute numbers the physical resources, in the form of shelter only, were not far removed from human needs by this time. The questions of the ability to pay for accommodation, of the standards of part of that accommo-dation, and of its distribution across the country and between cities and smaller towns remained. There remained also the unmet problem of slums. Of the $20 million appropriate under the NHA for slum-clearance measures, only $1,150,000 had been committed by the end of 1951. Under rental housing the position was slightly better. Of the $150 million appropriated, about $99 million had been committed. Most of the work done had been under Part I of the Act which was a facility for those who could afford it. In all, of the $480 million aggregate appropriation under the Act, the commitments were in the region of $333 million.

Notes
Chapter 2

1. *House of Commons Debates,* 1935, 4:3916
2. As early as 1919 the federal government had provided $25 million to local authorities across Canada by way of loan to the provinces to assist them in initiating local construction which would mitigate the unemployment that followed the war. It had in general been well administered and much of the money had been returned faithfully to the federal government. In 1930 a works program involving federal, provincial, and local authorities was attempted, but the lower levels of government became so involved in debt, and local authorities had raised local property taxes to such a point that many taxpayers no longer felt obliged to pay taxes at all, and the program was hurriedly dropped. Direct relief was then initiated. None of these however, could be construed as a national housing policy.
3. *Special Committee on Housing, House of Commons, Session 1935* (Ottawa: 1935, Queen's Printer).
4. *House of Commons Debates,* 1935, 4:3777.
5. Ibid., p. 3917.
6. Ibid., p. 3925, in quoting from the Ganong Committee's record of evidence to the League of Nations' survey on housing and the relief of unemployment.
7. Quoted in ibid., p. 3931, from a report by the American government to the League of Nations' survey on housing and the relief of unemployment.
8. At this time the life insurance companies were virtually the only lending institutions in the long-term mortgage field.
9. Local authorities were included, by amendment to the bill, to act as financial institutions.
10. Ibid., p. 3911. Over the years these activities have been subsumed by one or other federal authority such as the Central Mortgage and Housing Corporation or the National Research Council. The thinking at the time, however, was in terms of one instrument that could identify the economics of differing possibilities. The concept of a unified and on-going research instrument to look at all aspects of housing was hardly yet developed.
11. Quoted in ibid., p. 3945.
12. *House of Commons Debates,* 1937, 1:388.
13. *House of Commons Debates,* 1936, 2:1847.
14. *House of Commons Debates,* 1936, 1:392.
15. Ibid, p. 392.
16. Ibid., p. 393.
17. Ibid.
18. Ibid.
19. Ibid.
20. Ibid., p. 467.
21. Ibid.
22. Ibid., pp. 467-68.
23. Ibid., p. 479.
24. This Act proved to be one of the most used of all the legislative attempts made during the decade 1935-45. Up to March 31, 1944 some 125,720 loans had been

made, involving slightly less than $50 million total amount. Some 1,231 loans
had involved the government in losses of just over $400,000. The net loss was
only .806 percent. Some 98.4 percent of the principal amount had been repaid.
House of Commons Debates, 1944, 4:5979.

25. Speech of the Minister of Finance. Ibid., p. 3385.
26. Ibid., p. 34800.
27. *House of Commons Debates.* 1938, 4:3652.
28. *House of Commons Debates,* 1937, 1:739.
29. Ibid., p. 740.
30. Ibid., p. 742.
31. Ibid., p. 745-46.
32. All quotations are from the Minister of Finance's Speech on introducing the
Resolution to the House. *House of Commons Debates* 1938, 4:3651-661.
33. Ibid., p. 3674.
34. Ibid., p. 3661.
35. Ibid., p. 3653. Later, in the second reading debate, the minister remarked
"In fact . . . we have endeavoured in every way to get lending institutions to make
agreements with the dominion. It has been a slow process to persuade them to
enter into agreements at all." Ibid., p. 3774.
36. Ibid.
37. Ibid., p. 3654.
38. Part II of the Act expired in 1940 without any loans having been made for
rental accommodation construction. The ideas contained in the legislation,
however, are significant.
39. Ibid., p. 3654.
40. Ibid., p. 3672.
41. Ibid., p. 3655.
42. Ibid., p. 3655.
43. Ibid., p. 3656.
44. Ibid., p. 3672.
45. Ibid., p. 3780.
46. Ibid., p. 3656.
47. Ibid., p. 3669.
48. Ibid., p. 3673.
49. Ibid., p. 3674. In 1939 the federal government passed, but never carried
into effect, the Central Mortgage Bank Act. We have not examined the details
of this legislation, but its principles and purpose are briefly described in
footnote 96.
50. Ibid., p. 3675. *(The Canadian Year Book,* 1936, p. 915 shows that between 1920
and the end of 1935 the banks alone closed 1,245 branches across Canada.)
51. *House of Commons Debates,* 1938, 4:3771-72.
52. Ibid., p. 3774.
53. *House of Commons Debates,* 1939, 3:2718.
54. Ibid.
55. *House of Commons Debates,* 1944, 6:5975.
56. At the end of the Second World War, 77 percent of the federal life companies'
Canadian funds were invested in bonds, while only 10 percent were in mortgages.
See Royal Commission on Banking and Finance. 1964 Report (Ottawa, 1965),
p. 243.
57. *House of Commons Debates,* 1941, 3:2345.
58. *House of Commons Debates,* 1943, 4:3852-53.
59. Ibid., p. 3860.
60. Ibid., p. 3853.
61. This emphasis was derived from a report of a committee on postwar
reconstruction chaired by C. A. Curtis.
62. *House of Commons Debates,* 1944, 6:5973.
63. Ibid.
64. Ibid., p. 5975.
65. Ibid., p. 5976.
66. Ibid., p. 5977.
67. It should be emphasized that the minister viewed these measures much more

as a housing stimulation than as a slum clearance measure.

68. *House of Commons Debates,* 1944, 6:5980.
69. The term "urban growth process" in this context refers to the
national changes occurring in the distribution among metropolitan, small city,
and town communities of productive and consumer potential, population, etc.
70. *House of Commons Debates,* 1944, 6:5980.
71. Ibid., p. 6002.
72. Ibid.
73. *House of Commons Debates,* 1945, 2:1476. The provinces had yielded
fiscal conveniences to the federal government as a war measure in 1941.
74. *House of Commons Debates,* 1944, 6:6234.
75. Ibid., p. 6233.
76. Ibid., p. 5991.
77. Ibid., p. 6005.
78. This Royal Commission on Dominion-Provincial Relations, set up in August,
1937, and reporting in May, 1940, had made several recommendations on
improved methods of financing provincial responsibilities under the constitution,
including adjustment grants. The report was considered at the
dominion-provincial conference in January, 1941, but the conference broke
down on the second day in the face of opposition from the premiers of
Alberta, British Columbia, and Ontario. (*Canada Year Book,* 1946), p. 79.
79. *House of Commons Debates,* 1944, 6:6011.
80. Ibid., p. 6010.
81. Ibid., p. 6232.
82. Ibid., p. 6005.
83. Ibid., p. 5991.
84. *House of Commons Debates,* 1945, 2:1473.
85. Ibid., pp. 1473-74. The federal government was as adamant in the CMHC bill
as in the 1944 NHA to limit government assistance to "the people who are in
the business of lending money." Provinces and municipalities were
deliberately excluded, Ibid., p. 2033-34.
86. Ibid., p. 2050.
87. Ibid., pp. 2050-51.
88. Ibid., p. 1474. In this sense, CMHC should be seen as part of the
instruments needed in the model implicit in the 1944 NHA to encourage
lending institutions to invest in mortgages.
89. Ibid.
90. Ibid., p. 1483.
91. Ibid., p. 1476.
92. *House of Commons Debates,* 1946, 4:3683. CMHC in 1948 took over their
operations. Even this gesture to the federal government's alliance with them over
housing for the poor failed.
93. *House of Commons Debates,* 1945, 2:2014.
94. Ibid., p. 1986.
95. Ibid., p. 1990.
96. This Act enabled lending institutions voluntarily to become a member
company of the proposed bank and thereby to adjust the rate of interest and the
principal on outstanding long term mortgages carrying higher than current
interest rates and terms difficult for the mortgagee to meet. The interest rate had
to be reduced to 5 percent. All arrears of interest in excess of two years had
to be written off. The amount of the mortgage had to be adjusted downwards
to a point where it did not exceed 80 percent of the fair value of the property
mortgaged. In return, the bank would grant twenty-year debentures bearing
compound interest at 3 percent to the lending institution to cover half its losses
on interest and then full cost of the principal forgiven. The facility, in effect,
would have saddled the taxpayer with debt, but removed the mortgage from
the lending institution to the bank, whose jurisdiction was federal rather than
provincial, which it had hitherto been in respect of debt settlement. For details,
see *House of Commons Debates* 1939, May 6, p. 3665, and 1939, May 22, 4389.
97. *House of Commons Debates,* 1945, 2:1991.
98. Ibid., p. 2054.

99. Ibid., p. 2055.
100. Ibid., p. 2055.
101. Ibid. The alternative Mr. Low suggested was the 2 percent made to municipalities under the 1938 Municipal Improvements Assistance Act. These loans had been guaranteed by the provinces. The Act had been well used, proved effective for local governments, and had involved the dominion in no losses by non-payment. Why, he argued, should this not be tried again?
102. Ibid., p. 2056.
103. Ibid.
104. Ibid., p. 2057.
105. Ibid., p. 2046.
106. Ibid., p. 2048.
107. Ibid., p. 2048.
107. Ibid.
108. *House of Commons Debates,* 1952, 5:4491.

Chapter 3
Federal attempts to cope:
administration and money, 1952-1962

The Problems of 1952-54

The federal government since the end of the war and up to 1952, had faciliated the building of about two in every five permanent houses in Canada. Part I of the Act had been by far the most used. Other problems of a more collective nature, such as the housing of the poor, slum clearance, rental accommodation, and the dispersal of housing facilities to towns and small cities, had been tackled in one way or another since 1935 but without particular success.

By 1952 the pressing issue was the provision of serviced land to facilitate the rate of house construction then under way. Municipalities were becoming involved in heavy expenditure for sewer and water mains, roads, schools, and other services, and this expenditure required them to borrow money. The Minister of Resources and Development, R. H. Winters, remarked:

> Because of unwillingness or inability to borrow, the municipalities do not always respond as the need for additional serviced land arises. The financing problems are of a particular severity in metropolitan environs where the growth associated with a great city is apt to be thrust upon a junior municipality which is predominantly residential, and which lacks those commercial and industrial assessments that bulk so large in the ordinary municipal tax base. It is this non-residential property that has traditionally given some relief to the home owner in paying for expensive urban services.[1]

By an amendment to the NHA in 1949 a section had been introduced (Section 35) which gave some relief to municipalities for the installation of particular services on particular projects. After provincial governments had enacted enabling legislation, it was possible for a provincial government to go into partnership with the federal government to support a local authority with respect to public housing for the poor on a subsidized rental basis and to assemble and service land. The administrative formula worked out between 1949 and 1952 was generally one where 75 percent of the funds required came from the federal government and 25 percent from the provincial government. The provincial governments were free to share their part with local authorities in whatever proportion they saw fit. The ownership of low-rental projects was vested in the provincial-federal partnership, and a local housing authority was set up to manage the project. Land assembly and its servicing were funded on the same principle, but the local authorities had still to meet the cost of school construction, trunk main extensions, and the expansion of central municipal plant. These were normally met by property taxation. Only the particular project and its local needs were assisted through the partnership of the senior levels of government.

A 1952 amendment to the Act provided for the cost of certain new buildings erected on a site that was formerly a slum to be met under Section 35 with the same provincial-federal (25 percent — 75 percent) formula applied to it. The 1944 Act had provided for the federal government to pay 50 percent of the "excess acquisition cost," that is, the difference between the cost of the acquisition and clearance of slum land and the price at which it was sold to a limited-dividend company or a life insurance company. This 50 percent arrangement was to remain in the 1952 amendment, but it allowed in addition for the sale of the acquired and cleared site to be made jointly to the province and CMHC to conduct the redevelopment operations. This admendment added governmental agencies to the companies already empowered to build as a slum-clearance measure. The minister saw the opportunities presented by this amendment in these terms:

> The proposed amendments will permit the cleared area to be used either for housing purposes or for a municipal, provincial or federal public purpose, provided that the municipality makes available for a housing development an alternative area of a size sufficient to house at least the same number of persons as were living in the cleared area. The provision relating to the use of an alternative area will apply only where the slum area to be cleared is designated on the municipal plan for use ultimately for public purposes.[2]

This provision made it possible for governments at all levels to apply public money to slum clearance and the construction of public buildings on such sites. A feature of many Canadian cities, where public buildings are to be found adjacent to degraded areas near the city centre, dates back to this change in the Act.[3]

Similarly, 1952 was the date when public attention was first drawn to the financial plight of local city authorities, brought about by the increasing concentration of private investment within them. Opposition speakers in Ottawa commented,

> These municipalities are carrying on with the same limited tax base that they were given over 80 years ago . . . . Not a word has been forthcoming from the government as to any policy of seeking the solution that must be found to a problem of that kind.[4]

Suggestions were made as early as 1952 that the federal and provincial governments sit down together "to study the whole field of tax resources and work out an agreement by which there will be assured to the provincial governments, and through them to the municipal governments, adequate sources of tax revenue to meet the needs that are being placed upon the shoulders of the municipalities today."[5] These issues that had lingered on as a thorn in the flesh over the previous twenty years were coming to the fore. Either local authorities and the provincial governments were to be funded to do an adequate job of local planning with collective responsibility for policy, or the direction of urban affairs would remain under the direct influence of the federal government and the lending institutions. The events of 1970-71 bear witness to the results of this dilemma. The old way out, involving the right of both the individual and the federal government to contract with lending companies and thereby to circumvent the province was again in question.

The minister remarked as early as 1952 that:

> I have literally gone up and down this country explaining to provincial governments, to municipal governments and to anyone who would listen, that section 35 was on the statute books for those who wished to use it . . . They will find us most receptive.[6]

Alberta, however, moved in a different direction. True to its Social Credit philosophy it set up in 1950 a program of self-liquidating projects based on the principle of a revolving fund. It was initially capitalized to $5 million and later to greater amounts. Money was lent from the fund at 2 percent to municipalities for such projects as water and sewage systems, electrification, and school construction. It was the responsibility of the municipality to replenish the fund, with interest, on the due date and by 1953 the record in this respect had been good. Edmonton by this date had borrowed $3,900,000 from the fund.[7]

In 1953 Alberta introduced amending legislation to prevent the use of NHA (Section 35) money, which implied a provincial-federal partnership for land assembly and its servicing. If a municipality wished to benefit from the partnership plan it would have to go to the open market to get its money. Considering the 2 percent rate from the provincial fund this was unlikely, even if the provincial government was prepared to co-operate with the federal government.

The year 1952 was also the time when lending institutions were running short of ready cash for mortgages. Life insurance companies had been selling off government war bonds steadily since 1946 to about $800 million. The minister, R. A. Winters, remarked:

> Investment shifts of this kind and magnitude obviously could not continue indefinitely. Although the lending institutions have also been in receipt of a steadily rising flow of repayments on earlier mortgage loans, it has become increasingly clear that at some stage they would have to

reduce their rate of new mortgage lending from its recent level.[8]

To meet this situation, increases in the maximum rates of interest were authorized on NHA loans in June 1951 and September 1952. Also, in the summer of 1952, CMHC was authorized to make direct loans to prospective home owners in centres of up to 55,000 population "to compensate for a withdrawal from these centres of the operations of the lending institutions under the National Housing Act."[9] Thus, as lending institutions ran short of funds not only were interest rates increased, but decisions regarding where money was to be invested became confined to larger and larger centres of population. Government money, through CMHC, was used increasingly to meet the consequences of these trends. The federal government was coping increasingly through the application of its own resources. The minister remarked in 1954:

> The present situation is that the lending institutions are applying such an unusually large proportion of their new money to mortgage investment that a decline in mortgage money from this source must be anticipated. And even now their heavy mortgage investment is being supplemented by Central Mortgage which, in addition to its share of joint loans, is making direct loans at the rate of about $60 million a year.[10]

The cities were now really growing and the demand for finance was meeting the expectations of lending institutions.

In part this demand was stimulated by a tendency for local authorities to avoid arrangements calling for heavy municipal borrowing, especially in suburban municipalities undergoing rapid growth. The costs of urban residential sprawl were starting to show. Local authorities preferred to finance public services in new suburban areas by fusing the costs of services with mortgage financing. Instead of putting funds into municipal debentures, therefore, investors put them into mortgage portfolios and protected them, on occasions, with NHA insured loans. The municipalities' problems were now to keep control of technical standards in developing areas. In CMHC's opinion at this time, "the range and standard of municipal services in a number of areas are inferior to what was afforded new housing in the same areas thirty years ago."[11]

Increasing Federal Administrative Involvement, 1954-56

A second source of funds alternative to the lending institutions, was the banks. Within eighteen months they added $475 million in approved NHA loans. The minister recognized "that at the present time these deposits are rather fully employed in other directions" but these bank funds were unable to move into housing "because the Bank Act prohibits bank lending on the security of real estate mortgages." An expanded trading market in NHA mortgages was to be established under the Act. Up to this time life insurance companies were providing about 80

108

percent of all institutional mortgage financing.[12] The banks also had a wider geographic distribution, especially in smaller urban centres, than the insurance companies, though there remained no guarantee that the approximately 4,000 branches across Canada would be authorized to lend money on mortgages. The 1954 NHA brought banks into the lending picture. Their investments were especially safeguarded in the mortgage field as special provision was made for CMHC to purchase mortgages from approved lenders and "the mortgage portfolio of the banks will be eligible for loans from the Bank of Canada, as is presently the case for government bonds."[13] The insurance of mortgages was also elaborated, in that the borrower was obliged to pay a 2 percent premium towards insuring the risks of the lender.[14]

The second major change in the NHA of 1954 was the termination of the joint lending arrangements between CMHC and lending institutions, and the introduction of an arrangement whereby CMHC insured mortgages made by approved lending institutions to finance new residential construction. The chartered banks were to be included in those institutions already approved. Three types of insured mortgage loans were introduced: (a) those to assist in the construction of houses for home ownership; (b) those to assist in the construction of rental housing; and (c) those to finance the conversion of existing houses into multiple housing units. The amount of the loans was

> based upon a statutory percentage of the lending value [of the property] and will be subject to a dollar limit to be set by the governor in council.
>
> . . . The bill before the house contains provision that there will be an 80 percent maximum ratio in the rental field, but in the home ownership field the ratios will be on the basis of 90 percent of the first $8,000 and 70 percent of additional lending value. This has the effect that up to lending values of $16,000 the ratio of loan to lending value will be greater than it is now, at 80 percent, with corresponding lesser amounts of equity or down payment requirements.[15]

The period of amortization was generally 25 to 30 years, but the governor in council was to be authorized "to designate areas in which the period of amortization may be less than 25 years where economic circumstances or productive capacity of the area are not sufficient to justify the full 25 year term.[16] The governor in council was also authorized to determine by regulation the maximum interest rates to be charged by a lending institution for an insured NHA mortgage loan. This guaranteed flexibility in this area also, but it had to be "high enough to attract a sufficient flow of mortgage funds." Part 1 of the Act was now in reality intended to meet the needs of persons who could afford housing on an almost economic basis. Table 7 shows the upward trend in gross family income, from 1948 to 1955, of persons borrowing under the NHA.

TABLE 7. Gross family income groups as a percentage of total borrowers under the NHA.

Gross family income	1948	1949	1950	1951	1952	1953	1954	1955 1st and 2nd quarters
	%	%	%	%	%	%	%	%
Under $2,009	8.9	2.9	0.7	0.2	0.05	0.02	0.02	0.01
$2,100-$2,399	13.5	8.0	3.0	0.8	0.2	0.06	0.03	0.04
$2,400-$2,699	21.5	19.0	10.8	4.1	0.9	0.4	0.1	0.08
$2,700-$2,999	12.4	13.5	11.5	8.0	2.1	0.9	0.3	0.2
$3,000-$3,499	18.3	23.0	25.2	23.2	13.3	6.96	3.61	2.7
$3,500-$3,999	9.8	12.1	17.3	18.9	22.0	17.10	11.58	10.52
$4,000-$4,999	8.7	12.2	17.0	21.8	30.3	36.86	34.38	32.90
$5,000 and over	6.9	9.3	14.5	23.0	31.3	37.3	49.89	53.52

The 1954 Act superseded the principle of federal support for housing in general of all middle and lower income groups which had been inherent in the NHA up to this time, and opposition parties emphasized this feature of the new Act. The poor were now to be treated as a particular category requiring other provisions than Part I of the Act. This feature reappeared even more clearly in 1967. The 1954 Act left largely intact the slum clearance and limited-dividend corporation provisions of earlier legislation.

The 1954 Act also introduced an administrative measure that, though at first sight appeared to be trivial, became of importance later on. The purpose was to ensure that the construction complied with maximum standards, and under the new act, CMHC was to undertake the inspection. This had previously been done by the lending institution, but the banks were in no position to do it. In addition, the scale of building construction was increasing. The individual, custom-built home was giving way to mass, speculative development. CMHC in its brief to the Royal Commission on Canada's Economic Prospects, 1956, included in its submission a lengthy description of the process of mass construction and the need to safeguard the public's and the individual buyer's interests in the process. Not only did this measure increase the staff of CMHC but it tended to establish in Canada a centralized inspectorate that came to dominate the whole building field from construction plans to planning in general.[17] It led increasingly to the subservience of municipal and provincial planners to those who were in specialized positions backed by the source of the funds, in Ottawa. A planner in Edmonton who was associated in the late 1950s with planning in Alberta, remarked that CMHC officials treated the provincial officials "like kids, as if we knew nothing." He also claimed that their influence tended to stifle new thinking and innovation.[18] An opposition member in the House remarked in respect of this power awarded to CMHC:

> ... let no honourable member lose sight of the implications of the inescapable fact that under this bill CMHC becomes the sole arbiter with respect to every loan made under the provisions of this bill for all Canada of the standards and quality of construction.[19]

He also observed that CMHC now became the arbiter of the speed of construction as it had to approve every single advance or installment. As early as 1956 the effects of this administrative matter were felt. A member remarked in respect of CMHC activity in Toronto:

> ... the corporation is becoming increasingly bureaucratic in its attitude and behaviour. There is increasing evidence of an ivory tower complex and in some respects that bureaucratic attitude is verging on the autocratic. The corporation is becoming more and more remote from the people and their problems.[20]

The real danger indentified by the member was that the activities of CMHC would result in the loss of citizen involvement in housing, planning, and the growth of their city. Some of the citizens of the Toronto Regent Park North project had developed a feeling that CMHC was not interested in their participation, "that it is taking a 'hands off' attitude with respect to citizen interest."[21]

The administrative involvement of the federal government further increased by the 1956 NHA amendments. These placed the federal government in the centre of action concerning inner-city slum removal and at the very beginning of the process rather than at its conclusion. It was a very simple but crucial measure. There had as yet been no systematic large-scale withdrawals of old housing adjacent to, or intermixed with commercial use property. Fires, condemnation of properties and similar events and actions had provided an unplanned and unintended sort of slum clearance (or withdrawal). Now this process was to be intentional and systematic.

Additional amendments further enhanced the potential significance of this step. First, the area so cleared was no longer to be used only for public buildings or low or moderate rental accommodation but "may be redeveloped for the purposes for which it is best suited".[22] Second, these purposes included the sale of the whole or part of a cleared site to private enterprise for residential, commercial, or industrial uses, as well as the original purposes. The minister remarked:

> The prospect of redeveloping a blighted area into a commercial or perhaps industrial area which may be more appropriate to the district and at the same time more productive of revenues will, I believe, encourage a number of cities to participate in urban redevelopment projects. The prospect of having the federal government share the financial government share the financial burden virtually from the inception of a redevelopment project should provide an incentive as well.[23]

This arrangement involved a direct grant of 50 percent of the cost of acquisition and clearing, less any return on resale of the cleared land, direct from the federal government via CMHC to the municipality. If provincial legislation enabling municipalities to deal with the federal government directly did not require the provincial government to be brought into action, the provincial government would be entirely removed from this action. Theoretically, therefore, provincial governments could, if they wished, be excluded from any say in the policy affecting the inner core of their cities. At best the provincial government would be but a junior partner in the governmental ranks and, by virtue of the right now legislated to municipalities and the federal government to resell cleared land to private interests, could be denied further specific influence over the use of the land. This result is a clear example of the relative inconsequence of provincial decision. The extent of the provincial government's influence depended upon the rights afforded a local authority by provincial legislation and the extent to which the provincial government wanted to be party to a local authority's decisions and intents.

However, the fact is also evident that ever since 1935 the provinces had made little use of the NHA provisions for slum clearance. The minister was apparently forced, in a sense, to initiate amendments to the Act in 1956 due to a reluctance of the provinces to get on with the job.[24] The earlier remarks by the minister, in 1952, that he "had literally gone up and down this country" to encourage use of section 35 should not go unheeded. Similarly, city politics rather than lack of finance had contributed to the unwillingness of local government to get on with the job. The minister commented in reply to a question:

> We found that to be true in many municipalities across the country, and it is quite understandable. I have no criticism to make of civic administrators who find great difficulty in uprooting citizens . . . in demolishing their homes and having them to go to live elsewhere. Sometimes these problems have been so severe locally they could not be overcome regardless of the financing arrangements we might have made.[25]

For whatever reason, the provinces were reluctant to move in this area. No assistance had been given through the NHA to land assembly and other renewal projects up to budget time in 1956.[26] Neither lending institutions nor provincial or municipal governments appeared willing to commit themselves either collectively or individually. The provinces up to this time had been explicitly left the responsibility to assist municipalities in meeting the dearth of serviced land for new building projects, particularly on the growing perimeters of the major cities. Urban sprawl was already a major problem. The municipalities were in fact carrying the burden of cost on this land, though developers were moving increasingly into the field on their own account. Opposition members, as early as 1952, had urged the federal government to step in. In the 1956 debate, a member remarked:

> I affirm again as on previous occasions that the solution rests within the power of the federal government . . . (the problem) is not going to be solved without remedial action on the part

112

of the federal authorities. It is to be hoped that this type of action will come soon.[27]

Indeed it did; but by measures that again circumvented the provincial authorities, and enhanced the role of private enterprise in the process of urban development.

In the second reading debate on the 1956 amendment, the minister pointed out that right across the country towns and cities had been remodelled through the NHA and private investment. More than $8 billion from all sources, private and public, had been put into housebuilding. The single detached house had been the main type preferred by Canadians, but "our modern suburbs now accommodate no more than four families to an acre. This demand for living space has placed a severe strain upon the whole structure of local government." He continued:

> The suburbs have spread far beyond the boundaries of central cities and so the task of providing streets and sanitary services and schools has been imposed upon municipalities that, in many instances, had little previous experience and few resources for this purpose.[28]

Later he observed that ". . . Canadian cities have inherited a stock of housing which is caught in the relentless process of deterioration and obsolescence. The growth of cities has placed new demands upon the hearts of urban areas, with increasing traffic, growing commerce, and a changed pattern of living."[29] It was to meet this dilemma of cost to municipalities suffering urban sprawl from new housing on the one hand, and the degeneration of city cores by obsolescence on the other that the federal government moved the 1956 amendment to the NHA.[30] As previously described, this amendment placed the federal government four square with the municipalities at the initial point of action in core area clearance and permitted companies to develop the land cleared by municipal-federal joint effort.

The minister's case was empirically well founded. He described the process of ecological invasion by commerce, industry, and transport routes on older housing near the city centre and recognized that this invasion in turn contributed to the degradation. In such instances the reclaimed land might better be used for commerce and industry. The residents would be better housed elsewhere. He remarked:

> We cannot assume that expensive central area land is always the most logical place to house low income families. The use of such high cost land may make it necessary to house families at a high density or without adequate open space.[31]

Conversely, some non-residential land might better be used for housing purposes. City development has to be seen as a "continuous process of growth and change in urban land" . . . The minister concluded:

This view of urban redevelopment, as a vital part of a community's growth and regrowth, has led us to the conclusion that private enterprise might in some instances appropriately join with governments in bringing new life into the older and blighted areas of our cities, helping to restore them to a sound, productive place in a city's economy. We propose, therefore, that the federal government's aid to municipalities should not be applied exclusively to the redevelopment of sites for low rental and moderate rental housing.[32]

Just to make sure that the NHA had not been transformed into a general urban development program, the minister added: ". . . this federal aid to municipalities would be available only for urban redevelopment projects which would have the primary objectives of improving housing conditions, either through the elimination of poor housing or the provision of new housing."[33] Residents of the cleared area had to be rehoused, if only to avoid hardship. It was up to the cities to make the plans they considered appropriate to their particular problems and ambitions.

While federal aid was to be flexibly applied, two principles were to guide its conduct.

The first of these was "that land should generally be redeveloped for its highest and best use." This principle was justified on the basis of taxation, in that local and federal taxpayers should not be expected to subsidize land costs for a lesser economic use. Later in the debate the minister pointed out that local authorities had a great deal to gain from these projects. He remarked:

It almost invariably develops that the land redeveloped produces more revenue than it did previously to the redevelopment. I believe that when municipalities make detailed studies they will find that they are the level of government which really stand to benefit most directly from any of these redevelopment projects. And rather than having the weight of the financial burden bear on them I think they are in a very favourable position to benefit . . . [34]

The second principle was "that redevelopment is not likely to be effective unless areas of substantial size are acquired and replanned, so as to establish a new neighborhood character." Single lot development was clearly unsuitable. Traffic was likely to require new street plans. Local authorities had to be given elbow room to redevelop at a scale commensurate with their plans. The minister remarked:

It should be the purpose of redevelopment to revitalize the city by converting interior parts to a form as up to date as the new suburbs. A municipality will usually have to exercise its powers of expropriation to acquire sufficiently large tracts of land and to round out workable sites.[35]

The existence of an official community plan was the condition of federal assistance. A farsighted and systematic scheme to forestall the development of urban blight was the point the federal government wanted to identify in these plans. If reclaimed land could not be sold there was provision in the amendment for a municipal-federal leasing arrangement.

The federal government recognized that it could "only remove some of the road blocks in the path of redevelopment. It is not in our power to take direct action. The initiative must remain with municipalities." The provincial government's approval had also to be obtained, and some enabling legislation to facilitate municipal use of the federal legislation might have to be introduced in provincial legislatures. There was also "full opportunity for provinces to share with the federal and municipal governments in the costs of redevelopment."[36] Just how far the province was to influence the process was not clear. The role of provincial planning departments could readily be subsumed under that of the cities unless the province retained to itself the right to approve city planning proposals.

The studies necessary to make a success of this program were to be facilitated not through provincial authorities, but by extending Part V of the NHA so that CMHC could itself undertake them or finance by grant the necessary municipal studies.

The Trend to the Construction of Multiple-Family Dwellings, 1952-56

The events of 1952-56 were obviously important for what was to happen a decade later when the 1964 amendments to the NHA were introduced; but it is not easy to interpret the relation of the two sets of events. The federal government, true to its concern for the poor and for the blighted areas of cities, was elaborating its 1944 and 1949 machinery affecting slum areas. The 1952 amendment brought all levels of government into the building of new structures on cleared slum land as well as continuing the largely unused but existing provision through limited-dividend companies and rental housing provisions to have the poor accommodated on it. The "excess acquisition cost" principle of 1944 that helped pull the slums down, was enlarged to provide for federal assistance in the erection of governmental buildings on the cleared land. The lending institutions in the early 1950s were concentrating their efforts on supporting developers and builders in the suburbs on the city boundaries. Increases in mortgage interest rates helped them. The new financial provisions of 1954,

TABLE 8. All mortgage loans approved by lending institutions in new non-farm residential construction, 1952-56

Year	Number of Loans	Number of dwelling units
1952	33,828	46,026
1953	39,690	56,297
1954	61,448	84,916
1955	76,969	104,646
1956	56,733	76,739

Derived from *Canadian Housing Statistics,* CMHC, 4th Quarter, 1960, p. 17.

which introduced CMHC insurance on loans by lending institutions in place of provisions for joint federal-lending institution loans, gave lending institutions greater freedom of decision on the location of their lending as well as wider financial manoeuverability.

From 1952 to 1956 all mortgage loans approved by lending institutions for new (non-farm) residential construction moved as shown in Table 8.

TABLE 9. Dwelling units approved by lending institutions, 1952-56, by type of dwelling and type of loan.

	Single family dwellings			Multiple family dwellings		
Year	NHA	conv.*	ratio	NHA	conv.*	ratio
1952	21,130	9,952	1: .47	8,378	6,566	1: .78
1953	22,951	13,420	1: .58	9,658	10,268	1:1.06
1954	38,669	17,690	1: .46	11,755	16,802	1:1.43
1955	53,285	18,508	1: .35	13,094	19,759	1:1.51
1956	36,705	16,115	1: .44	4,753	19,166	1:4.03

*conventional
Sources as for Table 8.

Of these dwelling units the distribution between single and multiple dwellings and between NHA and conventional loans was as shown in Table 9.

Table 8 shows the rapid increase in the number of loans made for residential construction between 1953 and 1954, from 39,690 to 61,448, and the increase continued through 1955. Table 9 shows that lending institutions were favoring the use of NHA money for single-family dwellings. By 1955 the number of dwelling units approved under this heading reached 53,285 as against 13,094 NHA dwelling units of a multiple-family type. The conventional loans, i.e., non-NHA financing, for single-family dwellings increased between 1952 and 1955, but in its ratio to NHA loans tended to decline. On the other hand, for multiple-family dwellings conventional loans exceeded NHA loans after 1952 and the ratio between NHA and conventional loans in this category tended to increase strongly. Of the conventional loans, the number approved for multiple-family dwellings exceeded those for single-family dwellings during 1955.

It would thus appear that while governmental interest was turning increasingly to the city centre, NHA residential mortgage money was concentrated in residential suburban growth, and conventional lending was occurring with slow but increasing frequency in multiple-dwelling units. CMHC in turn had had to carry increasing responsibility for all types of accommodation in the smaller towns and cities, and under the 1954 Act was given markedly increased administrative authority and influence over urban development generally. The 1956 amendment placed CMHC in the very centre of down-town renewal and slum-clearance operations and at the same time increased the purpose for which cleared land could be used from public buildings and moderate rental accommodation only to "purposes for which it was best suited." These administrative intrusions by the federal agency coincided with increasing difficulty for city local

116

authorities in the funding of services needed for the growth they were experiencing. It would seem that CMHC was acting in such a way as to relieve the financial pressure on city local authorities by preparing the way for enhanced city income through a broader and more remunerative tax base in future years.

Early Approaches to the Problem of Municipal Finance

If the record of debate in *Hansard* is any indication, the 1956 amendment marks the point where the legislature was no longer in a position to identify the policy implications of changes in the NHA. It may be that other factors were influencing the members at the time, but the debate that ensued showed very little appreciation of the issues at stake.

The opposition parties, excepting the CCF,[37] favored the amendments and said that they generally supported the interpretation of the situation as given by the minister.

The attention of members may have been taken up by the new, emerging problem of tax relief for municipalities. In the Supply debate at the end of April, 1956, a lengthy discussion of this topic ensued. The Honourable George A. Drew, Leader of the Opposition, opened the debate in these terms:

> Those municipal councils, whether they be urban councils or rural councils, must deal with the wholly basic requirements of the daily life of our people. Through the school boards which are associated with the municipal councils in the local activities, they must deal with the problems of education as well as public works, public investment, streets, sewers, water supplies, light, unemployment relief, housing, health, welfare, their portion of main provincial and county highways and many other services which are more intimately associated with the daily needs of each one of us than many of the very important things that we are called upon to deal with here.[38]

Proposals had been submitted to the government and provinces as to ways and means of coping with rapidly growing municipal expenditures and inflexibility of revenue resources. Mr. Drew remarked:

> The offers that have already been made for financial adjustment between the Canadian government and the governments of the provinces have been described as unrealistic . . . One of the things that is certainly clear, and clear beyond all question, is that the present proposals which have been made in that field will not meet this urgent need of the municipalities.[39]

He suggested such measures as sales and excise tax rebates on purchases by municipalities and on land held by the federal government and therefore untaxed by local authorities. Provincial governments were already exempt from sales and excise taxation, but apparently were unable to confer tax concessions to creations of their own provincial legislatures.[40] In Mr. Drew's view, such tax concessions would be only a gesture and would not dispense with more serious solutions. The 1938 Municipal Assistance Act, involving very low interest rates for construction of self-liquidating projects, had been suggested by the Canadian Federation of Mayors and Municipalities as a possible principle on which new legislation could be drafted.

Other speakers emphasized that provincial revenues had been expended in support of education through local school boards and municipalities and several had already been pushed to the point of introducing provincial sales taxes. The cost of health and education could well, it was argued, be met from federal revenues and administered by the provinces and municipalities.

Solon E. Low, Member for Peace River, emphasized the practical steps taken by Alberta in handling this matter. He remarked: "In my province we are trying to practise what we preach". He then elaborated his experience, as former Provincial Treasurer of Alberta, in handling the 1938 Municipal Improvements Assistance Act. "I believe," he said, "it has proved itself to be an effective piece of legislation in every way . . . I know the great good we were able to do with the assistance of the Act."[41] World War II led to the suspension of the Act, and it had not been reactivated. Though a 2 percent rate of interest was unrealistic in 1956, Mr. Low argued:

> . . . we should lend them money at a much lower rate of interest than they are having to pay when they go into the money markets of the world and compete against one another for the sale of their debentures.[42]

The Bank of Canada had recently raised the discount rate to 3 percent and that in turn was harming the municipalities who would have to pay 6 percent to 7 percent for money they had to have. He remarked:

> In order to help to relieve that situation in my own province, the provincial government decided we would have to get into the field of lending and so we set up just last year a new corporation which is called a municipal financial (sic) corporation. It is a cooperative composed of membership from the cities, towns, the rural municipalities and the government. They each buy shares. The corporation then manages pretty well the distribution of financial assistance to the municipalities in the province . . . We have successfully obviated the necessity of our municipalities going into the money markets of the world and selling debentures there . . .[43]

He also argued for a much greater return for road building and maintenance to the lower levels of government from federal revenue on automobile taxation.

Mr. Low also raised the question of decentralization of industry. The larger cities had attracted industry which also paid taxes locally, though they also "create problems, including the problem of the fouling of water and all that sort of thing. But there are many municipalities where you find no industry at all."[44] He recommended that the federal government take the advice of the civil defence authorities and "assist the provincial governments in trying to work out some systematic pattern of industrial development so that there would not be this dangerous centralization . . . By wise direction from here (Ottawa) I am certain that a movement towards the decentalization of industry could be worked out which would benefit the municipalities to a tremendous degree." He also pointed out that for several years the Alberta government had paid local taxes in full on provincial property in towns and cities. He said, "we have been making a grant that was not only equal to but in excess of the full amount of taxes which those municipalities would have charged against the provincial property at the usual assessment rate."[45]

The Minister of Finance, W. E. Harris, replied by arguing that the 1938 Municipal Improvement Assistance Act was an unemployment measure. Also, "it would be quite impossible at the moment to find many municipal corporations which would use the Act even in its present form." In 1960, however, only four years later, the federal government amended the NHA to give local authorities considerable direct financial assistance in central sewerage works — as an anti-pollution measure. The reason he gave for this opinion was that on both occasions:

> when the provincial premiers were here last year and once again when they were here this year this question arose. On each occasion I told them that if they had any instances of municipal corporations not being able to borrow money for needed municipal purposes, I should be glad to investigate the reference they would make. To this date, I have not been given the name of a single municipality in this country that has not been able to borrow money for its purposes.[46]

The question of interest rate was covered by a self-righteous remark — "I have no doubt that all of us would like to borrow money at a lower rate than that which we think we are going to be obliged to pay when we set out to borrow." Local government apparently had no case in the minister's view for preferential interest treatment — at least at that time.

With regard to Mr. Low's description of the Alberta Municipal Financing Corporation, the minister indicated that he was "not as fabulously rich as you are"! He continued

> The province of Alberta is now in a position to make with its municipalities almost any arrangements that it might desire to make. They have the money in the bank and may do so. But the problem that faces the Minister of Finance here at the moment . . . (is that) it would be utterly impossible to raise by the present tax rate, sufficient revenue to carry out the proposals that they (the opposition) bring forward in the house.[47]

The irony of this matter was pointed out in debate by a member mentioning that the proportion of the tax dollar now going to the federal government had increased from almost 40 percent to 70.9 percent between 1930 and

1955. The proportion going to local authorities had dropped from 39.3 percent to 11.9 percent.[48] Though redistributions were involved, if holding the purse strings meant anything the federal government was in a powerful position. This aspect of the debate highlighted the change in emphasis from taxes levied to meet the daily needs of people — water, sewerage, education, roads, — met by local authorities, to taxes levied to support the complex superstructure of the nation as a whole — the modern airports, defence expenditure, national highways, a national civil service, and other items of the federal budget. A member explained the reluctance of local citizens to accept municipal office. He remarked that "anyone who has had service on the local level of government will realize that life can be one series of problems that are unsolvable." Buckpassing by the federal government in terms of the responsibilities of the provinces — "If you go to the provincial government they, in turn, say, 'Sorry it is not our responsibility. The federal government will have to deal with this matter.' Somebody has to take the responsibility for the tax situation that has developed in Canada . . . the federal government has to take the major responsibility in this regard."[49]

Much of the remainder of the debate was taken up with the problems of the Maritime provinces — a forerunner of the 1961 regional development legislation that was discussed in Chapter 1. Concurrently, however, the Minister of Finance at the 1956 federal-provincial conference had outlined to the provinces in the presence of municipal mayors invited to observe "the proceedings and learning from the proceedings of the financial arrangements that are now being made between the federal government and the provinces," how an additional estimated sum of between $100 and $130 million would be made available to the provinces by tax-sharing agreements. This opened up "quite a field of assistance to the municipalities, should the provinces desire to use the money in that way."[50] The question of relative need had to govern municipal no less than provincial and federal expenditures. This was, in the minister's view, his main objection to subsidizing municipal interest rates on money raised for self-liquidating municipal assets. There would be a tendency to concentrate on them rather than on other essentials of municipal service. Provincial premiers had complained too of the feature of conditional offers that obliged them to rearrange priorities to meet the conditional money when they preferred initially to develop other things.

The significance of this debate lies partly in its relevance to the problems of 1970-71, and partly in its showing how the manipulation of finance, in all its aspects, from taxation to conditional grants, has tended in recent decades to supersede the original purpose of the federal government's attempts to cope with rural and urban degradation. Though federal money remained important as a subsidy to on-the-ground developmental plans, the issues around which debate came to centre concerned rather financial manipulation and its implications for those manipulated. Money came to be the expression of a power relationship which increasingly obliged the provinces to do, through conditional grants and other fiscal arrangements, what the federal government required to be done. Need remained a criterion of decision, but increasingly the problem came to be seen as one of selective development. Manpower retraining, welfare, and medicare, are examples of this influence. In consequence, the political component of inter-governmental relations increased — an increase which was not lost on the Canadian Federation of Mayors and Municipalities in 1968-1970.

Increased Federal Direct Aid, 1956-1960, and Provincial Tax-Sharing Issues

In *Hansard* towards the end of the 1950s there is evidence that the federal government was running into interacting sets of problems within the administration of the NHA itself. After the boom of 1954-55 and the successful introduction of banks into the field of residential mortgages, the insurance and mortgage companies grew less and less interested in residential mortgages. Banks had by 1956 become the major source of residential mortgage funds. The prospects from investment in other areas of city growth had attracted money away from residential mortgages.[51] In an amendment to the NHA in 1957 the new Conservative government under Mr. Diefenbaker arranged for an increase from $250 million to $400 million on the amount that might be paid out of the consolidated revenue fund for facilities under the NHA; in May 1958 the amount was increased again, to $700 million. Limited-dividend corporation financing picked up in the recession of 1957 and the government's small homes loan policy (1,050 sq. ft.) was well received and used over $256 million during the winter of 1957-58.[52] Small urban apartments became popular in the construction industry. The sections of the NHA that authorized CMHC to make direct loans to borrowers unable to obtain finance from lending institutions, particularly in small towns, had to be strengthened. At the same time an amendment arranged for a lowering of the down-payment on houses, especially for the low-income group. An opposition member summed up the situation in these words:

> The banks had to be brought in because apparently at that time they were the only source available of investment money. At that time we in this group warned the government of the day that bank investments in the field of borrowing would last only so long, and then would level off. Today the banks, in the main, are only investing in housing the mortgage money that is repaid, and they are only investing that percentage in housing that has a relationship to the growth of the assets of the bank. Once again we have reached the end of the rope. Some day the government will have to realize that unless they are going to exert some pressure on the existing institutions they will have to take over this responsibility of supplying money.[53]

The rapid growth of Canadian cities during the late 1950s was sapping up money from lending institutions, interest rates were climbing, and housing in general had fallen rather low on the list of priorities of lending institutions. Land values had quadrupled between 1947 and 1957. Reference was made in the House to the growing number of advertisements appearing in newspapers under "Money Wanted" columns and offering high interest rates and raising fees for small second mortgages.[54] People with middle to low incomes appeared to be coping despite the NHA but at a very high price. The costs of general urban development were embarrassing the federal government which, in turn, was obliged to supply increasing quantities of its own resources to keep the scale of house construction at a suitable level — about 130,000 starts a year up to 1956 — and to meet the needs of persons with incomes below $5,000 a year.[55] Concurrently the federal government was supporting at low interest rates matters of national development such as pipe-line construction, highways, seaways and airports as part of the national development program. Housing, even of the poor, was increasingly a relative matter to the general onward development of the nation.[56] The requirements of people were becoming increasingly secondary to the things and processes implicit in the giant schemes of national, and particularly metropolitan city, development.

An opposition member remarked:

> I know that, if certain people had their way there would be a great deal of money available in the housing field. There is a very simple answer to the problems and that is to allow the interest rate to shoot away up high. I hope that is not going to be the philosophy that this government will adopt, namely that in order to obtain this money they will have to raise interest rates so high they begin to compete with industrial enterprise in our country.[57]

Towards the end of the decade housing investment in the Maritimes was falling off sharply, as was the case also in many of the smaller towns elsewhere across the country. From April to November, 1957, only about 240 loans, involving about $2¼ million had been made in the whole of the Atlantic provinces, which was less than that for the city of Windsor, Ontario alone. People in the Maritimes, where there was a shortage of homes, an abundance of lumber, and unprecedented unemployment, were unable or unwilling to use the NHA. The problem that had surrounded the federal government from 1935 to the war appeared to be coming back by the close of the 1950s. Its modern origin, however, lay not in prolonged national depression but in regional disparities of development and under-employment. The answers suggested in the House for the Maritimes were little different from those of the 1930s — longer amortization periods, lower interest rates, lower standards of construction, smaller homes, and making government money available. A maritime member concluded his speech thus:

> ... I again urge the minister to give very serious consideration to the possibility of amending the regulations and the standard requirements of the act in order to make it possible for the class of wage earners I have mentioned (less than $4,000 a year) to qualify for loans ... More new homes in the Atlantic provinces will mean work for our unemployed, a better

standard of living for our workers, additional markets for our
lumber and better living conditions for all.[58]

Quebec was similarly affected. Only the major cities in these regions were
receiving any mortgage finance from any source.[59]
    The problem was aggravated by the distribution of tax revenues
between the federal government and the provinces that had been a thorny
issue since the end of the war.[60] The financially weaker provinces claimed
that the bulk of the wealth and income of Canada was concentrated in
Ontario and Quebec, i.e. in Toronto and Ontario's industrial cities, and in
Montreal. Most of the head offices of companies and corporations doing
business all over Canada were situated there and taxed there. These
industrialized provinces therefore got an unfair share of the tax revenues
and estate duties from business done all over the country. A further
aggravation was the dearth of national developmental money in the poorer
provinces. Pipelines in the west, a seaway in central Canada, and the
opening up of the north were the centres of capital investment. The
president of the Atlantic Economic Council had remarked in 1959 during
a speech in Montreal:

> but once attention is turned east of Quebec to the Atlantic
> area, people think of aid, assistance, subsidies, subventions
> and the like . . . Let us stop thinking of the Atlantic provinces
> in terms of aid alone, and regard them as a region ready for, and
> worthy of, some of the same developmental projects that all of
> us now support in the rest of Canada.[61]

During 1957-58, Ontario had again been pressing the federal government
for a greater share of the federal-provincial tax distribution and
equalisation formula. This formula concerned personal and corporation
income tax and succession duty. It was a device to spread more evenly
over the provinces by distribution what had been collected unevenly across
Canada because of the centralization of wealth in the country. The federal
government did the collection, and, hopefully, by agreement with the
provinces, distributed revenue from these three sources in the interests of
the country as a whole. The formulae resemble an agricultural fertiliser
formula, e.g. 10-9-50 meant 10 percent of personal income tax, 9 percent
of corporation income tax, and 50 percent of succession duties, would be
turned over to the provinces, with an equalisation payment based on the
per capita average receipts of the two most wealthy provinces. Ontario
had been urging a 15-15-50 formula which would have given that
province over $100 million more than the 10-9-50 formula. The
Conservative government in late 1957 had used a 13-9-50 formula.
    Both rapidly developing provinces like Ontario and Alberta and
depressed provinces like Saskatchewan and the Maritimes could make
equally pressing cases for more money but from opposite points of view.[62]
The developing provinces needed more money to cope with the
consequences of development. The poor provinces required money to
cope with unemployment, personal impoverishment, and the lack of public
and personal amenities — the basic needs of their people. The federal

government tended to be caught in the squeeze on both the count of how much any province was to get and how much of its own resources were to be returned to the provinces generally.

Municipal governments since 1945 had greatly increased their expenditures, and so also had the provinces — by 246 percent and 381 percent respectively up to 1957. Federal expenditure, after considering transfers to the provinces, had remained approximately constant at $5 billion since the close of the war.[63] In 1958 the provinces were anxious to get their fiscal affairs straightened out and the federal government had just budgeted for an anti-inflationary surplus of $152 million. The times seemed opportune. The provinces' municipalities needed relief from "their pressing financial burdens" arising from essential public services in the expanding cities. The economic recession of 1958 exacerbated the financial situation of the provinces through reducing revenues from gasoline taxes, motor licence fees, liquor taxes and sales taxes. The Liberal opposition in 1958 was pressing for the instigation of a national development program "that can be shared in by all the provinces."[64]

During the federal-provincial conference in November, 1958, Ontario and British Columbia proposed a 25-25-50 formula. Ontario argued that the growth of the investment needed in Ontario demanded a greater provincial share of direct tax revenues, "so that Ontario and its municipalities could develop its services apace, with a developing economy and exploding population."[65] The Maritime premiers asked for some system of adjusting their per capita revenue to the national average. The western premiers "were in general agreement that the existing 10-9-50 formula gave little recognition to the rapidly expanding costs of the provinces constitutional responsibilities."[66] The conference agreed in principle to some supplementary assistance for the Maritime provinces, but not to a general tax-sharing formula. Supplementary assistance had to take a special or ad hoc form. In 1958 the federal government announced an annual adjustment grant of $25 million to the Atlantic provinces. A generally applicable formula of 13-9-50 would be applied to other provinces signing the agreement with Ottawa. This was the beginning of a policy that recognized regional needs and set off the ever-expanding co-operative relation between the federal government the the degraded non-city regions of the country that has ended, to date, in the Regional Development Incentives Act of 1969.

A system of unemployment relief by means of public works assistance in municipalities across Canada was in the formulation stage in November, 1958. It came to be known as the Winter Works Program, as its express purpose was to relieve winter unemployment. It came to be one of the larger items of federal expenditure on municipal public works. In 1959 it was administered by the Minister of Labour who had consulted the provincial premiers about it. The type of works in which the federal government was interested were listed and the munici-palities were encouraged to initiate the work, keeping careful account of wages paid in respect of it. After approval of each project by the provincial government, the federal government refunded to the municipality one-half of the direct cost of salaries paid over the winter months. It was a refund operation of projects initiated by municipalities within broadly defined areas of federal interest. The works would involve the municipalities in costs they would have to meet themselves, so it had a regulatory component. One of its purposes was to apportion employment over the seasons.

In 1959, by a further amendment to the NHA, the federal government again increased the aggregate amount which may be authorized from the consolidated revenue fund, from $750 million to one billion dollars in respect of housing falling under the category small home loans, limited-dividend housing projects, and housing assistance for primary industries (of which there had been very little). These were the areas where the lending institutions would not effectively co-operate and CMHC was virtually undertaking the work on its own account. It was a simple matter: where lending institutions didn't care to do a job, CMHC had to do it, and parliament had to vote public money with which to do it. The rate of increase of direct CMHC involvement in home mortgages over the period, 1954-58, is shown in Table 10.

TABLE 10. Rate of increase of direct CMHC involvement in home mortgages over the period 1954-58 (in millions of dollars).

Year	Dollars by approved lenders	Dollars by CMHC	Percentage distribution
1954	$433.4	$ 20.1	(96%, 4%)
1955	$559.0	$ 16.3	(97%, 3%)
1956	$387.7	$ 19.4	(95%, 5%)
1957	$260.9	$233.0	(53%, 47%)
1958	$512.0	$375.0	(58%, 42%)

House of Commons Debates, 1959, 2:1299.

Thus, while the provinces were pressing the federal government for a greater share of tax revenues — and Ontario in particular was seeking it to cope with the costs of its rapidly and ever-expanding cities — the lending institutions were increasingly letting the federal government down with respect to residential mortgage lending. There were severe housing shortages in the growing cities, and vacant and abandoned dwellings in non-city parts of the country from whence people had migrated; and any new construction in small towns and rural areas would not be financed at all by lending institutions. The rural-urban imbalance in Canada was impressing the federal government with its seriousness; but the pressures from the cities and the provinces were beginning to mount.

The 1958 figure involved 164,632 house starts. The minister remarked, after saying that "in Toronto metropolitan area there was more housing going on in that year than in any other part of Canada,"

> Then we have tried hard to increase the home building in the smaller centers of Canada. I would point out that the great demand is in the metopolitan areas. However, we have gone out deliberately to increase construction in the smaller centres. The CMHC officials wrote to every municipality with

a population of 1500 and over pointing out what could be done, the facilities available in obtaining loans and offering to send an official to that municipality for the purpose of discussing the positions with those holding office. We have had considerable success with that program as a result.[67]

Later in the debate the minister remarked:

It may be that in the rural areas and indeed in the smaller towns there is not the demand for new housing that we had expected.[68]

In 1958, in centres of under 30,000 population, the increase of house starts under the NHA was from 13,488 to 19,471 across Canada. A new "minimum house," of 848 square feet, was being experimented with, costing $9,000 to $10,000 in many parts of degraded and rural Canada from Newfoundland to British Columbia. The minister remarked:

. . . some of the very small homes which I have mentioned which are being built in various parts of Canada could be purchased by someone with an income much lower than the person would require to buy a home, say, in Toronto.[69]

The reality of rural and non-city personal degradation was being faced by CMHC, but at space and amenity standards that did not equate with those of the metropolitan areas. The federal government was still coping with the overall situation, but at a losing pace. The minister's policy was stated in these terms:

Loans will be made to prospective home owners who are unable to obtain loans from the approved lenders. In other words, they have first to go to the approved lenders . . . and if they are turned down by two, then they can go to CMHC and apply for a loan . . . The corporation is in a residual position.[70]

In May, 1958 CMHC took over the small home loans rather than expecting lending institutions to handle this type of work on an agency basis. CMHC had for several years been handling house construction in small towns on its own account but it was now extending its operations to all areas. Builders in particular were borrowing direct from CMHC on small home loans. Limited dividend rental units increased during the economic recession of 1958, from 4,100 units in 1957 to 7,000 in 1958. Churches and service clubs had joined in this activity as non-profit organizations, and particularly for aged persons. Limited-dividend rental units were under construction mainly in Toronto and Montreal.

Though supporting the 1958 NHA amendments, the Liberal opposition spokesman for housing warned that "the government itself

126

may not be as sensitive to the need or demand for new housing as individual lenders may be. The individual lenders are risking their own money and they have to be right." In using the construction industry to cope with an economic recession, there was a likelihood, in the opposition's mind, that an over-supply of housing could easily result — "that the turning on or turning off of lending operations are responsibilities that must rest with the government itself."[71] The demand for housing differed from one urban area to another, and for that reason, the opposition spokesman suggested "CMHC must be carefully watched.[72] On the other hand, the NHA was not really helping the lowest income group. The opposition feared that there was a surplus of middle-income homes, but that there was little substantial as yet for the family with an income below $4,000. As a result of the small-house (1,050 sq. ft.) building boom in Toronto the price of small lots had risen from about $3,800 in 1957 to about $5,500 in 1959. Paul Hellyer, in opposition, pointed out how this increase in turn increased the need for municipalities to receive assistance in the servicing of additional areas of land — assistance the federal government should seriously consider, if the cost of small homes was to be kept low and the demand for them increased in consequence.

By 1960 there were clear signs of a surplus of houses in many areas. Effective demand was declining, though the needs of the poor had not been adequately met. The Minister of Public Works, D. J. Walker, explained that the banks, life, loan, and trust companies had virtually stopped lending in 1959, other investments being more attractive to them. The amount of government lending was by now determining the incidence of housing starts. The minister remarked:

> It seemed likely, in view of the rates of building achieved in this period (1957-59), that the excess demand for NHA funds would not last indefinitely and that sooner or later a time would be reached when substantial increases in house building could not be brought about merely by making funds available on the existing terms, although much more could be achieved by improving the terms.[73]

The interest rate was raised at the end of 1959 to 6¾ percent from 6 percent but the banks, for legal reasons, were unable to take advantage of this highter rate. In the hope of admitting a new class of borrowers into the field, an amendment to the NHA in November, 1960 lowered the down-payment required.[74] This amendment would also save borrowers from having to arrange expensive second mortgages. The permissible repayment term was also extended from 30 to 35 years. Rental housing loans were also increased from 80 percent to 85 percent and the maximum loan amounts were increased. This was to encourage the construction of apartments. In this instance, the federal government was caught in the squeeze of hoping to help the lower income groups obtain housing, but at the same time of having to raise the interest rate to attract the lending institutions to invest in mortgages. A reduction in interest rates would only discourage lending institutions from making mortgage money available and CMHC would have to make increasing numbers of direct loans — a threat to its residual role. The minister remarked:

> Again I cannot forget the way in which the funds dried up toward the end of 1959, when an interest rate of 6 percent became totally unrealistic and when the borrowers turned in droves and in thousands to the government to help them out of their dilemma.[75]

The government's 1960 amendments were also designed to help urban redevelopment. City slum clearance and redevelopment schemes took off very slowly through 1957-58. Halifax, Montreal, Windsor, and Vancouver opened negotiations during this time. The regulations covering the federal part of this program were also worked out. The federal government paid 75 percent of the cost of the investigation leading to redevelopment, 50 percent of the cost of acquiring the land, and 75 percent of the cost of a new housing scheme to house people obliged to relocate.[76] The 1956 provisions that allowed private interests into the new-use aspect of cleared land remained. By 1960 virtually all major cities across Canada, except Calgary and Edmonton, had conducted studies of their obsolete housing with a view to urban renewal projects.[77] Some 300 acres of "blight" had been scheduled for slum clearance during 1958-1960. The estimated total cost of acquisition and clearance was over $22 million of which the federal government had offered its $11 million. The minister expected this part of the NHA to increase rapidly in the future as many studies had indicated its value. The statutory limit under this heading was raised from $25 million to $50 million to meet this anticipation.

The distribution of urban-renewal expenditure by population size of municipalities was broad. Table 11 shows the distribution of CMHC expenditure on this item from 1960-67 by municipal size. The distribution had favored cities of from 100,000 to 500,000 persons. There appears also to be some cyclical patterns of expenditure in the size ranges, but there is no available explanation for them. CMHC expenditure was steadily rising over this time. The Hellyer Task Force was appointed only in mid-1968.

The 1960 amendments allowed the federal government to pay 75 percent of the cost of acquiring and rehabilitating existing housing in urban renewal areas designated by agreement among the particpating governments. Studies and experience had shown, however, that in the large acreages designated for urban renewal there were several houses and apartments that were not so run down "or so plainly needed for other purposes that massive and complete clearance is necessary."[78] Complete demolition was not always required. Several buildings could still usefully be used to house the lower-income groups more cheaply than would new housing. The original act made no provision for the acquisition of suitable existing housing in urban renewal areas, and, in consequence, cities tended to wait "for severe blight to set in and then apply for total clearance aid. The proposed change may encourage municipalities to adopt and enforce by-laws governing the maintenance

TABLE 11. CMHC expenditure for urban renewal programs 1960-67 by population size of municipalities.

Municipal population	1960 $	1961 $	1962 $	1963 $	1964 $	1965 $	1966 $	1967 $	Total by population size
1,000,000 and over	22	1,083	31,912	778	996	917	50	5,761	
1,000,000 and over	22	1,083	3	1,912	778	996	917	50	5,761
500,000 to 999,999	1,406	1,010	694	140	347	668	2,167	1,677	8,109
100,000 to 499,999	311	416	1,672	718	2,510	2,326	2,820	3,887	14,660
50,000 to 99,999	420	368	1,818	1,397	644	992	776	1,817	8,232
Under 25,000 (sic)	45	19	5	10	16	59	91	854	1,099
Total	2,204	2,896	4,192	4,177	4,295	5,041	6,771	8,285	37,861

and occupancy of their housing stock and thus prevent rapid spread of blight."[79] By federal-provincial partnership the amendment permitted the augmentation of the stock of public housing by turning suitable buildings not required for demolition into government-owned rental properties. The minister remarked:

> We have a tremendous demand for such housing at the present time. We feel that this will aid the municipalities, and aid the federal government as well as providing more housing at lower cost.[80]

The governments were to be expected to move into low-quality house landlordship. Similarly, the Act was amended to provide for federal assistance for home improvement and maintenance to owners of rental properties, including apartment buildings. Urban accommodation that could be renovated and brought up to date by new plumbing and heating etc. was now to qualify for NHA assistance through supported bank loans. Rental housing stock across Canada now amounted to about one and a half million units. For this purpose the aggregate amount of loans that could be guaranteed under the Act was increased from $200 million to $500 million.

Federal Direct Aid to Local Authorities, 1960-62

Up to this time the federal government had assisted local authorities directly, with the approval of the provinces, in urban redevelopment programs, the winter works programs, and in 1960 a program of assistance to vocational schools. These were largely aimed at coping with urban unemployment.

The 1960 amendment to the NHA introduced steps to counter water pollution. The minister remarked:

> Great numbers of Canadians are now living in surroundings that are urban in every other respect except that they lack adequate sewage facilities. Less than one sixth of our urban municipalities have adequate sewage treatment plants in operation; perhaps two-thirds of our urban population are living in regions where seriously polluted surface waters are found.[81]

The riparian water users below the cities were taking court action, and, according to the minister, one town was delighted to be sued, "because that enabled it to get the provincial authorities to come forward with a grant which would permit the town to install a sewage disposal plant.[82]

The NHA had itself encouraged the building of houses in areas not properly serviced for sewage disposal. Although policy had been to confine NHA housing to piped mains, the amount of land within reach of the sewerage system had always been too limited or too costly. Subdivisions with septic tanks had been approved. Residential areas had always been less well serviced than other city areas; and the newest residential areas had suffered in particular.

130

Many house owners had decided to build beyond the piped system on larger lots which would accommodate septic tanks. Some of this had been supported by NHA facilities. When eventually the city caught up with them, and obliged them to connect to the sewer, they had found themselves with duplicate equipment and high taxation due to large lots and the cost of extending services to low-density occupation areas. For these reasons the federal government had decided to provide loans to municipalities to expand their sewerage systems by aiding in the construction of trunk sewers and sewer disposal works. This assistance was to be limited to central works. At the same time the policy on the use of septic tanks was to be tightened up. The minister, sensitive of the political implications of this move, remarked:

> We are bringing down a measure that will extend aid for
> purposes that everyone agrees must be served if Canadian
> urban development is to continue in vigorous, healthy and
> orderly fashion; and we are bringing it into the house in
> a form that focuses on the areas of most acute need and
> corresponds with the stated desires of Canadian local
> governments. Every local authority sincerely wishing to
> correct the evil of pollution will find through this measure
> a helping federal hand.[83]

The Canadian Federation of Mayors and Municipalities had frequently urged this step, but the minister recognized that some provinces and municipalities had already moved in this direction.[84]

To cover the provincial interest, these sewerage works were to be approved by provincial health authorities and the proposal to borrow under the NHA would require provincial approval. The minister saw the CMHC regional offices having informal discussions with provincial authorities before a formal application was made. He then remarked:

> However, it is to be understood that the province will not be
> the middleman here. We shall be dealing directly with the
> municipalities . . . Whatever the provinces want to do besides
> this is up to the provinces. We shall be glad to have them
> make whatever contributions they can make.[85]

The loan was to be limited to two-thirds of the cost of the proposed work, as recognized by CMHC. It was repayable over not more than 50 years, at a rate of interest close to the federal borrowing rate. To meet the situation of adjacent municipalities going together into one service the Act was to allow for joint ventures. A $100 million provision was authorized for this plan, but to get cities into action during the high incidence of unemployment over the winter of 1960-61 a quarter of the CMHC loan was to be forgiven where it was spent on work "put into place" by April 1, 1963.[86]

This 25 percent forgiveness provision, although introduced as a means of getting local authorities geared for action by the winter, was also in effect a means of reducing the rate of interest charged on the loan. This provision thereby made available to local authorities money at the rate of about 2 percent for sewerage works if they kept up to the prescribed time limit. This forgiveness principle was not a one-shot proposal, for it was used again in the 1963 Municipal Development and Loan Act. (This latter Act was an "urgent" national unemployment measure to get urban public works stimulated in a respectable guise.)

The response to the sewerage proposals was speedy. In September, 1961 the minister reported that requests for loans had come from all provinces in Canada and from municipalities of every size. Communities of less than 5,000 people had made good use of the facility. The minister remarked:

> In most of these smaller communities, sewage systems are being provided where they did not exist before. Furthermore, construction of sewage systems in the smaller localities has, in many instances, encouraged the installation of public water systems to replace individual wells.[87]

Some 106 loans had been made across Canada in the first nine months of the legislation receiving assent. Some 203 preliminary enquiries had been made and the minister, by further amendment to the Act in September, 1961, sought an increase in the statutory limit from $100 million to $200 million.[88]

The 1960 amendment also initiated CMHC loans to universities for student residences. They were at the rate of 90 percent of the cost of a project, carried the same rate of interest as limited dividend corporation loans, and were to be amortised within 50 years.

Opposition spokesmen tended to support the proposed amendments, but the Liberal opposition felt the urban redevelopment proposals did not go nearly far enough. They had pressed for a municipal grants assistance Act for several years, and they considered that to limit federal aid to municipal services to trunk sewers and plant was far too restrictive. They also pressed for a raise from 50 percent to 75 percent in the federal share of joint slum clearance schemes. The government was criticized for using housing primarily as "an economic pump primer" and for mismanaging the timing of incentives. The opposition argued that by raising interest rates, and thereby the cost of housing, the government was going against its espoused policy of helping those requiring federal help to acquire homes. The 6¾ percent interest rate seemed only to be getting the unemployed back to work, but producing houses the needy could never afford. The fear of unemployment was preventing people from taking on mortgages and large payments which they might never be able to afford.

By the same amendment the maximum charge on the Consolidated Revenue Fund for direct loans from CMHC was again raised, this time from $1.5 billion to $2 billion. The government expected the call on its funds in 1961 for direct CMHC loans to be $300 million. Some 40 percent of all NHA loans were made by CMHC in 1961 with funds provided by the government. Private funds for NHA lending had been "quite inadequate to meet the total demand."[89]

132

By raising the amount of money available to CMHC the government was hedging against the vulnerable position into which mortgages for new house construction had become placed. Any change in investment preferences by lending institutions could seriously affect the financing of single dwelling homes. The *1964 Royal Commission on Banking and Finance* observed:

> Thus, the relatively small share of the housing stock built each year provides the main source of demand for mortgage funds . . . the owners' equity in new housing has provided only 18 percent of the funds needed for construction since 1954, with 82 percent coming from financial institutions, government agencies and other outside sources. Borrowed funds are the principal source of finance for all but a relatively small number of houses and apartments built . . . The market for new housing can thus be powerfully affected by the way in which the mortgage market is organized and allocates funds among competing needs and by changes in the availability of mortgage funds.[90]

The lending institutions were becoming increasingly interested in metropolitan high rise office and apartment blocks. The considerably lower limit of the maximum loan on rental accommodation as against personally owned accommodation — a matter changed in 1963 when these were brought up to parity — was holding up the lending institutions' use of the NHA for their new interest.

The economy was picking up after the 1960-61 recession. Rates of interest were rising again. If the statutory provision of a 2¼ percent markup on the interest rate on long term federal government bonds for NHA loans had been implemented, the rate chargeable would have been 7¼ percent, but the government had managed to retain the 6¾ percent rate. [91] The attractiveness of corporate bonds and provincial and municipal bonds, was, however, threatening this rate. Lending institutions' funds were contributing only about 60 per cent of the necessary money as the rate stood.

In March, 1962 during the Supply Debate for Public Works, a member raised for the first time in the House the possibility of establishing a department of urban affairs.[92] John R. Matheson, Member for Leeds, Ontario, was discussing the problem of municipal financing and had quoted from the editorial of *The Listening Post,* organ of the Canadian Federation of Mayors and Municipalities, of February, 1962. Mr. Matheson remarked:

> It is the problem of paying. How are these municipalities going to pay for the things we know should be done in each of our towns and cities across Canada, and which can be done with a little bit of help. What these municipalities are asking for now is the full and continuing co-operation of the federal government in mobilizing the capital needed for such works, and that is why the comments made from this side of the

house (Liberal) are so germane to the growth problems
facing the local municipalities.[93]

Sewerage assistance was in the right direction, but "other basic needs
such as roads, subways, bridges, water supplies and conservation
projects" were required. The cities were growing and in the United
States the complexity and scale of the problems had brought suggestions
that the central government "establish a department of urban affairs.
While suggestions have been made in Canada that the federal
government should devote more attention to urban problems, there has
been no suggestion of such a department being established." The
persistent unemployment problem (719,000 persons out of work in 1961)
could be handled only by Ottawa — it is not enough simply to pass it on
to the provinces" — and the Public Works Department was the agency
"to whom we must look for assistance with respect to an expanded
public works program." In the same speech, the member also made this
comment:

> I think there is a genuine concern on the part of some of our
> municipalities right now lest they become too dependant
> upon provincial governments. They want to grow; they want
> to develop. They have at their helm and in their local councils,
> I know, some of the best brains we have available in our
> communities . . . [94]

The minister did not reply to these suggestions.
    The years 1962-63 show two other interesting developments in
the federal House. In December, 1962 Mr. Robert Thompson, Member
for Red Deer, Alberta, introduced a motion suggesting the setting up of a
department of federal-provincial affairs under the direction of a full-time
minister. He noted that Manitoba and Ontario had established portfolios of provincial-federal affairs — "they are looking toward something
that will tie the ends together at the federal level."[95] Fiscal relations
were a major topic envisaged for these departments, but in addition he
made the following comment:

> But again, behind all of this I would say that there is the
> basic issue of democratic government itself in Canada. More
> and more power assigned to boards means less and less power
> to elected representatives . . . My proposal here tonight is a
> means of giving provinces a chance to be heard on major
> policy decisions of the federal government, and even to get
> action on many matters which are neglected, of which
> resources and transport policy are two of the most
> conspicuous.[96]

The idea had its merits, but it involved the difficulty of federal
departments passing their particular proposals affecting the provinces
of Canada through a co-ordinating federal instrument. This they would
be unlikely to welcome (though, it should be noted, this was the

134

principle Mr. Andras managed to persuade the Cabinet to adopt in 1970 with respect to his "urban policy for Canada"). It was a much simpler matter for the provincial governments each to set up a provincial-federal co-ordinating agency both in their own capitals and in Ottawa, than it was for the federal government to do so.

In January, 1963 Arnold Peters, Member for Temiskaming, moved, under private members' business, a motion concerning a "Council to locate industry according to regional suitability." His idea was to legislate for assisting industry to locate in areas "which now have little or no industry."[97] He remarked that in Northern Ontario:

> . . . we have dozens and dozens of towns built around two basic industries (forestry and minerals) that were the backbone of the country's economy until the last few years, and now we see secondary industry in other areas rapidly approaching its sphere of supremacy and growth . . . we realize something must be done for the municipalities which grew out of those basic industries.[98]

Forestry, as a renewable resource, had a particular claim for the location of secondary manufacturing. Towns had been declining in the region. The member did not consider much help would come from the province of Ontario "when it believes all we should do is return these municipalities to an unorganized state where the province provides public welfare to take care of the people . . . (who) want to take care of themselves. They have a pioneering spirit and all they want are jobs so that they can continue to build their town.[99] The growth of Toronto, and of the "metropolitan industrial complexes" which were enticing industry and employing several hundred people but which were a liability to that city, was leading to the situation he wished to remedy. Manpower, housing, public amenities, and transport were all present in Northern Ontario — "the only thing that is needed is the direction of the federal government in locating industry in those areas . . ." Realistically, the member remarked at the end of his speech, "I will be very surprised if this resolution does not suffer the same fate as other resolutions and bills put before this house, which have been loved to death."

At this time also, the House debated legislation leading to the formation of the National Economic Development Board. It had just approved the setting up of the Atlantic Development Board, and in June, 1963, established an Industry Department. The National Productivity Council had been in operation for several years already. National economic planning was taking a distinctive form in the early 1960s. An opposition member, David Lewis, aptly pointed out that these boards were all under different ministers and in consequence the co-ordination of effort was likely to be minimal.[100]

In Alberta the Lieutenant Governor in Council had received a brief from the Alberta section of the Canadian Bar Association, dated January 10, 1963, bearing on the question of the administrative problems of government. This followed a previous report commenting on the proliferation of administrative boards, tribunals, and judicial and semi-judicial agencies within the province. The previous report had identified a number approaching 200, which was greatly in excess of what existed in Ontario. This, the Section had argued, had dangerous implications for the system of democratic government in so far as the policy to be administered by a tribunal or administrative agency was not spelt out clearly by government in its terms of reference. The system also had grave implications for the co-ordination of government policy. The left hand rarely knew what the right was doing.[101]

1. *House of Commons Debates,* 1952-53, 5:4451.
2. Ibid., p. 4453. In 1951 it was estimated that of the 100,000 houses identified as substandard in major cities, the majority were adjacent to the central business cores. Many were on small lots which inhibited larger scale development. The business cores were also expanding.
3. The federal government adopted a policy as early as 1949 of paying municipalities grants in lieu of taxes on properties of federal departments. Crown corporations were to be similarly encouraged. The Municipal Grants Act, 1952, formalized the federal position. In 1967 a review of crown corporation policies was initiated and the policies made uniform. Payments under the Municipal Grants Act increased from $31 million in 1963-64 to $40 million in 1967-68; Alberta municipalities received just over $2 million of these payments each year during this time. *House of Commons Debates,* 1968-69, 4:4468.
4. *House of Commons Debates,* 1952-53, 5:4457.
5. Ibid.
6. Ibid., p. 4492. This section referred to the federal-provincial partnership financial formula, and assumed close co-operation between these levels of government.
7. *The Edmonton Journal,* March 3, 1953. The Alberta Municipal Financing Corporation was set up in 1955 and superseded this fund.
8. *House of Commons Debates,* 1953-54, 2:1314.
9. Ibid., p. 1314.
10. Ibid.
11. *Housing and Urban Growth in Canada,* CMHC, 1956, p. 26.
12. *House of Commons Debates,* 1953-54, 2:1314.
13. Ibid., p. 1315.
14. Ibid., p. 1316. Under the joint lending schemes prior to the 1954 NHA insurance covered the lending institutions' business under the Act. Under the 1954 Act insurance was to apply to each individual loan to each mortgage, and could therefore be transfered with the loan. This was essential if mortgages were to be sold by the first lender to other investors and the mortgage market given greater flexibility and therefore attractiveness to lenders.
15. Ibid., p. 1315.
16. Ibid.
17. The paradox of this situation is seen in its relation to a statement by the Minister of Finance, Mr. Winters, during the 1953 NHA amendment debate. He than commented, "It is not the responsibility of the federal government to build houses . . . The basic policy of the federal government is to enable people to build houses by making available the proper economic climate and by doing what it can within its own sphere of influence to made credit available." *House of Commons Debates,* 1952-53, 4:4169.
18. Personal interview.
19. *House of Commons Debates* 1953-54, 2:1332.
20. *House of Commons Debates,* 1956, 3:3171.
21. Ibid., p. 3175. The minister's reply is contained in *House of Commons Debates,* 1956, 4:3332-33.

22. *House of Commons Debates,* 1956, 3:3168.

23. Ibid. The minister's supposition is not entirely born out by the facts. The problem is one of increased difficulties for a local municipal council over deciding for what, and how to develop its blighted areas. If the range of choice increases, the danger of internal council conflict and of local officials versus the councillors increases. If the range of choice remains restricted this potential for conflict is correspondingly limited, and the likelihood of speedy municipal decision and action is increased also. Edmonton's urban renewal scheme since 1961 illustrates this problem. There is also the problem of slum citizens' objections to being moved en bloc.

24. As was shown in the 1956 debate, Toronto had initiated a major low rental housing project — the Regent Park North project — without CMHC entering the picture. Certain local authorities had taken some initiative as early as 1943, but with limited general extent.

25. *House of Commons Debates,* 1956, 4:4004.

26. The column "Guarantees to approved lending institutions in request of land assembly projects under the National Housing Acts 1944 and 1954 (December 31, 1955)" has a "nil" amount against it in the budget appendix Table XLVI, "Other outstanding guarantees and contingent liabilities." *House of Commons Debates,* 1956, 3:2441.

27. *House of Commons Debates,* 1956, 3:3170. In 1956 the capital cost of the full complement of neighborhood and community services to be provided by lower levels of government was between $1, 500 and $2, 500 per house, or $5,000 to $10,000 of outlay per acre of residential development. *House and Urban Growth in Canada.* CMHC, Ottawa 1956, p. 25.

28. *House of Commons Debates,* 1956, 4:3301.

29. Ibid. The cost of slums was a matter of increased municipal concern from 1955-58. *The Financial Post* of December 14, 1957, carried a long article on the subject. In Montreal slums were reported to provide 6 percent of the total city tax revenues, but 33 percent of the total population, 45 percent of major crimes, 60 percent of tuberculosis victims, 35 percent of fines, and 45 percent of total city service costs.

30. The differential in cost between acquiring land in downtown Toronto and Montreal and in developing virgin land was about $250,000 in the city and $8,000 an acre serviced, and $2,000 an acre unserviced in the suburban areas. *Housing and Urban Growth in Canada.* CMHC, 1956, p. 33.

31. *House of Commons Debates,* 1956, 4:3302.

32. Ibid.

33. Ibid., p. 3303. The 1964 amendment to the NHA explicitly included commercial and industrial, as well as residential purposes.

34. Ibid., p. 4006.

35. Ibid., p. 3303.

36. Ibid.

37. The Co-operative Commonwealth Federation, which later changed into the New Democratic Party.

38. *House of Commons Debates,* 1956, 4:3393.

39. Ibid. p. 3394.

40. The Minister of Finance replied (Ibid p. 3406) that it had been a principle of the Canadian constitution that the crown in the right of the province is not taxed, but this does not extend to municipal corporations.

41. Ibid., p. 3399.

42. Ibid., p. 3400.

43. Ibid., p. 3402. Mr. Low was referring to the Alberta Municipal Financing Corporation. The needs of local authorities by 1956 were likely to be greater than the fund could contain. The new instrument permitted the province to supply finance to the corporation from sources outside the province. The original revolving fund was limited to intra-provincial sources.

44. Ibid., p. 3401.

45. Ibid., p. 3402.

46. Ibid., p. 3403.

47. Ibid.

48. Ibid., p. 3409. Another member pointed out that in 1929 the federal government took 6.4 percent of the gross national product and the provincial and municipal governments together 8.7 percent. In 1954 the respective figures were 19 percent and 8.5 percent (p. 3460). These figures also did not take into account federal transfers.

49. Ibid., p. 3430.

50. Ibid., p. 3463.

51. Consumer credit became a significant matter about this time, particularly through instalment buying. By 1963 consumer credit had escalated to about $4 billion.

52. The small homes loan was a consequence of technical changes and reduced standards that CMHC had managed to devise as a contribution to low and middle income housing needs. It was used extensively in the metropolitan cities, especially in Toronto.

53. *House of Commons Debates,* 1957-58, 3:3506.

54. Ibid., p. 2505.

55. The average income of persons using the NHA in 1957 was $5,800, but the average income across Canada was $3,300. The 1957 amended regulations would permit persons with income of $3,450 to qualify for loans. (Ibid., p. 2518).

56. From 1955 to 1957 NHA approvals by the life companies dropped from $227 million to $96 million and those of loan and trust companies from $42 million to $9 million.

57. Ibid., pp. 2507-8.

58. Ibid., p. 2518.

59. In the first quarter of 1958, of 3,536 house starts in Quebec, 2,997 or 85 percent were in the city of Montreal (Ibid., p. 133). Manitoba was similarly affected.

60. An excellent analysis of the issue is contained in Moore, A. M., Perry, J. H., and Beach, D. I. *The Financing of Canadian Federation the First Hundred Years.* (Toronto: 1966, Canadian Tax Foundation), Canadian Tax Papers No. 43, especially chapters II and III. In Alberta the increase of revenue from the federal treasury was from $89.6 million in 1956-57 to $147.9 million in 1959-1960. Of the latter amount some $59.0 million was an unconditional grant and $88.9 million conditional grants. These two types of grant represented some 44 percent of the money spent by the Government of Alberta. *House of Commons Debates,* 1962-63, 3:2365.

61. Quoted in *House of Commons Debates,* 1958, 1:732. The Atlantic provinces had in fact been assisted in power development facilities in 1957.

62. In 1957 Ontario opted out of a federal agreement on corporation income tax and imposed its own 11 percent rate of tax. This was 2 percent above the standard provincial share across the country but the premier, Mr. Frost, felt "the main fruits of the tremendous economic expansion in that province were being enjoyed by business corporations . . . and he regarded many expenditures of his government as relating to and assisting this expansion." (Moore, Perry and Beach, Ibid., p. 56.) No equalization payments were made to Ontario because its economic growth relative to other provinces kept its per capita tax yield the highest in Canada for several years.

63. House of Commons Debates, 1958, 1:734.

64. Ibid., p. 736.

65. Moore, Perry and Beach, *Financing of Canadian Federation,* p. 59.

66. Ibid.

67. *House of Commons Debates,* 1959, 1:684.

68. *House of Commons Debates.* 1959, 11:1242.

69. *House of Commons Debates,* 1959, 1:685.

70. Ibid., p. 686. In rural areas a prospective borrower was expected to try only one private lender before approaching CMHC.

71. Ibid., p. 690. During the period 1953-58 net family formations amounted to 513,000 while there were 724,700 dwelling units built. House completions were dropped to 120,000 in 1960.

72. Ibid., p. 691.

73. *House of Commons Debates,* 1960-61, 1:90.

74. This device had worked well in 1957 when the formula under insured loans was changed from 90 percent of the first $8,000 of lending value and 70 percent of the remainder, to 90 percent of the remainder. The 1960 amendment provided for 95 percent of the first $12,000 and 70 percent for the remainder. The rates were set on the lending value of the property as distinct from the purchase price.

75. Ibid., p. 91. Bank approvals on NHA loans fell from $300 million in 1958 to $175 million in 1959, and to only $1 million in 1960.

76. *House of Commons Debates,* 1958, 1:132.

77. *House of Commons Debates,* 1960-61, 1:92. The minister explained Calgary's and Edmonton's position in terms of their being "almost new cities and they may not need it at the present time." Edmonton initiated its studies in 1961.

78. Ibid.

79. Ibid. However, as early as 1956, CMHC had observed that "The vigorous enforcement of housing codes has the effect of lowering the selling price of unredeemable slum property, by raising the costs of maintenance. Hence redevelopment costs are likely to be less formidable." *Housing and Urban Growth in Canada p. 32.* There appeared to be an inherent quandry implicit in actions of the type the minister hoped to effect.

80. Ibid., p. 93.

81. Ibid.

82. Ibid.

83. Ibid., p. 94.

84. The significance of this measure was interrupted in 1963 during the debate on the Municipal Development and Loan Act, as being a principle that opened the door to direct federal-municipal financial arrangements. The Canadian Federation of Mayors and Municipalities in particular saw it as being a precedent that would permit later evolution and expansion.

85. Ibid., p.94.

86. In December, 1962 this period was extended to March 31, 1965 and in 1964 it was extended in 1967.

87. *House of Commons Debates,* 1961, 8:8485-86.

88. By the close of 1962 some 360 loans to the value of $85 million had been made. Ontario and Saskatchewan in particular had taken up this provision of the NHA.

89. Ibid., p. 8487. However, there were, allegedly, some 4,037 completed but unoccupied homes across the country at this time.

90. Royal Commission on Banking and Finance. *1964 Report.* (Ottawa: 1965), pp. 268-69.

91. A reduction to 6½ percent was achieved later in 1961.

92. *House of Commons Debates,* 1962, 2:1446.

93. Ibid., p. 1445.

94. Ibid., p. 1447.

95. *House of Commons Debates,* 1962-63, 3:2363.

96. Ibid.

97. Ibid., p. 2945.

98. Ibid., ARDA was not being applied to Northern Ontario.

99. Ibid., p. 2946.

100. Ibid., p. 2938. The Economic Council of Canada was established in 1963.

101. *House of Commons Debates,* 1963, 2:984.

Chapter 4
The swing to the downtown city centre:
1963 to 1969

Planning and the Growth of Manufacturing
      After assuming office early in 1963, Lester B. Pearson's
Liberal government enacted measures which greatly increased the
federal impact on urban areas. From the records of *Hansard,* this
impact appears in some respects to have been unintentional or vicarious.
The setting up of the Economic Council of Canada and the establishment
of the Department of Industry were, at face value, unconnected with
urban areas. The debate from the government benches made little
reference to urban areas. The Municipal Development and Loan Board
Act and the amendment to the National Housing Act were, of course,
directly connected with urban development and were explicitly stated
as being so. This apparent insensitivity to the obvious relation between
economic growth and city expansion may be accounted for, in part at
least, by the federal emphasis on regional rural development that
typified the end of the 1960s.
      This apparent insensitivity, however, is ironical in view of the
government's emphasis during 1963 on the role of planning. "Planning"
was in some quarters a dirty word and in others was associated with the
bogey-man of socialism.[1] Mr. Pearson, when introducing the resolutions
respecting both the Economic Council and the Department of Industry
had to tread carefully in respect of this topic, particularly as a hard hitting
speech by David Lewis of the New Democratic Party (NDP), on that
party's ideas of planning, had been made as recently as the closing
sessions of the previous (25th) Parliament.[2] The Prime Minister, in
introducing the resolution remarked:

> I, myself, think that planning, far from being a word to arouse
> suspicion, is a very good word indeed. However, it has to be
> used with a certain amount of caution; that is to say, it is a
> good word, provided that when we use it we know what we
> mean by it. We must not fall into the trap, in my view, of
> thinking that something called planning is, itself, a magic
> key to economic progress. It is merely a means to an end.[3]

In extracting the basic feature from the various types of planning
mechanisms tried in Europe with considerable success since the war,
the Prime Minister observed that:

the experience which is common in the various countries, is that all the countries where the planning has been instituted have all succeeded in establishing by consultation between government and the public in its varying manifestations of public activity, a broad consensus about the objectives and methods of economic policy and broad agreement on the targets and goals which should be achieved by economic activity. The government's hope . . . is that we can establish an economic council of Canada which will be an effective instrument for creating in Canada this kind of economic consensus, the kind of economic understanding that we need if we are to make the most of our resources, achieve and maintain high levels of employment, make our economic growth adequate for that purpose and compete successfully, as we must, in the new trading world.[4]

The proposed council was envisaged as deliberately keeping close contact between private activities of various kinds and the government. Its functions were to appraise economic trends and assess economic problems. The Prime Minister continued:

This appraisal must not, of course, be made in vacuo . . . but must be made to serve as a basis for sound policy decisions by government, by business, by labour and by other economic groups. In other words, if planning in government or planning between government and private organizations or agencies outside government is to be effective, it has got to be more than merely an academic exercise.[5]

This purpose of appraisal was even more clearly spelt out in respect of private corporations and government activities a little later in the speech. Mr. Pearson remarked:

When the economy has been studied as a whole, when its prospects and its potential have been assessed, the need which has been recognized in most of the free economies of the world is to relate these general prospects, and these general needs, to the particular plans of individual industries and of government agencies at all levels, and bring these together so that each will know what the other is proposing and hopes to do. Our great corporations, our provincial governments, our public agencies — they already plan. Where major investment projects costing tens of millions of dollars are involved, such planning is done many years ahead. But at present, all this partial planning within our economy is not related; it is not co-ordinated.[6]

The economic council was seen as "bringing together the thinking of government and the thinking of our great industries, our trade unions, our farm organization . . . " Planning meant consultation among powerful groups "in order to replace haphazard influence by conscious guidance. It means both government policies and private policies will be more broad-based and long-sighted than at present."[7]

The Leader of the Opposition, John Diefenbaker, in reply to this resolution cautiously accepted the principle, but was concerned about the potential for direction inherent in a council with paid membership and entitled "directors." He remarked that "if these directors are to have the powers that directors normally have then . . . we are opposed to any agency or device which will provide bureaucratic control over the business life of Canada."[8] He argued that businessmen were already beginning to worry — "Business had a right to be required to consider the welfare of the state at all times." Economic growth had to be the prime consideration and the reduction in unemployment which it would entail had to be assured.

A. B. Patterson, Member for Fraser Valley, wished that the resolution could have been discussed together with "the setting up of the municipal development and loan board, because we are convinced that this measure is one of the most important which will be brought before the house this coming session."[9] He did not, however, elaborate on the connection between the proposal and the future of the cities. As its publications demonstrate,[10] the Economic Council since its inception has been concerned with urban affairs.

Immediately following the resolution on the Economic Council, the Prime Minister moved for the adoption of a resolution setting up a Department of Industry. Whereas the test of the value of the Economic Council's work "will be whether it succeeds in identifying what I might refer to as the emerging points of expansion in our economy," the"point and purpose of the Department of Industry . . . will be to assist in transmitting the various ideas into effective action."[11] He argued that agriculture and fisheries had their own ministries and that mining was served by the Department of Mines and Technical Services, but "there is no department of industry, no department of government especially concerned with the needs and opportunities of manufacturing industry . . ."[12] The bill was to be one "to create a department which will be for manufacturing industry what the Department of Agriculture is for farmers." The new department was to keep close and practical contact with industry:

> . . . to make sure that industry gets service from government. It will be a department to which manufacturers can come to find out what is going on, to get advice and help in their problems. New and expanding enterprises in particular will look to it to see that government policies make their paths as smooth as possible. It will be concerned with translating into specifics the more general ideas about our economic growth that we hope will be generated in the economic council.[13]

The Prime Minister hoped that the department would remain small. Up to December, 1964 there was provision for the temporary appointment of people who were not civil servants but who had specific knowledge of manufacturing industries. The department was to be a "focus point" to give clarity and direction to government action in encouraging industry. Secondary industry was seen as the force that would produce Canada's future wealth, reduce unemployment, and encourage new immigration to Canada. Protectionism was not a realistic policy for Canada in the 1960s — "Canada's need is for industries that will fit into the new patterns of international trade which are now emerging and to which we will have to adapt ourselves.[14] Sophisticated industrial processes in particular had to be developed. The department was not to shore up weak industry by protection, but to help industry adjust to a changing world with new opportunities.

Mr. Pearson was concerned with the provincial governments' interests in industry and its welfare — "That is their constitutional responsibility as well as their natural duty." He argued that the setting up of a federal department of industry would:

> . . . in no way lessen or interfere with provincial responsibilities. The new federal department will not in any way create new federal responsibilities. Its concern will be simply and solely to discharge more efficiently and effectively the responsibilities which already fall on federal authorities. By providing a purpose for federal action, I believe the new department will make it easier for provincial departments of industry to do their work. Therefore, far from being hampered or interfered with, provincial action in support of industry will be, we hope, assisted by this development. Opportunities for fruitful federal-provincial co-operation will be improved.[15]

Mr. Pearson was quite correct in the last sentence of this quotation. While the richer provinces would undoubtedly object to federal interference in their ability to attract industry to themselves, the poorer provinces, particularly the Maritimes which had experienced population emigration and a paucity of industrial investment, would welcome federal initiative to get it there.[16] The federal government's dilemma was how to get into law a procedure that would permit it to favor certain provinces by incentives to industry and by close co-operation with provincial governments, and at the same time appear to be respecting provincial jurisdictions — at least for those provinces who found it convenient to be jealous of this right. The arguments raised in the House concerning a solution to this dilemma are revealing.

During the committee stage, Charles M. Drury, Member for Westmount and minister designate of the new department, argued that just as provinces have a responsibility in relation to industrial matters within their own provinces, so "does the federal government in relation to industry generally within Canada. A similar situation has arisen with regard to other federal departments, the Department of Agriculture, for example, which has duplicates in each of the provinces."[17]

Concerning one reason the bill had not been submitted to the provinces before being passed by the House, the minister argued:

> . . . inasmuch as we are dealing with a field for which the government is exclusively responsible, it is unnecessary and even undesirable to submit it to the wishes of the provincial governments.
>
> When the federal authority acts within its own jurisdiction, it has to make its own decisions. It is neither necessary nor desirable to risk any measure being vetoed — if I may use that expression — by the provincial governments.
>
> As far as the present legislation is concerned, it is clear that the federal government has the right, and even the duty, to look after the industrial problem at the national level. That is the object of the bill and there is no suggestion of conflict with the provinces.[18]

The minister did not explicitly state what he meant by the words "industrial problem." He went on to explain the relation between unemployment and automation. The answer to at least that "problem," as he saw it, lay "principally in accelerating very greatly the rate of industrial growth which has been experienced in this country over the past years."[19] Apparently the minister did not appreciate the inherent contradiction in this policy, namely, that the very purpose of automating the industrial process is to create added profits by deliberately reducing the need to employ industrial workers. His reference to "very greatly" would be the only qualifying correction, but the amount of new automated or highly technical industry necessary to be a realistic answer to unemployment would be immense. Further, the scale of such industrial production, in the absence of a greatly increased export market, would exacerbate the significance of consumer demand to buy the goods produced.

The federal government by setting up the Department of Industry was placing itself in a position where it could meet the provinces across the country hand-to-hand over industrial matters, while co-operating more fully and in a different way with some provinces than with others. The Area Development Agency part of the bill was:

> the first time that a federal government has made provision for a specialized organization to concentrate on area problems in all regions of Canada. Other agencies have been limited in their activities to particular regions, such as the Atlantic provinces, or to specific sectors of the economy.[20]

An opposition member from Quebec pointed out that the provinces were there precisely to look after area problems. And the minister himself recognized that in introducing this bill, he is following a new procedure which constitutes another interference in a provincial matter . . . "[21]

The proposed Area Development Agency (ADA) was expected to play an important role. The ADA "will create in Ottawa a small group of people whose special responsibility on behalf of the Minister of Industry, will be to make sure that various federal policies are conceived and co-ordinated in ways which will be a maximum help to the areas of maximum need."[22] It was intended to co-ordinate rather than execute and in this capacity would "not interfere with provincial action to the same end." The provinces were seen as being given an easier and more effective role.[23]

Opposition members asked if the federal government had consulted the provincial governments before setting up the new Department of Industry. The new department was tantamount to being a challenge to the autonomy which provinces had hitherto enjoyed with respect to industry. Quebec in particular was likely to be concerned over it. Too little processing of raw materials had hitherto been done in Canada and Quebec's incidence of unemployment had been proportionately high for some time — some 40 percent of the unemployed were in Quebec.[24]

Thus, with a 1963 budget deliberately intent upon stimulating industrial manufacturing by income tax depreciation allowances, and with a new Department of Industry and a new Area Development Agency, the Liberal federal government showed that it intended to rejuvenate economic activity by means of a planned process. Many of the ideas implicit in the new legislation were reproduced in 1969 and 1970 in the proposals to implement a national urban policy for Canada, but they were introduced in 1963 in terms of setting up both co-ordinating and research agencies, e.g. the Economic Council and the Area Development Agency, and administrative bodies, e.g. the Department of Industry. The emphasis in both 1963 and 1969 was on national scales of implementation, and both sets of legislation arose out of fear and a premonition of what might happen if steps were not taken on this scale of co-ordination and planning.

The Municipal Development and Loan Board, 1963-68

On the day after the debate on the preceding two resolutions, the Minister of Finance, Walter Gordon, introduced a bill to set up the Municipal Development and Loan Board. This bill was introduced under the same pretext as the 1935 Dominion Housing Act and the 1938 National Housing Act, namely to combat unemployment by national measures.[25] The House was aware, said the minister:

> . . . of this government's determination to do everything possible to combat serious unemployment in this country. One of the constructive ways in which this can be done is by assisting municipalities to proceed with needed capital works, many of which have been long deferred, and to help them expand and accelerate current programs.[26]

Concurrently with this unemployment there existed countless works that could be undertaken in municipal areas to the benefit of their

146

citizens. "It is this situation that the municipal development and loan act is designed to meet." The construction industry was most likely to benefit. This industry was also the one most likely to offer jobs to the predominantly unskilled unemployed of whom the minister said, "Some of these are Canadians born on farms who have moved into urban communities. Many are newcomers to Canada facing difficulty in establishing their families here."[27]

The Leader of the Opposition, Mr. Diefenbaker, shrewdly observed that the principle of the bill differed very much from the expectations of the Canadian Federation of Mayors and Municipalities (CFMM) as expressed in their brief to him, when Prime Minister, on November 9, 1962. In the view of the CFMM, the principle of a municipal loan fund had already been recognized in 1960, in the legislation authorizing sewerage loans to municipalities. The proposed legislation was intended to provide loans to meet specific developmental expenditures on municipal services, and was only vicariously aimed at coping with urban unemployment on a convenient basis. The principle of the sewerage legislation should in the view of the CFMM be extended to all municipal development, including rapid transit.[28]

The program was seen by the minister as being particularly timely, as municipalities from one end of Canada to the other had developed projects which they could not afford but were anxious to undertake. Unemployment would, therefore, be relieved on a wide geographic front and the coming winter would be a timely opportunity to start.[29] The program was to be dovetailed to existing winter-works incentive programs, but would not overlap with such activities. The bill authorized a limit of $400 million to be spread over three years and provided for loans of up to two thirds of approved cost to municipalities, available for a period of almost three years — up to March 31, 1966.[30] Municipalities could, in effect, therefore, turn the $400 million into $600 million of effective work. One quarter of the amount of each loan could be forgiven on work completed by this time. The rate of interest was based on the government's own long term borrowing rate and therefore considerably lower than the rate normally available to municipalities. Loans were generally made for a 20 year period.[31]

The express approval of provincial governments was required. The minister remarked:

> (The bill) provides that loans may be made only after a
> municipality has secured explicit provincial approval for
> eligible projects and for related borrowing by way of
> debentures. The operating procedures proposed are equally
> consistent, we believe, with full respect for the constitution
> which places the municipalities under the sole and exclusive
> jurisdiction of the provinces.[32]

The loans were to be for projects whose important and useful nature could be demonstrated and which the municipalities would themselves have carried out sooner or later. The federal government was not to become "a lender of last resort" to the municipalities. Only capital works of a type listed in the bill were to be eligible, and this did not include sewer construction or slum removal (already provided for through CMHC), hospital construction (already provided for under other federal legislation) and educational projects (which had become closely identified with provincial jurisdiction).[33] The listed items, however, enabled "approximately one half of the capital expenditures for which municipalities normally borrow to qualify under the bill."[34]

Administratively arranged, the loans board was to work in close co-operation with CMHC which was already in close touch with municipalities. CMHC field staff were to assist the board and thereby forestall the growth of a new staff attached to the board. Apparently provincial services were not to be brought into the administration beyond the point of approving the project and the loan. The minister remarked:

> While it is contemplated that CMHC will provide many of the administrative services under the Act, the prime initiative for developing the loan program will remain with the loan board. The responsibility for decisions with respect to loans and for the administration of the act will rest with the board.[35]

Mr. Diefenbaker asked explicitly: why has this legislation not been submitted to the provinces? As each project would require provincial approval it seemed only sensible to him that a federal-provincial meeting should have been arranged "to review all aspects of municipal finance."[36] He also hoped that municipal representation would be arranged for such a meeting. The bill as presently proposed provided for a federal board to determine if provincially approved projects were to be funded, and apparently on criteria determined by the federal authorities. The bill had the characteristic of being hasty legislation. He remarked:

> Is the government going to pass legislation, defy the rights of the provinces by passing it, and then come to a conference later this fall on a date as yet undetermined and say "Here is your bill of fare; it has passed the parliament of Canada."[37]

Mr. Gordon, Minister of Finance, replied to the question on provincial consultation in these terms:

> This has not been done. It is the government's view that it is the right of parliament to have first opportunity of discussing this plan on the resolution stage, and then when parliament has expressed its views it will be appropriate to discuss the plan with the provincial authorities.[38]

The issue, as Mr. Diefenbaker saw it, was one of steady increase in the demands of governments below the federal level for money "so that it will not, in its own economy, have to raise its own taxes to meet its own requirements." Opposition speakers during this debate raised more cogently than at any time since 1944 the implicit threat to provincial jurisdiction contained in the bill. Members from Quebec in particular identified the nature of the problem. Paul Martineau, Member for Pontiac Temiscamingue, quoted the opinion of Pierre Laporte, Quebec's Minister for Municipal Affairs, as saying:

> If the federal government, whichever party is in power, has money to spend for examination and solution of municipal problems, that money should rightly belong to the provincial authorities because they are the only ones to have any authority to deal with those problems.[39]

Horace A. Olson, Member for Medicine Hat, explained that in the case of Alberta, where the Municipal Financing Corporation had long been in existence, the federal minister could conveniently deal direct with this provincial agency. There was no need for a special board to be established in Ottawa. He remarked:

> There will be no interference with provincial rights if the government will deal with the municipal finance corporation. On the other hand, if you set up another board, whether or not it is in conjunction with CMHC, and try to deal directly with the municipalities I think you will run into some constitutional problems and perhaps bring about some disagreement with the province that really is not necessary.[40]

He suggested that the minister encourage other provinces to set up a central borrowing agency as had Alberta, as such a procedure offered excellent opportunities to do the thing the minister hoped to do by questionable means.

In general terms the Social Credit members from Alberta welcomed the bill. To them it was a step in the direction of public authorities using public money for a public purpose at a reasonable rate of interest. It demonstrated the wisdom of Alberta's own revolving-fund idea and the municipal shareholding concept implicit in the Alberta Municipal Financing Corporation. The bill reflected only the inability of private capital to be effective in public matters. The local authorities had been unable across the country to raise the developmental capital they required at rates they could afford. The federal government was at last, in the proposed bill, recognizing something Social Credit had been arguing for a long time.

The Prime Minister's view, however, as reported in *The Globe and Mail* of May 30, 1963, was that his government had no intention of competing with or replacing existing sources of finance: "Our purpose is to provide an additional source so that municipalities can undertake more capital works on terms they can afford."

From a practical perspective, some members recognized that many municipalities had already borrowed up to their province's allowable limit, and that other municipalities were in no financial

149

position to borrow at all.[41] Both of these situations would require special provincial arrangements or else the federal government would pre-empt the provincial statutes. The bill, being based on the principle of an unemployment measure, would probably be ineffective, as high unemployment and impoverished municipalities tended to go together. Many members saw in the bill merely an attempt to assist the metropolitan areas and wealthier towns once again. Others saw in it a means of continuing federal tax money inputs into municipalities without facing the more general question of a revision of taxation rights for municipalities in general. John H. Horner, Member for Acadia, Alberta, recognized the difference between federal initiative in the winter works program, and this bill, which did not have the seasonal component in it, nor the specificity implied in the sewerage program.[42] He identified its similarity to the 1938 Municipal Improvements Assistance Act, but in the present bill there was not the regulatory provision of the 1938 Act covering how much any municipality might borrow (the provision had set this limit according to the percentage of municipality's population to the population of Canada, with a general minimum covering small municipalities whatever their population). He remarked:

> . . . but I fear that under this legislation loans will be made on a wide open basis to the larger municipalities, and that they will gobble up the greatest part of the $400 million, possibly within the first year.[43]

He felt that "a definite favoritism to Toronto, Bay Street interests, and to investment brokers" had been shown in the recent budget debate. A per capita basis of distribution was, in his mind, the only fair one. With regard to provincial interests in the bill, he argued that co-operation among the three levels of government remained essential "because the provinces, through their direction of road programs and water development projects can control and regulate the growth of municipalities, towns and cities."[44]

A few days following this debate an unsuccessful motion was put to adjourn the business of the House to consider an urgent matter. The Premier of Quebec, Jean Lesage, had, according to a member, "vehemently denounced as a very serious infringement upon provincial autonomy, the proposed federal assistance to municipalities, and various other bills or resolutions submitted to the house by the government."[45]

The Prime Minister announced shortly after, that the bill would be reintroduced for second reading after the federal-provincial conference towards the end of July. He remarked:

> This is legislation which it is urgent to have in force soon so the municipalities can plan their work for this winter with knowledge of the financial assistance for which their representatives have repeatedly asked and which the government believes to be desirable for the encouragement of employment.[46]

The reference to "representatives" may have been only a slip of the tongue, but the phrasing of the sentence is suggestive of the influence organized local authorities were having in their relation to the federal government through the Canadian Federation. The Prime Minister suggested that any amendments could be added after discussions with the provinces.

The conference reached "full agreement on the proposals of the federal government to promote employment by financial assistance, with provincial approval and co-operation to municipal works."[47] The federal government had undertaken at the conference to propose features in the bill that would enable "the measure to be applied in forms adapted to different conditions in the various provinces."[48] The range of municipal works was to be broadened so as to include those in any province "which the province and the federal government believe to be productive of increased employment." If a province wished, it could make agreements with the proposed federal Municipal Development and Loan Board providing for provincial responsibility for granting and administering the loans to municipalities, subject only to certain federal safeguards for accountability and report to parliament.

The Leader of the Opposition, Mr. Diefenbaker, summed up events in these terms:

> . . . the provinces, . . . succeeded 100 percent in attaining their objective. What is going to happen is that the provinces will have available tremendous amounts of money from the federal government, not only for the purposes originally decided upon by the government for the projects which were referred to, but for a whole lot more projects.[49]

Later in the debate he commented:

> All the provincial premiers gave approval. Why should they not? . . . They will have the right to spend practically as they wish in the municipalities, subject to whatever control may yet be revealed. It is a wonderful thing so far as the provinces are concerned . . . How different were the provisions of the communique from the provisions of the resolution which was presented to parliament . . .
>
> The scheme now presented bears little or no relationship to the original . . . This plan bears little or no relation to anything proposed by the Liberals in the election. It now resembles the winter works program of the former government. They went all the way around and came back to the position we had taken in regard to this question on the winter works program.[50]

In the same speech, Mr. Diefenbaker pointed out that the winter works program had been cut by six weeks or 20 percent by the Liberal administration and a tax increase put on building materials and production machinery in the recent budget. These actions were hardly consistent with a coherent policy to cope with unemployment.

The Social Credit member for Red Deer, R. M. Thompson, hoped that shortly legislation would be introduced to set up a municipal development bank "that would provide a source of social or public capital to take care of the public needs on a continuing basis.[51] He felt the proposed board could be but a temporary measure. In this he proved correct, but not for the reason he hoped. The $400 million was provided as agreed to, and the Municipal Development and Loan Board concluded its business in 1968 without any additional funds or legislation being provided to continue it.[52]

Like the winter works program and the urban renewal program, the Municipal Development and Loan Act never became a permanent feature of Canadian urban financing. Most short-term measures, with the exception of the urban renewal project, have been measures to cope with urban unemployment. Though such measures have been applied to both urban and rural regional degradation, ad hoc attempts tried in urban areas have been more frequent. If the manipulations introduced so frequently by amendment to the NHA are included in these ad hoc attempts, there has been scarcely a year since 1950 when some alteration or scheme to cope with urban unemployment has not been attempted.

The crux of the matter in 1963 was the original federal intention to use CMHC and the loan board as its instruments for dealing with the provinces and the municipalities. The federal-provincial conference had broadened this to permit provinces to deal more autonomously with the board and to handle their local authorities in a much more independent way — independent even of federal intent — if they wished to do so. But if policy was merely to hand over to the provinces more money, the simplest way would have been to increase by a few percentage points the federal-provincial tax-sharing and equalization agreements. No special board or federal program of municipal development would then have been necessary. Municipal loans, however, would then have been made from the provinces, not from the federal government through the loan board. There would also have been little, if any, certainty that the additional money would have been spent on local public works to combat unemployment. Further, the lending institutions might not have been brought into the scheme if the provinces did not wish it. As it was, the municipalities normally arranged their "own financing for the construction of the project once the loan commitment from the Board was obtained."[53] Social Credit members in the House had urged that the money be made available from the Bank of Canada rather than from private lending institutions.[54]

The minister persisted that the bill was to encourage additional public works and additional employment. "It is not the purpose of this bill primarily, or even indirectly, to ease the financial plight of the municipalities."[55] The federal government was not to become a lender of last resort. Mr. Gordon remarked that

152

> ... the provinces made it clear that the federal government
> has no jurisdiction over the municipalities and the question
> of their finances, good, bad or indifferent, is the direct
> responsibility of the province concerned and of no one else.
> So at this point the emphasis is naturally on additional
> employment.[56]

Though the federal government, under the cloak of pollution control, had got through sewerage works as an innovating principle of municipal-federal relations, it was having to stay very closely in the case of the Municipal Development and Loan Board Act to the depression of 1935 and 1938 in its approach to national unemployment. The Canadian Federation of Mayors and Municipalities had been led to think in 1962 that a Liberal administration would move strongly towards establishing a closer and more formal municipal-federal link. Mr. Lesage, and the Quebec Legislature's unanimous vote of concern over provincial rights, had led to a watering down of what appeared to be the bill's original intent. It is little wonder, therefore, that the loan board quietly and unceremoniously wound up its business in 1968. After the federal-provincial conference and the government's amendments to the bill, there was doubt whether the board was needed at all.[57] As events turned out only four of the pronvices opted to administer their own affairs, i.e. Quebec, Ontario, Manitoba, and Saskatchewan, and the remainder used the board's services with CMHC as designed in the original bill. The evidence is not conclusive as to whether the Liberal administration had in mind the inception through the loan board of a more formal financial relation with the municipalities, despite its assurances of respect for provincial jurisdictions, but Quebec and the Conservative opposition certainly smelt a constitutional rat and the other provinces enjoyed additional largesse in their handling of municipal problems.

As part of the agreement with the provinces, the bill was amended in certain important respects during the second reading. Among these was an amendment requiring that the $400 million be divided among the provinces in proportion to their 1961 population. Mr. Gordon explained this as a measure to ensure

> ... that a disproportionate share of the $400 million loan
> fund will not go to some provinces because they are in a
> position to proceed rapidly with certain projects.[58]

The provinces had been particularly anxious to see this provision inserted — though it was said to have been a federal proposal at the conference — despite the announced intention of the bill to be a means of coping with urban unemployment whose incidence was not equally distributed by province.

The unanimity of provincial agreement again shows the complementary character of the fears of the provinces: those provinces with high unemployment and poverty feared that the rich provinces would use their influence to acquire a larger share, and the richer

provinces feared that the federal government would manoeuver to ensure
that the poor and high unemployment areas got a disproportionate
share. The only way around this reciprocal fear was an equal per
capita distribution, despite such a provision's putting into question
the announced purpose of the bill. As the Social Credit member for
Red Deer had previously suggested, equality of distribution was "the
only fair way."

Fundamental Changes in the NHA, 1964: The Downtown Centre
The 1964 NHA amendments were ostensibly aimed at
increasing the powers of CMHC. An increase was authorized from
$2 billion to $2½ billion for direct loans by the corporation; but in
addition the minister responsible for the bill, J. R. Nicholson, who was
Postmaster General, anticipated that the new powers would
"represent a basic change in our concept, perhaps I should say a
completely fresh approach, to some of the most vexing housing
problems facing the country."[59] There was to be a double-barrelled
approach — one at low-income housing and the second at urban renewal.
Flexibility of objectives and of ways to achieve them was the new
feature of the Act. This flexibility was to provide expanded opportunities
for lending institutions and local metropolitan authorities.
Though the average standard of housing in Canada had
improved greatly, the hard-core slum environs of the cities still
caused human misery and degradation. Some 90 percent of the entire
housing output associated with the NHA over the previous ten years
had "been provided for the middle income or upper income classes."[60]
The minister continued:

> I submit it is clear from this pattern that Canadian housing
> policy has been heavily committed to the support and aid of
> the private market; and rather to the production of housing
> than to its distribution, which has been left almost entirely
> to these private market forces.

The "filtering down process" of housing from one class to another had
contributed to the housing of the poor, but this process "is too indirect.
It is too uncertain; it is too slow, and it is too expensive in the long
run."[61] Public housing must be the means for raising the housing
standard of the poor and of the urban slum dweller.
Since 1949 some 12,000 public housing units had been
constructed, but their distribution was scattered. Only 9,000 of them
had been let at subsidized rents related to the tenants' ability to pay.
The federal subsidy for these houses was an annual $1.7 million "and
in my opinion that is a shockingly low sum to pay for a country as
rich as Canada."[62] Yet "well over 100,000 families in Canada" were
stated by the minister to be unable to go to the private market for
accommodation or to use the NHA. He remarked:

> In my view, and I speak as a minister of the crown, our best
> accomplishments in public housing are not impressive. In the

view of the government it represents the greatest single area of failure in our federal housing policy.[63]

Along with minor matters,[64] the bill proposed municipal ownership, after provincial approval, of public housing projects for the very poor — a proposal that had been suggested, but turned down, almost two decades before. "The federal government through CMHC is to provide long term capital assistance in the form of loans and in the form of grants for such projects."[65] In addition, the federal government was to pay a portion of the annual subsidies or operating losses — which had hitherto been a municipal, provincial, individual gift type of operation to keep rents low enough for occupants to afford. It had been an operation that had rarely come off, and the minister saw the amendment as "encompassing nothing less than a decent standard of housing for all Canadians."

The provinces were to initiate the plan and to pay part of the cost. Provincial rights were to be respected by having provinces "designate" the municipalities to work with CMHC in the provision and operation of the scheme. The minister remarked:

> It will be largely up to the provinces and to the local government bodies designated by them to acquire and to build and manage these projects. The public housing contemplated . . . may consist of new dwellings or may consist of dwellings acquired or leased from the existing stock of units . . . The provision for provincial and municipal ownership . . . is considered fitting because of the wide range of responsibilities which must be assumed by the provinces, or rather by the designated municipalities.[66]

The bill had been discussed with the provinces and they were in agreement.[67] The provinces and the municipalities were not to be compelled to use this enabling provision. The existing application type of initiative from below was to be retained in the legislation. The minister, however, offered a veiled threat. He remarked:

> . . . the government has a flexible attitude toward the new legislation itself but not toward the objective. If within a reasonable time the legislation fails to produce the pace of activity that is needed to bring about our ultimate goal, it will have to be reviewed. I believe, however, that as long as there is hard evidence of provincial dedication to the same goal . . . we will reach that goal together and we will reach it in our and not in somebody else's lifetime.[68]

Several of the provinces, including Alberta, moved at this time to establish their own provincial housing and urban renewal agencies. These agencies tended to work co-operatively with the federal government in programs to provide housing for low-income families and the elderly. The provinces were beginning to move in the area of public housing both by federal-provincial sharing arrangements and by a new special provision. The 1964 amendment offered the provinces long-term, low-interest loans equal to 90 percent of the cost of a project proposed by them and approved by CMHC. The provinces came to use this source of funds increasingly both for housing the needy minorities and for urban renewal projects. By this measure the federal government was stimulating both provincial organization in housing and urban renewal and also provinces' acceptance of new responsibilities hitherto held more closely by the federal government. The provinces were themselves, at last, getting directly into some aspects of housing.

The bill was introduced at a time when lending institutions favored the construction of high-rise apartment blocks because of ease of administration, large-scale operation, and central siting in city cores. Table 12 shows the distribution of single and multiple family dwellings approved for mortgage loans by lending institutions under conventional and NHA loans for the period 1952-1970.

The table shows the very erratic nature of NHA loans for both single and multiple family dwelling units. Though still erratic, conventional loans for both types of dwelling unit show greater consistency.[69] From 1962 conventional loans for multiple family dwellings showed a sudden and marked increase from 27,953 in 1961 to 42,348 in 1962. Though considerable support through NHA for this type of dwelling was given in 1961, when the number of loans approved reached 14,588, the 1964 NHA amendment raised this figure to 15,960 and 16,967 in 1964 and 1965 respectively. The number of NHA supported

TABLE 12. Single and multiple family dwellings — conventional and NHA loans, 1952-1970

Date	Single home construction		Multiple family dwellings		Total of all dwellings	
	NHA	conv.*	NHA	conv.*	NHA	conv.*
1952	21,130	9,952	8,378	6,566	29,508	16,518
1953	22,951	13,420	9,658	10,268	32,609	23,688
1954	38,669	17,690	11,755	16,802	50,424	34,492
1955	53,285	18,508	13,094	19,759	66,379	38,267
1956	36,115	4,753	19,166	41,458	41,458	35,281
1957	23,472	13,305	1,898	22,593	25,370	35,898
1958	38,340	12,280	8,084	32,464	46,424	44,744
1959	22,860	13,861	3,825	33,021	26,685	46,882
1960	14,609	14,390	7,204	27,774	21,813	42,164
1961	24,055	13,512	14,588	27,953	38,643	41,465
1962	23,521	14,017	10,377	42,348	33,898	56,365
1963	20,416	18,488	10,809	58,113	31,225	76,601
1964	12,237	20,486	15,960	73,439	28,197	93,925
1965	8,549	22,318	16,967	67,903	25,516	90,221
1966	4,256	16,424	10,311	38,065	14,567	54,489
1967	5,983	18,151	21,171	50,435	27,154	68,586
1968	20,194	23,310	41,407	62,726	61,601	86,036
1969	19,301	23,812	29,394	57,996	48,695	81,808
1970	17,870	15,148	35,159	26,641	53,029	41,789

*conventional

single dwelling loans fell off markedly after 1964. The NHA was, therefore, being used to support the multiple dwelling loan concurrently with the already established preference of conventional lenders. The rush to the suburbs that had been a feature of the previous decade was over. Lending institutions and the construction industry had swung their interests into urban renewal. The NHA amendment of 1964 was to confirm and facilitate this swing.

With regard to urban renewal, "For the first time federal legislation is put forward which will encourage and assist municipalities, with appropriate provincial authorization and supervision, to conduct broad programs of urban renewal." The difficulty with the previous legislation, the minister thought, had been that although half the cost of clearing blighted property had been paid by the federal government, it could get into the operation only "so long as there is housing before or after on the cleared site."[70] Urban renewal had now to be extended to non-residential property. The minister remarked:

> The development of fine cities in Canada requires that municipalities be able to clear areas of blight and slums, whatever their present use may be, whether it is commercial, industrial or residential.[71]

In addition, the application of federal urban redevelopment grants was to be extended from acquisition and clearance to the cost of preparing cleared land for disposal for the re-use proposed. Funds could be provided for worn-out municipal services, street and traffic improvements in the selected areas, and for sidewalks and off-street parking in the approved urban renewal areas.

> . . . we can no longer rest content with a federal urban renewal policy which is confined to clearance and redevelopment alone. Such a policy by implication accepts the process of decay and rot as if it were something inevitable and natural. We know there is no automatic private market process which regenerates urban areas as they decline. Therefore, the government believes that if there is to be such a regenerative process, it must be developed as a matter of public policy.[72]

The effect of the measures was therefore to place the federal government four square with municipal and provincial governments in the redevelopment generally of city depressed areas. CMHC was authorized to join the provinces and municipalities in rehabilitating urban renewal areas in accordance with officially prepared plans. Industrial, commercial, or housing uses could be applied in these plans. Luxurious office accommodation could be fitted in with apartment buildings. The limit of federal help to residential and slum areas *per se*, which had been so clearly stated by Mr. Winters as minister responsible for the NHA in 1956, had been expanded to a general context. Concurrently, the concept of designated areas of a city became increasingly important. The term "scheduled" portions of a city came to reflect both the delineation made by the local authority in terms of its plan and the area for which federal assistance was operative. The importance of scheduling particular city areas for urban renewal assumed a national political and administrative significance. The minister envisaged that CMHC would "negotiate with the various municipalities interested, and when an area has been designated loans will be made available in that area."[73]

The scheme carried with it a preventative as well as remedial quality. The bulldozer had to be employed after deterioration had reached the point of no return, while timely intercessions could readily forestall this process and save many areas of the city core from reaching such a deteriorated state. The average cost of clearing an acre of land in most cities had worked out at about $100,000, but in Toronto and Montreal this had been $300,000 per acre. "Under these circumstances," commented the minister, "it becomes necessary or advisable for the federal government to move in and assume a major share of the cost and, as is proposed by this legislation, lend money to municipalities or in some cases make funds available through grants to correct the situation."[74] Though a part of these costs was offset by recoveries from re-use, experience had shown "that the loss of about one-third of the gross expenditures on the most comprehensive redevelopment projects must be borne and is being borne by the governments concerned."[75] The federal government, in the national interest, was "prepared to absorb in future a substantial portion of these losses."

The minister's remark, quoted above, that "We know there is no automatic private market process which regenerates urban areas as they decline," and the federal government's readiness "to absorb in future a substantial portion of these losses" suggest that the 1964 amendment was intended deliberately to support a policy which retained in the downtown centres a high concentration of activity which would not continue without federal assistance. This suggestion implies in turn that were the "private market process" to operate unhindered the nature of future cities would become very different from what the 1964 amendment encouraged them to become.

The federal government, by concentrating on urban renewal in the way it did, was subsidising the "private market process" to accomplish regeneration. The high values given to downtown land explained why regeneration was difficult, but such values were also the expression of speculative expectations that the land would be taken up for yet more intensive uses. The popular image of the downtown city skyline was of multi-story blocks. If land values were the only hindrance to the "private market process" then the question arises whether the concentration always assumed to be so essential, and hence so pronouncedly a feature of cities, is really as beneficial as is commonly supposed. If the benefits of concentration are equal only to the costs of land, then the whole question of city form, of concentration as presently aspired to, is in urgent need of fundamental study. It is more likely that the federal government was again being used by lending institutions and the construction industry to assist in evolving the popular image of the virile metropolis that was current at the time.

Certain institutions do benefit from concentration but others do not. Lending institutions in particular had to assure for themselves a safe, long-term investment with adequate returns. Local governments saw the opportunity for an expanded and rewarding tax base, though the problem of providing schools for children resident in high-rise blocks was ominous. So, too, was the cost of building transit routes to serve such concentrations. The propriety of using public monies to further the type of city concentration which suited certain institutions but not others, and which foreseeably could lead to a series of additional costs to local authorities, was not publicly debated in the legislature. The use of downtown degraded land in the interests of the public generally by the provision of sporting arenas, public parks, and the like, was only halfheartedly considered. The legislature was predominantly interested in how to get rid of blight and how to build more houses. The high-rise solved both problems; but the minister was not entirely satisfied with the answer.

He envisaged a preventative or conservational component to the federal urban renewal legislation of 1964. He remarked:

> The economic and social characteristics of redevelopment should spur us all in the search for devices and techniques which will prevent the deterioration of areas to the point where clearance and the bulldozer offer the only remedy.[76]

Clearance was too simple a technique. A municipal program was needed which would stop structural and environmental decay and encourage the economic and social renewal of areas about to begin to decay. What appeared to be required was to clear degenerated areas, to rehabilitate persons and areas caught in the grip of decay but which had not gone too far, and to conserve areas threatened by decay. "Urban blight usually casts its shadow before it and I firmly believe that it can be turned back, if the warning signs are heeded, but the situation must be attended to when these warning signs first become noticeable."[77] A combination of public and private action could, the minister hoped, restore many of the older and threatened residential areas of the major cities. It was particularly in these areas that CMHC was to be empowered to make loans and grants to provinces and municipalities to assist in meeting the costs of such programs; to insure loans made by approved lenders to owners of existing houses in urban renewal scheduled areas; and to make loans and contributions to provincially or municipally owned housing agencies or to contribute to the operating losses of limited-divided corporations. To facilitate private improvements "and the fluidity of property markets in renewal areas," the NHA insured loans provisions would be extended to existing houses "in designated areas." If the private lending institutions would not operate in this area, CMHC was to fund directly. The conservation aspect of the minister's plan was one "which by its very nature requires the adoption and enforcement of zoning and maintenance bylaws by the cities, and it falls largely within the purview of provincial and local governments."[78]

This extension to existing houses was in fact never seriously taken up until 1967, and then it was taken up overwhelmingly by CMHC itself until 1970. The NHA loans approved on existing housing from 1964-1970, by approved lenders and CMHC itself, were as shown in Table 13.

TABLE 13. Loans for existing housing 1964-1970.

Date	Approved lenders Units	$	CMHC Units	$	Total Units	$
1964						
1965			2	25	2	25
1966			8	82	8	82
1967	5	51	3,746	34,962	3,751	35,013
1968	5	50	3,660	34,158	3,665	34,208
1969	685	10,245	3,789	42,408	4,474	52,653
1970	5,344	77,875	2,149	24,268	7,493	102,143

*Derived from *Canadian Housing Statistics* (Ottawa 1970: Central Mortgage and Housing Corporation), Table 40, p. 35.

The minister's conservational hopes were largely disregarded until the housing crisis of 1967 changed the situation once again. Municipalities, with provincial approval and with backing of lending institutions and the construction industry, were in the meantime hell-bent on getting the high-rises built. The overall policy of the federal government was selectively handled by those agencies at the point of action, and the federal government was reluctant to alter the course of events. There was little purpose in lending money to improve existing buildings if their continued degradation would enhance the likelihood of their being demolished, and the space being used for further high-rise construction. The ownership of them was sufficient to ensure the right to determine further use; their standard was better left unimproved.

The Act now permitted a province to designate a declining area in any municipality, whether city or rural town. The Act was not limited to metropolitan blight. It was up to a province to designate its sub-standard areas.[79] The minister knew that there was no certainty that the provinces would take up these new amenities. However, he also felt that CMHC should move cautiously.
He remarked:

> ... should think that we would want to see how this scheme works out in some cities and municipalities where the stagnation and slum conditions ... are presently existing. We should make an attempt to clean this up before we branch out into too wide a field.[80]

Some citicism was made of the proposal to designate particular urban zones in principle. A member remarked:

> We have now had some experience of designated areas by government, and it seems to me that we must be very careful in the way we consider the proposal . . ."[81]

His point was that had the proposal been introduced a long time before, some of the urban sprawl, with its attendent servicing and education costs might have been contained through the speedier development of city centres and adjacent zones. As the proposals now stood, an area within a large urban centre had to be designated a slum area before the proposed amendment to the Act could be applied. Meanwhile older houses beyond the designated area, and in the smaller towns elsewhere, were continuing to decline with no provision to fund their purchase and rehabilitation. The minister's proposal "had gone far enough." Many working people had availed themselves of the provisions to build new homes and too little support had been offered for the purchase of older properties and the improvement of existing assets. Indebtedness on new construction had been a burden for many. Loans for the purchase of older homes should therefore have general application, rather than application to designated zones.[82] The minister later replied that the amendment proposed was not limited to slum areas, but designation could be applied to areas where blight was starting in order to deal with it in good time. It was already clear that designation was to have a convenience quality attached to it — a quality to be determined by the views of the local authority and approved by the province.[83]

The debate also elaborated certain suggestions made on previous occasions. Three members suggested different types of enquiries about how to make the NHA effective. One suggestion included a royal commission to examine the establishment of a separate department of state concerned with urban growth and development. The minister commented "I know both Honourable members who suggested this appreciate the difficulties that lie in the way." He continued by saying:

> Having regard to the difficulties that you run into when you try to get the provinces to accept amendments such as are incorporated in this bill — and the course agreed upon represents months of careful negotiations . . . With property and civil rights in the background — the field in which a minister responsible for urban growth and development could work would be rather restricted, I would think.[84]

This, no doubt, is the substance of the issue surrounding the 1970 proposals for an urban policy for Canada and the creation during 1971 of a Ministry of Urban Affairs.

It is not incongruous that the House moved shortly thereafter to consideration of the Canadian flag and on June 18, 1964, to request an amendment to the BNA Act on old-age pensions and supplementary benefits. A broad scheme of social insurance required an amendment to the constitution. The constitutional problems associated with property and civil liberties in urban areas will no doubt require the same. The issue before the provinces, from the evidence so far provided, is whether or not they wish, or are willing to accede to, the federal government's playing the key role in the affairs of municipalities within their current legal jurisdiction. In the budget speech in April, 1965, Mr. Gordon raised the question in fairly clear terms. He remarked:

> The achievement of Canada's economic goals . . . will require the use of the whole range of policies available to us and to provincial government and local authorities. These include not only general policies, fiscal and monetary, trade and industry, but also particular policies.[85]

Among these particular policies was "the planning and proper use of our land, the development and the redevelopment of our cities and towns." Roads and other utilities to assist production were also included. He then remarked:

> That is necessary if business, labour, agriculture and other private interests are to play their full part in carrying forward the progress of our economy and improving our productivity. All this implies that the federal government must work with the provincial governments and that the latter, in turn, must work not only with us, but with the municipalities.[86]

While it was proper in the minister's view that the federal government's responsibility for fiscal, monetary, and trade policies was primary and indisputable, such policies had, if they were to work to best advantage, to be co-ordinated with "plans and policies in areas which come under provincial jurisdiction."[87] Provinces and local authorities were now spending more than the federal government, so even from this perspective, as well as that of economic growth and stability, a unitary approach was desirable — "An essential part of the job of good economic management in Canada is to achieve a reasonable harmony in the policies of the different governments."[88]

It was this debate that initiated the first proposals on the Canada Development Corporation, though the subject had been raised in 1963. The Royal Commission on Taxation had been appointed in September, 1962 and its report was awaited. It is little wonder, therefore, that the 1965 amendments to the NHA only provided for increases in the amounts for expenditure under various sections of the Act. The amount which might be advanced to CMHC for making direct loans to borrowers was increased from $2½ billion to $3¼ billion,[89] and the maximum amount of all loans in respect of which insurance policies might be issued was raised from $6 billion to $8½ billion. Other increases on minor items were from $100 million to $300 million for public housing projects.[90]

Since the passing of the 1964 NHA, the minister, Mr. Nicholson, and officials of CMHC had toured the provinces to bring home to local authorities and provincial administrations the greatly increased provisions of the new legislation. The minister was "greatly encouraged" by the co-operation he had received.[91] What the minister referred to as "intensive education programs" had been held after each of the provincial conferences to get the municipalities familiar with the new legislation. Provincial legislation to implement the federal provisions had now been passed in Alberta, Saskatchewan and Manitoba, and in other provinces. Alberta and Ontario had established their own housing corporations, and Quebec moved in this direction in early 1965. Some 60 urban renewal studies had so far been started, which, in the minister's view, suggested that a nationwide campaign was underway "to reclaim and modernize vast sections of our towns and cities."[92] The new financial provisions were expected to ensure "that the NHA will continue as a vital legislative instrument to materially assist the urban growth process, to aid our lower income families, and . . . strengthen the tradition of close and effective co-operation in housing and allied matters among Municipal, Provincial and Federal governments."[93]

New Organizational Measures and the
Financial Risk of High-rise Blocks

This process of gearing up provincial housing instruments across Canada, which typified the mid-1960s, occurred simultaneously with organizational plans of the federal government.[94] By mid-1965 federal speeches in the House openly included ideas about a Department of Housing and Urban Development, with a full time minister, with CMHC an integral part of it, with the CMHC President made a deputy minister of the new department, and similar notions. A speech by J. Macaluso, Liberal Member for Hamilton West, referred to the advisory role to the federal government of this proposed department, and continued:

> It could exercise leadership in co-ordinating urban activities at the Federal level and provide assistance and information to the Provincial and Municipal Governments. It could encourage comprehensive planning at all levels of Government. This department could also conduct continuing studies on housing and urban development problems.[95]

Cities everywhere, he felt, were looking "for a better administrative pattern under which to mesh the many functions of government that relate to community rebuilding." The federal government had to take the lead. In addition to this idea he supported the setting up of an Institute of Urban Development "to plan for the growth and development of an entire metropolitan area."[96] And to meet the demand for professional and skilled persons in the upcoming planning process, he proposed federal support for "a government-supported training scheme similar to that which we have in the labor colleges. An

163

institute of urban development would help to train local officers in a
wide range of administrative proposals dealing with urban affairs."[97]
These training facilities were envisaged as forming part of the new
proposed department "or perhaps even in one of the universities of
Canada."[98] The similarity between these proposals and what eventuated
by 1971 is striking.

The Minister for Citizenship and Immigration, J. R.
Nicholson, under whom the NHA was administered in 1965, was also
emphasizing that "the whole act of revitalization of our communities
must spring from local initiative . . . The challenge — the ultimate
responsibility is entirely local."[99] The federal government apparently
was only setting up "timely provisions" — both administrative and
financial. The inherent contradiction between local initiative, planning,
and control, on the one hand, and the growth of federal ideas about
trained personnel, institutes, and a Department of Housing and Urban
Affairs on the other, was apparently of little consequence at this point.
It exemplified the long-existing compromise between federal and
provincial constitutional interests, but concurrently showed that the
federal government had no intention of relinquishing its part in the
process. The federal government, perhaps unwittingly, was devising the
new organizational machinery required to initiate what eventually came
to be referred to as a "national policy" on urban development. The
emphasis was moving gradually from national policies on unemployment,
slum measures, pollution, and other maladies to a policy of a direct
approach to urban development *per se,* rather than to its effects.

In resting his case on the importance of local initiative in
the process, the minister was not entirely on insecure grounds for the
major cities by this time were vocal, co-ordinated, and proven in their
capacity to produce the wealth the nation required. The minister saw
the expression of local initiative in these terms:

> if the city takes the initiative, the municipality takes the
> initiative, and the province is behind it, the machinery and
> the funds, provided they are voted today (Second Reading
> Debate) will be available . . . [100]

But local initiative was not entirely unencumbered.[101] Though real
estate developers, backed by lending institutions, were ready for large
scale construction, the city councils were by no means so happy.
Urban renewal generated a great deal of public concern and personal
objection. Those directly affected, and involved in eviction and
compensation proceedings, as well as those threatened by the growing
institutional ownership of whole city blocks, raised sufficient
political concern for elected officials to take heed. The tendency of
discrete ethnic groups to dwell in the twilight zones around city cores —
e.g. the Chinatowns and Italian suburbs of the metropolitan areas —
added an organizational and racial component to local struggles. The
public advantages of greater concentration were largely in terms of more
efficient economic use of urban land and a moderness of appearance.
The costs were political opposition and social unrest. The urban

political disturbances in the USA, associated with ethnic minorities, brought this matter home very clearly after 1965.

Much of the research money spent on urban renewal studies was applied to studies of the social consequences of moving people from established neighborhoods and the means of coping with the political repercussions of such measures. The contrast between the circumstances of the persons resident in, but evicted from, blighted areas, and of the persons moving into the new apartments erected in the city centre emphasized the conflict. Some metropolitan and provincial authorities took pains to diversify the type of accommodation erected and included a number of public housing projects with those intended for rental accommodation. But whatever the mitigating measures were, the rush to make Canadians apartment dwellers, obliged them to accept the status of rent-payer than dwelling-owner and mortgage-payer. Although legal measures were introduced to permit the purchase of single apartments or of condominiums, these did not catch the public's imagination until 1970, as Table 14 shows:

TABLE 14. Mortgage loans approved for condominium tenure under the NHA 1967-70

	Dwelling units	$
1967-69	4,665	76,751
1970	8,729	152,275

*Derived from *Canadian Housing Statistics* (Ottawa: 1970, CMHC), Table 64, p. 57.

There was much publicity given at this time to the advantages, and even the necessity, of super-concentrations of population in city centres. Images and drawings of cities of the future and other mind-boggling prognostications of what the future held in store were common. Lending institutions by their support of large, block construction, rather than support of the individual home owner and the consequent spread of risk this entailed, were engaging in risky investment practices. The condominiun idea was not popular enough to reduce this risk. Federal support for the scheme in principle as well as in practice was essential. Vacancies in high-rise apartment blocks could not easily go above five to seven percent for long periods if the financial stability of these investments was to remain.[102] In this sense they were a high risk investment and were strongly subject to popular taste. A lot of eggs were being put into one basket.

Advertising the popular image of the good city life with emphasis on the genuine conveniences is important to the continued viability of cities. A reduced birth rate will similarly assist them. But rapid transit and ease of exit from the city centre will threaten them, as also will a change in taste for single dwellings in quiet country homes, or a belief that children require a different environment for their upbringing. Apartment blocks not infrequently contain childrens' recreation areas as well as adults' swimming pools and gymnasia. Developers are fully conscious of the necessity to provide amenities that will attract a wider range of clientele than newly-weds, professional and working childless couples, and the elderly. The struggle is genuinely present between those interested in turning the mass of the nation's population into sophisticated high-rise urban dwellers and those who prefer smaller city, town, and country amenities.

The presence of the new provincial agencies could open the door to a renewed influence by provincial governments — an influence virtually denied them since 1935 — on the locale of home mortgages. This is clearly a critical research area for the future. Although it is popularly assumed that everyone likes to live in the city, this assumption could well be a rationalization for the apparent inevitability of rural-to-urban migrations and the growth of city populations. It occurs to us, for example, that the rural residential parcels surrounding Calgary, the country residential settlements that fringe Edmonton in several directions, and the willingness of several thousand city workers to travel by car daily to their homes in remote country districts, is evidence of a considerable proportion of city workers who prefer to reside in the country far away from the city and on property they can call their own. If the lending institutions can be levered off their control of mortgaged dwelling locations a very different pattern of residential preference — different from the suburb as we know it today — could very easily emerge. Rapid transit to a widely scattered and extensive city hinterland could readily be the key to such a trend. But the matter is not one merely of residence and down-town city centres. The whole array of occupational activity between residential services on the one hand and and intense commercial and financial activities typical of city centres on the other, should be studied with a view to its potential as an instrument of decentralization.

The political process which may accompany the influence of new provincial housing agencies is a further important research area. Conflict will be pronounced between the city owners and a provincial housing agency which is influencing the locale of residential dwellings in outlying small towns or remote rural settlements, or aiding through land assembly, public amenities, or rapid transit the movement of population away from city centres. As previously suggested, institutionally owned, large-scale, downtown apartments are a risky investment. The moment the conditions necessary for their success are threatened, virtually the whole modern process of city concentration is threatened with it. Provincial-federal relations could in turn become involved in this political process, for the current form of city concentration has been influenced by federal legislation, supported by CMHC, and carried through by the plans of municipalities. However, the provinces are no longer the odd man out. The relative inconsequence of provincial decision need no longer be as pronounced as it appears to have been; but whether the opportunity will be taken up is quite another matter. In just over 30 months after the 1964 legislation, some 16,000 public housing units for the provinces had been developed under *provincial* auspices as against 11,700 in the previous 15 years.[103] But it was largely in this relatively inconsequential area — inconsequential to the main drive of city dynamics — that the provinces were acting. The issue is raised again in Chapter 7.

166

The 1966-67 Housing Crisis and the Relative Freeing of Interest Rates
Reference to Table 12 will show that in 1966 the number of single and multiple family dwelling loans granted dropped off very markedly. Both NHA and conventional loans were affected. New dwelling starts from all sources had reached a record high of 166,000 in 1964, but by 1966 a severe shortage of housing and of dwelling construction had emerged. The Economic Council described the housing situation at this time in these terms:

> Over the whole period 1961-66, the growth in the physical volume of housing construction has thus averaged only about 4 per cent per year, compared with a rate of growth in real Gross National Product well in excess of 6 percent. This has meant that at a time when the number of new households being formed was rising sharply, the share of total available resources being devoted to the provision of new housing was significantly smaller than in the early 1960s.[104]

The council then argued that "this situation has not developed as a result of any conscious choice, based on an ordering of the national priorities." The situation has "for the most part, been inadvertent, reflecting simply the emergence of taut monetary and credit conditions during 1965 and 1966, in a situation of developing excessive over-all demand pressure in the economy."[105] Housing construction had played its traditional role of "economic regulator" to offset excesses in demand "elsewhere in the system."

In May, 1966 the minister, Mr. Nicholson, was unprepared to provide additional money through CMHC for private housing, except in support of the aged and the poor. The flow of institutional mortgage investment for single homes had dropped off sharply, but builders were clamoring for additional money and workers were being laid off. The interest rate was raised to 6¾ percent and was effectively 8 percent in some areas.

The minister's action must be judged against a broad perspective. He was anxious to cool off construction in the face of rapidly increasing inflation and interest rates. His objective in early 1966 was to cut by about 15 percent the 1965 record figure of private dwelling construction. He therefore declined to make additional money available over and above the $450 million provided for CMHC direct loans to individuals and builders that year, despite the clamor from builders. The builders could intensify their own search for funds — "They cannot expect the government completely to solve such problems for them."[106] As lending institutions had other interests at this time it was obvious that the builders of private dwellings were heading for a slump. The recently increased amount of maximum loan, to $18,000, had tended to absorb the available supply of funds into fewer and more expensive units, hence the minister's concern for the poor and aged.

The 1964 amendments had encouraged metroplitan high-rise construction, and the ratio of multiple to single dwelling units had risen from about 2:1 in 1963 to almost 3:1 in 1965. The metropolitan centres had experienced this boom in addition to the "developing excessive over-all demand pressure" from the economy generally. Manufacturing was moving steadily, along with the population to whom it offered jobs, to the metroplitan areas. Accommodation was again a genuine problem.

The 1966 amendments to the NHA, introduced in October when the year's statistics on housing were available for review by the minister and the prospect of winter unemployment lay ahead, emphasized increases in direct loans from CMHC. Private lenders by that time were supporting the industrial expansion of the country and had cut back on urban high-rise apartments as well as family dwellings. To meet this, the loan ratio was increased from 85 percent to 90 percent of the value of the building for the traditional construction industry. This brought the construction industry up to par with the loan ratio applied to provincial housing instrumentalities when borrowing from CMHC. It was aimed at assisting the investment potential of the construction industry, particularly the new large-scale urban structures. The government did not intend to expand greatly its own provisions, but nevertheless increased from $8½ billion to $9 billion the aggregate amount of all loans which might be insured under the Act, and increased from $3¼ billion to $4 billion the maximum charge on the Consolidated Revenue Fund for lending by CMHC. Concurrently, the government took steps to introduce an amendment to the Bank Act which would again facilitate the commercial banks' contribution to the mortgage field. The banks' acitivities had ceased effectively in 1959 due to increasing rates of interest and to regulation under the Bank Act. The government now proposed to bring banks into line with CMHC and other lending institutions. A special spring program of 20,000 starts to be funded by direct loans to builders from CMHC was initiated as an emergency measure. No presale guarantee was provided by the builder on these loans, i.e. there was no home owner before the units were started and in this sense the building was speculative.

The emphasis of the government's own efforts was to be on homes for the aged and for low-income families, and on accommodation for students. The minister then added:

> At the same time there has been no hesitation and no holdback in respect of federal government aid to the growing number of municipalities who are embarking on programs of civic improvement with National Housing Act assistance and to certain other municipalities with special needs. This is most important to resource based communities in this country.[107]

Federal support for housing in remote resource towns was to continue as another item of minor activity. The minister made special mention of the oil sands at Fort McMurray, and the "hundreds of millions of dollars . . . being poured into this development" as illustrative of the type of activity this additional money was needed to support.[108] The small-scale, special items of federal activity were to be increased, but the more general and larger activities associated with family homes were to be held back.

This amendment of the Act also introduced certain "improvements" obtained at the suggestion of provincial ministers. For the first time loans were now to be made to persons who wished to purchase, improve, and occupy an already existing home. This measure aimed at assisting those who could not afford to purchase or build a new house, and the minister specially mentioned persons moving off the land and starting up again in the cities.[109] Such a house had to be repaired and in this sense this provision facilitated the preventative quality of the urban renewal legislation and of the various house repair Acts from 1937 onwards. This measure was envisaged as partly a winter works project, and the banks could readily assist its funding. If lending institutions declined to do so then CMHC would do so directly. A $10,000 loan ceiling was placed on these purchases. The 1964 Royal Commission on Banking and Finance had recommended that government guarantees be extended to existing houses after observing that:

> Experience in the United States, where government guarantees extend to existing houses, indicates that better financing terms on older housing may have little effect on urban development and that as long as people wish to buy their own separate housing, sheer space consideration will force an outward move from the centre of the city.[110]

Presumably suburban developers and peripheral city land speculators had to be considered. The measure was welcomed by members from rural Canada also who felt that it provided the opportunity for small-town dwellers to buy local houses under the NHA and thereby circumvent their difficulty of getting money for new construction in such areas.

The rate of interest was causing increasing concern. The Canadian Labor Congress had presented a brief to the government expressing its concern over the plight of the poor. NDP members in the House were emphasizing that a $15,000 mortgage paid off over 25 years at 6¼ percent interest would involve an interest and principal repayment of $29,500, or almost double the original loan. At 8½ percent interest, which was now not uncommon on first mortgages, the interest payment alone would total $21,000. They were also emphasizing the hardship caused by urban renewal as the homes which evicted persons had to buy were 20 to 30 percent more than their own accommodation. Many were having to occupy apartments. The law was not concerned about the situation of the persons affected, but about the value of the homes being taken for other purposes. The provinces handled expropriation legislation, so the minister was unable to do much about it. But these situations, in the view of some members, underlined the importance of establishing a department of housing both to deal with the current hardships experienced by urban dwellers as a consequence of urban renewal and to stimulate house construction.

On March 20, 1967 an attempt was made to initiate an emergency debate on the housing crisis. CMHC had announced that in the month of January, 1967 the number of detached dwelling starts had dropped by 38.5 percent compared to the same period in 1966; apartments had dropped by 17 percent and row housing by 78 percent. The "disastrous drop in housing starts, high mortgage rates and the crippling rise in the prices and the rents of homes" was the evidence provided for this unsuccessful attempt.[111] Reid Scott, Member for Danforth, in attempting to convince Mr. Speaker of the urgency of the crisis, remarked:

> In the middle of this hurricane of discontent sits the minister, calm, indifferent, serene, unconcerned and hiding behind the British North America Act. His sole contribution to this crisis has been to suggest the release of more mortgage money and all that will do, Mr. Speaker, is to build more homes that our people cannot afford to buy anyway.[112]

The Supply Debate for the Department of Labour, under which CMHC was then administered, offered the next opportunity. Some weeks before this, the difficulties of persons occupying limited-dividend housing and public subsidized housing had been raised. Their rents were being assessed on gross take-home pay and were becoming impossible to meet. The opposition attacked the government for the latter's not having a housing policy which was realistic in the face of a tight money policy, high interest rates, and inflation. The minister was quoted from the Ottawa *Citizen* in the House as having said a few days previously:

> Housing problems are going to be serious for an indefinite period . . . but I would hope the crisis period is over.
> If you're going to live in a city you're going to have to live in an apartment.[113]

Over the Easter recess, 1967, the Prime Minister made a speech indicating that a review of housing policy and a new initiative in the problem was to be made. When the House resumed, a blunt question was asked the Acting Prime Minister, Mr. Paul Martin, "Whether the government is considering a new agency or perhaps a department of housing and urban affairs."[114] There was no definite reply. On April 11, the minister, J. R. Nicholson, stated that "Marked progress . . . has been made in the house building program of late, and I think it is reasonably safe for me to assure honourable members that this year we will have the largest spring housing start program in the history of Canada.[115] Housing starts were expected to reach a rate equivalent to 170,000 per annum. With regard to low-rental housing, which had been a special point of several opposition members, Bryce S. Mackasey, Parliamentary Secretary to the Minister of Labour, pointed out:

The Housing Act puts housing at the disposal of the municipalities and housing corporations of the different provinces, and it is up to the provinces to show a little more initiative and to take advantage of the very enlightened legislation which is available, and the huge sums of money which go untapped and unused year in and year out because of the lack of initiative on the part of the provincial authorities.[116]

The immediate parliamentary crisis was momentarily over. The minister's optimism, though it later proved to be unfounded, rested on the stated support of lending institutions and the provinces. The minister had held conferences with most of the provinces, and these were followed "more recently by meetings with the representatives of the principal groups of private mortgage investors in this country, operating in both the conventional and NHA fields, including the banks, trust companies and assurance companies. Yesterday I met for four hours with the presidents and senior vice-presidents of every major assurance company in Canada, and of many of the smaller ones.[117] The minister confidently expected a resurgence in building starts, up to a rate of 170,000 per annum.

The government had been caught in the dilemma of having to dampen the general economy by a "tight money policy," as it was called in 1966, and to carry much of the burden of financing new construction. The private investors "simply had to be brought back into the field" and the chartered banks were expected to play a significant role, as they had done in 1954. The price demanded by lending insitutions was, however, already clear.

In November, 1966 a new formula governing the maximum interest rate under the NHA was approved. It was now to be one and

TABLE 15. NHA interest rates on approved lenders' home ownership loans, 1961-1971.

November	1961	6½%	January	1969	9⅜%
June	1963	6¼%	June	1969	9⅜%**
January	1966	6¾%	July	1969	9.39%
November	1966	7¼%	October	1969	9.87%
April	1967	7 %	January	1970	10.06%
July	1967	7¼%	April	1970	10.29%
October	1967	8¼%	July	1970	10.03%
January	1968	8⅝%	October	1970	9.86%
April	1968	9¼%	January	1971	9.64%
July	1968	8⅛%			
October	1968	8¾%			

*The table is derived for the period November 1961 to January 1969 from Kellough W. R. and Beaton W. "Anatomy of the Housing Shortage" in Matsushita, R. (Ed.) *Issues for the Seventies: Housing,* McGraw-Hill, p. 57, and the period June 1969 to January 1971 from *Canadian Housing Statistics,* CMHC 1970.

**June 27, 1969 — maximum interest rate on NHA insured loans was abolished.

a half percent above the long term yield on government bonds rather than a maximum rate fixed by the governor in council. The minister considered it a "realistic move," and added:

> By allowing this automatic adjustment on a quarterly basis, according to the return on the long term yield on government bonds, the rate now for the first time in history is sure of a competitive place among investment returns generally.[118]

The 1964 Royal Commission on Banking and Finance had recommended a similar step.[119] Lending institutions' representatives had recently assured the minister "that this has been the most significant move in bringing them back into the field on an increasing scale."[120]

The movement in interest rates on approved lenders' home ownership loans from November 1961 to January 1971 was as shown in Table 15. The table shows that the rate dropped from 7¼ to 7 percent between November, 1966 when the announcement was made, and April, 1967. It also shows the steady rise that followed. The minister now expected "a stable, not a spasmodic, flow of funds into housing," and added:

> What possible chance was there to get a mortgage company, trust company or any other investment institution to lend money at a rate of interest of 6¾ percent, and before that 6¼ percent when they could get rates of 7¾ percent or even 8 percent or more on money lent for the building of a warehouse or a factory or something of that nature? There was an insatiable demand for funds in the years 1964, 1965 and even more so in 1966. There was demand for every available dollar for the construction of major power projects, pipe lines and projects in all these fields.[121]

The minister was pleased to note that the rate had fallen since his "realistic move" and expected it to decline further by the end of June, 1967. Private lenders were coming back especially in metropolitan apartments (see Table 12). Housing shortages were acute in Toronto and Montreal, no doubt as a consequence of the jobs created there during the "insatiable demand" of 1964-66, and of international immigration.

Construction costs increased rapidly in 1966 as against an average annual increase of 1.4 percent in the period 1956-1966. Table 16 shows the average construction cost per square foot of new single-detached dwellings financed under the NHA and the annual percentage increase. Higher interest costs and higher construction costs were moving *pari passu*. A loan of $10,000 amortized at 7¼ percent over 30 years carried the same debt service as $11,100 over the same period amortized at 6¼ percent. The one percent increase in interest costs had the same effect as an 11 percent increase in building costs. With both forms of cost rising substantially in 1967 the proportion of Canadians capable of affording new housing was limited.

TABLE 16. Average construction costs, 1956-1970.

Year	Average cost $ per sq. ft.	Percentage increase	Year	Average cost $ per sq. ft.	Percentage increase
1956	10.22	4.18	1964	11.01	3.09
1957	10.41	1.86	1965	11.62	5.54
1958	10.56	1.44	1966	12.56	8.09
1959	10.78	2.08	1967	13.04	3.82
1960	10.65	-1.21	1968	13.68	4.91
1961	10.61	- .38	1969	14.62	6.87
1962	10.56	- .47	1970	14.97	2.39
1963	10.68	1.14			

Derived from *Canadian Housing Statistics, 1970* (Ottawa: March, 1971, CMHC), p. 70.

But as the country's housing stock of something like 5½ million units had been built at lower interest rates than those prevailing in 1967, the buyers' preference for older units carrying lower rates of interest was likely to increase. The price of these properties was therefore likely to rise *pari passu* with the increasing costs of 1967. The lending institutions and the construction industry were in a changed and profitable situation in 1967. The secondary mortgage market was likely to boom.

The government was criticized for fixing the interest rate at 1½ percent above long-term bond yields. The security on NHA mortgages was the same as on bonds, but bonds carried a greater liquidity and were cheaper to administer than mortgages. The 1964 Royal Commission on Banking and Finance had noted that there was very little trade in outstanding mortgages and the mortgage market "does not have a forum in which prices are continually adjusted to shifting demand and supply pressures . . ."[122] One avenue for action by government was to increase the marketability of mortgages in order to reduce the 1½ percent differential between mortgage and bond rates. Mac T. McCutcheon, Member for Lampton Kent, argued:

> If trading in mortgage money were to operate on almost an over-the-counter basis, as is the case with bonds, the construction industry could plan for much longer periods at a time. This would mean a greater improvement in efficiency as well as lower money costs and I firmly believe this is one way — indeed, it may be the only way — in which we can make the best of a bad situation.[123]

The construction industry had admitted to its own inefficiency, but the current "method of financing each year's operation after a mad scramble each spring for funds is one of the main causes of present difficulties."[124] Mr. McCutcheon saw the answer to construction inefficiency in terms of a regular, planned flow of mortgage money, allotted over a two to five year period. This would help to forestall the use of the industry for an "artificial tinkering" with the supply of funds and thereby become a dampener to the business cycle. The flow of funds should be based on demand.

The lending institutions were already assured of long-term rewards from high interest rates arranged through amortisation of loans over 20 or more years. The construction industry saw similar advantages in greater stability. Mr. McCutcheon possessed insight from an additional perspective. He remarked:

> . . . only the federal government has the facilities to be able to envision a nationwide situation. Provinces and municipalities just cannot have this type of over-all perception.
> In my opinion we missed a golden opportunity to rationalize our house building requirements when in our haste to implement the Canada Pension Plan we let the funding of the plan slip through our fingers, as it were, and allowed the provinces first claim on the assets.
> This fund . . . could have provided the massive injection our housing industry required on a temporary basis, that is to say, until we get caught up. Then in an orderly fashion the mortgage bank concept could have taken over.[125]

The member was referring to a long-standing organizational difficulty over responsibility for administering cost-sharing programs between the federal and provincial governments. Since 1966 the federal policy had been to encourage the provinces to take a fiscal equivalent, but only Quebec had done so. However, where security programs involved the accumulation of regular premium payments and eventual benefits to recipients, such as old age pensions, the provinces were quite anxious to comply. Such measures provided provincially available funds for investment by the provinces under their own discretion.[126]

To the minister's dismay, in September, 1967, the 1½ percent above the long-term bond rate proved inadequate to attract the lending institutions to NHA insured loans. He remarked:

> Despite introduction of this self-adjusting formula, which got satisfactory results during the first quarter, the NHA rate throughout the year has been substantially below conventional rates, and for the past six months it has offered no significant premium over high grade corporate bond yields. As a result since March 31 private lenders have shown very little enthusiasm for NHA insured mortgages.[127]

His new answer was to invoke Section 4 of the NHA to permit a spread of 2¼ percent. This was done to attract private funds into housing "and to enable the government to concentrate its future lending in the important social areas of greatest need, namely, public housing, housing for elderly people, housing for students and urban renewal."[128] Although the interest rate on home ownership was to go to 8¼ percent in the coming quarter, there was to be no change in the NHA interest rate on loans for public housing and the other areas listed by the minister. Canadians able to afford home owner and rental accommodation on a commercial lending basis would now be obliged to do so, and the NHA was to be used by government for its identified social needs. Some $300 million had been allocated to these needs in 1967.

The minister's explanation for the general problem that housing had become was in these terms:

> No country can grow as fast as Canada is growing and have a concentration of population in certain urban areas without having housing problems. But I do want to make it perfectly clear that these problems are largely centred in the metropolitan areas of this country, and the record shows that fact quite conclusively . . . the situation in these specific areas is not indicative of the housing situation which prevails in the majority of our cities and towns . . . the housing problems that arise in metropolitan areas such as Toronto, Vancouver and other cities the size of Hamilton and larger arise not so much out of a reduced volume of housing — in fact there has been a very substantial increase in housing — but out of the unprecedented pace of general development and growth in these areas."[129]

The 15 percent of starts in 1967, over 1966, had been "largely possible by the vast infusion of federal funds to support housing." Federal expenditure on housing was expected to exceed $900 million in 1967 which was by far the largest disbursement in history. Direct assistance for home ownership and rental housing would be double that given in 1966, which was in turn a record year. At the same time, as the Economic Council observed," . . . the accelerated increase in government spending in 1966 and 1967 is outpacing the growth of government revenues at existing tax levels."[130] The Acting Minister of Finance, Edger J. Benson, felt that the high federal contribution to housing in 1967 could not be repeated.[131] The private lenders were still not pulling their weight. The banks were only just gearing up their mortgage lending — at about $10 million a month over the past quarter. The banks "have concentrated their investment . . . in the more attractive market of consumer loans," and the buoyant state of the Canadian economy had discouraged a rapid return to mortgage financing.[132]

The Economic Council was of the opinion, however, that:

> "housing has tended to bear too large a proportion of the burden of cyclical adjustments in the post-war period. *The use of housing as an economic regulator should not be continued to such an extent in the future.* (Emphasis original.) Especially with the sustained high rates of new household formation over the years ahead, housing cannot be permitted to bear a major part of the load of any over-all demand constraint in the medium-term future without courting serious risks.[133]

175

The minister was piqued that no advice as to what might be done had been offered in this Review. Other countries besides Canada had been trying to solve the problem. A "completely controlled economy" and "for the government to intrude into the field of private enterprise and create special economic controls" might provide solutions, but in a private enterprise economy "we suggest we must strike a balance between the need for funds for housing and the need of funds for other purposes, including social welfare measures . . ."[134] The government had been under pressure to free the mortgage rate entirely, which would have given a new appeal to NHA mortgages as they carry the NHA insurance feature. The minister then argued that:

> Most of this borrowed money goes into multiple dwellings
> — apartment blocks — and people who build apartment
> blocks do not build them just for the pleasure of providing
> people with accommodation; they do so for profit. They are
> in business to make a profit.[135]

The minister was convinced from his discussions with lending institutions that this new arrangment would create funds for rental projects, multiple dwellings, in the large urban centres where accelerated growth was creating the most urgent need.[136] He was correct in this, for multiple dwelling structures in Canada rose from 71,606 in 1967 to 104,133 or an increase of 45.42 percent in 1968. (See Table 17).[137]

Alberta's 1967-68 Boom

The distribution of the above growth is, however, interesting. The table below shows the number of multiple dwelling structures under NHA and conventional mortgage loans approved by lending institutions by province, for the period 1962-1970, and the number of single detached dwellings for Canada as a whole over the same period.

A very rapid increase is observable between 1967 and 1968 in only certain provinces. Table 18 shows the absolute and percentage increase for each province for these years.

To explain the shift in emphasis to three Maritime provinces and to Alberta and Manitoba — but not Saskatchewan — is beyond our powers. It may have been the consequence of federal regional development policy in the maritimes and the particular opportunities available to investors in the two prairie provinces; but we are unable to ascertain if this was so. It may have been a return to the philosophy of the last century — that when interest rates are rising, go to the prairies; but we doubt that! The high absolute figures for Quebec and Ontario are to be expected from the pressures on Toronto and Montreal for accommodation, but the relatively low percentage increase for these two provinces is striking. Lending institutions seem to have turned momentarily against them.

Metropolitan concentration was causing increasing concern. Land costs, costs of servicing available land, and the profits and operations of land speculators, were the subjects of public criticism.

176

TABLE 17. Multiple dwellings by province and single detached dwellings for Canada, 1962-1970.

| | Multiple dwelling structures | | | | | | | | | | | Single detached dwellings |
Year	Nfld.	P.E.I.	N.S.	N.B.	Que.	Ont.	Man.	Sask.	Alta.	B.C.	Canada	Canada
1962	59	87	961	552	17,589	22,366	1,130	588	4,452	4,941	52,725	37,538
1963	197	82	1,231	437	21,747	27,854	2,204	1,396	4,668	9,106	68,922	38,904
1964	113	106	2,390	849	25,793	38,995	1,613	2,117	4,549	12,853	89,399	32,723
1965	52	103	1,991	637	24,779	39,150	2,503	1,752	4,119	9,784	84,870	30,867
1966	50	56	1,209	344	15,047	19,465	1,225	1,226	2,945	6,784	48,376	20,680
1967	89	21	725	526	19,842	33,889	1,636	2,161	3,677	9,040	71,606	24,134
1968	82	49	2,018	1,737	29,470	41,481	4,060	2,723	10,422	12,091	104,133	43,504
1969	95	102	3,302	1,133	21,072	32,476	4,022	1,771	10,774	12,581	87,390	43,113
1970	119	52	1,307	423	14,197	26,696	4,064	38	7,289	7,359	61,800	33,018

Derived from Canadian Housing Statistics, 1970 (Ottawa: March 1971, Economics and Statistics Division, Central Mortgage and Housing Corporation), Table 38, p. 33.

TABLE 18. Absolute and percentage increase by province of multiple dwellings, 1967-68.

Province	Absolute increase	Percentage increase
New Brunswick	1211	230.2
Alberta	6745	183.4
Nova Scotia	1293	178.3
Manitoba	2423	148.2
P.E.I.	28	133.3
Quebec	9628	48.5
B.C.	3051	33.8
Saskatchewan	562	26.0
Ontario	7592	22.4
Newfoundland	-7	-7.9

Derived from Table 17. The provinces are arranged in descending order of percentage increase.

The estimated land cost for new bungalow type construction under the NHA from 1960 to 1967, for selected cities rose as shown in Table 19. Alberta's three main cities experienced considerable land cost increases between 1960 and 1967, but considerably less than Toronto. Between 1949 and 1966 the average cost of urban serviced land in Canada increased by over 350 percent, which was far more than the increase of cost of house construction (100%) or financing (45%). The Parliamentary Secretary to the Minister of Public Works, J. B. Stewart, pointedly raised the need to examine the cost of metropolitan concentration. He commented:

> ... as our national economy grows and as our society develops there may well come a point at which the cost of concentration will exceed the savings of proximity ... Manufacturers, financial corporations and the other great entities which make up our economy tend to locate their businesses and head offices in great centres. One thing leads to another ... Whether this is a good thing in economic terms is a question which is often obscured. As a result there is a kind of inward momentum or inertia in the business community and in the minds of those who determine the answers to those questions.
> I suggest to you that the savings of proximity in transportation and communications are very real but there may well come a time when the costs of concentration overbalance the savings of proximity.[138]

What he did not mention, however, was that the benefits of concentration tend to accrue to private business, whereas costs tend to fall on the taxpayer, whether municipal, provincial or federal. The argument for a new municipal tax base to permit local authorities to cope with their problems is derived from this situation. The federal government, however, was scarcely in a position to interfere with this trend, though its 1964 legislation in particular had stimulated metropolitan concentration. A member did suggest that CMHC "ought to tell builders that mortgages will not be guaranteed where the cost of the lot exceeds a reasonable amount," but such authoritarianism was hardly welcome.[139] Similarly, municipalities and provinces should assemble and develop land and sell it at reasonable prices to prevent the private developer making exorbitant profits.[140]

In a speech in the House the President of the Toronto Metropolitan Home Builders Association had been quoted as arguing that the difficulties blocking private and multiple dwelling construction in Toronto were an insufficiency of serviced land, unstable mortgage financing conditions, an inequitable tax base and, lastly, restrictive construction bylaws and conflicting building codes. The answers suggested were not new — the mass production of homes by planning which would extend water and sewer facilities onto virgin land, a modification of the educational tax burden to permit municipalities to spend more by opening up virgin land for development without having at the same time to worry about where the consequential education tax revenue was to come from, the adoption of a universal building code, and a streamlining of the land development process. The builders were said to be ready to meet public needs, but:

> the way had to be cleared by a change of attitude on the part of mortgage companies and municipalities — mortgage companies which preferred to finance downtown high-rise apartments and municipalities which do not encourage multiple housing because of inherent education costs involved in connection with accommodation for families with children.[141]

TABLE 19. Estimated land costs for new bungalows financed under the NHA, 1960-67

CMHC Field Office	Land cost 1967	Percentage change in land cost		
		1960-67	1963-67	1965-67
Calgary	$3,585	30.4	24.4	16.7
Edmonton	$3,709	23.1	14.8	4.7
Halifax	$1,968	24.5	5.3	
Halifax	$1,968	24.5	-5.3	-2.5
Lethbridge	$2,231	34.0	39.1	28.1
Toronto	$8,306	63.7	67.7	43.8
Vancouver	$3,979	25.0	17.9	13.2
Winnipeg	$3,111	10.7	6.5	-4.0

Extracted from figures in House of Commons Debates, 1967-68, 7:7212
The estimated cost of new bungalows financed under the NHA rose from $23,056 to $24,878 (7.9 percent) in Toronto; from $17,980 to $18,980 (5.6 percent) in Calgary; and from $17,954 to $18,967 (5.6 percent) in Edmonton, Ibid. p. 7213.

It would appear from these remarks that the decision of lending institutions had been very deliberate. The sudden absolute and percentage increases in Alberta's multiple-dwelling construction between 1967 and 1968 may have had less to do with the "inherent economic potential" of Alberta than with a decision of lending institutions and Albertan-based builders that Calgary and Edmonton had, at that particular time, advantages over the eastern metropolitan areas. The vacancy rates in privately-initiated apartment structures of six units and over from 1963-68 in Calgary moved as shown in Table 20.

TABLE 20. Vacancy rates in Calgary and Edmonton in privately initiated apartment structures of six units and over, 1963-69.

Year	Calgary	Edmonton
1963	14.4%	9.2%
1964	11.6%	13.0%
1965	8.0%	6.5%
1966	5.8%	2.8%
1967	1.6%	2.8%
1968	1.3%	2.8%
1969	1.7%	3.7%

Canadian Housing Statistics, 1970 (Ottawa: 1971, CMHC), Table 19, p. 18.

Alberta's own situation, and particularly Calgary's, were propitious for making profits on apartment-type structures.

The lending institutions' decision determined that Alberta should boom in 1967. Alberta's cities had what Toronto did not have at that time — suburban space for single detached dwellings. It is quite conceivable that had the lending institutions not favored Alberta, the much publicized growth boom of Calgary and Edmonton, and of Alberta's economic potential generally, would never have come about. There is no magic in growth booms or in economic potentials *per se;* someone makes a decision before they become a reality and can thereupon be used for propaganda purposes to attract additional business to them.

In terms of absolute increase Quebec and Ontario led the field, but the less industrialized provinces, such as Alberta, had by far the largest percentage increase. The NHA loans, approved by lending institutions, supported conventional loans in this change of construction locale. NHA mortgage loans in Alberta, approved by lending institutions between 1967 and 1968, rose from 1,128 dwelling units to 6,968 units.[142] Table 21 shows, for the period 1962 to 1970, the number and ratio of single detached to multiple dwellings in Alberta, and, for comparative purposes, the same for Ontario.

Table 21 shows that the construction boom in Alberta in 1968 was in both single and multiple dwellings, with a distinct increase in the proportion of multiple units to single units, compared with the pre-1968 period. Comparatively, in Ontario there was a considerable absolute

TABLE 21. Single and Multiple Dwellings in Alberta, 1962-1970, and comparison with Ontario

Year	Alberta (a) Single	(b) Multiple	Ratio (a) : (b)	Ontario (a) Single	(b) Multiple	Ratio (a) : (b)
1962	3244	927	1:0.29	9761	7377	1:0.76
1963	2158	719	1:0.33	10057	8038	1:8.80
1964	1377	346	1:0.25	7069	13	
1962	3244	927	1:0.29	9761	7377	1:0.76
1963	2158	719	1:0.33	10057	8038	1:8.80
1964	1377	346	1:0.25	7069	13804	1:1.95
1965	1141	26	1:0.02	4934	14254	1:2.89
1966	476			2658	9410	1:3.54
1967	927	201	1:0.22	2476	17054	1:6.89
1968	4148	2820	1:0.68	8607	24662	1:2.87
1969	3661	2398	1:0.66	8092	17889	1:2.21
1970	3928	3673	1:0.94	6693	20240	1:3.02

Canadian Housing Statistics (Ottawa: March 1971, CMHC).

increase in the number of single and multiple dwellings also, but the proportion of multiple dwellings over single dwellings was almost four times as great as in Alberta. Calgary and Edmonton, it seems, were only gearing up for the multiple-dwelling and high-rise boom. So long as suburban land for single detached dwellings remains available this boom may be slow in coming compared with the Ontario situation. The ratio of single to multiple units in Alberta in 1970 was close to that of Ontario in 1962, but the absolute numbers of units constructed were less than half.

Though Alberta's metropolitan centres continued to expand throughout 1969, their booming growth was considered in the budgetary measures of June, 1969, which were aimed at selectively dampening the inflationary tendencies in the economy. The first method of dampening was to intensify competition in the industrial centres of the country by putting into effect immediately the final tariff reductions of the Kennedy Round due to be implemented on January 1, 1972. The second measure was aimed at the construction industry because of its tendency to lead the upward movement of costs and prices. By deferring the depreciation, or capital cost allowance, for tax purposes on commercial buildings for a period of two years, the Minister of Finance, Mr. Benson, hoped to dampen new capital investment in the booming metropolitan centres of Ontario, Alberta, and British Columbia. The deferment was not to apply to housing, industrial buildings, utilities, or public institutions, but to commercial building and as such was aimed at the high-rise office blocks and at wholesale and retail construction. It was not to apply to regions where unemployment was high. The cut-off point was a population of 50,000 as recorded in the 1966 census. It was in the larger centres of the booming provinces, where commercial building construction appeared likely to rise by more than 25 percent in 1969, and total building construction by more than 10 percent, that his policy was to apply.[143]

This was a deliberately discriminatory proposal and was related to the interlude between the time of the budget and the start of Mr. Marchand's program of regional development, then under debate in the House.[144] The measure only deferred and did not cancel tax advantages. It was a measure aimed at spreading capital from commercial high-rise to housing and industrial purposes. Philip Givens, Member for York West, and a former mayor of Toronto, remarked:

> This is bound to affect the conduct of the lending institutions with respect to plans six months hence . . . in six months there will be a remarkable and definite change. Anyone who has ever been involved . . . with construction knows that the first two years are not big earning years in commercial buildings because they have a high breakoff point. It is not until there is approximately 80 percent occupancy that you start to make a profit.[145]

The budget proposals were aimed directly at the decisions of lending institutions and developers in the fast-growth centres of Canada. The building booms of Calgary and Edmonton then subsided, regulated by the same external sources that had begun the booms in the first place. Once again, Alberta's affairs were managed from places outside the province and the decisions made reflected the views of these outsiders about Alberta.

1. Paradoxically, "socialism" had been bandied about freely in the House during the Conservative government's tenure of office and particularly when the extensive and rapid increases from the general revenue fund to the CMHC were taking place from 1957 to 1961
2. See *House of Commons Debates,* 1962-63, 3:2938. The Liberal Party was itself also divided on the question of "planning."
3. *House of Commons Debates,* 1963, 1:792.
4. Ibid. Over the previous six years there had been chronic deficits in Canada's balance of payments and a currency exchange crisis in 1962.
5. Ibid., p.793.
6. Ibid.
7. Ibid. Mr. Maurice Lamontagne, President of the Privy Council, who guided the bill through the House, argued the case for planning in terms of business cycles being generated through an involuntary accumulation of inventories that could not go on indefinitely. This economic instability was to be ameliorated by closer co-operation between public and private sectors and more flexible and selective policies. The Economic Council was to assist in this. *House of Commons Debates,* 1963, 3:2085
8. House of Commons Debates, 1963, 1:795.
9. Ibid., p.796.
10. Some of these publications are:
The Canadian Economy from the 1960s to the 1970s. Fourth Annual Review.
Illing, Wolfgang M., *Housing Demand to 1970.* Illing, Wolfgang M., Kasahaia, Yoshiko, Denton, Frank T., and George, M.V. *Labour Force Growth to 1980.*
Anderson, Isabel B. *Internal Migration in Canada 1921-61.*
11. *House of Commons Debates,* 1963, 1:801
12. Ibid., p.802.
13. Ibid.
14. The Department of Trade and Commerce in fact was already active in promoting industry. An assistant deputy minister was in charge of a promotional branch -- see the Department Annual Report, 1962, pp.27-30. The staff of the department reportedly jumped from 274 in 1963-64 to 786 in 1964-65. See *House of Commons Debates,* December 2, 1968, p.3369.
15. *House of Commons Debates,* 1963, 1:803. In the budget debate of 1963, import replacement, particularly in the automobile industry, was emphasized as one technique. *House of Commons Debates,* 1963 2:997.
16. Mr. Louis Robichaud, former premier of New Brunswick, has reportedly changed his mind about the policy of industrialization in the Maritimes. Peter Calamai, in *The Calgary Herald* of August 14, 1971, reports Mr. Robichaud as having regrets over some of the concessions made to attract industry to the Maritimes, Mr. Robichaud has since become Canadian Chairman of the International Joint Commission to Control Pollution.
17. *House of Commons Debates,* 1963, 2:1692.
18. Ibid., p.1693.
19. Ibid., p.1694.

20. Ibid., p.1643. Up to December 31, 1967, Alberta had submitted 17 applications under this program involving some 714 new job opportunities. Ontario, by contrast, had submitted 239 applications involving some 18,164 job opportunities. Over Canada, some 847 applications had been made for 49,957 job opportunities. *House of Commons Debates,* 1967-68, 7:7578.

21. *House of Commons Debates,* 1963, 2:1697.

22. *House of Commons Debates,* 1963, 1:803. The then Minister of Finance is cited in *House of Commons Debates,* 1963, 2:1690 as having said in 1961, "In my view, the federal government should appoint a separate minister with direct responsibility for directing policies designed to revitalize business activity in depressed areas all across the country."

23. Some provinces, especially in the Maritimes, prior to ADA legislation, had provided tax incentives to encourage a particular location of industry.

24. *House of Commons Debates,* 1963, 1:874.

25. During 1962, the GNP had increased 8 percent, a point of importance to the Conservative opposition. Over the previous five years, the annual average of unemployment had been 6.6 percent of the workforce, i.e. about 425,000 persons.

26. *House of Commons Debates,* 1963, 1:888. The economic strategy implicit in these loans was to be their immediate effect on unemployment while the Department of Industry's import-replacement policy was gearing up. The Minister of Finance expected the effect of the loans to be felt within six months. *House of Commons Debates,* 1963, 2:997.

27. *House of Commons Debates,* 1963, 1:888.

28. Ibid., p.889

29. The winter works program of the Conservative government had already cost about $900 million.

30. The minister was chided over the $400 million figure as he had recently been chairman of the Royal Commission on Canada's Economic Prospects, Ottawa, November, 1957, wherein the estimated gross new investment, 1956-80, on "social capital" was $47.5 billion. The forecast for the decade 1956-65 was $16.2 billion. See the final report, Table 15.2, p.308.

31. *Annual Report of the Municipal Development and Loan Board* March 31, 1968, p.6.

32. *House of Commons Debates,* 1963 1:889.

33. The federal government, in 1960, had assisted municipalities by aiding vocational school development to train and retrain the unemployed. Before the bill was passed, and after the federal-provincial conference of 1963, a number of additional municipal services from those proposed at this time were included. Schools, hospitals, and matters of provincial discretion were added.

34. *House of Commons Debates,* 1963, 1:889.

35. Ibid.

36. Ibid., p.892. The Minister of Finance, in reply, pointed out that the provinces had not been consulted when the Conservative government had put the sewerage bill before the House; nor for the winter works program, nor for the Technical and Vocational Training Assistance Act. *House of Commons Debates,* 1963, 2:1264.

37. *House of Commons Debates,* 1963, 1:892.

38. *House of Commons Debates,* 1963, 2:1264. A few moments before this, the Prime Minister, in reply to a question during Question Time, had indicated that he had received a request from the premier of Quebec requesting postponement of consideration of the bill until the provinces had had their meeting with the federal government in August.

39. Cited in *House of Commons Debates,* 1963, 1:912.

40. Ibid., p.914.

41. The terms of the scheme required, in effect, that the municipalities contribute 84 percent of the cost, plus interest, and the federal government provide 16 percent. The NDP members recognized this as not being much of a federal contribution to cope with unemployment. *House of Commons Debates,* 1963, 3:2929.

42. The sewerage program, over the two-and-a-half years of its existence had, to mid-1963, accounted for just over $100 million covering 442 loans.

43. *House of Commons Debates,* 1963, 2:1259. The amount budgeted in the first year was only $70 million.

44. Ibid., p. 1260.

45. Ibid., p. 1596. A text of the premier's letter and of the premier's charge is contained in *House of Commons Debtaes,* 1963, 3:2232.

46. *House of Commons Debtaes,* 1963, 3:2168.

47. Communique on the concluding session of the conference. Cited in Ibid., p. 2713.

48. Ibid.

49. Ibid., p. 2714.

50. Ibid., p. 2910.

51. Ibid., p. 2715.

52. One amendment was made, namely: to extend for six months the period for which 20 percent of a loan made could be forgiven to September 30, 1966, but the date March 31, 1966 remained the last date on which new loans could be made.

53. *Annual Report of the Municipal Development and Loan Board,* March 31, 1968.

54. *House of Commons Debates,* 1963, 3:2912-17.

55. Ibid., p. 2931.

56. Ibid.

57. Ibid., pp. 2966-69.

58. Ibid., p. 2908.

59. *House of Commons Debates,* 1964, 4:3714.

60. Ibid., p. 3716.

61. Ibid.

62. Ibid.

63. Ibid., p. 3717. The 1961 census showed that of the 4.5 million houses in Canada, some 200,000 in urban areas had only cold water facilities, and 168,000 in urban areas had no installed bath or shower.

64. Among the minor provisions was one extending the time on loans to the provinces for sewage works. The 25 percent forgiveness provision was also extended.

65. *House of Commons Debates,* 1964, 4:3717.

66. Ibid. This new provincial responsibility contributed to the provinces setting up their own housing and urban renewal instrumentalities.

67. Ibid., p. 3801.

68. Ibid., p. 3717.

69. In 1963 the maximum loans allowed on rental property were brought up to those allowed on individually owned properties. Prior to this date they had been considerably lower. The previous policy of favoring home ownership over rental accommodation was superseded by this provision.

70. *House of Commons Debates,* 1964, 4:3717.

71. Ibid., pp. 3794-95.

72. Ibid., p. 3795.

73. Ibid., p. 3796.

74. Ibid., p. 3718.

75. Ibid., p. 3793.

76. Ibid., p. 3794.

77. Ibid.

78. Ibid.

79. It might be pointed out here that it was this legislation that initiated the move of the Alberta government to establish the Alberta Housing and Urban Renewal Corporation, 1967. A similar step was taken in most other provinces.

80. *House of Commons Debates,* 1964, 4:4076.

81. Ibid., pp. 4051-52.

82. Ibid., p. 4061.

83. Ibid., p. 4075.

84. Ibid.

85. *House of Commons Debates,* 1965, 1:431.

86. Ibid.

87. Ibid.
88. Ibid., p. 432.
89. Loans under these provisions were running at about $300 million a year at this time.
90. Ontario had been particularly active in this area, but British Columbia and Saskatchewan had also taken advantage of this part of the Act. The Ontario Housing Corporation had a very ambitious project planned. In general, the minister remarked, the response from the provinces "has not been as encouraging as we would have liked." *House of Commons Debates,* 1965, 2:1314.
91. *House of Commons Debates,* 1965, 1:658.
92. Ibid., p. 660.
93. Ibid., p. 662.
94. Although Mr. Lester Pearson introduced fundamental changes in the departmental system of the federal government by means of the 1966 Government Reorganization Bill, these changes did not include reference to urban areas.
95. *House of Commons Debates,* 1965, 2:1251.
96. Ibid.
97. Ibid.
98. Ibid.
99. Cited in Ibid., p. 1256 from a speech by the minister, December 17, 1964, at a symposium in Ontario of provincial and municipal representatives. The minister expressed similar approval of the initiative taken in Quebec under its new Housing Act. Ibid., p. 1311.
100. *House of Commons Debates,* 1965, 2:1314.
101. An indication of this is shown in the difference between the amounts federally approved for urban renewal study projects and the actual amounts spent on such studies. Over the period January, 1963 to December, 1967, approvals totalled $2,069,000 and actual expenditure $1,048,000. In particular, since the amendment to the NHA of June, 1964 providing for federal support of urban renewal scheme studies, approvals were $1,840,000 and actual expenditure only $832,000. When it came to the crunch, about half of federally approved expenditure was not taken up. *House of Commons Debates,* 1968, 1:975.
102. Personal interview with a CMHC regional representative in 1970 when vacancy rates were beginning to cause concern. The vacancy rate in apartment structures of six units or more in June 1967, varied from one percent in Vancouver to 2.5 percent in Halifax. *House of Commons Debates,* 1967-68, 7:7209. By 1971 the vacancy rate in some cities had reached over 10 percent and was a cause for concern. The matter is discussed more fully in Chapter 6.
103. *House of Commons Debates,* 1967, 3:2590.
104. Economic Council's *Fourth Annual Review,* p.24.
105. Ibid. From 1962 to 1965 the annual growth rates in consumer credit balances outstanding was between 12.5 percent and 16.4 percent. It dropped to 8.3 percent in 1966 and rose to 10.9 percent and 11.9 percent in 1967 and 1968 respectively. *House of Commons Debates,* 1968, 2:1306.
106. *House of Commons Debates,* 1966, 5:4617.
107. *House of Commons Debates,* 1966, 9:9133.
108. Ibid., p. 9133.
109. Ibid., p. 9134. This measure should not be confused with the existing provision where an owner of an existing house could obtain CMHC finance up to $4,000 to renovate his property. The new provision concerned support to purchase and then improve an existing house.
110. Royal Commission on Banking and Finance, *1964 Report* (Ottawa: 1965, Queen's Printer) p. 278.
111. *House of Commons Debates,* 1966-67, 13:14169.
112. Ibid., p. 14170.
113. Ibid., p. 14377.
114. *House of Commons Debates,* 1966-67, 14:14416.
115. Ibid., p. 14767.
116. Ibid., p. 15026. The same approach, i.e. that of provincial responsibility, was made by Mr. Bryce Mackasey to a similar urgency debate motion on

September 25, 1967. *House of Commons Debates,* 1967, 3:2422.

117. *House of Commons Debates,* 1967, 1:93. At further discussions, later in 1967, the minister had been asked by lending institutions to make it clear whether the government wanted more money for housing or wanted it put into government bonds. "They tell us that they cannot have it both ways" and would co-operate if they knew what the government wanted. *House of Commons Debates,* 1967, 3:2777.

118. *House of Commons Debates,* 1967, 1:94.

119. *1964 Report,* p. 285.

120. *House of Commons Debates,* 1967, 1:95.

121. Ibid.

122. *1964 Report,* p. 282.

123. *House of Commons Debates,* 1967, 1:377.

124. Ibid.

125. Ibid., p. 378.

126. As of March 31, 1968 Ontario was holding $728.6 million, British Columbia $186.1 million, Alberta $113.3 million and other provinces, except Quebec, lesser amounts. *House of Commons Debates,* 1968-69, 4:3649.

127. *House of Commons Debates,* 1967, 3:2576. The government was, in effect, fixing a maximum rate of 8¼ percent in the hope that the actual rate would be determined by supply and demand below this figure. The lending institutions wanted flexibility. Different rates could now operate in different parts of Canada. Ibid., p. 2775.

128. Ibid., p. 2577.

129. Ibid., p. 2586. He again emphasized the point in summing up the debate. See Ibid., p. 2772.

130. Economic Council's *Fourth annual review,* p. 261.

131. *House of Commons Debates,* 1967, 3:2617.

132. For a brief analysis of the economic issues involved see the Economic Council's *Fourth Annual Review,* pp. 23-26., and elsewhere.

133. Ibid. p. 265.

134. *House of Commons Debates,* 1967, 3:2588.

135. Ibid., p. 2589. Later, on October 3, 1967, the minister clarified this point by saying that when housing was to be built for profit, such as apartment blocks, and when there was a shortage of money, only special circumstances such as the needs of resources towns for multiple dwellings would induce the federal government to provide funds. Ibid. p. 2771.

136. Ibid., p. 2589.

137. The number of multiple dwelling structures financed under NHA over the same period rose from 40,439 to 59,378 or an increase of 46.83 percent.

138. *House of Commons Debates,* 1967, 3:2758.

139. Ibid., p. 2764.

140. Ibid.

141. *House of Commons Debates,* 1966-67, 14:15173. The vacancy rate in apartments of six or more dwelling units as at June, 1967 was 1.1 percent in Toronto, 1.8 percent in Calgary, and 2.3 percent in Edmonton. *House of Commons Debates,* 1967-68, 7:7209.

142. *Canadian Housing Statistics* (Ottawa: March, 1971, CMHC).

143. *House of Commons Debates,* 1969, 9:9419-20.

144. Ibid., p. 9417.

145. Ibid., p. 9903.

Chapter 5
Federal attempts to cope:
gearing-up national urban policy,
1967 to 1969

This Chapter deals with the series of crises which surrounded the federal government from 1967 until its eventual decision to move towards a national urban policy for Canada. It describes the resignation of two ministers responsible for housing, J. R. Nicholson and Paul Hellyer, and the constitutional issue raised by the Prime Minister, Pierre Elliott Trudeau, following Mr. Hellyer's resignation in April, 1969. Since this issue raised the question of provincial and federal rights over housing and urban affairs, it is the context within which the 1970-71 federal proposals of a national urban policy for Canada are to be understood.

Early Thoughts On a New Federal Initiative, 1967

During the supply debate of the Department of Labour, J. R. Nicholson, who was Minister of Labour and responsible for housing, outlined the federal policy which was to be in effect from September, 1967 onwards. This policy was centered on those aspects of housing which fell within the purvue of the provinces, namely: public housing for the poor, limited dividend corporations — "which seem to have been quietly forgotten in recent years"[1] — urban renewal, and auxiliary services at the municipal level to support additional dwelling construction. He considered the availability of mortgage funds to be but one aspect of the total situation, for if funds were made available to build, say, 300,000 houses a year, the municipalities could not service the required land. The centres of population growth in particular were badly affected. He commented:

> I must say that in view of our rapidly expanding population the problem is bound to be with us indefinitely in those areas where growth takes place . . . Toronto is perhaps the best example in Canada of situations such as this, partly because of the unusually high percentage of new Canadians who have moved to that city within a relatively short period of time. This situation requires that federal, provincial and municipal governments work together in closest co-operation in order to provide the long-range planning which is necessary to supply the services to meet a greatly enlarged housing program.[2]

In Toronto, the minister argued, there were no serviced housing lots available at a price much less than $12,000 per lot.[3] He continued:

> We also know that in some of the municipalities surrounding the city of Toronto the problem is that the town councils would like to see more apartment buildings erected within their boundaries, not individual homes. The reason for this is very simple. More schools are required and the municipalities need money to pay the teachers; yet the major tax base is in the city of Toronto. This is true in every large metropolitan area in this country.[4]

The minister's answer was joint planning and a joint course of action by the three levels of government. "This is necessary," he said, "in order to provide for the arterial roads that are needed, serviced lands, schools, churches, shopping facilities, and all the other pieces that go to make up our urban fabric."[5]

He had also suggested to the Prime Minister "that some form of federal-provincial discussion take place to enable urban development in Canada to keep pace with requirements in a realistic and practical way."[6] The BNA Act was identified as a serious difficulty in solving the "housing problem." This conclusion is important for three reasons. First, it indicated that the provinces were adopting a stronger position towards urban affairs than they had done previously. Secondly, the constitutional issue actually did come to a head less than two years later, in April, 1969, and led to Mr. Hellyer's resignation. Thirdly, this conclusion was the basic idea behind the consensus stated by Dr. N. H. Lithwick in his 1970 study *Urban Canada: Problems and Prospects* (see Introduction, note 17) to be required for an effective urban policy for Canada.

The NDP opposition in the House was quick to chide Mr. Nicholson on the grounds that his inability to be effective in urban affairs led him to hide behind the BNA Act. The attitude that "we can do nothing because under the Constitution housing is under the authority of the provinces" seemed disastrous to the practical NDP.[7] As both the NDP and the Progressive Conservative opposition made clear in April, 1969, housing was a matter of national concern and had therefore to be dealt with nationally irrespective of the constitutional jurisdiction to which it had been assigned in 1867.

For a long time members of all parties in the House had suggested the appointment of a minister responsible for housing and urban affairs, but the government was moving slowly. Opposition speakers harped on the inability of the federal government to legislate for the needs of the poor and the elderly. Current interest rates for an $18,000 maximum loan at 8¼ percent mortgage over 25 years involved the payment of $42,084. The interest charge would be $24,084 or $6,084 more than the original loan. Unlike the apartment-block owners, the lending companies had no responsibility for repairs and maintenance in single dwellings, yet they had this high financial return on them. Current government policy over interest rates was diametrically opposed to the purposes of the NHA concerning the provision of housing for the lower and even middle income groups. The average annual income of NHA borrowers in 1967, in metropolitan areas, was $8,143 and in major urban areas $7,852.[8] As the cost of housing was now just under $20,000 per unit the NHA regulations themselves required an income of between $7,000 and $8,000 per annum to qualify for a loan.[9] In recent years, since 1964, over 80 percent of the total federal commitment to housing had gone into NHA insured loans, 10 percent into non-profit loans for housing elderly persons and students, and only 6 percent into public housing. The poor were not being considered, though the rate of interest on public housing was to be kept at the customary 6¼ percent.[10]

Public housing, however, carried with it the inevitable provincial-federal jurisdiction conflict. Federal money had long been available, but the provinces had not requested it. The new federal initiative, if the government was now serious about housing for the poor, had to tackle provincial-federal co-operative measures. Ian G. Wahn, Liberal Member for St. Paul's, said:

> Up to the present time parliament has taken the view that the provision of sufficient public housing is essentially a welfare matter within the constitutional jurisdiction of the provinces and their municipalities. I contend that this view is long outdated . . . Surely it is now entirely clear that under existing conditions the provision of public housing in the large rapidly growing urban areas is a question of national urgency involving the peace, order and good government of Canada.[11]

Public housing, by this argument, was no longer to be a welfare, and hence provincial matter, but one of national urgency. It would have placed public housing in the same category of federal initiative as unemployment measures had been since 1935 and sewerage since 1960. When pitiable situations existed, the federal government could act and had acted. Mr. Wahn felt confident "that if parliament will accept the federal responsibility, effective action can be taken without constitutional change."[12] The reason, he said, for provincial and municipal reluctance to act on public housing was:

> . . . that additional public housing in the large urban municipalities . . . will under existing conditions impose an additional, unwarranted and indeed unbearable burden on the home owner.
> . . . the urban home owner at the present time is bearing an unfair and regressive tax burden.[13]

The issue was not the small capital cost which a municipality had to put up, but rather "the hidden charges" which a municipality had to bear. "These include the cost of providing water mains, sewage systems and municipal services of all kinds, and particularly schools for the large numbers of children in the public housing projects."[14]

> Surely it is entirely clear that if the municipalities are to welcome public housing projects these projects must be made financially attractive to the municipalities. This is a financial, not a constitutional, problem and it can be solved.[15]

On the other hand, the minister, when closing the October, 1967 debate, repeatedly emphasized the importance of educating the provincial and municipal authorities as to the range of facilities available to them through the NHA. He had clearly been impressed by his recent conferences with officials, by a national conference on housing, and by his visits in person to particularly difficult areas of the country, such as Sudbury. He remarked:

> On a non-political basis we are getting good cooperation from most of the provinces, and this is due to our active educational program. That program is now getting results.[16]

This co-operation had led to four recommendations which appealed to the minister. They were:

> (1) a comprehensive planning of urban regions and the acquisition of lands for transportation corridors and the open spaces required for urban growth; (2) new community programs to stimulate orderly and comprehensive development of new suburban areas within the context of regional and urban plans; (3) housing programs to serve as an integral part of other combined federal and provincial anti-poverty measures in specific area; and (4) housing for moderate income families, "not for those with incomes of less than $5,800, but say for those with incomes perhaps between $4,500 and $7,500."[17]

These recommendations were to receive further study. They were taken up in December, 1967 by then Prime Minister, Mr. Pearson, on the occasion of a federal-provincial conference. The approach involved the provinces on every point.

With the advantage of four years' hindsight, this 1967 conference, and Mr. Nicholson's educational attempts with provincial officials preceding it, have particular significance.[18] Enhanced federal-provincial co-operation was expected to have resulted from educating provincial and municipal officials about the provisions of the NHA. Mr. Nicholson, as mentioned in the previous quotation, had referred to the non-political basis of "good co-operation from most of the provinces." However, the 1967 federal-provincial conference was cited by the government in the House at a later date as an illustration of federal ineptitude in its handling of the political aspects of urban co-operation. On September 17, 1970 in his speech to the Union of

British Columbia Municipalities in Penticton, B.C., the current minister responsible for housing, Mr. Andras, remarked:

> That conference (1967), I regret to say, was not too productive . . . The federal government offered a remarkable and, in fact, rather interesting, set of proposals: these included establishment of a coherent planning mechanism at the federal level, federal aid to regional planning, investigations of transportation corridors and . . . The provinces really wanted cash. And they questioned what they were presented: wide-reaching federal proposals that were, frankly, just laid on the conference table before them without warning or consultation. We said, in effect, "there . . . here's what *we* are doing for you." Things don't work that way anymore, and the provinces were not ready to accept that approach."[19]

The year 1967 appears to mark the point of a considerable change in the relation of provinces to the federal government.

It also seems that Mr. Nicholson had been influenced by the local officials he had met while touring the country, as the new emphasis was to be on regional rather than municipal and local planning. The concept of a "community program" to provide for social development by bringing into the planning process members of the public and interested parties was then in fashion. Also in vogue was an emphasis on combined governmental approaches to regional problems, such as those which were being experimented with through ARDA and similar rural regional activities.

The minister remarked:

> With regard to serious study of the proposed new communities program, a suggestion has been made that the federal government should go in with the provinces and municipalities in undertaking a comprehensive new communities program of the kind that I have just spoken of, whereby the federal government might provide special incentives for large scale comprehensive development of suburban communities in certain urban regions.[20]

In this scheme the federal government might contribute "what the three levels of government agreed would be a reasonable amount" — from 40 to 60 percent.

Another new idea was "resettlement programs" whereby people living in remote communities and occupying shelters which were almost valueless but which were their own, would be concentrated where a resource existed. The obvious cases were appearing in the Maritimes where ARDA, and FRED and other agencies were gearing up their activities. This also was to be studied with the provinces. A conference with them was scheduled after the provincial elections were over, towards the end of the year.

On December 11, 1967 the then Prime Minister, Lester B. Pearson, announced at the federal-provincial conference on housing and urban affairs the establishment of a national advisory housing council, possibly with a full-time secretariat and research division. He outlined also four proposals he intended to implement. These were in essence those Mr. Nicholson had outlined to the House in October. The Prime Minister's suggestions had been limited in their timing of application by the phrase "when our resources permit."

On December 13 the NDP tried unsuccessfully to obtain an emergency debate on housing "particularly in view of the failure of the federal-provincial conference on housing to deal with the crisis, caused primarily by the lack of any new and effective proposals by the federal government."[21] Later the Prime Minister was asked when the council would be set up, but he replied "There seemed to be a difference of opinion at the conference as to how this work of co-ordination and research could best be done."[22] Further discussion with the provinces was necessary. There was little support from three metropolitan centres. "The problem is to keep pace with this development in terms of the number of houses required . . ."[23] Land and its increased costs were the most difficult item, but this came under municipal and provincial jurisdiction. Municipal government, the government closest to the problem, was extremely complex. There were 18 cities in Canada with populations over 100,000 but there were 260 municipal jurisdictions covering these people. More money from Ottawa was not the answer. Nor was federal participation, "for the simple reason that the provinces have the primary responsibility in this matter, not the sole but the primary responsibility."[24] The federal government had been told this clearly at the conference, "and that the federal government should be very careful in intervening beyond its jurisdiction in this field." But in addition, it remained a national problem.

The way out for the Prime Minister was his four proposals. They all would improve and enlarge the scope of federal lending procedures. They would also require the full co-operation of the provinces, and "in due course, massive amounts of money, provincially, municipally, and federally."[25] In concluding his speech the Prime Minister said:

> In particular there were the four proposals which were put forward and which could lead to very far reaching federal and provincial developments in the field of housing; that indeed could lead, if the provinces so desired and within their own constitutional jurisdiction, to an even greater participation than that which has taken place in earlier years by the federal government in a field of very great and serious importance, one that is likely to become even more so.[26]

The federal government was holding out an even larger incentive than hitherto, but the fish were shy to bite.

The proposed council was to be arranged on a federal-provincial basis, and the Prime Minister was "a little surprised" that this ideal also did not get immediate acceptance from provincial premiers. The Economic Council had made the case for it. The Prime Minister quoted the relevant section from the Fourth Annual Review (p. 268):

> The essential need is for a synthesis, a comprehensive philosophy, a co-ordinated concept of urban development. This applies both to the largest metropolitan areas, where expansion and decentralization need to be framed within the setting of the broad urban region, and to the city complexes of more modest size where rates and problems of growth will nevertheless still be formidable . . . in no area of government affairs are there more glaring gaps and deficiencies of data, information and understanding than in urban problems and government. This is not to deny the many useful efforts to improve the situation. But there is an immense need for more and better co-ordinated study and research in this field.

The idea of the council was "to meet this need on a federal-provincial and not merely a federal basis."[27] The council was not intended to become "merely another committee of government officials . . . to produce new but inactive uses for old papers and reports . . . " Mr. Pearson's view was that the proposed council "would have the same relationship to government in the field of housing and urban development as the Economic Council. It would consist of outside experts in this field." It was to be "an impartial and influential body that could act as a kind of public conscience, a spur for urban development in Canada, encouraging government at every level to do the necessary things in this field."[28] He saw it serving a useful purpose in support of proposed annual meetings of provincial and federal ministers in the housing field. It was to further

> more intelligent, planned action on a national basis so as to help not only the federal government but each provincial government in the field of housing . . . when the provincial governments give it further consideration they may also decide the proposal is a useful one. However it is up to them, if they do not wish to particpate that is their responsibility, and no doubt they will continue to operate through their own provincial bodies in this field.[29]

The Member for Danforth, Reid Scott, was very outspoken on the constitutional issue. His interpretation of the provinces' position was that "they are incapable of solving the problem and that they are all desperately seeking federal initiative in this entire area." If necessary, to meet the needs of the Canadian people, the federal government for the next five years should "so reorganize our financial affairs as to provide $1.5 billion a year for the housing industry." This would equate expenditure on housing to that of national defence. If this sum did not meet the need, "the balance could come from private sources." This suggestion was a reversal of the role government had hitherto played relative to the lending institutions. By lending the government's money for specific purposes, "we could influence housing policy without interfering with the constitution." He then added:

> This is what is done at the present time. It is a trite phrase to say the CMHC are just mortgage brokers. Everyone knows that today by laying down conditions under which money will be lent to NHA tremendously influences the type of houses that are built, their location, their services and everything connected with the housing field.

There is no reason for not carrying this further.[30] Ian Wahn, in defending the government against the serious situation which had developed in Toronto and in supporting the national approach of his government argued:

> The Toronto housing crisis is not caused by local conditions or by internal growth . . . people are flocking to Toronto from every part of Ontario, from every part of Canada, from every part of the world. During the last six years one quarter of all immigrants to Canada have come to Metropolitan Toronto. No wonder we have a housing problem . . . [31]

Housing was just one aspect of the national problem "resulting from the inevitable growth of great urban areas."

Mr. Nicholson, in concluding the debate, argued that there was "general agreement among all ten provinces with the four broad and very significant proposals . . . ," but details had to be worked out.[32] The federal government had, he argued, already indicated its willingness "to commit to CMHC, for investment in 1968, funds substantially in excess of those budgeted for 1967 in these areas of greatest need . . . " These were the areas of regional planning, land assembly, suburban area development, and homes for moderate income families. Topics placed for discussion on the agenda of the conference had not all been well received. They had included pollution, urban traffic congestion, suburban resistence to low cost residential development, urban land costs, and the fragmentation of urban government planning. The minister continued:

> . . . but to say the least it seemed to some of us that at least some of the heads of provincial delegations were not too anxious to discuss these sensitive matters. They seemed to feel that the federal government should not take anything but an academic interest in these questions.[33]

Mr. Nicholson then suggested that these issues were far from being in hand, and gave an example from Ontario where, "in certain circumstances, you have to go through 42 different agencies in order to get permits to proceed with building of housing . . . They (the provincial delegations) did not try to come to grips with that problem."[34] He then laid the blame for what happened at the conference fairly on the provinces. He said:

> If there is reluctance on the part of some of the provinces to go beyond the exercise of their primary constitutional jurisdiction and reluctance to discuss the plans they have for exercising their prerogatives, then something is wrong and this is where the conference failed. If it failed it was because it was a federal-provincial conference and at such a conference one must expect contributions at both the federal and provincial level.[35]

The minister was learning, apparently, that politics can be and are played at provincial levels no less than at the federal. The game at the federal level had become increasingly one of retaining federal influence over the urban process — money was no longer proving enough. There is little reference in the evidence examined as to which provinces constituted the threat to federal initiative, but Quebec had been objecting to political infringement of its constitutional prerogatives for a decade at least, and Ontario had increasingly demanded greater autonomy over its financial disbursements for almost as long. British Columbia had maintained an independent approach to Ottawa on a variety of issues for many years. On the other hand, the Maritimes were benefiting from close federal co-operation through ARDA and other programs, and were unlikely to challenge the federal government. The prairie provinces, and particularly Alberta, appeared to take a middle-of-the-road, uncommitted position.

Coping with the Issues 1967-68

While the above abortive attempt at a new federal initiative was under debate, the minister was struggling with the practical problem of adding additional incentives to lending institutions in order to ensure the funding of a respectable number of new housing starts. The economy was booming and the familiar reluctance of lending institutions to invest in mortgages at such times had re-appeared. Concurrently, due apparently to international trends, interest rates were rising rapidly, thereby compounding the problem of providing housing cheap enough for even the middle range of Canadian earners to afford.

In the 1967 budget speech, the Minister of Finance, Mitchell Sharp, had seen the shortage of savings in Canada, and hence the paucity of capital, as contributing to the housing problem.[36] Canadian rates of interest "must be high enough in relation to those of the United States that they will attract into Canada the capital required to supply our deficiency . . . There is nothing we can do about it unless we can increase our own savings . . ."[37] **During the same debate** an NDP member pointed out that the direction of Canadian savings was also an issue. John Gilbert, Member for Broadview, pointed out that Canadian life insurance companies did about 50 percent of the insurance business with the remainder being done by American and British companies.[38] Total investment by insurance companies was about $12 billion in 1965, but only about 65 percent of the $12 billion was invested in Canada. The remainder was invested elsewhere. The mutual funds in Canada were also scattering their investments, and they "have no social conscience whatever."[39] There was a wide expectation that price increases would continue over a long period, and investors were becoming concerned over the real value of long-term bonds. They were demanding higher yields in order to hedge against this contingency. Investors were also seeking liquidity in the form of short-term securities in order to be less dependent on borrowing in the future.

The NDP launched a critical attack on the government's urban policy in its Budget Debate. John Gilbert, Member for Broadview, recommended an immediate cut in the mortgage rate to 6 percent under the NHA and 7 percent on conventional loans. The virtual freeing of the interest rate had let it rise to 8¼ percent and the conventional rate to from 8 to 9 percent. An increase in mortgage rates had not necessarily meant an increase in the number of house starts; but it had ensured an enormous profit to lending institutions. He remarked:

> We can say unequivocally . . . that in no small part the mortgage crisis has been caused by the private lending institutions, who have ignored their social responsibilities in meeting the housing problem . . . They have lent their funds for the construction of large hotels, motels and luxury apartment buildings and have ignored NHA lending. More especially, CMHC has failed to fulfil the original purpose for which it was set up.[40]

A borrower had to have $8,000 income to qualify for a NHA loan and "that means that two-thirds of the population are out of the picture." He proposed that the government fix the number of starts required each year and consult the lenders.

> It should get definite commitments, so as to ensure an annual volume of housing starts and then adjust its lending program accordingly. If it does not get agreement from the private lending institutions, it should take legislative action to direct into housing a percentage of the investment portfolio of these companies. After all, . . . the savings accumulated by banks, insurance companies and trust companies are the savings of the Canadian people, and the Canadian people should have some right to direct where these monies should be invested.[41]

197

The amount of mortgage money invested in Canada from the United States was insignificant, so no differential, he argued, should be recognized in this respect.

The section of the NHA (Section 35) which enabled the three levels of government to acquire land on a shared-cost basis had been virtually ignored. The NDP urged governments to take advantage of this measure. "They must be the wholesalers of land." This party would also create a publicly-owned building organization "which would tender competitively on major public housing projects, thus providing a yardstick for building costs and serving as a leader in the advancement of building technology."[42] There were other suggestions; but the NDP's approach was characterized by increasing government involvement in the actual, practical task of getting building underway. It involved getting government's hands dirty on the job, rather than looking from a distance and playing the management role; it involved control, to a limited extent and by co-operative means, of the decisions made by lending institutions.

This speech was followed by one from R. K. Andras, Liberal Member for Port Arthur. Since the debate concerned the budget, his speech dealt with some matters tangential to urban development. He did not reply to the NDP's proposals on the subject, but developed further ideas of his own. In view of his position, in June 1971, as Minister of State for Urban Affairs his 1967 views are significant.

As Member for Port Arthur in northwestern Ontario (Thunder Bay), Mr. Andras was particularly sensitive to the disparities in regional growth in Ontario. The golden horseshoe, extending down to Niagara, Windsor and back to Toronto, he said:

> is creating so many problems and demanding so much of the attention of the Ontario government that it simply cannot afford to devote sufficient energy, time, effort and money to many of the other sections of the province in order to plan the kind of development that we want to see take place in those sections. In my opinion many other provinces, classified as "have not" provinces, have co-operated a great deal more than Ontario with the federal government, particularly through ARDA programs, in seeking stimulation for the economies of their various areas.[43]

He had recently made specific recommendations for an economic development plan for the northwest Ontario region. His negotiations with the federal government had been encouraging, but he had been unable "to move the Ontario government to any action whatever."[44] Ontario had not co-operated with the federal government in ARDA as had the Maritimes. This had led him to some "rather radical thoughts about our political set up," including the possibility of making a separate province of northwestern Ontario. He added:

> I am not sure that this is a wild idea. I think that for some time to come the Ontario provincial government is going to be

198

preoccupied with the demands and the problems of southern
Ontario, so that it will not be able to turn much attention
to the areas of northern Ontario which demand planning and
development.[45]

An institution of regional development might be another interesting
idea. "I believe we need a real study into the formation of a national
program for regional economic development . . . ", but there was a
jurisdictional problem, as his efforts with the Ontario government
had shown. The federal government can act "only if it is invited to
participate." He added:

> Something has to happen to get these areas going which do
> not enjoy the same rate of growth as the six or seven very
> affluent areas of the country. I believe that during the
> discussions next month in the federal-provincial conference
> which basically will discuss federal-provincial relations, this
> matter of regional economic development should be placed
> on agenda and thoroughly discussed in order that jealousies
> and jurisdictional problems and other impediments can be
> removed.[46]

With regard to revenue from taxation of corporations and individuals,
where 35.4 percent of taxes came from corporations and 64.6 percent
from individuals, Mr. Andras had this to say:

> I make no defence of corporations, except to say we are
> bound to recognize, whether we like it or not, that business
> and industry constitute one of the major segments of our
> society, investing money, taking risks, producing goods and
> providing incomes which individual citizens enjoy. All this
> is responsible for the standard of living we have reached. We
> cannot afford to kill the goose which lays the golden egg.[47]
>
> . . . there is an economic base from which all these blessings
> (social reform measures) flow, and we have to protect that
> base. The time has now come for us to stop and temporarily
> digest the social reform measures we have passed, so as not
> to overload the economy. It is time now to turn to the theme
> and to the priority, and for a short period at least as a
> government to concentrate our investments into economic
> development, and let the gross national product grow so
> that the tax base is increased.[48]

The basic issues which were to confront Mr. Andras in later years
were then being studied. The 1969 Regional Development Incentives
Act and the 1969 review of urban problems in Canada still lay ahead.

The removal of the 11 percent federal tax on building
materials was seriously considered at this time. The issue had been an
"old faithful" for many years. Premier Johnson of Quebec had agreed

to remove the additional 8 percent sales tax on building materials in his province if Ottawa would do this. The cost of a $15,000 home was expected to be cut by $1,300 if these measures were taken. In earlier debates government members had replied by asking why builders of luxury accommodation should be spared the 11 percent tax just to reduce the cost of the smaller and cheaper homes at a time when the government needed the tax revenue and had to get it from somewhere in any event. To cheapen the cost of homes by the removal of this tax was only asking the government to receive less revenue while leaving intact the profit margins of the private interests concerned with housing.

Another suggestion made by Gerard Laprise, Member for Chapleau, was for the federal government to authorize any Canadian citizen who buys a new one-family dwelling for himself to deduct the property taxes in full from his taxable income until the house was fully paid for.[49] Another member took up the point by saying that this provision "is made in so far as business and industrial properties are concerned. If the principle is applicable in those particular areas, why could it not apply to home ownership?"[50] These measures were designed deliberately to encourage home ownership rather than renting accommodation.

Though the condominium idea was slowly beginning to be accepted by 1968, the above suggestions were in effect counter to the general trend towards apartment living. It may be significant that British Columbia, (which has been more successful than other provinces in keeping its non-metropolitan population away from Vancouver) and most recently Alberta (if the introduction of the former premier's pre-election promise of a $1,000 grant for specific persons buying their own home, ever reaches the statute book) should be the two provinces involved in measures of this type. The significance is not only that both were Social Credit government ideas, but that they were prepared provincially to take measures aimed at comprising the national trend initiated by lending institutions and supported by the federal government in its 1964 NHA amendment.

In the midst of this political struggle, the federal government was attending to "the most acute problems associated with rapid urbanization in Canada" which were being experienced in Ontario.[51] Dwelling starts in Toronto in 1967 were expected to be a record. About 50 percent of these starts were financed under the NHA. Almost 10 percent represented accommodation for low income families, elderly citizens, and students. The federal government, like the honest broker, was continuing to meet the needs of people that the province was anxious to overlook. As Mr. Andras had observed in an earlier speech, the Ontario government was not interest in the remoter areas. The provincial government was concerned with providing the provincial infrastructure for its growing production. The Toronto city government was interested in its tax base, and in increasing high-rise concentration and the system of expressways to cope with it.

In dealing with the 1968 situation the minister had authorized CMHC to step up money for individuals who wished to build their own homes and arrange financing through direct CMHC loans. He had requested CMHC to pay particular attention to rural areas where lending institutions were still reluctant to lend. The limited-dividend program was to be substantially increased. It already guaranteed a 5 percent profit to entrepreneurs who set up limited-dividend companies, and there were some tax advantages. The minister thought that that was enough, but new arrangements had to be worked out to revive the program. He also had cut back on speculative builders' loans — "Let them go to the private lending institutions to borrow money and make their profit in the usual way."[52]

Direct loans to provinces and municipalities for public housing, land assembly for housing, sewage treatment plants, and other facilities were to be made available on a short-term basis of 10 or 15 years at low interest rates. The provinces would be able to acquire land through this measure, but not to hold onto that land "for 50 years and [it] would not become the property of the province, with the taxpayers of Canada paying the shot and the asset being turned over to the provinces . . . "[53] There would have to be no profit for the province in the arrangement. Greater activity was also to be expected in the urban renewal program.

On February 19, 1968 a resolution amending the NHA was introduced by the President of the Treasury Branch, E. J. Benson. He had replaced Mr. Nicholson as the minister responsible for housing.[54] The bill allowed for a reduction of the down payment on new houses by increasing the 95 percent limit upon which CMHC could make or guarantee loans to $18,000.[55] Previously the 95 percent applied only to the first $13,000 of a loan. Thus in future for a mortgage with a lending value of $18,000, only $900 would be required as down payment Lending values above $18,000 would be covered at a flat 70 percent of the addition, and the maximum amount to which CMHC could go on any one loan would be determined later and reviewed by the Governor in Council.

The NDP argued that the amendment did not help dwellers in the cities where house values were in the region of $25,000. The gap between $18,000 and $25,000 was too great, as the buyer with a small down payment was forced into secondary financing at 12 to 15 percent interest. The average price of single-dwelling houses in Toronto had reportedly moved from $21,914 in 1965 to $34,869 in January, 1968. Inflation and rising house prices had made the 1968 NHA amendment out of date. It had also done nothing to reduce land costs. The cost of land in Toronto had reputedly increased by 500 percent in ten years, and the provincial governments seemed happy to accede to such increases. Similarily, the NHA interest rate was now 8⅝ percent and conventional rates were yet higher. The amendment, in effect, had done nothing, the NDP argued, to alter the availability of housing to the mass of Canadian people.

Shortly after this debate, the Minister of Finance, Mr. Sharp, had to act to "buttress confidence in the Canadian economy and the Canadian dollar in the midst of mounting international financial uncertainties"[56] Cuts in expenditure and restraints on price increases, wages, and other costs and incomes were planned despite the government of the United States having exempted Canada from many of the controls it had introduced. In January, 1968 the bank rate was raised from 6 to 7 percent — the highest rate since the turn of the century — and the chartered banks agreed to discourage the use of the bank credit to facilitate abnormal transfers of funds abroad by Canadian subsidiaries of foreign countries. At the same time Canadian exports to a wide range of countries were increasing, and the balance of payments on trading accounts were continuing to improve. Recent inflation had raised interest rates on the borrowings of all levels of government, and many municipalities and home owners had become reluctant to borrow. Governments were borrowing on the United States' capital market.[57] The federal government's course of action included a freeze on the numbers employed in the civil service, and measures to regulate employment, for, the government argued, inflationary tendencies develop as full employment is approached. "We have found that at a level of unemployment of $3\frac{1}{2}$ percent in 1965 and 1966, our prices began to increase sharply. Our cost increased much more rapidly than did those of competing economies."[58] This, plus the "growing tendency" of people to expect prices to rise year after year, were, Mr. Sharp thought, the basic issues. Workers, no less than investors, were seeking arrangements that hedged against rising prices. Tommy Douglas, the New Democratic Party Leader, then questioned much of this reasoning, and argued "we are facing a situation in which a large part of the economy dominated by large corporations has been able to establish administered prices which are not sensitive to the laws of supply and demand."[59] The freeing of interest rates was "putting available capital up for auction to the highest bidder, and therefore, capital is not going where it is needed according to social requirements."[60] Small business, the aspiring homeowner, and the lower levels of government were poorly placed in this situation. An answer, as seen by Mr. Douglas, was a massive government-sponsored housing scheme to build 250,000 to 300,000 houses a year for people with ordinary incomes. This would help to catch up on the deficit between the 200,000 new houses a year proposed by the Economic Council and the number of houses which had been actually constructed in recent years — a deficit of about 25,000 to 50,000 units a year. This would have a multiplier effect in the economy, as well as coping with threatened rising unemployment.

On October 4, 1968, Mr. Hellyer, who was the new minister responsible for housing, announced that the original estimate of 175,000 new housing starts in all areas of Canada "is now virtually assured," and the final figure could be close to 185,000.

> However, distribution of new housing starts as between rental accommodation and single family dwellings for home ownership continues to cause concern. Multiple dwelling starts for the first nine months are 26 percent higher than the comparable total for 1967, whereas the rate for single family dwellings is 8.4 percent less than 1967.[61]

The original estimates were for 100,000 multiple units for rental purposes, and 75,000 single family dwellings. It was likely that the latter would fall short. To alleviate the shortage of family accommodation, CMHC was authorized to make, from within its capital budget, $170 million available "for commitments for home ownership dwellings during the balance of the year." This represented some 9,000 units of new construction "in the form of single family dwellings and condominiums together with 2,000 loans on existing dwellings."[62] Of the 9,000 units, some 3,000 were for individual home owners and 6,000 were available for merchant builders.

In effect, Mr. Hellyer's announcement made public the increased residual role of CMHC — this time to support the single family dwelling. For long, CMHC had supported rural construction, the home in the more unpleasant urban area, the poor, and other "unwanted" sections of Canadian society. It was now to support, as a deliberate act, additional funding for single-family dwellings if the number required fell short of estimates. The lending institutions were once again exerting their pressures on the type of home that they would support. This situation needs to be understood in conjunction with the second of Mr. Hellyer's announcements.

Effective October 7, 1968, CMHC was to accept applications for loans from merchant builders without a presale requirement. Builders had been unable to obtain loans for single family housing during the summer, despite the record level of interest rates. To meet the obvious favoring of some areas over others in this situation, the minister added, "These loans will be distributed across the country on an equitable basis with emphasis on houses of moderate cost."[63] This, too, was aimed at "restoring the balance" between rental and home-ownership houses. The principle had been introduced earlier, but the risk to which public money was being exposed had prevented the elaboration of the principle at that time. The principle, in effect, enlarged a second range of contract facilities which circumvented the provinces. As well as contracting with lending institutions, the federal government was now contracting also with merchant builders.

The winter works program had been cancelled in favor of "more rewarding types" of public investment, such as manpower retraining.[64] Late in November, 1968 the government was asked if it was considering the reintroduction of low interest loans to municipalities to assist in their intermediate term capital expenditure programs. The Minister of Finance replied that the government was constantly considering:

> the growing requirements for social and development capital . . . Municipal needs are balanced against those of the private sector and other governments and agencies, by a competitive capital market. At present the federal government is making every effort consistent with its responsibilities to limit its own demands on the market and thus to assist in the improving the access of other public and private borrowers.[65]

Later, the minister was asked if "in view of the very large profits announced by the banks of Canada," the minister would consider reintroducing the ceiling on interest rates, particularly for mortgages. The minister replied:

> I think the lifting of the ceiling on interest rates has meant that the marginal borrower in Canada has been able to borrow money at lower rates than when the ceiling was on.[66]

By January, 1969 the interest rate had risen to 9⅜ percent. The minister responsible for housing, Mr. Hellyer, assured the House "that the level of interest rate is a matter of concern to the government . . . "[67] He had no specific answers at that time.

The way in which the federal government handled these specific issues suggests that there was little the government could do. By raising the loan limit to 95 percent of an $18,000 loan, it had effectively driven to the limit the assistance it offered on down payments for insured loans. Housing had been placed above the means of most Canadians unless they made considerable sacrifices and were prepared to pay large sums in interest. The unwillingness of the federal government to subsidize interest rates on housing, other than for schemes designed deliberately to aid the very poor, made it the object of political attack. The federal government was caught in a hopeless situation and the provincial governments were unwilling to help it out. In depending on the provinces in order to make effective Mr. Nicholson's 1967 policy, the federal government exposed itself to the risk of ineptitude in handling housing in general, and provided provincial governments with the lever they had lacked since 1935.

The Hellyer Task Force, 1968, and the Crisis Over the Constitution, 1969

In August, 1968 a task force under the chairmanship of the Honourable Paul Hellyer, Minister of Transport and minister in charge of housing was established. The task force began its work in Ottawa in mid-September, 1968 and the chairman hoped it would report by the end of the year. Thereafter legislation would be introduced "probably in the latter part of this session, but hopefully in time to have some influence on next year's construction program."[68] After obtaining from all interested parties their ideas on the matter, the task force was to carry out a genuine search for the facts. Not unnaturally, the minister was asked what additional facts he could possibly need after consideration of the reports and statistics already available.[69] While the task force was hearing evidence, questions were asked frequently in the House as to whether municipal officials would be given time enough to prepare briefs; why it refused to hear the submission of the Toronto real estate board; and similar questions.[70] It was referred to as a travelling circus and an on-the-road commission. The minister replied that "the response to the work of the task force has been so great it is quite impossible to hear all of the representation that might be made by larger organizations." He hoped to hear from a wide mass section, and to get varied points of view.

While the task force was collecting evidence, the minister froze the process within CMHC whereby the requests by local authorities for federal assistance in urban renewal and public housing projects were approved. In November, 1968, CMHC was instructed to defer consideration of new applications for urban renewal schemes. Existing schemes, in large and small urban centres, would continue, but new proposals were to wait until receipt of the task force's report.[71] Urban renewal studies not yet in operation were also to be suspended.

The situation as at the end of October, 1968 was that 126 schemes had been approved for preparation at the planning and study stage since June, 1964 when the NHA amendment was introduced. The federal government had paid out $1.2 million on such preparations, with an outstanding commitment of $1.6 million. Of these 126 schemes Alberta had proposed 11. In addition, 21 municipalities had applied to prepare studies.

Eight municipalities had applied to implement a scheme already approved which would have involved the federal government, at its 50 percent share of cost, in an expenditure of $24.9 million. Of these eight, one was in Alberta, namely, the Medicine Hat project involving the federal government in about $1.3 million. All of these were to be held up.

Since the scheme's inception the federal government had approved for completion some 49 projects with an estimated federal commitment of $163 million. Of this commitment only $49 million had been expended up to the end of October, 1968. Some of the larger schemes would be completed in only five to seven years. In Alberta the only project underway was the Calgary (Churchill Park) project, involving the federal government in an estimated $3.3 million.[72]

The minister responsible for housing remarked in explanation:

> In our (the task force) studies we have found that the traditional method used in urban renewal, of taking a large area, razing the whole area and rebuilding the whole thing, while it may be appropriate in certain circumstances where the land is to be changed, in other circumstances may not be the least bit appropriate. In some cases we have been razing perfectly habitable houses . . .[73]

It was necessary, in the minister's view, to change the guidelines so that proposed studies would not "come up with the same kind of solutions which the task force feels may not be adequate . . ."[74] In late February, 1969 the matter was still held up pending the policy review. At that time, the minister considered it inevitable that projects involving "large commercial development, purchases from entrepreneurs, factories, hotels and worn out stores" could easily be postponed a few years until "we have produced enough housing in this country to meet the urgent needs of Canadians."[75] In March, 1969 he stated that "A lot of urban renewal funds were going into primarily commercial redevelopments."[76] Similarly, public housing proposals were being held up, allegedly, because one province (the Opposition suggested Ontario) was seeking inordinate amounts of money under the program.[77] But the minister had had a rude awakening over public housing from another perspective. He had sought and talked with many of their occupants and had learnt first hand of the stigma and rejection felt by them. Large, conspicuous blocks particularly constituted a genuine sociological problem both for occupants and for their administration.[78] By early March a number of small public housing projects — those that provided "good family accommodation" — had been authorized, but large structures remained frozen. A federal minister had been experiencing the political agitation of affected citizens normally felt only by the mayors.

The significance of the Hellyer task force report lay not in the details of its recommendations — many of which had been long discussed — nor in the pragmatic, region-by-region, problem-by-problem approach the report suggested. From the political perspective, its significance lay in the extent to which the federal minister and CMHC were to intrude into details of decisions about the local suitability of federally funded programs. The minister froze urban renewal and public housing because the task force came to the opinion that many programs were wrongly conceived or were being abused. The issue is summed up in the minister's own words in these terms:

> Without going into the details of each individual submission [by the local authorities] at this time ... We will ensure that where they do not qualify there are other alternatives for us to explore in the same community, different sites or limited dividend or some other alternative ... We will ensure that just as many units are built, but they may be under a different program if we are satisfied that a different program will be more advantageous.[79]

Later in the same speech, in reply to a question on the proportion of projects now allowed to go through, Mr. Hellyer replied that the number of units approved was not really the issue, but rather:

> the detailed analysis of what we have done because I think it would meet the criteria ... which will permit the kind of housing we want to be built to go forward and, at the same time, will indicate to the various people involved what we should not do to make sure that there is an adequate flow in alternative programs to keep housing at a satisfactory level during the year.[80]

It was a matter of establishing what later came to be called the "guidelines" for municipal activity.

As a result of Mr. Hellyer's most recent freeze policy, however, local authorities and provinces were no longer in a position to submit their requests to the federal government under one or other section of the NHA, i.e., to model the details and standards of construction on the requirements and regulations of CMHC in order to ensure approval; but were now to be directed into federal assessments of the *in situ* suitability of their request, its conceptual adequacy in the local situation, and to receive alternative proposals if CMHC felt them to be more desirable.[81] This approach constituted one more step towards the centralization of decision in Ottawa. The Hellyer task force's approach generated precedents for the later "urban policy for Canada."[82] It was also a fundamental constitutional issue, raised, as other issues had been, at a time of national economic, financial, and housing crisis. It was one aspect of the issue for which Mr. Hellyer was to pay dearly in April, 1969.

The report of the task force was tabled in the House of January 29, 1969. The minister considered that the report was "the most comprehensive review of housing and urban problems undertaken in Canada since the Curtis enquiry almost 25 years ago."[83] The first opposition speaker, Robert McCleave, Conservative Member for Halifax-East Hants, raised the fundamental issue of provincial involvement in the task force's affairs. He commented:

> The task force, I suggest, would have been better informed, and its report would have been better received, if the studies had involved more provincial consultation and if the task force had better reflected all three levels of government. One of the main recommendations calls for direct federal-municipal dealings. There are no references to provincial housing corporations although these were, after all, established to deal with problems which may be unique to their provinces and municipalities.[84]

Other opposition members were less charitable. The report was referred to as "a colossal fraud on the Canadian public," with only "pitiful and pathetic" solutions offered to the housing crisis. A Social Credit member, after noting that the interest rate had been allowed to rise to 9⅜ percent while the task force was on tour, observed that this interest rate over 30 years on a $30,000 loan, returns $45,000 in interest. CMHC, in his view, had become a collection agency. To pay interest at this rate an income of $9,000 a year was necessary, and 90 percent of the Canadian people were said to earn less than $9,000 a year. He remarked that if the Prime Minister "really wants to help the Canadian people, he just has to resort to the methods used in the case of undeveloped countries."[85]

Municipalities were becoming increasingly concerned over possible cut backs in urban renewal projects. The minister was non-committal over the prospect of formal discussion with the provinces and municipalities on the matter of changing the urban renewal program.[86] By mid-February, 1969 he expected informal discussions to be held "in a few days." The object in mind was "to find ways in which all levels of government in Canada as well as the private sector can, by co-operating together, meet the needs of the

Canadian people in respect of housing in an even more satisfactory way than has been done in the past."[87]

The federal-provincial conference of mid-February, 1969, dealt with constitutional issues. These were expressed in terms of the spending powers of the two levels of government as well as in the specifically legal issues of the Constitution.[88] In the debate in the House, the Prime Minister, Pierre Trudeau, raised the matter of "current pressures which bear upon all levels of government." Many of these "have scarcely been defined, let alone brought under control." Among these was environmental pollution, the challenge of which cannot be met effectively

> in our federal state without some constitutional reform or clarification. It is important that we know which level of government is responsible and, if both, in what way they are are ready to co-operate through the use of the spending power and other devices to permit these problems to be tackled properly.[89]

He then included urban renewal and urban transport as additional examples of this matter. He continued:

> These problems cannot be dealt with properly because the present constitution is either silent or vague about the level of government which has the legal competence to tackle them. Until the constitution is brought into the 20th century in some of these respects, governments are to a large degree powerless to solve the problems either by acting alone or in co-operation with other levels of government.[90]

This is a very different constitutional position from that of the federal government in introducing the 1935 Dominion Housing Act, the 1938 National Housing Act, or even the amendments to the NHA of the early 1950s and early 1960s. It aimed deliberately at stimulating downtown city centres and made other intrusions into supposedly provincial affairs. The Leader of the Opposition, Robert Stanfield, argued that the provincial premiers were not:

> impelled by the urgency to work out revisions to the constitution. They were not so much incensed at anomalies or inequities in the present constitution . . . as they were at the way in which the federal government has been exercising the federal power and interfering in provincial financial jurisdictions.[91]

More specifically, on this matter, he commented:

> The provincial premiers were virtually unanimous in condemning the federal government for withdrawing from

certain programs after it had got the provinces involved in them.[92]

David Lewis, Member for York South, pointedly observed that the Prime Minister had not dealt with what he himself said "was the most pressing problem, namely, the division of power, the extent of the federal spending power, and the like." The provinces had been asked to recommend to the federal government the extent to which the latter should distribute money to assist regionally degraded areas or to meet the needs of urban areas. These were the very issues, in fact, on which the provincial premiers were divided. The Prime Minister, in his opening address of the debate had himself pointed out the diversity of provincial requests. He said:

> Some of those [provinces] who objected to the federal use of the spending power were the very same ones who urged us, for instance, to solve the problems of housing or pollution .. [93]

Should the federal parliament exist as a tool of the provincial governments or is it expected constitutionally to direct the affairs of the country irrespective of provincial claims?

The fundamental issues of how public policy was to be applied, whether federally, provincially, or by co-ordinated action and agreement, were not dealt with either in the conference itself or in the February 14 debate in the House of Commons.[94]

Mr. Lewis stated that the NDP's position was:

> ... unequivocal. After some years of study and discussion there should be a new constitution which would strengthen and not weaken the capacities and powers of the Canadian government and parliament to care for all the people of Canada. It must strengthen and not weaken .... to enable them to establish minimum and equal standards across Canada in income, public services, educational opportunities, health and welfare, decent housing, clean air, and unpolluted water for Canadians in every part of this country regardless of their background and origin .... This national objective will not be achieved by reducing the federal spending power.[95]

For this reason Mr. Lewis expressed concern over the recent federal policy of expecting provinces to tax themselves if they needed money. Many provinces did not possess the resources to tax further, and such a federal policy was likely to dissuade such provinces from welcoming an enhanced federalism. Later in his speech Mr. Lewis made particular mention of the need for an enhanced central government to play "its full role in the attempts to solve the new urban problems which affect the quality of life of most Canadians."[96]

He continued to argue however, that stronger provincial governments were also needed:

> ... it is impossible to run this country, whether it is a medicare plan, a housing plan or anything else that is involved, all from Ottawa. We believe that it is necessary to decentralize the choice of policies in many instances, and certainly to decentralize the administration and the carrying out of policies through the provinces and indeed through the municipal governments within the provinces.[97]

The NDP would not retreat from its position that "if you insist that in every case every province must be treated in exactly the same way the result may well be immobility for Canada."[98] The arrangements with the provinces had to be flexible so that, as in the case of the Quebec Pension Plan, if one province wished to arrange matters in a particular way it did not negate the possibility of a similar plan under different arrangements with other provinces. Similarly, any new constitution had to include provision for "consultative and planning machinery that would take in all 11 governments in Canada."[99] Fiscal policy could only be made effective when income and expenditure are properly related among the levels of government. Mr. Lewis remarked that the fiscal authorities were handicapped:

> ... if every level of government, without relation one to another, is able to go to the market as it pleases, when it pleases, and without knowing what the total effect on the monetary policy is or may be at any given time.[100]

A major recommendation of the task force had been the setting up of a Department of Housing and Urban Affairs. The government had introduced the Government Organization Bill to establish new departments and to cope with regional development, but had not included the proposed urban affairs department in this bill. In March, 1969, it was apparently still reviewing the constitutional implications of the proposal. On March 18 the Prime Minister said that he knew of no plans to set up a new ministry as the task force recommended.[101] In the meantime, the opposition was centering its criticism on the ever-increasing cost of money, the ever-declining proportion of the Canadian people capable of paying from their income for the cost of a new house, the paucity of public housing, the treatment afforded public housing in the task force report, and similar topics.

Mr. Hellyer, in his reply to this criticism, introduced for the first time the notion of inevitability in the growth of metropolitan areas. It was in the cities that the action was occurring. He added:

> More and more people are moving to the great metropolitan centres, and this seems to be an irresistible trend. There is opportunity in the cities ... There is the variety that many people seem to want, and consequently this trend to

urbanization is very well established, particularly so in our own country . . . [102]

He saw the solution in terms of looking at a variety of situations, "at the way different people are affected in different parts of the country, to see whether some solutions can be found that will meet the needs of the people in the various areas."[103] The range of housing choice had to be as broad and flexible as possible, and the range of choice should not be that of "officialdom, politicians or bureaucrats but the choice of the individuals directly concerned."[104] This choice had to be available for all Canadians, rich and poor. Many briefs presented to the task force had argued for higher subsidies, but Mr. Hellyer's objection was that subsidies have to be paid for by the taxpayer. If the net result is a redistribution of income, "then we must look at all these relative changes and see how advantageous they are to each particular group being served."[105] The obvious first decision of the task force was to increase the total supply of housing as shortages were, supposedly, "a contributing factor to high costs."[106] Vacancy rates were very low in most metropolitan centres. Research into the relation of supply and price had not been conducted, but a preliminary enquiry by CMHC had concluded, "that there is a definite relationship between the two, and that by increasing supply you will affect prices, which will go down."[107] A vacancy rate of 3 to 5 percent in the major centres was thought to be adequate to reduce prices in the market place.[108] The goal of one million houses over the five years 1970-75 was expected to achieve something on the supply side. Some $20 billion would be required for this program, of which $10 billion was to come from private lenders.[109]

The "on and off" nature of the mortgage market since the war, Mr. Hellyer argued, had hindered the introduction of economies of scale in house construction. No sooner had manufacturers geared up to large-scale production than the supply of mortgage money was restricted. Other builders, the minister thought, had gone out of business when the supply of mortgage money declined. About half the builders in Canada had been in the business for less than five years. Larger organizations with greater amounts of capital were needed to generate the research and development necessary.

The report had also recommended that NHA mortgages be extended to cover all existing housing. The average working man could not purchase the available houses costing $7,000-$13,000 for lack of equity, though his income was enough to meet the payments. By applying to older housing the NHA loan principles now current such working men would soon afford the small down-payment of 5 percent and come to own their own homes. The second and third mortgage was the bane of a working man's existence.[110]

Mr. Hellyer explained the past failure to include such provisions in the NHA in these terms:

I think the reason . . . was that it was felt the emphasis should be put on new production and in this way the filtering down process would take care of the needs of people of all income

211

groups. The system did not work satisfactorily and one of the reasons was that the financial terms available for used housing were much less advantageous than the financial terms for new housing.[111]

In this view he overlooked the critical issues of the control that lending institutions had possessed over metropolitan and selected city growth — a control that ensured the viability of their long-term investments in high-rise city blocks. The NHA had for decades been the instrument of this control, but to extend the NHA provisions to used housing would have compromised this control by enlarging the scope of federally-supported housing assistance to all types of dwellings, rather than to those which critically determined the future of city development. Lending institutions would have become encumbered with extensive investment in the very dwellings hindering the implementation of the schemes they envisaged, as the recent freeze on urban renewal had shown. The speed of urban change would be retarded. City councils would be faced with less remunerative sources of revenue from old housing than more remunerative from new city blocks, and the provinces would have had to become involved increasingly in the funding and operation of their cities. As events turned out, under the pressures of 1969, the amendments to the NHA of that year did provide for this opportunity.[112]

The cost of money had not been part of the task force's mandate, "but we could not ignore it because we felt it was probably the most important contributing factor to the increase in costs in the last few years."[113] All the governments in Canada were advised to treat this problem as a matter of priority. The task force did not indicate how the cost of money might be tackled, save by freezing the interest rate. The mark-up of 2¼ percent above the Government of Canada bond rate was too high. The rate had been floating at something less than that for the previous few months, and both CMHC and the banks had been making loans at 9 percent, which was ¾ percent below the limit.[114] In his assessment of the tactics of lending institutions, Mr. Hellyer commented:

> There is something in the pyschology of lending institutions in that they use the government rate in their communications with their customers. They say, "After all, the government set this rate and we have little discretion in respect of it."[115]

The fundamental constitutional issue over housing was raised by the Leader of the Opposition on March 4, 1969, after Mr. Hellyer had completed his explanation. Robert Stanfield quoted Mr. Trudeau's earlier remark that "until the constitution is brought into the 20th century in some of these respects governments are to a large degree powerless to solve the problems either by acting alone or in co-operation with other levels of government."[116] Mr. Hellyer had been accused of ignoring the provincial governments when the task force was touring the country. Mr. Stanfield continued:

212

Clearly, the Minister of Transport (Mr. Hellyer) was operating in an area of divided jurisdiction. Nevertheless, he acted from the beginning in this matter without taking cognizance of the proper role of the provinces in solving the housing problem. It would have been much wiser to involve the provinces. They could have enlightened the task force considerably about certain aspects of the problem .... The minister concerned turned his back on the provinces, and I will not be surprised if he achieves nothing substantial in the solution of the housing problem.[117]

He argued that Mr. Hellyer had "certainly very little ground .... to stand on" in the light of Mr. Trudeau's constitutional remarks. "Because of the Prime Minister's views, the position of the Minister of Transport lacks credibility."[118] The task force had recommended that in certain instances — for low-cost housing — the 11 percent sales tax on building materials be abolished, but Mr. Benson, Minister of Finance, had indicated he had no intention of accepting the recommendation.[119] Mr. Hellyer, it seemed, was getting into an untenable position. Mr. Stanfield suggested that the minister should have the courage of his convictions: "his position is patently phony and insincere."[120] To Mr. Stanfield: "The report and the minister himself are complete washouts."[121]

By early April, rumour was rife that a split had occurred in the federal cabinet. One issue in this matter was the failure of Mr. Hellyer to announce government policy arising from the task force's recommendations. Apparently the minister "had not been able to persuade his cabinet colleagues."[122] Mr. Hellyer's own view of the position was: "The reason is really the extent and the range of the proposals being made. They are numerous, and also quite far reaching in effect."[123] In consequence, the legislation took time to prepare. The Prime Minister, Pierre Trudeau, in March and April, 1969 replied "No" to questions asking if it were the government's intention to set up a department of housing and urban development.[124]

Perhaps from desperation, Mr. Hellyer announced on April 16, 1969, that "a new approach to providing housing for low income families will be undertaken in the city of Ottawa under a special arrangement."[125] This case was apparently cited to illustrate the new approach, namely, the construction in a single neighborhood of row housing units of which half were to be sold as condominiums and the other half rented. It also indicated that federal intent was being implemented to the specific details of federally-sponsored programs. Opposition critics were quick to point out that this did not equate a general statement on housing by the minister; nor did it obviate the current necessity for municipalities to negotiate in every detail, in each and every project, with the minister. An NDP member commented:

... we deplore his piecemeal approach ... This is only a token performance in solving critical housing shortages in the city of Ottawa.[126]

213

About the same time, the government was being pressed both in the House and by the Federation of Mayors and Municipalities to indicate its intention about extending the 25 percent forgiveness provision on municipal loans to local authorities for urgent capital works. The current program was due to end in March 1970, and the local authorities were obliged to plan a year ahead. The task force had recommended that "The federal government should make direct loans to municipalities or regional governments to assist them in assembling and servicing land for urban growth." Though this recommendation had reference to land assembly policy rather than to general servicing of land, it contained the essence of further direct links between local and federal governments.

In late April, the Canadian Federation of Mayors and Municipalities raised the question of official municipal representation at the June federal-provincial constitutional review conference. The federation was looking into the method or procedure for making effective their request to participate. The Prime Minister had suggested that:

> If they had any such submissions to make, they should not be made to the federal government directly, but to the secretariat (of the conference), which is at the disposition of provincial governments, as well as the federal government.[127]

Mr. Trudeau interpreted the current constitutional requirement and the requirements of federal-provincial meetings thus far as leaving it to the provinces "to decide how their representation should be composed." He continued:

> I suggest that if the provinces decide to bring as part of the provincial delegation representatives of the municipalities, it would, of course, be their right to do so. As things now stand under the constitution and arrangements . . . the federal government cannot by itself invite the municipalities.[128]

The question of CFMM itself making proposals enabling municipal governments in the future to participate actively in the deliberations of intergovernmental bodies was the issue to be referred to the conference secretariat. The NDP Leader, Tommy Douglas, asked if the Prime Minister would be prepared:

> to consider having placed on the agenda of the conference the advisability of setting up an urban affairs council on which all three levels of government would be represented, for the purpose of discussing the co-ordination of the three levels of government on matters affecting particularly large urban municipalities.[129]

The Prime Minister thought "that such initiative would be premature on our part."[130]

However, the division of powers between the federal and provincial governments was already under official discussion. The Prime Minister than added:

> This, it would seem to me, would be the proper way in which the question of municipal representation and jurisdiction under the constitution should be arrived at . . .[131]

The federal government would "be very happy and anxious to discuss" all aspects of municipal representation and the division of powers, but the municipalities were to initiate the move through their provincial governments, rather than have the federal government take the initiative.

The conference, proposed for June 11 to 13, would not be televised because officials of governments would be present. Some provinces had been anxious that officials be present. On this point, Mr. Trudeau said:

> This mixture was requested by some of the provinces themselves. It was not a federal initiative, but we agreed to it because it seemed like a plausible and acceptable idea.[132]

The conference being held in camera, it would also be difficult for opposition members of the federal legislature to be present.

On April 24, 1969, the Prime Minister informed the House that he had that day received Mr. Hellyer's resignation "as a member of the government," effective April 30, 1969, and that he had recommended that it be accepted.[133] Mr. Hellyer's decision had been made as a consequence of differing views between the Prime Minister and himself about the proper methods to tackle the problem of housing. It was a matter of whether housing and urban affairs were properly a matter for federal initiative. There was no doubt about them being national problems, but the division of governmental powers over them was constitutionally determined. Asked by a member whether the Prime Minister intended to call a federal-provincial conference to get agreement between the two levels of government "on the constitutionality of the housing problem and take a decision in the best interests of all Canadians," Mr. Trudeau replied:

> . . . many federal-provincial conferences have been held on housing, and it was precisely because no agreement was reached to give increased powers to the federal government that we are now in such a predicament.
> Also, a little more than a month ago the minister met in Toronto with the provincial ministers responsible for housing, and the matter was then discussed once again.[134]

The provincial governments had apparently forestalled the possibility of additional powers being assumed by the federal government. The NDP had favored a delegation of provincial responsibility for certain critical aspects of housing and urban affairs to the federal government. This would have involved an open agreement about the best way to handle what had clearly become a national issue. Quebec was known to be sensitive, but provincial agreements with the federal government could, in the NDP's view of the constituion, be made by any province so wishing. The technique had been used in the case of the Canada and Quebec pension plans and it could be extended.

The Prime Minister's position on housing, rather than on the constitution, was that it was difficult to substantiate an assertion that there was a housing crisis. The task force had indicated that Canadians could rightly claim to be among the best-housed people in the world. It was therefore difficult to argue "that housing is the most pressing national problem facing this country."[135] Why should it come ahead of education, of financial progress and development, or of equalization of opportunity? The rate of house construction was about 200,000 units a year, which provided the five year estimate of a million units suggested by the Economic Council. This rate of construction had followed from a number of legislative and policy actions. The Prime Minister indicated some of these as being the automatic adjustment of the NHA interest rate to the general interest rate, the Bank Act changes of 1967 resulting in the re-entry of the banks into mortgage lending, lower down payments on houses, CMHC's direct home ownership loans, and similar measures.[136] The lending institutions had greatly increased the money supply for housing loans by 27.2 percent from $2.1 billion in 1967 to $2.7 billion in 1968. He added:

> While all types of dwellings contributed to the increase in starts in 1968, apartment and row houses, with 36.5 percent growth, accounted for most of last year's performance.[137]

The Atlantic provinces had shown the largest relative gain, 31.7 percent followed by the prairies at 27.1 percent, but growth was general. New starts in urban areas "increased at a record annual rate of 227,000 units in the first quarter of 1969."[138] With the implementing of many of the key recommendations of the task force "an even greater part of our resources will undoubtedly be channelled into providing shelter for Canadians in all parts of the country."[139] Housing the poor still remained a problem but "it is nevertheless quite evident that the priority given by the federal government to its housing policy is now, as in the past, showing good results."[140]

The Prime Minister argued that it was not appropriate for him to speak in detail "of the process of cabinet consideration of housing policies," but many ministers had had to determine the implications of the task force's report, which took time. The amendments to the NHA which were then being drafted would reveal the government's decision, but "The amendments which will be offered at that time will, of course, deal with those matters which are essentially under federal jurisciation."[141]

The amendments were to cover these points: an increase in the flow of mortgage funds from the private lenders; permitting loan value ratios and limits to be set from time to time by the governor in council; extension of the maximum amortization period from 35 to 40 years; extending to housing generally the same terms as now applied to new construction, except that the maximum loan on existing housing would be $18,000; amending the NHA loan regulations to establish the maximum loan for home ownership or rental accommodation at $25,000; approval of a form of mortgage with a five year-roll over,[142] but with monthly payments calculated on an amortization of at least 25 years; and reducing the rate of mortgage insurance fees by 50 percent. (Up to the end of 1968, the insurance fund had paid out $81 million, and the reserves then amounted to $224 million.) Other provisions to stimulate limited dividend and non-profit housing companies were also to be introduced.[143]

Consultation with the provinces on other housing matters had to be continued. The way in which the federal government dealt with provinces and municipalities was just as important, in the Prime Minister's view, as making amendments to the NHA itself. He said:

> It is absolutely essential that the federal government, before it launches into programs which could have important implications for matters within provincial jurisdiction, should consider these implications and consult closely with the provinces.[144]

The task force had made at least 16 recommendations that bore on the responsibilities of provinces and municipalities. Many were entirely outside the responsibilities of the federal government, others included both federal and provincial responsibilities. The latter included the federal loans for housing and for land assembly, and there was the question whether this should not be done by the provinces. Many provinces, not just Quebec, objected to federal instrusion in such matters. The Prime Minister then commented:

> If, on the other hand, money is lent to provincial governments, is it not desirable and necessary to ensure that reasonable conditions are established for the use of that money, and that the ultimate beneficiary has some idea of the source of the money? And can these reasonable conditions be established with reasonable consultation?[145]

This argument is reminiscent of that held quite seriously in the federal House in the later 1930s. Discussions had been held with the provinces and would continue. The Prime Minister felt it very necessary for governments to work together to reach the basic goal of providing Canadians with housing. This inter-governmental co-operation was his approach to federalism.[146]

The alternative approach was to argue that when problems largely within provincial jurisdiction become serious and widespread enough, then whatever the causes that may have brought them about,

217

the federal parliament should "be able to act, to legislate, to spend, to lend, to start shared-cost programs, regardless of what the constitution says about provincial jurisdiction and regardless of the reaction of provincial governments."[147] This position assumes that because the federal parliament is the only body capable of national action it should act in national problems, and further, that the federal parliament can transfer at its own initiative a provincial matter to itself when that matter is held to be national in scope. The Prime Minister did not share this point of view, though he claimed to understand it.[148] In his view it was proper that the rules of the game be honestly changed — a new constitution agreed upon with the provinces—and conferences to that effect had been initiated as early as February, 1968.

Mr. Hellyer's resignation had been brought about by this fundamental difference of opinion over the roles of government on the one hand and the urgent need to cope with the misery, the poverty, and the state of human habitations—"the real problems of people in their day-to-day living"[149] — as a practical reality needing urgent solutions. Apparently, under the constitution, in Mr. Stanfield's words "the governments of Canada are largely powerless to deal with problems such as housing, urban renewal, and urban transport."[150] Had this been the position taken by the federal and provincial governments in the past, then "there would never have been any progress in this country."[151]

The basic issue in the minds of these two leaders was centering on the issue of what could be achieved on the one hand by co-operation of governments, with patience and understanding, and on the other by continuing the federal policy initiated under conditions of national emergency in 1935, whereby the federal government acted and supposedly got results. It was a fundamental difference. In Mr. Trudeau's mind, co-operation was required both to arrange governmental activities on urban affairs and to re-arrange the rules of the constitutional game.[152] To Mr. Stanfield it was a matter of getting on with the job and producing results that improved the lot of urban Canadians and letting the niceties of the constitutional game be taken up separately. He commented:

> The British North America Act will be with us for some time yet. Ways have been found for over 100 years to attack problems under the present constitution through federal-provincial co-operation . . . The country cannot stand still. Problems will not wait for the constitution to be reviewed and revised.[153]

The attack on the Prime Minister for arguing that housing may not be Canada's first priority was bitter, particularly from Quebec members and those from the older cities of Canada where dilapidation of structures was pronounced, and poverty and scarcity were resulting in overcrowding. Similarly, the cost of housing, caused largely by interest rates and inflated land costs, had effectively put it beyond the reach of even the average income groups, despite the government's declared policy for many years to meet the needs of all Canadians, including those of lower and average income. The Ralliement Creditiste Leader, Real Caouette, emphasized the immorality of paying $84,000 in all to own a $20,000 home.[154] The Prime Minister's proposals for amendments to the NHA, extending this period to 40 years, only exacerbated the inequity of the financial system by putting the final cost of the home to over $100,000.[155]

The Liberal Member for Don Valley, Robert Kaplan, speaking in defence of the Prime Minister's position, outlined "the errors in provincial policies which have created this crisis."[156] He recognized that any solution to urban problems would inevitably lead to an increase in the number of tenants, rather than homeowners, and he identified the growing tenant-landlord conflict as symptomatic. Yet, "it is a shocking fact" that municipalities were still denying tenants the right to vote in local elections. "With the past shortage of accommodation they have lacked any bargaining power."[157] Tenant-landlord relations were within provincial jurisdiction, but there had been little action. The education costs of municipalities could be relieved by the provinces taking them over directly — "in a broader geographic perspective, no money is saved by keeping children confined within old neighborhoods."[158] The solution envisaged by Mr. Kaplan was to place the cost of education "above the municipal level and that ratepayers be freed from the education tax " This he saw as permitting "municipalities to accept residential development without regard to the education consequences."[159]

Mr. Kaplan's second major point concerned land banks. As land adjacent to city boundaries was already controlled by developers and speculators, provincial acquisition would "only involve the transfer of huger sums of money from the treasury to private pockets without bringing the land purchased any closer to development."[160] He argued that "If sensible fiscal arrangements were to be made by the provinces with their municipalities . . . I believe that so much land would be opened up that prices of raw (unserviced) land would fall as the demand was met."[161] His assumption was that lending institutions would be willing to finance the houses destined to be built on this land rather than finance the more remunerative downtown developments. Provincial financial arrangements with municipalities on this point may not in themselves be sufficient. Provinces might well become obliged to instigate their own arrangements for residential mortgage financing in addition to land banks. Similarly, more direct provincial involvement in city services generally may be a necessary condition.

Mr. Kaplan's third point was that high standards of construction and regulations on house values to be built, and on lot frontage, in given areas of a city , which municipalities imposed, could be controlled only by provincial, and not by federal legislation. The provinces, therefore, in Mr. Kaplan's view, held the key to action which would materially assist housing and urban development. He commented:

> The actions of the Minister of Transport fail to focus attention where it primarily belongs, that is on the provinces and municipalities.[162]

Much of the debate during this political crisis avoided the question of setting up a Ministry of Housing and Urban Development. A member remarked that in the standing committee, Mr. Hellyer had intimated that in his view this ministry was not one of the most important recommendations in the task force report.[163] As recently as February, 1969, Ontario had issued a position paper on the constitution for the visit of the task force, wherein "Mr. Hellyer was told the federal government should not expand much into the housing field . . . beyond the present role of providing most of the public funds."[164] Bryce Mackasey, Minister of Labour, in defending the Prime Minister, emphasized the need to get one point clear:

> Let us first get the decks cleared and try to understand who is complaining and who is insisting in 1969 that the constitution be respected in the field of housing. It is not the federal government but the provinces, not necessarily only the province of Quebec.[165]

Ontario had told Mr. Hellyer quite frankly "not to come into direct contact with the municipalities."

The House had had before it over the previous year a number of private bills requesting changes in name and capitalization of several federally-registered lending institutions. These bills had created some uneasiness in the House, partly because requests to increase authorized capital were being made "at a time when everyone is calling for great restraint,"[166] partly because authorized increases were needed not to increase business but to pay for takeovers of other companies,[167] partly because they demonstrated increasing United States penetration of the Canadian financial market,[168] and partly because the bills did not reveal the government's own attitude or policy.[169] There were other considerations, but the time appeared to be one when the re-organization of the capital market was pronounced.[170]

While these difficulties were being sorted out in the House of Commons, the rate of building construction was increasing. The high rate of interest, and the possibility of writing mortgage contracts — only the NHA mortgages having the roll-over five year clause — covering long periods at existing interest rates had made mortgages attractive investments. The distribution of starts over residential homes and multiple rental units was again favoring the latter in the large centers. The inevitable process of concentration was still apparent.

The 1969 Amendments to the National Housing Act

The Prime Minister announced his appointment of Robert K. Andras as minister responsible for housing on May 5, 1969.[171] Mr. Andras was to be Minister Without Portfolio. Mr. Andras had spent the previous 10 months in association with the Department of Indian Affairs. Asked, during Question Time, whether the Prime Minister was considering the establishing of a separate ministry of housing and urban development, the Prime Minister said that no steps were being considered beyond those already announced.[172]

Mr. Andras assumed his responsibilities at a very difficult time. The cost of living index rose from 123.2 to 124.6, or an 1.1 percent increase, in the month of April, and by 1.9 percent in the first four months of the year. The House had before it a bill to amend the NHA and was moving towards the second reading. Mr. Andras received rapid briefing sessions to prepare him to answer oral questions put to him by the opposition. He was constantly being asked when he would bring forward the long awaited "guidelines" on urban renewal and public housing which the local authorities had been promised. The protracted nature of the debates on the Criminal Code Amendments and the postal services, which were carried on before and after he took office, was his only advantage. To cope with the cost of living problem Mr. Trudeau announced that "There will be a need for the government to introduce some very severe expenditure cuts which will hurt different vested interests in the country."[173] He had in mind matters affecting the 1970-71 fiscal year which would cut into expenditures and programs now in existence. Shared-cost programs with the provinces were an area of concern which the Prime Minister had spoken about on previous occasions.

Mr. Andras's remarks, when introducing the 1969 amendments to the NHA, emphasized more strongly than previous ministers had done the predicted population increase of Canada's metropolitan areas. As much as 80 percent of Canada's population by 1980 was expected to be urban; and of this, one-third was expected to reside in Montreal, Toronto, and Vancouver. The quality of life in these centres caused him concern. Public concern over "pollution, overcrowding, traffic congestion, inadequate recreational facilities, alienation, deprivation and the inertia of some of our institutions" could no longer be neglected.[174] He did not see these issues resolvable "by methods of the past." No single government held the key to a solution. Joint planning and co-operative endeavors seemed to offer the only solution.

Immediate federal policy was to support in principle and to give high priority to the continuation of federal assistance for increasing the supply of housing for low income groups. While research and investigation was underway into the factors contributing to people's dislike of public housing and their sense of humiliation in having to live in it, the federal government intended not to curtail or to freeze existing proposals. Projects already submitted to and approved by CMHC would go ahead. Provincial governments had already been so advised. All applications "as they are put forward" will be considered, and acceptable provincially-supported projects will be authorized "within a generous but not unrestricted budget." He then added:

> But we will not let this decision prevent the immediate intensification of discussions with the provinces with a view to improving the physical and social characteristics of public housing. We hope to reach agreement with each province quickly as to the type most suitable to its particular area.[175]

In Mr. Andras's view, the earlier freezing of projects had not been a mistake, but the time which had elapsed since the freeze had stepped up the necessity to act in less ideal ways—"time came upon us very quickly."[176]

Mr. Andras was, in effect, backing off from the stand attempted by Mr. Hellyer, where the federal government was intruding more pronouncedly into the details of federally supported schemes *in situ* and within municipal jurisdications. His approach now was in terms of types of projects suitable to the different provinces. Just what this involved in terms of politically dividing the provinces in their relations with the federal government or in deciding what was to be considered suitable in any "area" or province, is not clear. The provinces, however, were to be introduced as an essential component in the relation of urban municipal authorities to the federal government, and in this sense Mr. Andras's approach further strengthened the potential for provincial initiative.

With provincial consultation the federal government now proposed to intensify research into "the wider aspects of low income housing." Its social and psychological aspects in particular were to be studied — "We want to develop new concepts for improving our techniques for providing this type of social assistance."[177]

The task force's findings on the resistance to subsidization and to public housing generally had profoundly influenced federal thought, but its proposed research was to determine the ways of getting around this resistance rather than to remove the economic situation which gave rise to the necessity to subsidize and to provide for public housing.

Mr. Andras argued that in terms of existing legislation "there is scope to improve our methods of increasing the supply of subsidized housing and its quality."[178] Purchase of the existing stock of housing for occupation by the poor rather than the construction of new units, had been successfully tried by Ontario, and Mr. Andras saw it as having potential. Subsidizing housing acquired under lease arrangements was also to be considered so long as provincial housing authorities were the prime lease holders. Such measures would not increase the stock of housing, but shift the ownership of it into public hands and permit its occupation on social rather than on financial grounds. Additional help was also to be given to limited dividend companies and non-profit organizations by increasing the loan level from 90 to 95 percent.

The amendments of 1967 to provide loans through CMHC up to $10,000, for the purchase of used housing by individuals, had proved useful "in many communities; but again, particularly in our major centres, it is obvious that larger first mortgages are needed."[179] The proposed amendment now provided for 95 percent financing up to a maximum of $18,000 and permitted the loan to be used for either purchase or improvements. Home improvement was no longer to be a basic condition for the loan. The largest centres in particular were expected to benefit. The effect of the amendment could be that private lenders were now relieved of any obligation they may have felt to fund the purchase of used houses, though the incidence of second mortgages at high interest rates would decline. CMHC was now to take over an ever-increasing part in the financing of used housing.

Several other details were included in the bill. Many of these —such as amortization periods to go to 40 years, and a clear inclusion of condominiums as "houses"—extended earlier provisions of the NHA. None involved significant changes in principle. The system of mortgage insurance was to continue, and the flow of funds from lending institutions was of particular concern. A greater volume of private lending than ever before was required. In evidence before the Standing Committee on Health, Welfare, and Social Affairs the minister remarked:

> The flow of funds from private sources is a matter of great concern to me . . . We are, as you know, amending the NHA to make it possible for those companies to borrow on a short-term basis to invest in mortgages. That is the force and purpose of the five year roll-over provision.[180]

This provision was about the last step it was possible to make to facilitate private investment from the lending institutions. It was a change from the long-term investment policies which had typified mortgages since 1935. Mortgages were now to be included in the short-term arrangements of lending institutions under the NHA.

Despite Mr. Andras's awareness of the importance of lending institutions, no commitment had been obtained from them as to the amount of money which they intended to put into mortgage financing in the current year. The chartered banks, loan and trust companies, and the life insurance companies had indicated that a greater total amount could be expected. The President of CMHC then added:

> However, they will not commit themselves to this. Their intentions at the beginning of the year are subject to the developments of the market as the year goes by.[181]

The input by the various types of lending institutions was fluctuating in mid-1969. The banks were increasing, but life insurance companies decreasing their mortgage financing. In general these tended to offset each other. The government's program remained largely dependent on the whim and fancy of lending institutions making careful use of opportunities, NHA and private, to maximize their profits and security.

The arrangement since 1967, of pegging the NHA interest rate to the bond rate with quarterly adjustments, had worked against the interests of borrowers. Anyone watching the bond market could predict the forthcoming interest rate and plan his investments accordingly. Mr. Andras commented:

> That prejudgement or predetermination could and undoubtedly has had an influence on occasion on the investment intentions of approved lenders.[182]

223

By freeing the interest rate such irregularities or manipulations of the supply of mortgage money would be removed. The bill proposed the removal of the 2¼ percent maximum mark up above the long-term Canadian borrowing rate. This measure was soundly criticized by the opposition as being a government capitulation to the lending institutions. The NHA rate was then at 9⅜ percent and many mortgages were being written at 10 or 11 percent.[183] The argument that mortgages had to be competitive with other forms of investment was used in reply. The alternative, in the minister's view, was a "closed economy" with the pegging of wages, prices and profits.[184]

The aggregate amount of loans insured under the NHA was to be raised from $11 billion to $15 billion, which was expected to be adequate to the end of 1971. Other increases in statutory limits along with a variety of housekeeping measures were also proposed.

The urban renewal program was to be amended to provide for 50 percent federal assistance to provinces and municipalities for the rehabilitation of existing houses in renewal areas rather than their demolition. The task force had found habitable houses being demolished as a part of the renewal scheme. The amendment would facilitate their renovation after acquisition by public authorities and thereby give local authorities greater flexibility in renewal schemes. One idea behind the the measure was the provision of mixed accommodation in renewal areas, mixed in terms of the income of persons and the type of dwelling present. This was to obviate the closed character of a ghetto and to encourage varieties of persons to reside together. The possibility of one level of government or another providing public recreation services (such as community centres) in renewal areas—and built in as part of the total scheme by deliberate planning and subsidy—was to be looked into further. Mrs. Grace MacInnis, in the Proceedings of the Standing Committee, commented, "It is a new approach. The old idea was boxes for beds; we are getting away from that now into the idea of amenities."[185]

Similarly, to counter inflated land costs in the major cities, the 90 percent loan provisions to municipalities, after provincial consideration and approval, for the acquisition and servicing of land for public housing, was to be extended to all housing. Provincial consent for such loans and schemes was to continue as under the existing legislation. Such loans had to be taken up before March 31, 1972. The provinces had indicated their approval, and even eagerness, for this extension from public housing to housing in general, and some support had come from the Canadian Federation of Mayors and Municipalities.[186] A case was made in the standing committee for the inclusion of builders in the assistance now proposed to a province, a municipality, or public housing agency. A member explained the situation in Metropolitan Toronto in these words:

> I point out that most of the subdivisions are not conducted, or in any way run, by municipalities, but by private individuals .. by the time you acquire land and subdivide it you have put

in approximately $50,000 to $60,000 per acre for three-and-a-half years.

Consequently there are now four subdividers in the whole of Metropolitan Toronto with land for sale. There are 12 subdividers, but the other eight use their own lands. They will not sell. Consequently there is a scarcity of land and the price goes up.

A builder of 50 or 60 homes could, if he had the money, acquire the land without the speculator and put in the services, which the municipality would be perfectly agreeable to have him do. The only thing he needs is money ... I am not speaking about the speculator—one who will sell the land; I am speaking only of the one who will build on his land ... He does not necessarily have a direct loan so long as he has a guarantee.[187]

Mr. Andras recognized that there would be no "constitutional barrier, any more than there is for NHA insurance loans directly to individuals" and others.[188] He intended to look into this further. He had, perhaps, found the same solution as was used in the 1935 Dominion Housing Act to circumvent the lower levels of government on this particularly important aspect of urban development.

Mr. Andras recognized in the House that this proposal of federal assistance to lower levels of government was "the means by which our towns and cities can take direct action in molding their physical growth in the way they wish."[189] This measure was capable of fundamentally altering the power relationship among governments of all levels, and between private developers and lending institutions on the one hand and governments on the other.

In pressing for the establishment of a Minister of Housing and Urban Affairs an opposition speaker pressed on the government to consider the inter-provincial and also inter-state (on the American side of the border) nature of predicted megalopolitan urban growth around the Great Lakes and down the St. Lawrence. The Edison Company of Detroit had commissioned a Doxiadis group to study Detroit, and the group had found the whole region from Milwaukee to Quebec City to be the proper area of its enquiries. Two Canadian provinces and some five or six American states were involved in this complex. It appeared to the opposition that such developments would involve the federal government inevitably and it should begin its work expeditiously.[190] In the light of this type of situation the amendments to the NHA then under discussion seemed trivial. A new dimension to urban affairs in Canada was being introduced into federal legislature. It would also seem from reading *Hansard* debates and standing committee minutes that by June, 1969, there was an atmosphere of greater co-operation among the political parties than had been apparent for several years. The reason is not clear. But it may have been that the issues of power which urban affairs typify were commonly understood to be under review. The opposition was not satisfied with the adequacy of proposals for low income housing, but it did appear to appreciate that Mr. Andras was taking measures to compromise at least some of the centres of power that had come to dominate the Canadian urban scene over recent years.

1. *House of Commons Debates,* 1967, 3:2590.
2. Ibid., pp. 2590-2591. The vacancy rate in December, 1967 in Toronto was reportedly 1 percent, the lowest vacancy rate in North America. There were 11,000 families on the Metro Toronto waiting list. *House of Commons Debates,* 1967, 5:5709.
3. The average figure for land costs in Toronto for single detached dwellings was $9,667 in 1969. *Canadian Housing Statistics, 1970,* p. 71.
4. *House of Commons Debates,* 1967, 3:2591.
5. Ibid.
6. Ibid.
7. Ibid., p. 2597.
8. *Canadian Housing Statistics, 1967,* p. 66.
9. For a long time the rule of thumb applied was a maximum of 27 percent of gross income available for housing costs. The average family income at the time was somewhat less than $6,000 per annum.
10. The income level for occupancy of public housing was adjusted upwards to $7,000 per annum for the major metropolitan areas, and somewhat lower elsewhere later in 1967.
11. *House of Commons Debates,* 1967, 3:2609.
12. Ibid.
13. Ibid.
14. Ibid.
15. Ibid., p. 2610.
16. Ibid., p. 2771.
17. Ibid., p. 2773.
18. See the discussion of Mr. Trudeau's speech on the Canadian Constitution, January 1970, Chapter 6, p. 269.
19. Press release, CMHC., Ottawa, September 17, 1970.
20. *House of Commons Debates,* 1967, 3:2773.
21. *House of Commons Debates,* 1967, 5:5368.
22. Ibid., p. 5374.
23. Ibid., p. 5695.
24. Ibid., p. 5696.
25. Ibid., p. 5697.
26. Ibid., p. 5698.
27. Ibid.
28. Ibid.
29. Ibid.
30. Ibid., pp. 5702-03.
31. Ibid., p. 5710.
32. Ibid., p. 5715.
33. Ibid., p. 5716.
34. Ibid.,
35. Ibid., p. 5717.
36. *House of Commons Debates,* 1967, 3:2731.
37. Ibid.

38. The 1964 Royal Commission on Banking and Finance, (1969 Report) p. 239 had found that "the Canadian insurance industry is more international than most sections of our financial system."

39. *House of Commons Debates,* 1967, 3:2838.

40. *House of Commons Debates,* 1967, 5:5291.

41. Ibid.

42. Ibid.

43. Ibid., p. 5295.

44. Ibid.

45. Ibid., p. 5296.

46. Ibid.

47. Ibid., p. 5294.

48. Ibid., p. 5295. Mr. Andras did not appear to recognize that all previous moves to "let the gross national product grow" had resulted in development in metropolitan areas rather than in northern Ontario.

49. Ibid., p. 5705. In fact, the two Social Credit governments of British Columbia under the Home Acquisition Grant Fund of 1967, and as proposed by Premier Strom of Alberta in an election speech in early August, 1971, had provided grants to particular categories of persons buying their dwellings for the first time. This is not the same suggestion as Mr. Laprise's but is on similar principles.

50. Ibid., p. 5708.

51. Ibid., p. 5717.

52. Ibid., p. 5718.

53. Ibid., p. 5719.

54. Mr. Nicholson became Lieutenant Governor of British Columbia. The circumstances surrounding his ministerial resignation have not been identified in this study. From *Hansard* debates it would appear that Mr. Nicholson's sincerity and dedication were respected by all parties in the House, but the circumstances surrounding housing and urban affairs within which he was obliged to work left him impotent and ineffective.

55. Loans on used houses had fallen off during the year, but the minister was ignoring the matter.

56. *House of Commons Debates,* 1967-68, 7:7332. Sterling had recently been devalued. The United States was expressing concern over its rising balance of payment deficits over the outflow of gold, etc., and had imposed mandatory control over direct investments by U.S. controlled businesses in other countries.

57. Interest rates in the United States were at this time 2 percent lower than in Canada. Conventional mortgages in the U.S.A. were between 6½ percent and 6¾ percent in March, 1968, as against 8½ percent in Canada. Ibid., p. 7591.

58. Ibid., p. 7337.

59. Ibid., p. 7366. The prospect of setting up a prices review board was under discussion at this time.

60. Ibid., p. 7368.

61. *House of Commons Debates,* 1968-69, 1:797.

62. Ibid.

63. Ibid.

64. *House of Commons Debates,* 1968-69, 3:3359. The Minister of Manpower and Immigration remarked, "We believe that the work we are doing in the training field will be more effective in coping with the problem of unemployment than the former winter works program." Other programs, through FRED and ARDA, Western Farmers, etc., were also a part of the new approach. Ibid., 4:3907.

65. *House of Commons Debates,* 1968, 3:3121-22.

66. *House of Commons Debates,* 1968-69, 4:3487.

67. Ibid., p. 4365.

68. *House of Commons Debates,* 1968-69, 1:25.

69. Ibid.

70. See, for example, Ibid., p. 559, p. 626, and p. 628.

71. *House of Commons Debates,* 1968-69, 3:2517.

72. Reply to question 698, *Sessional Paper No. 254,* House of Commons, Ottawa.

73. *House of Commons Debates,* 1968-69, 3:2972.

74. Ibid.
75. *House of Commons Debates,* 1968-69, 6:5902.
76. Ibid., p. 6164.
77. Ibid., p. 5975-76.
78. Ibid., p. 6165.
79. Ibid., p. 6258.
80. Ibid.
81. Before approving some metropolitan urban renewal schemes, the minister made personal site visits. See, for example, *House of Commons Debates,* 1968-69, 7:7340-41 and 7519.
82. Some 16 of the task force recommendations concerned matters that were the direct responsibility of the provinces, not the federal government.
83. *House of Commons Debates,* 1968-69, 5:4881.
84. Ibid., p. 4882.
85. Ibid., p. 4884. Loans at 3¼ percent and 1 percent had recently been made to such areas as an aspect of federal policy on the international front.
86. Ibid., p. 4892.
87. Ibid., pp. 5369-70.
88. See, for example, Ibid., p. 5527.
89. Ibid., p. 5524.
90. Ibid., p. 5524-25.
91. Ibid., p. 5530.
92. Ibid. He was referring in particular to personal welfare provisions such as medicare and the Canada Pension Plan.
93. Ibid., p. 5527.
94. Federal-provincial relations had become strained since February, 1968 when budgetary cuts had been introduced. The freezing of new urban renewal and public housing projects over the summer and fall of 1968 had done nothing to engender a co-operative atmosphere.
95. Ibid., p. 5544.
96. Ibid., p. 5548. The issue at stake was that certain provinces would get poorer while the rich continued to get richer. Such a situation was already apparent and federal policy, as ARDA and FRED demonstrated, was to deal with it regionally rather than specificially provincially.
97. Ibid., p. 5545.
98. Ibid., p. 5546.
99. Ibid.
100. Ibid.
101. *House of Commons Debates,* 1968-69, 6:6748.
102. Ibid., p. 6159.
103. Ibid.
104. Ibid.
105. Ibid., p. 6160.
106. Ibid.
107. Ibid. In the 1956 brief from CMHC to the Royal Commission on Canada's Economic Prospects, entitled "Housing and Urban Growth in Canada," the relation of prices to supply and demand is stated explicitly on page 10, but no research is indicated to support it.
108. This whole proposition is questionable. Calgary, in October 1971, was reported by CMHC as having a 10.3 percent overall vacancy rate in apartment buildings, but the rents had been reduced only in particular cases. It is interesting to note that though the overall rate was 10.3 percent, the city centre had a rate of 17.2 percent at that time.
109. *House of Commons Debates,* 1968-69, 6:6160.
110. Ibid., pp. 6161-62.
111. Ibid., p. 6162.
112. It might be pointed out in this connection that the home-improvement loans provisions had not been particularly well used; only about $177,000 had been involved in a year in the whole of Canada.
113. Ibid., p. 6162.
114. Ibid., p. 6163.

115. Ibid., p. 6163.
116. *House of Commons Debates* 1968-69, 5:5525.
117. *House of Commons Debates,* 6:6183.
118. Ibid., p. 6184.
119. Ibid.
120. Ibid.
121. Ibid., p. 6185. Mrs. Grace MacInnis, New Democratic Party Member for Vancouver-Kingsway, was more charitable. She felt that the unusual step of a minister heading a task force had been deliberate. This step had foreclosed the possibility of government pigeonholing the task force reports. She felt "the Minister of Transport decided not to run that risk." *House of Commons Debates,* 1968-69, 7:8028. Her speech was made after Mr. Hellyer had resigned from the Cabinet.
122. *House of Commons Debates,* 1968-69, 7:7421.
123. Ibid., p. 7432.
124. See *House of Commons Debates,* 1968-69, 6:6748 and 7:7520.
125. *House of Commons Debates,* 1968-69, 7:7572.
126. Ibid., p. 7573.
127. Ibid., p. 7794.
128. Ibid.
129. Ibid.
130. Ibid.
131. Ibid., p. 7795.
132. Ibid.
133. Ibid., p. 7893. James Richardson became Acting Minister for Housing until this now important post could be filled again on a regular basis.
134. Ibid., p. 7896.
135. Ibid., p. 7977.
136. Ibid.
137. Ibid., p. 7978.
138. Ibid.
139. Ibid.
140. Ibid.
141. Ibid., p. 7979. The constitutional legality of the Hellyer Task Force's recommendations was submitted to two academic legal scholars who submitted a memorandum to the government. See *House of Commons Debates,* 1968-69, 9:10298.
142. This term referred to the writing of mortgage contracts with negotiable five yearly interest rates. It was a means of bringing to the mortgage market the short-term borrowings of lending institutions.
143. *House of Commons Debates,* 1968-69, 7:7979.
144. Ibid.
145. Ibid., p. 7980.
146. Ibid.
147. Ibid.
148. Ibid.
149. A phrase of Mr. Hellyer's, used at the press conference following his resignation.
150. *House of Commons Debates,* 1968-69, 7:7983.
151. Ibid.
152. A later speaker, on the government side of the House, put the matter in explicit terms by saying, "I hope . . . that the federal government will be able to obtain, with the co-operation of all the provinces, some direct access to our cities. This is a priority subject for federal-provincial constitutional discussions." *House of Commons Debates,* 1968-69, 7:7992.
153. Ibid., p. 7984.
154. Based on the assumption of a 9⅜ percent interest rate over 30 years.
155. *House of Commons Debates,* 1968-69, 7:7988.
156. Ibid., p. 7993.
157. Ibid., p. 7992.
158. Ibid., p. 7993.

159. Ibid.
160. Ibid.
161. Ibid., pp. 7993-94.
162. Ibid., p. 7995.
163. Ibid., p. 8008.
164. A press release quoted in the House. Ibid., p. 8016.
165. Ibid., p. 8016.
166. *House of Commons Debates,* 1968-69, 6:5827.
167. Ibid.
168. *House of Commons Debates,* 1968-69, 5:502, and 8:8488.
169. *House of Commons Debates,* 1968-69, 5:502.
170. We have not gone further into this matter in these studies, but the topic appears to be a rewarding one for further study.
171. *House of Commons Debates,* 1968-69, 8:8292.
172. Ibid., p. 8357.
173. Ibid., p. 8466.
174. *House of Commons Debates,* 1968-69, 9:9174.
175. Ibid., p. 9176. In fact, as late as July, 1969, most urban renewal projects had not been approved. The minister first hoped to visit each site, but later on indicated that municipal representatives were visiting him, and "we may work both ways." *House of Commons Debates* , 1968-69, 10:11221.
176. *House of Commons Debates,* 1968-69, 9:9176.
177. Ibid.
178. Ibid.
179. Ibid., p. 9177.
180. *Minutes of Proceedings and Evidence,* No. 39, June 5, 1969, p. 1693.
181. Ibid., *p. 1719.*
182. Ibid.
183. *House of Commons Debates,* 1968-69, 9:10119.
184. Ibid., p. 10132.
185. *Minutes and Proceedings,* p 1753.
186. *House of Commons Debates,* 1968-69, 9:10134.
The reason for the limited time, to March 31, 1972, imposed on this matter was not indicated in debate. However, as further amendments to the NHA would appear to be necessary about that date, Mr. Andras may have been giving the lower levels of government a chance to act effectively before expanding the provisions to private builders in addition to the public authorities.
187. *Minutes and Proceedings,* pp. 1763-64.
188. Ibid., p. 1764.
189. *House of Commons Debates,* 1968-69, 9:10134. The point was raised again a few days later. See vol. 10:10617, where the provinces were said to have taken the measure as a "real incentive, facility, and instrument for planning."
190. *House of Commons Debates,* 1968-69, 9:9184-85.

Chapter 6
Urban policy for Canada,
1969-1971

The Need for Co-ordination
 The emphasis of the Department of Regional Economic
Expansion (DREE), established in 1969 under Jean Marchand (see
Chapter 1, pp. 37-55), was on the co-ordination of federal efforts in
regional development. The disparities in living standards and
opportunities of people across the country had been discussed at recent
constitutional conferences. The provincial governments had recognized
the importance of the problem. DREE, as a new department, was "to
get down to the roots of the problems which have produced the existing
disparities . . . and help make the basic economic and social changes
needed to create new employment and earning opportunities . . ."[1] It
was an intensified effort on an old problem. Economic growth had to be
dispensed widely enough across Canada to bring employment and
opportunity to the slow growth regions.
 The new department's policy was to provide incentives to
industry to establish itself outside the metropolitan centres. The
departmental structure had first to be created to implement the policy,
because up to 1969 various unco-ordinated programs in a variety of
departments had been in vogue. The services and knowledge of these
other departments and agencies had first to be centralized. When the
federal structure was in order, co-ordination and co-operation with
the provinces could be made effective. The DREE legislation had
stipulated that co-operation with provinces "and the participation of
local groups in the drawing up and implementation of development
programs for special areas" would be its *modus operandi*.[2] DREE was to
enter into agreements with the provinces for the joint implementation of
programs, and where agreements were unnecessary the proper
co-operation would be maintained.
 In the case of DREE, the problem which the minister
encountered was that of building up an adequate administration and
executive instrument. The policy of regional development had been
generally agreed to by the provinces. The actual implementing of the
specific programs themselves was likely to be the area of difficulty. In
the case of urban affairs, however, the reverse was true. CMHC had
built up a considerable administrative and executive capacity with long
experience of dealing with provincial governments. The critical issue in
urban affairs was agreement at the level of policy. Nevertheless,
CMHC was caught up in its own set of problems.

At the time of the 1969 amendments to the NHA, Robert Andras, Minister without Portfolio, but responsible for housing, had no staff or office. He was dependent on CMHC for advice and suggestions. Steven Otto, Member for York East, with twenty years of experience in the construction industry, outlined the difficulties the minister might have if he relied solely on CMHC, for that organization was itself caught up in an intractable situation from a practical point of view. This situation included the following features:

—Not only was there a shortage of housing in the metropolitan areas, but for the past 50 years the construction industry had built houses to last 30 years. The decay of the existing stock was therefore increasing.

—In Toronto the cost of accommodation was absorbing something like 50 percent of the take-home pay of even the middle income group, and while Canadians could tolerate 25 percent of take-home pay the 50 percent was applying to both rental and owned accommodation.

—The root of high urban costs was not so much the equipment inside the house, as the high cost of land - "when the price of land is running between $10,000 and $12,000 on the outskirts of the city and between $23,000 and $80,000, in Toronto itself, you cannot put a $6,000 house on it."[3] The construction industry had done its part in keeping costs down.

—The lending institutions of Canada were capable of transferring money across political boundaries. The local building society, typical in Britain, had not evolved in Canada. The shortage of mortgage money was not solvable by local initiative and saving. Where the technique had been tried in Canada it had failed. The Nova Scotia Savings and Loan Company had recently altered its charter "because it was found the building society operation did not work in Canada."[4]

—CMHC continually demanded an assurance that a lending institution was interested in putting up money on a project before CMHC guaranteed a loan. In this way CMHC was avoiding open competition with lending institutions and not using the powers it had been granted to generate the competition needed to reduce mortgage costs.

—Sewage-disposal systems, municipally organized and provincially administered, were the crux of land cost."[5] By requiring larger and larger sewage systems, embracing wider and wider catchment areas and trunk sewage routes, the land available for development was restricted to these routes. Its value rose in consequence. Had research been applied to developing small scale, even lot-sized, sewage systems the area of land opened up in consequence would have forestalled rising prices due to limitation of supply - "If the periphery around Toronto were not tied to the trunk sewer system, land would be available from one side of the city to the other. In that case the speculators would have nothing to speculate with."[6] The builder would put in his own services.

—Private industry had made innovation on a broad front and had sought approval for others from CMHC. However, it had experienced difficulty in getting new ideas approved.

In summing up his argument Mr. Otto considered CMHC to be "absolutely useless in most of the fields in which it is empowered to act."[7] A complete shakeup was required, and a new organization established — "The minister is not going to get very far with the organization he now has."[8] He gave no indication of the organizational form required.

By the end of June, 1969, there is evidence in *Hansard* that Mr. Andras was already well aware of the federal impact on urban municipalities. He was also starting to assess the organizational form he needed. He opened an address in the House with these words:

> . . . the federal government has a significant and pervasive stake in the future of the urban environment of Canada. There is no doubt about that . . . Its record shows it is aware of the responsibilities inherent in that fact. The role of the government has been an effective one, one that has been accepted by provincial, and municipal governments and authorities throughout Canada. This effectiveness and acceptability arise in large part out of the influence of the National Housing Act.[9]

He continued by arguing that the federal legislature "has kept abreast of changing municipal requirements by constantly updating the NHA." However, the federal govenment had no prerogative "in the actual physical planning of our municipalities."[10] He continued, significantly, as follows:

> There have developed in many large urban communities complex, complicated, overlapping networks of municipalities in a single urban area, each responsible, autonomously almost, for its own planning, its own struggle for a balanced assessment between industrial and residential use, and all without regard to the larger urban area of which it forms a part. There is in most urban places the lack of an over-all plan of urban development for the whole area in which future growth is to take place. Consequently, instead of urban regional plans for the development of industry, housing, education, transportation, open spaces, recreation, pollution control and urban renewal on a regional basis there exist in many cases municipal restrictions to exclude those activities which do not produce sufficient municipal taxes to carry them.[11]

The provinces were responsible for the co-ordination of urban regional planning, and only they were empowered "to take the direct action which is required to provide the necessary solutions." The federal contribution to urban affairs had not in fact been limited to housing. Airport facilities, railway and terminal facilities, university assistance, hospital subsidization, and an array of federal departmental activities had made obvious contributions.

Recently, an argument had been advanced that just as the federal government was originally involved with transcontinental rail and road services, it was now obliged to get involved with urban transit, if only because the majority of Canadians were urban residents. It was, however, not involved. Mr. Andras then argued a very significant point. He said:

> In the first place, it is not the federal government, but the provincial and local governments which determine the pattern of urban settlement, whether low density or high density, suburban or downtown. It is simply a myth that the pattern of suburban growth in the country has been determined by the kind of mortgage insurance aid offered under the National Housing Act. These lending aids are equally available whether a building is suburban or downtown, high-rise or low-rise, compact or dispersed. The premise of this argument, then, is nonsense.[12]

Mr. Andras's argument follows from the assumption that because lending aids are equally available in a legal sense, the means of their application on the ground are equally impartial. As the evidence contained in this book shows, this assumption is false. The lending institutions, rather than either the provincial or the local governments, have been the predominant deciders of most issues on the ground.

The CMHC's increasing responsibility for single dwelling finance in small town and rural areas because of the resistance of lending institutions to service such areas, bears ample witness to the questionable nature of Mr. Andras's argument. The "pattern of urban settlement," in so far as it relates to the cities themselves, has been influenced possibly more by local authorities than by provincial governments; though it may be unwise to generalize this point to Canada as a whole. In Alberta the provincial government has tacitly refrained from interference in local authority development.

Mr. Andras's argument that the NHA has not determined the pattern of urban settlement ignores the lending institutions and their influence. As recently as June 5, 1969, when the Standing Committee met to consider the 1969 NHA amendments, there are many examples of this influence.[13] Lending institutions have not merely provided much of the needed capital; they have also been selective in the purposes for which they lend and the persons to whom they lend. There is also some evidence to suggest that CMHC has, both in terms of its own decisions and certainly in terms of its role as an instrument of government policy, been similarly selective. The federal govenment cannot abnegate the facts of the past thirty-five years merely on the grounds of the constitutional division of powers. Mr. Andras, perhaps of all federal ministers responsible for housing, has had the courage to identify this federal role publicly.

Federal responsibility for urban transportation systems, including roads, was a questionable matter. Mr. Andras argued that such systems serve predominantly the local population using them and thereby compromises the case for federal assistance. Though he did not mention it, a distinction may also be drawn between housing as a service to the individual needs of Canadians and transport as a general public amenity and city service. There would appear to be a different order of responsibility based on this distinction, though the point tends to emphasize the questionable constitutional legality of the 1935 decision of the federal government to support housing rather than Mr. Andras's current case against federal support for urban transportation. The federal government, as a matter of fact, had become increasingly involved with urban transportation research. It had contributed $75,000 towards the expenses of the first Canadian urban transportation conference and federal agencies concerned with transport had increased their research in this area. The minister then added:

> But this is something quite different from taking a direct position, city by city, or province by province, in actual urban transportation activities.[14]

Quite apart from the monetary considerations of such a direct position, the minister appeared to be sensitive to the problem of selective criteria implied by such activity. Precedent could be used embarrassingly by both provinces and cities to argue their case for equal treatment.

The more fundamental matter, however, was possibly the constitutional issue once again. The proceedings of the June 5, 1969 Standing Committee meeting show Mr. Andras to be well aware of this point. Asked "whose responsibility it would be to introduce policy on the better economic use of land whereby rights-of-way utilized by hydros, railways, expressways and other utilities, rather than being dispersed and operating separately, could be amalgamated . . . ", Mr. Andras replied:

> . . . with the possible exception of your use of the word "railways" that the rest of it, and perhaps even that to a degree, would be much more directly a provincial jurisdiction under the Constitution.[15]

By the federal provision of funds, however, Mr. Andras thought that "a considerable degree of persuasion" could be brought to bear.

The minister was also facing a dilemma regarding urban renewal, which had "grown quite rapidly, from relatively insignificant proportions to one of the most important areas of concern in the short span of the last half a dozen years."[16] The consequences of the 1964 NHA amendments and the interests of the lending institutions in high-rise commercial and apartment blocks were creeping up on the federal authorities. In this instance, the dilemma was between federal policy and the interests of ethnic minorities, particularly the residents of the many Chinatowns across the country, who were served eviction notices as urban renewal schemes were approved. Mr. Hellyer had met the dislike of the residents of public housing; Mr. Andras was confronted by the objections of the representatives of ethnic minorities. Mr. Andras remarked:

> Perhaps because of its very rapid growth we find today serious questions being asked from many directions about urban renewal, such as questions about citizen participation.[17]

In some cases nobody had taken the trouble to visit citizens and consult with them "about bulldozing their homes and demolishing this area, the very place where they have felt safe and secure." Mr. Andras wanted to consult such groups "before we move blithely ahead in the name of progress,"[18] and before he removed his own dilemma by granting final approval for urban renewal projects. It was important to Mr. Andras that the federal government does not "rush ahead with any programs without giving full consideration to those kinds of representations."[19]

Citizen participation was considered essential to these operations. In Mr. Andras' opinion:

> participation must cut in at a very much lower level than it has in many of the urban renewal projects of the past. Careful consideration must be given to the rehabilitation of structures which must be saved. Municipalities should be prepared, surely, to adopt and enforce bylaws of maintenance and occupancy standards. Those bylaws are necessary if we are to get on with the job; otherwise renewed areas may deteriorate and fall back into the condition they were in originally.[20]

There were about 148 urban renewal plans that "have to be acted on pretty quickly." He hoped to visit these sites as soon as possible. In this he was following Mr. Hellyer's earlier example.

This emphasis on haste, after the years of research and planning that had gone into each of these plans, is a complex matter to interpret. The minister had been under pressure in the House from members clearly pressured, in turn, from municipal levels. Delay cost money for both public and private interests. In many instances, urban renewal affected highly remunerative sites near city centres. Municipal mayors were catching the discontent of frustrated financial and commercial interests and of their own city planning staffs as well as of the increasingly organized opposition of threatened minority groups. The lower levels of government were dependent on quick and decisive action by the federal authorities to generate a *fait accompli* locally and to provide the scapegoat for blame in the event of excessive local concern. In hoping to see citizen participation cut in at a very much lower level, Mr. Andras was responding more to his own situation and responsibilities than to the realities of leaders at the local level.

When the Standing Committee on Health, Welfare and Social Affairs was discussing the 1969 amendments to the NHA, Grace MacInnis, Member for Vancouver-Kingsway, questioned the minister on the involvement of people affected by public housing proposals and similar large scale operations. She hoped they would not be faced with a *fait accompli*, but that officials would engage in serious consultation with them. The minister agreed wholeheartedly and stated his experience of the last ten years as being that:

> packages developed in the back room in Ottawa or anywhere else, even though they may be the most enlightened plans in the world . . . are just doomed to less than success . . . I think there is a great psychological requirement to let people have a piece of the action.[21]

Local officials consulting with those affected and with provincial authorities was the ideal practice as the minister saw it. The cities could easily get held up by the provincial governments if consultation at this level was disregarded. But Mr. Andras did not feel it was a federal responsibility to:

> direct and demand that the provincial governments invite the participation of municipalities . . . I think if we attempted to take that kind of hard line, my feeling, rightly or wrongly, is that in the end we would delay the whole process because we would get other factors involved in the consultations.[22]

The invitation had to originate at levels at least below the federal level. If citizen participation was to be taken seriously as an essential part of the procedure then the city or city-zone became the only meaningful point of its application. Yet it was precisely at this level where authorities felt unable, through compromise and conflict of interest, to act with confidence and foresight.

Compromise of a proposal was relatively easy at the municipal level if the groups affected by the proposal could obtain the assistance of professional personnel who could demonstrate any compromising fact to an interested and suspicious public.

The point comes out clearly in a reply made by Mr. Andras in the proceedings of the Standing Committee. Asked whether guidelines for the whole country could be laid down for developments that involved the bulldozer and public resentment, Mr. Andras indicated he preferred to sit down with provincial and local ministers and officials to see what is locally possible as opposed to what is totally desirable. Though anxious to move as quickly as possible, Mr. Andras recognized the following issue:

If the authorities at the municipal level will, of their own volition, recognize the concern that has been expressed in the debate so far and begin to introduce, or to think about, change without an edict from any level we would hope that some effect will immediately be felt in these (programs) in the early stages and as they progress.[23]

Citizen participation, though an apparently necessary requirement in a supposedly public act such as urban renewal, is an impossibility if large sums of private money are involved and time is an important consideration. The difficulties of electing or selecting citizens to become involved, of explaining to lay persons even a part of the implications of what is involved after professionals and specialists have mulled over the issues for years, of indicating the reasons for particular decisions having gone the way they did in terms of the choices available, and the like, turn such a policy into tokenism or a sham which disaffected citizens are quick to identify. Urban renewal decisions are inevitably political and therefore potentially inflammable. A policy of generous removal expenses and incentives to encourage individuals to relocate — in brief, the application of policies and principles already found necessary in the case of industry in regional development programs — might prove more practical than assuming that the political facts of renewal can be erased by citizen participation. Such participation is a cheap and convenient way out, but one that may not always prove feasible.

There is a distinction to be drawn between selling the idea of the necessity for renewal of blighted areas, and threatening the livelihood and amenities of persons directly affected by it. Few people would, in the abstract, disagree with its principle, but the ethnic content of Mr. Andras's dilemma is a consequence of existing organizational networks in affected areas. Its ethnicity is a matter of pre-existing organization and such organizational capacity is capable of expansion to wider segments of urban degraded zones than those with readily identifiable ethnic characteristics. If the urban policy for Canada as it emerged over the following two years is to become a reality, then the costs of urban renewal should include the costs of incentives to residents of high density city areas to move elsewhere. Such costs are already part of federal policy on regional industrial location, and the affected citizenry, particularly if encouraged to participate in renewal schemes, may shortly come to identify themselves with such a policy. The "negotiable provisions" afforded industry seem to set a precedent.

Mr. Andras, during this speech, emphasized "that it is only through the expression and resolution of these creative tensions that the urban artifacts we create will be given authentic vitality."[24] Co-operation among governments, among governmental departments, among private sector interests, and between this sector and governments was seen as the essential for future development effectiveness. Mr. Andras saw it as taking many forms, from zealous support and genuine community involvement to painful conflicts of interest.[25]

239

David Lewis, Member for York South, attacked Mr. Andras's sophistry on the ground of inaction. He cited "the avid, legalistic mind" which made him Minister without Portfolio, rather than Minister of Housing and Urban Affairs, and which failed to provide him with a staff or with the national council on urban affairs suggested by the Economic Council of Canada. Mr. Lewis's speech was intended to generate the organizational mechanism needed to allow the federal government "to take the initiative to call the provinces together, and the major municipal regions of Canada . . . not merely to discuss them (problems) but to make some kind of plan."[26] Mr. Lewis remarked:

> But we do condemn it for its refusal to recognize that its role is not and must not be merely the role of the largest treasury in Canada, making money available for housing or urban renewal, for its refusal to recognize that the role of the central government of Canada must be a deliberate, determined and conscious attempt to find solutions for the urban problems facing Canadians from coast to coast.[27]

The opposition parties had in the past recommended in different ways the same kind of initiative. Mr. Andras reminded the House that in December, 1967, and in the spring of 1968, at federal-provincial housing conferences, the provinces had shown "a less than enthusiastic response" to such a federal suggestion. Mr. Lewis's interpretation of the source of the problem, however, was "the legalistic, straight-jacketey approach which the Prime Minister takes to the Canadian constitution."[28]

Steven Paproski, Member for Edmonton Centre, pleaded for the recognition of Canada as an urban society and for the recognition that all federal policies from wheat sales to inflation affected urban development and the life of urban residents. The unco-ordinated and rapid growth of metropolitan centres contributed to problems. He remarked:

> If our major cities were already working models of efficiency and high quality living, urban growth of the proportions I have indicated would not tax their existing facilities very much. But our metropolitan areas are conglomerations of mounting deficiencies and heavy backlogs of essential works still to be done.[29]

He was anxious to see the federal government generate "a new model for Canadian cities of the 1970s." While the government refused to contemplate direct programs in the cities there was little hope of implementing any model. In Mr. Paproski's view federal and provincial officials discussed vital matters of city concern, but city officials were not told — "they are kept in the dark and the progress and plans for their cities are held up."[30] Participatory democracy seemed to mean "the right to protest after something harmful has been done."[31]

Other members argued that so much money had been poured into the urban centres that the rural areas had suffered. Greater control exercised at the federal level would help to cope with this issue also. If a constitutional conference could be called which would result in the handing to the federal government of control of economic development something satisfactory for both rural areas and metropolitan cities might be done. In reply to a question in the Standing Committee as to whether CMHC had, or intended in the future "to introduce indirectly what may be described as sound tools of planning because of the fact that it provides the funds for certain purposes", Mr. Andras hoped that the operation of housing policy federally would have that effect, but he preferred to see it done with the "participation of the other levels of government so that it is not a unilateral edict from the federal government." He feared that in that event a delay in the process — "because you get everybody very angry and very upset" — would be the only result.[32]

Mr. Andras met with the leaders of lending institutions in early July, 1969. They had agreed to meet "at least twice a year with more formal and precise agendas in order to make these meetings more meaningful."[33] The constitutional conferences with the provinces were also to continue. The minister expected to meet with provincial housing ministers in July and August, 1969.[34] CMHC officials were working ever more closely with local and provincial planning authorities, but without constitutional authority or official support. The federal government would give careful consideration to resolutions of the Canadian Federation of Mayors and Municipalities that were presented to it, but the federal government considered it inappropriate to request the provinces to include municipal representatives in provincial delegations at federal-provincial conferences.[35] This was the position at the close of parliamentary session in October, 1969.

The Political Struggle and the Clarification of Ideas
During the third Federal-Provincial Conference on the Constitution, in mid-December, 1969 the opposition staged a debate in the House on urban problems. They were seeking the establishment of a parliamentary committee "to concern itself with the problems of urban people of Canada."[36] Mr. Stanfield envisaged its responsibilities as being:
(1) to provide a national forum and a national focus for the discussion of urban problems and their consideration;
(2) to hear directly from municipal governments and provincial authorities in a public way on how the federal involvement in our cities can be made more effective on a continuing basis;
(3) to discuss and make periodic recommendations to Parliament and to the government on specific problems and opportunities for federal action or assistance; and
(4) to provide an opportunity for some of the members of Parliament on the government side of the House to make the kind of representations about urban problems that they are unable to make now except perhaps privately.[37]

Though there was some political advantage to be gained from these efforts, the insinuation of a feeling of impotence on the part of the opposition and of some government members over the government's decisions on urban areas was well founded. Mr. Stanfield spoke on this theme, and although the federal-provincial conference was open on this occasion, Mr. Andras had been putting off for several months his statement, first promised in the summer, on urban renewal and public housing. He had been under constant pressure to make a policy statement. In November he had explained the delay as due to "long consultations with my counterparts in the provincial governments" whose recommendations he was still considering.[38] It would appear that they were considering how to organize a department of urban affairs and housing, and how to relate it to CMHC. The federal role in the cities, whether within the existing constitution or under an amended one, was the overall question. Mr. Stanfield saw his proposed parliamentary committee as symbolizing the concern of the federal parliament with urban Canada.

The NDP wanted the motion to go one step further and the House to recommend the setting up of a separate ministry of housing and urban affairs with a full-time minister. This party added further reasons for the involvement of parliament; namely, the Presidential Commission of the USA had found violent crime to be primarily a phenomenon of the cities and concentrated among youths of the 15 to 20 age group, and had forecast that high-rise apartment blocks would become fortified cells protected by private guards and security devices. John Gilbert, Member for Broadview, concisely expressed the urban problems of Canada as being "poverty, unemployment, a housing crisis, drugs, alienation of youth, and the changing role of the family."[39]

Government members opposed the motion on the basis that such a committee would be a means of inquiry "into the activities of the provincial level of government."[40] This argument referred, apparently, to inquiry by politicians rather than by officials of CMHC whose duties had for decades taken them into intimate involvement with provincial and municipal decisions on urban development. A second point of debate was that a committee would be party to only a small fraction of the federal influence, as other areas of recognizable effect, such as air transport, were dealt with elsewhere in the federal parliamentary machinery. Similarly, activities of the Department of Regional Economic Expansion (DREE) would influence the cities, but its affairs were channelled through other means.

Mr. Andras expressed regret at the superficial level of much of the debate. The urgent need was, he felt, to obtain a "precise and meaningful understanding of our urban environment and its problems" at all levels of government. The matter was incredibly complicated. Not only were the urban areas the nub of the socio-economic development of Canada, but each city had responded and adapted to the forces affecting it in unique ways. Each city therefore had its peculiar characteristics and would require specific responses to its problems. He remarked:

I think the thing that has impressed itself on me more than anything else is that each part of the social system that is a city and an urban area is highly interdependent in ways that defy simple analysis. I am stressing these points because I sincerely believe that many of us are failing to appreciate how little we understand about this system.[41]

He then cited several examples of the unanticipated consequences that followed from previously well intended but *ad hoc* measures: in the name of urban renewal, viable communities had been destroyed and hardship inflicted on those it was intended to assist; public housing measures had on occasion locked the poor into even more rigid social ghettoes; metropolitan expressways had increased the demand for land in city cores which in turn denied housing to the local residents because of rising land costs: assessments had gone up in downtown areas and so had taxes making it profitable for businesses to retire to the suburbs leaving the poor to carry the increased tax, and so on.

Mr. Andras's review of urban renewal and public housing policy had been conducted with his provincial counterparts, but he added in response to a question that he had also been consulting representatives of the municipalities, "I think with the consent and support of the provincial ministers."[42] He had met also with the Executive Committee of the Association of Mayors and Municipalities. Municipal representatives from Ontario had attended the federal-provincial conference the very day Mr. Andras was speaking in the House, but they had come at the invitation of their provincial government, not the federal government. The federal government had offered "no opposition . . . to their presence at this conference."[43]

The analysis being made of urban renewal and "of all the housing programs under the NHA" marked, in Mr. Andras's view, "the first phase of our attempt to understand this complicated urban process. I say also that the second phase necessarily involves an incredibly deep and careful analysis of that process in all its complexity."[44] That enquiry had just been launched and Mr. Andras hoped to place recommendations from it before the House by the late spring. There was to be no apology for the need for further study. Interviews had been held with urban experts from many industrialized countries, "and I find somewhat to my horror that I know of no country, not even among the most advanced industrial western nations, that truly has an urban policy."[45]

This was the first time that Mr. Andras had introduced the concept of "an urban policy" as broadly conceived as this. The general content of the conception is shown in the above remark. He was not holding off on a statement merely about urban renewal and public housing. His understanding of his ministerial responsibilities had gone much beyond that by December, 1969. However, the issues which he enunciated as "the critical urban problems" with which he was trying to deal were rather banal. He said:

For example, we want to know who are the urban poor. Are they in the main unemployable, or are they temporarily unemployed? No evidence collected to date permits us to answer even this simple question. We want to know why there is such a squeeze on the revenues of urban governments, and what can be done about it. We want to know what alternatives there are to the current treadmill of more cars, more highways, and then more cars. We want to know what alternatives there are to monotonous suburbs and decaying inner cities.[46]

It would appear from these questions that the major works on urban life, government, and planning which had been published during the past century in Europe and America had passed Mr. Andras by. He was apparently seeking to make the same discovery as did Charles Booth in his *Life and Labours of the People of London* published at the turn of the century. Some basic facts about urban living, despite the developed techniques of the modern census, of sampling, or of the records of the Department of Manpower, seemed to be missing or were inadequate to meet the demands Mr. Andreas expected to impose on them. This search for clearer and more adequate facts of detail and trivia is particularly interesting in view of the next part of Mr. Andras's speech. He continued:

But part of the problem, and I plead with honourable members to understand this, or join me in the attempt to understand it, in trying to answer these specific questions is that they cannot be answered or dealt with in isolation. Where you put a public housing project of any significant size, where you put an airport or an expressway, has a shaping effect on urban society. These matters are interrelated, and they cannot be dealt with as has been the case in the past, as if the city was a multi-ring circus and what was going on in one ring had no relationship to what was going on in the other rings.[47]

Earlier in his address he had mentioned the uniqueness of Canada's cities in terms of their responses to socio-economic forces. If one adds up the standard of fact he required, the determination of the interdependence of one part on all other parts, and of the uniqueness of individual cities, one can get an impression of the immense task Mr. Andras had set himself. He had aimed to understand what he referred to as the "urban process," to a degree which assumed a condition of total knowledge. One danger in the approach was that of missing the wood for the trees. But the methodological risk was one of over-emphasizing the structural, descriptive quality of the city and under-emphasizing the dynamic and power component. A condition of true perfect knowledge assumes familiarity with both.

Mr. Andras was not, at that time, unaware of the dynamic component. He continued by stressing the need "to understand fully how the problems arise. We have to start treating them not in terms of their symptoms but in terms of their causes. We also need better data on how they are connected to social, demographic and economic change."[48] He saw his task to be to search for "the key determinants" of the urban process, to facilitate the isolation and evaluation of:

> the possible alternative strategies for governmental intervention to manage that system effectively. Its objective is to direct the urban systems so as to alleviate the critical urban problems and to pursue actively our primary social goals in a country which is becoming essentially urban.[49]

The provinces and municipalities were intimately involved. Their interests and legitimate roles had to be continually kept in mind. This was where Mr. Andras's discussions with them had come in. He saw himself working closely with them "to arrive at a joint consensus of goals and strategies." Understanding was the prerequisite of effective action, but the co-ordination of activities had to be "in terms of the objectives and the conception of the urban process."[50]

These early remarks by Mr. Andras suggest a perspective of approach. His approach was in terms of intervening in a social process, but the intervention had to be deliberate at both the point of critical consequence and as to the direction in which the change must be effected. The objectives, and the conception of what the urban process was like, required explicit statement. The pattern or paradigm to be used to gain the understanding sought was the model of structure and interrelatedness of the parts. It was reminiscent of the model employed in 1938 when the first National Housing Act was introduced.[51] The model was aimed at solving the national housing problem; the modern one at solving the whole urban problem. Housing was approached through inducements to lending institutions and others to act in ways the model required they should act. Insofar as Canadians have become, depending on the value judgement you have, either one of the best or the worst housed people in the world, the model had proved to be an instrument for deciding on at least some course of practical action. Ironically, this model led to the costly, concentrated metropolitan centres of today, almost annual amendments to the NHA, the persistence of urban poverty, regional rural degradation, and the host of pathologies mentioned daily in the press. Perhaps these phenomena are not strictly caused by the NHA or any paradigm implicit in it. But is the paradigm adequate in those situations for which the federal govenment has assumed a responsibility in conjunction with an ambivalent jurisdictional right? The paradigm has practical value at the level of the applied and final act -- at the level of architect and engineer in constructing the house or bridge, or perhaps of the town planner with free scope to lay out the initial plan for a new city. It is a paradigm appropriate to physical matter with relatively known constants. But it is a paradigm singularly inappropriate under conditions where:

245

(a) there exist a series of public authorities capable of action independent of the assumptions implicit in the model, and
(b) there exist a series of organized companies and corporations possessing capital and resources of their own that may or may not, at will be disposed to act in the public interest, but undeniably in their own interest.

The paradigm ignores the political nature of the real urban process.
The model has to be applied in situations of intense political struggle. Even in the federal government itself, between the minister responsible for housing and CMHC, this is apparent. In Mr. Hellyer's recent book, *Agenda: A Plan for Action*, one reads:

> On a day-to-day basis there is a tremendous amount of two-way pressure between the government and the Corporation. There is pressure to make loans to specific companies, to make loans to specific places and on occasion to make special arrangements . . . Pressure groups form, become aware of their own political influence, and governments react.[52]

The Prime Minister has for years been engaged in conferences with the provinces over amending the 1867 constitution or generating a new one. Behind these inconclusive debates has lain the ogre of control of wealth-producing cities. The CFMM has explicitly declared the importance of Canadian cities to the economic well-being of the nation. The frequent meetings of the heads of lending institutions with ministers responsible for housing to ascertain the anticipated extent of private lending in the mortgage market and the consequences of their decisions for public support through CMHC to ensure an adequate number of housing starts each year, are others of the political arenas within which the model has to be adjusted.
Yet the very thing which the model does *not* contain is the assumption that the federal government can act decisively in this political arena. Mr. Hellyer's resignation was associated with the continued right of the federal government to intrude increasingly into city municipal affairs in the face of the 1867 constitution. The provinces, armed since the mid-1960s with housing authorities of their own, tied closely to Ottawa through shared-cost agreements and tax-sharing agreements, and conscious of the immense wealth generated by metropolitan centres, have become increasingly unwilling to permit the continued influence of the federal government in their local authorities. The lending institutions, assured of the continued recognition by Canada of the international determinants of interest rates, and assured of ever increasing demands for capital from commercial and industrial sources anxious to increase employment opportunities concurrently with added automation, supporting a strong export drive of Canadian manufactures and meeting the expectations of Canadians for an ever higher standard of consumption, have entrenched themselves with the highest, long-term rates of interest and return on money

since confederation. Yet the federal government persists in using models of urban development which ignore the assumption of power and direction inherent in the qualities normally associated with the autonomy of a nation state.

The feature which typifies this situation more than any other, is the determination of federal ministers to play the game with honour, integrity, and the public interest uppermost in their minds. This has been the characteristic of Mr. Nicholson, Mr. Hellyer and Mr. Andras, to mention only the most recent. It has been applauded in the House and recognized by the public. The feature is beautifully demonstrated in Mr. Andras's eventual statement, on December 18, 1969, concerning urban renewal. He had been pressed and politically embarrassed in the House for almost a year to make this statement. When it finally came he said very explicitly:

> . . . in the absence of clearly defined economic and social goals, including the provision of housing for the most disadvantaged income groups, the program appears to have served a multitude of often contradictory purposes which were never foreseen in the original definition. For example, as a result of urban renewal activities to date, there has been a net loss in low income housing stock.[53]

While the study of the causes of the urban process was underway, Mr. Andras could not see:

> the wisdom or justification for an expansion of government intervention, or major new dimensions, in programs such as urban renewal, some forms of which are doubtful in their results. We see rather a need for more emphasis on low income housing and such investments that provide clear and more immediate benefits.[54]

Certain renewal schemes would be allowed to continue. But if even only those schemes which had reached the point of final implementation, after the preliminaries were completed, were all allowed to proceed, "the federal treasury alone would be involved in ultimate expenditures approaching $400 million and loans up to two-thirds of the total grant. Provincial and municipal expenditures would have been on a similar scale."[55] The costs of urban renewal were coming home to roost, which, in addition to the moral aspect of urgently needed homes for individuals and families, had led the minister to conclude that urban renewal, as presently arranged, was not in the public interest.

This decision hit the interests of local authorities and lending institutions. The 1964 and subsequent amendments to the NHA had proven rewarding to them. Urban renewal had been one of the instruments whereby city cores could be transformed at public expense. It had contributed to the high-rise commercial and apartment developments of these areas. The federal government, in its recent sponsoring of conferences and research on urban transportation, had also been showing an enlightened interest in contributing to the costs of this area of public problems — problems increasingly generated by the mode and extent of the concentration that had already come about. To soften the blow of the minister's decision, some 12 projects spread over most provinces, and additional to the six already negotiated and approved in August, would be allowed to continue with maximum cost figures approximating $25 million annually up to 1974. That was to be the limit of federal support "at least until the urban policy review is completed next year."[56] Communities with schemes unapproved would be encouraged to amend their programs to facilitate use of other sections of the NHA.

Urban renewal was the example used by the minister to illustrate the need for a constant review and evaluation of programs. "Unforeseen weaknesses and changing priorities" made such evaluations necessary to avoid a waste of scarce resources. The long-promised guidelines on public housing were still held up on the grounds of consultation with the provinces. When their submissions were in hand, Mr. Andras envisaged the writing of a composite proposal, "Then I believe we shall have to go back to the provinces with that composite proposal in order to get some kind of consensus, and at that time I will be glad to make a statement."[57]

A week before Mr. Andras's statement on urban renewal, the House had been debating amendments respecting incorporation, operation, and administration under the Trust Companies Act.[58] Though it is not possible to do more than outline some of the amendments proposed, it is clear from *Hansard* that they were intended to affect mortgage financing.[59] Bills covering amendments to other types of lending institutions followed in short order. The first bill affected the activities of federally-incorporated trust companies, of which there were then nine doing about one-third of the trust company business in Canada. The bill had four principal purposes:

> First, to provide certain expansions in the investment powers of trust companies; second, to establish a better and more flexible system of controlling companies if they should get into financial difficulties; third, to extend the prohibitions against investments and loans where there may be a conflict of interests, and, fourth, to establish a letters patent system of incorporating companies and amending existing charters.[60]

With regard to the first, the bill purposed to bring the investment powers of trust companies into line with those of insurance companies, i.e., trust companies would be permitted to make mortgage loans on the security of leasehold as well as freehold real estate, make investments outside Canada in any country in which they were doing business, make investments in real estate for the production of income which qualified on the basis of an earnings test, and to make investments in real estate for the production of income in larger parcels than was presently permitted. They were also to be relieved of the restriction limiting the amount of any mortgage to 75 percent of the value of the real estate unless insured through a government agency. They were to be granted the right to own subsidiary companies in certain circumstances, including trust companies outside of Canada.

Provincially-chartered trust companies would, under the amendments, be permitted to obtain a federal charter not by a special act, but by letters patent. This facility would be granted, however, only with the concurrence of the province of incorporation. The general purpose of the amendments was stated as being:

> ... it is considered that its approval would assist in increasing the supply of funds available for mortgage lending, particularly for housing purposes, and increase the ability of federally incorporated trust companies generally to provide services to the public.[61]

The opposition parties sensed something suspicious in these proposals; but not having had the opportunity to examine the matter ourselves, we prefer not to comment. It is, however, an obvious future research area.

The "Urban Canada" Studies (1970)

Though CMHC was engaged in studies continuously through these years, and had research potential of some $15 million, the decisive studies of 1969-1970 were those of Dr. Harvey Lithwick, Professor of Economics at Carleton University, and a small, tightly co-ordinated group of external and public service experts. They reported directly to Mr. Andras, who was a member of the cabinet. Mr. Andras considered that the impact of the study on the Canadian political and administrative process was great.[62] In a few short months Dr. Lithwick produced a major report entitled, *Urban Canada: Problems and Prospects,* and submitted it to the minister on March 9, 1970.[63] This report was followed by a series of research reports and monographs on a variety of urban topics.[64] In addition, several other public bodies were engaged in urban analysis about this time. The Economic Council of Canada, the Canadian Federation of Mayors and Municipalities, and the Science Council of Canada, to mention only a few, have reported between 1967 and 1971 on various aspects of urban affairs. Dr. Lithwick's work was by far the broadest and in many ways the most significant.[65] His study, for these reasons, has been made central to this analysis.

The following criticism of parts of Dr. Lithwick's study is made in full recognition of its immense breadth and significance for Canada. The spirit of our criticism is in the spirit of Max Weber's observation, "Every scientific 'fulfilment' raises new 'questions'; it *asks* to be 'surpassed' and outdated. Whoever wishes to serve science has to resign himself to this fate."[66]

For our own analysis the future, as envisaged in possible or likely urban forms, and the decisions of critically placed persons who bring about these forms, are of particular concern. The choices likely to confront the Alberta provincial government and its major local authorities are the raison d'etre of this part of our study. Our analysis is centred, therefore, largely on the assumptions and prognoses made in Dr. Lithwick's study.

Assumptions

His major report is divided into three parts. The third, "Urban Prospects," is the most cogent because in it are laid bare some alternative policies available to the federal government as well as the restrictions or conditions which surround the implementation of such policies.[67] Though the prognostic aspect will be considered in the next sub-section, it is necessary to start with one of Dr. Lithwick's major conclusions.

Chapter 5 opens with a fundamental conclusion:

> . . . it (urban prospects) is more a study of what might be than what is, since even according to a restricted definition, no governmental bodies, federal or provincial, can be credited with the development and execution of an urban policy in Canada at the present time. What substitutes for it is a complex set of unco-ordinated, often contradictory, essentially random public policies provided in the wake of strong economic forces which essentially set the agenda for urban growth.[68]

Part II of his study contains the evidence and argument for these conclusions. Though we have no argument with the assertion that strong economic forces essentially set the agenda for urban growth, we do not accept that no governmental bodies can be credited with the development and execution of an urban policy in Canada. The difference between us requires elaboration. It rests partly on the notion of "policy" and partly on the conceptual approach to the issues.

In a section dealing with "The Theory of Public Policy," Dr. Lithwick argues that in Canada:

> There appears to be no agreement anywhere on objectives, only vague and often one-sided views about resources, and little imaginative work on policy development. Thus, there is an enormous conceptual gap at the pinnacle of policy development that colours all derivative policies and frustrates any attempt to bring order into the overall policy system.[69]

There is, in his view, an urban policy vacuum at all levels of government: "no city appears to have any clear set of urban goals," there is no "full blown notion of urban policy" at the provincial level, and at the federal level "there has never been any federal urban policy in name or in practice.[70] By policy, Dr. Lithwick has in mind as essential requirements:

(1) An agreed-upon set of urban objectives;
(2) A full understanding of the limits of public policy in the urban field;

250

(3) A procedure for directing resources to achieving these objectives with these limits — in other words, strategy development.[71]

These requirements assume, in their practical application, that kind of social arrangement typified by a commitment to a public cause. It resembles communities in a state of legitimate war — clear and undisputed leadership co-ordinating people and resources to achieve an agreed-upon common end. Dr. Lithwick comments, "But any intention to harness public policy to a set of comprehensive urban goals suggests the need for a new kind of vertical integration within the hierarchy of government and horizontal coordination with each tier."[72]

    The specification of urban objectives at the local level is envisaged as being most difficult at the stage of collecting together disparate interests, particularly those of the local citizenry. Local government does not necessarily reflect such interests, as Dr. Lithwick correctly observed.[73] He explains these difficulties as due to the "ineffectuality" and "the under developed state" of local government. "The organizational forms and the short planning horizons are throwbacks to the town-meeting politics of the last century."[74] Local government "lacks decision making authority, as a result of its constitutional status." There is an inherent contradiction in this analysis. Citizen involvement and clear-cut decision by a rationally-oriented, constitutionally-untrammeled authority mix like oil and water. One cannot have both in an effective administration. The administration of a metropolis is not, for good reason, that of a commune. Dr. Lithwick argues:

> Consequently, the priorities in urban decision making reflect those of rural-oriented provincial legislatures, jealous of their own political power and fearful of the large urban centres with their economic power and their cosmopolitan outlook. The individual urbanite has very little say in the decisions that affect him most. Had the urban system been managed better, this problem might be relatively remote. As we have stressed, policy in the urban area has been totally inadequate.[75]

Dr. Lithwick believes that by neighborhood councils, local chapters of national parties, and similar arrangements, citizen interests can be "plugged into the policy system," and done in a way which fits into the present constitution.[76] When this is achieved, then disparate interests must be aggregated by resolving conflicts. "Preferably this should entail discussion, debate, analysis, further discussion, and hopefully resolution. In cases of severe conflict, adjudication procedures must be developed."[77] Above all, there must be "Overall consistency with national objectives," and to ensure this a federal presence with clear objectives is necessary.

    Dr. Lithwick's proposals, however, are confused, inadequate, and impractical. The reality of the urban situation is not as he portrays it. The city is known as a place of opportunity. Opportunity, however, is not the same thing as a readiness to innovate. Contrary to popular belief, we suspect that in matters of socio-economic and political organization the city is characterized by conservative attitudes and almost straight-jacketed, structured relations. The difficulties in "reforming" urban government, in getting lending institutions to try condominium dwellings (CMHC had to lead the way in almost every province), are examples of this conservatism. This conservatism has very little, if anything, to do with a rural-oriented provincial legislature, or the town-meeting politics of the last century. Opportunity is perhaps more accurately described as existing within rather narrowly defined limits, but the limits are definable in a variety of circumstances, from those applicable to large versus small manufacturing, large versus small retailing, through lending institutions to professional persons and skilled workers. It is this structured situation that provides high monetary returns and removes the uncertainty associated with other types of high opportunity situations, e.g., as in near anarchic conditions in a political context.

Its very dynamic expresses both opportunity and exploitation of every resource. The social meaning of organized capital is not its steady accumulation but opportunistic investment resulting in a relative advantage over peers and competitors. But such investment is very tightly legally controlled to ensure its security. Within the city are undertaken the most detailed studies of structural controls and manipulatory mechanisms applicable alike to competitive governments and competitive corporations. The city is the centre of political manoeuvre and must remain so if the process of wringing our surplus cash and acquiring advantages over others is to be its prevalent tone. The city is the centre from which acquisitive people influence the affairs of others in both the immediate and remote hinterland. This tone exists internationally no less than within Canada. Dr. Lithwick's approach, however, requires the direction of urban affairs by the federal authority in an undisputed and publicly recognized fashion. He argues, "It replaces the existing concept of many semi-autonomous decision-making centres with one in which the machinery of government is an organic whole."[78] It may be recalled, however, that Lester Pearson, when introducing the bill to set up the Economic Council of Canada in 1963, had remarked that a broad consensus "about the objectives and methods of economic policy and broad agreement on the targets and goals which should be achieved by economic activity" was what was needed.[79]

There is, however, little possibility of achieving any "agreed-upon set of urban objectives" in a socio-political situation of this kind. Even if verbal agreement was attainable the chances of effective application on the ground are slight, for such effectiveness would require the application of the principle contained in the agreement at every point of human decision on any practical issue. The decision of a property owner to seek the re-zoning of his land from residential to commercial, no less than the decision of the federal government to hand to provincial governments rights over critical urban development matters, would need to be made with altruism rather than self-interest in mind.

252

The principal form of current co-operation is the written contract. Punative sanctions by governments are conspicuously rare in urban administration and control tends to be exerted by refusal of financial requests coming from below. Contract and company law is not the epitome of urban relations by coincidence, nor is constitutional and administrative law the epitome of government by default. Self-interest through political manoeuvre in the variety of forms it takes, from profit opportunity through bureaucratic entrenchment to professional camaraderie, is the dominant ethos of urban behavior. It is not the Protestant ethic which guides behavior. What guides behavior is the game of the competitive manipulation of peers within more or less structurally effective parameters according to implicitly agreed-upon rules aimed at the diminution of influence in some and the elevation of it in others. This is the case whether provincial, metropolitan, or municipal affairs, or whether corporations, companies, or public utilities are involved. In our view, the appropriate conceptual framework is provided by F. G. Bailey's *Strategems and Spoils*[80] rather than by any model implying agreed-upon objectives, or the rational applications of means to ends within a collective consensus.

Dr. Lithwick envisages the necessity of obtaining a clear notion "of society's objectives" if the public sector is to perform its task effectively.[81] This unattainable consensus enables him to conceive the possibility of the rational allocation of resources, of devising appropriate means to ends, and of reducing costs to the public good. Men's decisions could then be guided by objectively acquired evidence, the intrusive elements of politics be pushed aside, and the careful calculation of repercussions and effects he made before the decision was taken. This is the utopian condition of perfect knowledge which Mr. Andras also sought, It is blatantly unrealistic. However, Dr. Lithwick does identify the major contributing factor to the present urban situation: that the alleged absence of agreed-upon goals encourages conflict. "Battles are bound to continue over such matters as constitutional authority and revenue needs because there is no context for these discussions."[82] His difficulty is precisely that the real context is not discussion about the form urban policy should take but the competition that exists among political units. Goals there are, but they are perceived only in political terms, not in rationally discussed, co-operative terms.

Urban strategy, as Dr. Lithwick sees it, is the directing of resources towards achieving urban objectives. When objectives have been formulated, and a fuller knowledge of the limitations obtained, then priorities, specific goals, and appropriate means, can be formulated. Finally, it becomes necessary to fortify the strategic process by achieving specific targets in given times — "the cumulative attainment of which will ensure ultimate goal achievement.[83] This was in essence the "kind of machinery" needed for the implementation of an urban policy in Canada, but the manpower to make it effective "just does not exist in Canada at this time." Dr. Lithwick continued:

> The few competent persons available are diffused throughout the system — some in government, others in university and

still others in consulting. There is no concentration of effort, and no consequent advance in the technology of policy making in the urban area. In other words, the scarcest resource for the foreseeable future will be manpower.[84]

The two steps immediately needed were to conserve and rationalize the energy of those available and to generate an intensive training program. He recognized that a large institute of advanced research might achieve both research and training functions. But the condition under which greater knowledge is power is the presence of a structural context that permits effective action. This, we argue, if not already available, is unlikely to be made available to the federal authorities, and therefore mitigates against the effectiveness of Dr. Lithwick's argument and proposals. The proposal would be effective if social and political life could be arranged to permit its application; but to identify the essential requirements of the concept of "policy" in such terms, and in the face of the historical situation of governmental behavior, is to beg a major question.

There is an ambiguity in Dr. Lithwick's assessment of federal influence on extant urban policy which points to an important matter. At one point the following observation is made:

> The Federal government has wide jurisdiction over economic and social problems, and implementation procedures which directly impinge on the nature of urban policies adopted by provinces. Because of this, planning must be stratified, but it also must be integrated. *Clearly, the Federal Government plays an important part in the development of urban policy.*[85] (Our emphasis.)

When discussing the federal role in urban policy, and after dismissing as naive the constitutional expectation of provincial paramountcy over municipal matters, Dr. Lithwick identifies two roles played by the federal government in urban Canada:

> One is a *policy role,* entailing the conduct of public policy that has either a direct or an indirect impact on urban Canada. Policies with direct impact include such areas as housing, where explicit urban programs — such as urban renewal, public housing, land assembly, and sewer treatment programs — are part of the arsenal. The indirect effect arises as a result of the fundamental interdependence of urban units and the economy. With primary responsibility for economic affairs — macro as well as micro — the Federal government has a massive influence on the location, growth and structure of individual urban areas and ultimately, on the urban system.[86] (Emphasis original.)

The second federal role is considered to be a completely passive one, provided by the presence of federal buildings and utilities occupying urban space, and the taxes and salaries paid. The general tenor of his argument is that "the federal government has had a very limited *direct* policy role in the cities."[87] (Our emphasis.) Only two agencies, CMHC and the National Capital Commission, had a clear urban focus, though DREE was said to be moving towards an urban focus.

The various themes contained in these quotations seem to boil down to a recognition of the importance of the federal role in extant policy through vicarious responsibilities of the federal government, such as macro and micro economic affairs. Although the government's *direct* policy role in the cities is said to be limited — and the institution of major consequence is identified as CMHC — its *indirect* impact, arising from the fundamental interdependence of urban units and the economy, is said to be a massive influence on the location, growth and structure of individual urban areas, and ultimately on the urban system. If this is correct, then we must enquire whether or not urban policies may be means of accomplishing policies implicitly and explicitly required in other directions. In other words, is the supposedly limited nature of *direct* urban policy the consequence of the convenience afforded the federal government of using urban affairs — including CMHC and other direct implements of application — to execute policies in other directions? The low priority of housing and urban affairs in the ministerial ranking system would support such a position. On the other hand, our impression is that there is no more constantly recurring theme in the record of *Hansard* since 1935 than housing and urban phenomena. Bilingualism, offshore mineral rights, and others come and go, but housing and the NHA is a steady annual.

If policies in other directions were being served through housing and urban construction, then the issues towards which such manoeuvering was directed would be endemic in Canadian affairs and would require regular and continuous treatment. Our analysis supports this contention. Our view is that the NHA is a critical component of the struggle between the federal and provincial levels of government for influence over local authorities. Federal support for and federal use of lending institutions instead of provincial governments has been deliberate for many decades. The NHA was originally, and has continued to be, the principal federal instrument for circumventing the constitutional prerogatives of the provinces over housing and other aspects of urban development. The close connection of CMHC regional officials, of municipal specialists, of developers with applications for approval of their various plans, and of lending institutions, with themselves and with the federal minister responsible for housing — who administers the greatest financial resource in the country — has led effectively to the inconsequence of provincial decisions on urban affairs. The 1964 amendments to the NHA, which facilitated the spate of high-rise, and city-core commercial and residential development, illustrate the structure within which the federal government was acting. The provinces have always had to be "consulted," to "approve of," to have municipal requests "passed through," etc., but only since about 1967 have provincial "initiatives" had to be taken into account. It is no coincidence, we argue, that 1967 was also the time when certain

provinces initiated a review of the constitution, and had also
established, almost across Canada, provincial housing instrumentalities
of their own. Their instrumentalities were frequently associated with
urban renewal, as was the case in Alberta. Urban renewal, as Dr.
Lithwick observed, was perhaps the most controversial of all CMHC,
programs.[88] In his discussion of the problems of local citizen
participation with local authorities in the "collection stage" of
generating agreed upon urban goals, Dr. Lithwick remarked:

> In the increasingly contentious area of urban renewal, for
> example, it has become apparent that local government has
> tended to act more in the interest of articulate and powerful
> groups — the elite-developers, financiers and businessmen
> — and against the interests of weaker, though usually larger
> groups. Again, in highway planning and land zoning, this
> bias in local politics has arisen.[89]

The provinces were surely not unaware of the potential of these forces,
though, as is discussed below, they were rather ambivalent about
getting too intimately involved with them after the initial experience.

After a succinct review of urban renewal and slum clearance
legislation and objectives,[90] Dr. Lithwick comments as follows:

> There have been problems in the administration of the
> federal program. The success— even the instigation — of urban
> renewal depends upon the initiative of the municipality
> concerned: it must apply for federal assistance. Despite a
> comprehensive educational program directed at the
> municipalities by the Corporation, this critical factor may
> not be realized. Municipal political considerations may deter
> renewal action: the introduction of an unpopular urban renewal
> scheme entailing large disruptive effects may cost the
> enterprising administration a large segment of its popular
> support. But the ready availability of money under the NHA
> for purpose of urban renewal studies and schemes *should
> offset such political considerations* and help to remedy
> ignorance of renewal goals and processes.[91] (Our emphasis.)

As was mentioned in the previous section to this chapter, local
authorities are dependent on the federal initiative — on the federal
minister's final approval of the renewal scheme — to cope with the
political and popular reactions that occur on the local scene. Ethnic
minorities have been vocal both locally and federally. The availability
of money does not offset political considerations when large segments
of population are disturbed and political office is dependent on the votes
of the people. Both Mr. Andras and Mr. Hellyer found it difficult to act
with good conscience in urban renewal. The provinces sought to enter
the political fray with their own provincial instrumentalities, but were

conspicuously silent over their newly won initiative when the political repercussions became clearer in 1968-69. It is precisely, we argue, at the point where explicit issues are raised and revealed openly in their political significance, that no level of government from the local to the federal is capable of effective action. Urban policy, therefore, must be vicariously implemented and the federal government in particular has been a master at this approach.

Dr. Lithwick's analysis verges on this issue, but does not grasp its full significance. In a very apposite and insightful conclusion, he remarks:

> It is obvious that policy directed at the city must discriminate among other objects of public concern. Yet it is the absence of just this abstraction of urban from other policy that has been so apparent in the past. For a great number of possible reasons, the federal and provincial legislatures of this country have been beset by tension between demands of policies of equalization and demands for policies of selective development. The cross-pressures of political life have pushed public policy towards the middle ground, militating against specialized treatment of unique cases. Thus, despite the unique material needs of urban centres, they often have been treated as general categories.[92]

Tensions, however, beset the federal government in its specifically urban role — not to mention those of rural regional degradation and "equal opportunity" for all Canadians.

Two important concerns of the federal government came vicariously to be served by housing and urban developmental projects, namely, the interests of lending institutions, and the interests of the Canadian population in shelter that could be afforded, of cities that could be lived in decently, and of work provided through the construction industry when the economy needed a boost. Policy in these ostensibly separate areas has been remarkably consistent, although this consistency has resulted in the growth of widely disparate circumstances for the two parties concerned. On the one hand, banks and lending institutions generally have come to gain remarkably well. Certain lending institutions were granted added facilities to procure federal charters by letters patent, and other organizational conveniences were granted them by legislation in 1969-1970. Rates of interest, whether determined by international considerations, by inflation, by captured markets, or what have you, have been unprecedentedly high for long-term borrowings in recent years. On the other hand, the cost of housing has exceeded even the middle-income Canadian's salary, particularly in the metropolitan areas; he is becoming obliged to live in apartment dwellings whether he prefers them or not, and urban poverty has become a national issue attended to by parliamentary commissions and research activities from one end of Canada to the other.

This does not imply that the federal government was necessarily aware of what it was contributing. In this sense, Dr. Lithwick is correct in his conclusion that there has never been a deliberate and discriminatory policy for urban areas. But the problem faced primarily by ministers responsible for housing over the years was one of getting enough house starts underway each year to meet the political challenges in the House — challenges based on humane and publicly sensitive grounds. So long as the economy continued to grow, enough money could be found to keep all aspects of government policy afloat. Government policy essentially was to keep the balance, to keep the growing going, to prevent embarrassment over sensitive and visibly serious conditions, and to let market forces set the trend.[93] Commerce and manufacturing were pleased with population and resource concentrations. So long as the Canadian public could be convinced that city growth symbolized the prosperity of Canada and that the individual's personal losses on selling his farm or small town business were just part of the inevitable course of progress, there was no direct challenge through the ballot box to politicians. Public policy had only to patch up the wounds: to care for those left out of the general "prosperity."

Housing for the poor and the replacement of city slums and unsightly areas — both visible conditions — were part of the "special" programs the federal government has interested itself in since 1935, but with notably few results. Urban policy was an adjunct to policies in other directions rather than a policy on which other things depended. There is indeed truth in Dr. Lithwick's conclusions, but the difficulty is that they fail to recognize adequately the structural constraints within which Canadian cities have grown and which in turn have directed that process of growth with its attendant phenomena. Dr. Lithwick is content to let the matter rest on the basis of competition for urban space. The federal government has not only been largely party to the process, but has been deliberately party to it. The situation in which federal ministers have been placed has required they act in certain ways. The structural directives to action have scarcely changed for three decades. The current constitutional conferences, Mr. Hellyer's resignation over a clear matter of policy, the costs of urban renewal, and especially the unequal distribution of benefits from urban renewal between organized capital, on the one hand, and the personal lives of Canadians on the other, all bear witness to the strains under which this structural arrangement is currently laboring. The critical issue for urban policy in Canada is not so much the absence of a policy as the selection and deployment of the instruments available to the various parties involved, particularly governments, in the current structural arrangement, to ensure a re-alignment of inter-connection and influence. The Canadian population is also one of the parties in this game as the poverty studies, interest rates, rural-urban migration, consumer debt, and other phenomena demonstrate.

Dr. Lithwick's analysis viewed urban affairs from the perspective of a process understandable through models common to academic economics.[94] Such models are appropriate only in situations where the goals are defined and the choice is between various known means to these goals. The political economist, on the other hand, is of necessity bound to consider the decisions of men crucially placed in the structure of economic power. It therefore became particularly difficult for Dr. Lithwick to identify those instruments whereby the application of a federal policy on urban affairs could be made effective. He had to rely on attaining an initial consensus and agreement on urban goals. In his discussion of alternative policies, he makes correct reference to the political contexts of policy application, particularly to the rights of provinces in the constitutional context, but there is no reference in his analysis to such things as the structurally advantageous position of the lending institutions, the ability of private corporations to make use of governmental aid through the competitive struggle among provinces and metropolitan cities, or reciprocity in the processes of urban growth and rural regional degradation.

It may be argued that the "complex set of unco-ordinated, often contradictory, essentially random public policies provided in the wake of strong economic forces" does subsume the emphasis we prefer. But the critical task, as we see it, from the perspective of formulating policy for political instruments, is to determine the points at which the tables can be turned; that is, to determine which acts will free governments to set policy effectively and will free "economic forces" to fill in the map. Should the NHA and its series of amendments since 1938 be construed as deliberate government policy? Dr. Lithwick is inclined to see it as an example of the unco-ordinated or even random instances of federal policy. Our view is that it was an essential instrument of power and therefore of policy.[95]

In fairness to Dr. Lithwick we wish to emphasize two points. First, he is very conscious of the possible alternative interpretations of the evidence. He remarks, "We have attempted to sketch several of the dimensions of the urban system (in Chapters 1 and 2 of the *Report*), but are under no illusions that we have completely or even accurately portrayed that system." (Parenthesis ours.) Second, it is clear from several sections that he is fully aware of the importance of structural and organizational matters. In a brief section on "Institutional Machinery" he comments:

> In other words, a choice of organizational structure is a choice of which interests or which values will have preferred access or be given greater emphasis, particularly in the meta-policy stage of determining assumptions and setting priorities of policy making. Organization *is* strategy so that if, for example, urban poverty policy specified participation by the poor in decision making (as it surely should today), institutional provision for this aspect of the program would be essential for its effective operation.[96] (Emphasis and parenthesis is original.)

The third of Dr. Lithwick's essential requirements for a total policy system is the specification of objectives. (The first two are the development of strategies and the comprehension of constraints.) The development of strategies is dealt with under a section headed "Policy in the Unconstrained Future."[97] At this point, we should indicate Dr. Lithwick's final preference for the future of urban development, in order to avoid giving the impression that he subscribes to urban development merely through an unconstrained future. His final preference is for growth to be managed in such a way as to ensure that the "economic dynamic of presently large centres must not be destroyed; the labour force and markets must remain accessible"[98], but that at the same time growth must not add to land-use problems of the metropolitan centres. New cities, capable of attracting increasing economic activity to the point of becoming fully-fledged, mature components of the national urban system, must be created. They should be located "on the primary arteries" which link existing centres. He derives this preferred future from an assumption that the future of urban development can be the consequence of choice, through agreed-upon goals, rather than through a determinism in the decisions of men within the extant politico-economic system. The "unconstrained future" refers, therefore, to the continuation of processes already extant, namely, those which have generated the current crop of problems.

The way in which Dr. Lithwick sets off the unconstrained future against a future achieved by agreed-upon goals is fascinating. Dr. Lithwick writes:

> It is our conviction that the central problem of this approach (that solutions of a conventional sort have limited effect) to the unconstrained future . . . is that it forces us to accept the *inevitability* of a continuation of the processes inherent in the present. Because these processes are abstract and powerful, and have served the needs of those groups who have benefited most, there is great pressure not to tamper with them. If it is wrong, at least it is familiar, and we can patch up some of the excesses through public policy.[99] (Parenthesis ours.)

He then introduces the fact — beautifully analyzed elsewhere in the report and to be discussed below — that "the urban system contains serious contradictions that frustrate the attainment of our present social goals . . ."[100], and foresees prospects in the unconstrained future as even worse than the present situation. He then argues:

> The major alternative open to us is to reject the central assumption that the future is inevitable — that we must as a nation, passively adjust to its demands upon us. Rather, we must consider how we might possibly shape the future urban system so that it can serve our objectives, rather than thwart them.[101]

In the latter quotation the "urban system" is abstracted to the point where it is beyond, and not part of, the decisions of men. It is treated as if the interests vested in it — with 75 percent of the Canadian population

260

already with some stake in it — can be dispersed and the federal authorities be provided with the god-like task of turning into reality the agreed-upon goals of the nation. The abstraction is pushed a stage further by recognizing the uncertainty of anticipating "the kinds of desires that society at large will have in the future."[102] To personify "society" in this way is to simplify matters to where human intentions and "society" become dialectic in nature, and thereby annul the range of choices which the present does in fact provide. The real prospect in these terms is to move to the revolution forthwith! But Dr. Lithwick is more sensitive than that.

The reform of policy making by the federal authorities is seen to rest on three innovations: a national urban council, an urban research unit, and adequate delivery systems. There appears to be a correlation between these instruments and the essential requirements of a total policy system. The first two are considered to be "unobjectionable" innovations. No constitutional issues are involved, and the benefits to all concerned would appear to be substantial.[103]

A national urban council was envisaged as being the formal structure to facilitate the formulation of consistent, meaningful, and acceptable urban policy. It was a forum "where the interests of the various groups involved in the urban policy system could be presented, where objectives could be reconciled, and where feasible plans could be drawn up."[104] A technical staff would be charged with the development of consistent long-term objectives. Short-term goals would be reconciled with the longer ones and alternative programs would be deliberated and selected by the council. The execution of acts would then be consistent and actors would be assured that the goals specified would be met. This concept was elaborated to include regional councils developing regional plans. Their membership would consist "of local federal officials (such as CMHC's regional officers), relevant provincial authorities and representatives of the relevant urban communities..."[105] (Parenthesis original.) The primary purpose of these instruments was to develop the "rational, national urban view, without which we foresee little prospect of dealing effectively with our urban problems."[106]

This proposal, in effect, duplicates the current provincial-federal governmental system, though regional councils need not, perhaps, be limited to provincial boundaries. Its only difference is its putting federal and municipal officials by right into provincial matters. The proposals could be construed as a means of removing urban affairs from political party and governmental competition. It enhances the contribution of technical expertise to decision-making. Dr. Lithwick explicitly had the French planning model in mind. A national urban council, however, was proposed by former Prime Minister Lester Pearson to the federal-provincial conference of December, 1967. At that time it was envisaged more as an instrument for housing than one for general urban policy. But even at the housing level, the provinces had been very cool towards it and the proposal was dropped. Goals, altruism, and a social order prescribed collectively are hardly the practical tools of urban development under present political arrangements.

The urban research unit was envisaged as developing from scratch "much of the information essential to the effective conduct of urban policy."[107] It was also to construct relevant models of the national urban system in order to identify beforehand the implications for that system of the application of any specific policy decision. It was also to be two-tier with the national unit concentrating on the macro-urban system and the regional units becoming expert in their specific areas.

The delivery system is recognized by Dr. Lithwick as the nub of political difficulty. It is the point of strategy development. Jurisdictional conflicts are endemic to the delivery system. Emphasizing the federal role of his study, Dr. Lithwick examines three choices in depth. All three would yield some improvement, but the third, which involves a reconsideration of the whole policy system, is "theoretically the ideal solution."[108] The first of these choices involved no fundamental change, but rather an improvement in the efficiency of the present delivery system.[109] For example, lack of previous awareness of the impact of federal activity in urban affairs has led to indecisive actions and uncertainty of results. Correcting this lack of awareness should improve actions and results. For another example, the correction of conventional notions about urban poverty[110] should lead to programs dealing more effectively with it. Thus urban poverty was found not to be typically a problem of unemployment or underemployment, but rather "the situation of the aged and the handicapped — the unemployables."[111] But, adds Dr. Lithwick, this does not imply that the relative incomes of other groups are adequate. Thus, by clearly identifying particular groups and their discrete needs the present delivery system could be made more effective. There was a great deal the federal government could do merely by improving the present delivery system. This was achievable largely by improving its own "*awareness* of urban reality."[112]

Dr. Lithwick found in his research that he was "unable to discover sufficient information on the dimensions of the problem, the federal impact on the urban systems, their causes, and their effects to prescribe a particular course of action." He added:

> The need for fundamental research into such areas as the environment and the community would appear to be a most relevant federal objective at this time.[113]

We would support this suggestion, and particularly the study of small-scale, even one house, sewage systems which do not pollute the environment. This single technical discovery alone would radically alter the present layout of city suburbs with their dependence on sewer trunk lines, the high cost of land tied to developers' land holdings and service provisions, and would enlarge the possible choice of community types available to urban dwellers.

His second policy option, U-11, involves a total federal approach. This approach is a further step from — not an alternative for — the first. It rests on the co-ordination of federal delivery systems and their impact. It would imply that urban policy of the federal government was "not only headed in the direction of our objectives, but operating complementarily permitting the various parts to reinforce each other in that task."[114] The obvious technique — interdepartmental committees that encourage awareness of each other's role — is rejected on the basis of it being "a generally ineffectual approach." It fails because agencies argue for their particular interests rather than focusing on the common needs.[115] In an insightful analysis of current federal departmental practice and attitude, Dr. Lithwick remarks:

> Our enquiry into the conduct of most relevant federal agencies, however, reveals that they are generally insensitive to the urban problems they help generate. Our interviews with and questionnaires to most agencies reveal that generally they are single-objective oriented, and that these objectives are set in Ottawa, without an urban perspective.[116]

This evidence clearly indicates the socio-political complexity of intra-governmental machinery alone. Our own evidence on the Alberta provincial government machinery and attitude supports Dr. Lithwick's federal findings. The highly interdependent nature of the urban would make this feature particularly handicapping. Dr. Lithwick argued for "a distinct spokesman for the Federal Government's urban objectives so that these objectives are always clearly articulated and promoted as a guide to the delivery of policy. All federal agencies with an urban impact would need to consider their policies in the light of these objectives..."[117] It would not be a matter of courtesy, but priority, that the relevant authority could claim this attention. The Cabinet was seen as the level for the resolution of conflict among participating authorities.

There could hardly be a less realistic proposal! The dictum of Cabinet secrecy represents not only a symbol of Cabinet and party solidarity, but a hiding from the public of conflicts between elected and appointed authorities. The cameraderie that exists among a minister, his department, and its officials is important. This is not to say that the Cabinet is a centre for horse-trading between ministers and civil servants; but rather that the emotions and hopes of people with pride in their work and in their contribution to the solution of particular Canadian problems is put on the line, put to the test, by every minister proposing before the Cabinet a particular course of action. Mr. Hellyer and the task force proposals show this. The minister's own reputation within his department is dependent upon the success he may have within the Cabinet. Adverse Cabinet decisions can be a critical test of the loyalty of men and of the efficacy of a government department. Dr. Lithwick's proposal suffers the dual handicap of assuming (i) that a relatively junior and only recently established minister of housing and urban affairs would get other urban-influencing ministers and departments effectively to follow his call on urban policy, and (ii) that the Cabinet could be an enduring instrument for the reconciliation of conflict. The condition for the success of Dr. Lithwick's proposal is a near-dictatorship with a hireling Cabinet. This is hardly typical of Canada at the present time.

The third policy option, U-111, offering the theoretically ideal solution, envisages a re-allocation of the delivery systems — spending as well as legislative power — over the various levels of government. It involves fundamental constitutional changes. Dr. Lithwick argues that the process is already underway, but from the bottom up — "The growth of metropolitan governments is a response to the need for urban services that transcend narrow jurisdictional boundaries."[118] He argues correctly that the "final form of the metropolitan governments is a compromise between functional requirements and the preservation of political power." The political competition in this instance is identified as being between provincial governments and major cities. The way out for the cities has been a desire for alternatives such as city-provinces and changed constitutional status. But Dr. Lithwick does not appear to appreciate fully what the consequences of this alternative will be. While the growth of metropolitan city government is certainly a search for more appropriate scales of urban governmental organization and urban planning, it is equally a response to the consequences of inordinate concentration and the escalating public costs which have accompanied such concentration. By taking to itself the right to locate industry anywhere in the country, the federal government would in turn be threatening the jugular vein of metropolitan centres. City governments are unlikely to treat this with equanimity. Dr. Lithwick's proposal therefore only throws to the federal level the political conflict hitherto occurring on the provincial level.[119]

The politics of federal action, as Dr. Lithwick sees it, rest on the relationship between the national economy and the urban system. This relationship is expected to expand as urban populations, global economic planning, and the interdependency of urban concentrations increase, and the need for co-ordination becomes increasingly apparent. He argues:

> The more we move into national economic planning, the more essential will be the need for associated special planning. Such specific matters as industrial location, inter-urban transport and communications, and inter-urban migration will be of direct federal concern. In contrast, a number of highly local functions, such as public housing, urban renewal, and even the location of federal facilities - post offices, other federal buildings, transport routes - will fall into the domain of local government.[120]

It would seem from this vision that the federal government's problem is being unable to see the wood for the trees. Mr. Hellyer's and Mr. Andras's concern for public housing and urban renewal, their compulsive desire for on-site inspections, and their wish for "participation" by affected persons was misguided conscientiousness. Such matters in the future would become increasingly local affairs while industry would be located by federal direction, the appropriate linkage of city with city would be facilitated by transport corridors, and people would be linked by systems of migration from one urban node to another. The constitution becomes merely a variable in this streamlined urban economic vision — it (the policy option) seems to establish the relevant political roles on the basis of purely functional analysis.[121] The vision may, he admits, because of this political component and because of the state of our knowledge, never be achieved. But "the constitutional reforms presently underway" should not treat this policy option as irrelevant nor should the "merits of the ideal approach" he deprecated.[122]

The provinces appear to be left out of consideration except in so far as a category of "provincial urban goods" is assigned them, but this is not elaborated.[123]

Dr. Lithwick fails to appreciate that the relationship between the national economy and the urban system has been precisely the typical concern of federal activity since 1935. The locus of decision regarding where housing will be built, however, is now transferred from lending institutions to the government itself. Urban migration has for long been of federal concern as CMHC and NHA, in their attempts to house the migrants, well demonstrate. The change in federal planning, in Dr. Lithwick's view, is rather one of scale, to a *national* urban *system* rather than isolated metropolitan centres, and of the centralization of power and authority to make this scale effective. Dr. Lithwick's suggested changes weaken or remove many of the presently existing checks and balances on federal power.

There is also a point Dr. Lithwick does not consider. He assumes increasing national planning, and discusses its relation to special planning. But Dr. Lithwick forgets that "space" to private corporations means western-world space, i.e. outside the areas under communist-type planning. The modern corporation is international, and unless other nations of the world move towards similar national planning, the politico-economic environment of Canada may come to prove less and less attractive if Canada alone were to proceed on a planned basis. We do not wish to elaborate the point, but the federal government is precisely the point in Canadian political and national economic affairs where this aspect cannot be ignored. We suggest that a Canadian national urban policy may not easily take precedence over Canadian international economic policy, just as it may prove impossible to achieve as a deliberate policy inside the nation itself.

In addition to policies assuming an "unconstrained future," Dr. Lithwick considers certain policy options in a "constrained future." The constrained future emerges at the time when "we are prepared to design the future."[124] The chances of such a constrained future emerging are considered quite good, if only because "the *increment* in urban population over the next 30 years will be almost twice as great as the current urban population."[125] New facilities and construction to meet the increment would provide the opportunities to design the future. The need for replacement of existing degraded facilites will also provide such opportunities.

The urban options under this condition are envisaged as:
(1) Policy option C-1: Limiting Urban Growth. Though this option is controversial in itself, the federal government may readily manipulate

Canadian immigration policy. The rural population could also be fixed by some means and thereby the population growth of urban areas could be regulated. This option is recognized as conflicting with other national objectives such as growth in itself and a regional balance, and may be "politically unacceptable."[126]

(2) Policy option C-II: Managing Urban Growth. This is Dr. Lithwick's preferred option. It was outlined above, but needs some elaboration. Whereas limiting urban growth may reduce the benefits of concentration, this option attempts to retain such benefits while reducing costs. The option is seen as forestalling the consequences on costs of scarce urban land by opening up new urban amenities — "Improving access within our existing urban areas ultimately has been self-defeating because it has led to more sprawl; more congestion, and so forth."[127] It is an attempt to enlarge the range of choice available to businesses and persons whose current alternatives are to locate either in metropolitan centres or in poorly developed small towns or rural areas.

The *modus operandi* for achieving this second option is outlined by Dr. Lithwick in three supporting programs:

(a) Limiting sprawl at the pressure points. Here the task is to identify such points — though just what constitutes a "point" is not mentioned — and to procure the consent of the relevant municipality and province, or plurality of these, for federal initiative there. It would appear that Dr. Lithwick is really suggesting the development by federal initative in certain extant suburban developments whose growth has been stunted by metropolitan cores affecting them. He is by no means clear on this point. The suburb identified, i.e., the point, is then subjected to raising population densities, assisting growth in specified ways such as approval of land use plans, land assembly, mortgage control, etc. This would ensure the right type of growth for the needs of the overall metropolitan system. It sweeps aside much of the initiative now resting with the other levels of government.

(b) The second supporting program is one envisaging support for urban infra-structures already existing in currently small areas linked to the main urban system. This appears to be aimed at satellite developments, though Dr. Lithwick seems to be at pains to avoid this terminology. He recognizes that most of this type of development would fall to junior levels of government with co-ordinated assistance through the N.H.A., transit facilities, and new federal buildings.

(c) Developing New Communities from the grassroots up in such a way that they become fully planned in themselves and in integration with the general metropolitan system. High-speed, mass transit systems would be provided so as effectively to remove the automobile from such urban systems. Public acquisition of land would yield to public authorities all incremental land values. It offers all the opportunities of pre-planning of right-of-ways, for example, which were thought to accrue to the Mexico Cities, Canberras, New Towns, and the like, of this world, but the purpose in this case is to make the perfectly planned commercial and industrial city rather than a national shrine or garden city. Dr. Lithwick recognizes that the concept is not new, but sees its uniqueness in its integration with a full (national?) urban system and its dynamic processes.[128]

The point Dr. Lithwick emphasizes in discussing this policy option is that it is a *national urban policy,* rather than merely a federal urban policy. It assumes the co-ordination of decision and the integration of action among all levels of government and of their planning and regulative instrumentalities. The national urban policy would co-ordinate all interests, not merely that of the federal alone. The national urban council is the means. The federal urban policy, by contrast, is associated with national economic development, internal and international mobility, and regional disparities — "The national dimension of the urban system makes such as (sic) federal policy essential, particularly if we sincerely intend to design the future."[129] The specific federal role is seen as being "highly aggregative in the preferred option."[130] This presumably means coercive. Dr. Lithwick sees the federal interest "in largely macro issues" as offering more scope for junior levels of government — "Because the developmental problems would be modified, the extant problems in cities would be more manageable." Most of the planning functions, "indeed the whole municipal sphere, would come under its (provincial) jurisdiction."[131] (Parenthesis added.)

Prognoses

Dr. Lithwick develops an intriguing, but admittedly speculative, analysis of the future urban process under conditions of an unconstrained future. He makes this analysis in order to strengthen his plea for deliberately constraining the current urban process. The essential problems, as he sees them, are the increasing costs derived from inherent contradictions within the process. He identifies the broad national urban trends as:

> the growing polarization of economic activity in the major metropolitan areas, the shift towards labour-intensive service activity, the rapid population expansion to meet these demands, the increasing importance of in-migration as a source of this population and the consequent draining of rural and small urban areas, and the growing importance of inter-urban links which will reinforce the dominance of the largest elements in the macro-system.[132]

The expansion of the cities will apparently produce great economic benefits. Real incomes will rise from 50 to 100 percent per capita which could provide the individual "with an enormous potential range of choice, not only of commodities, but of life styles themselves, permitting the attainment of individual and collective welfare beyond any level conceivable at present."[133] But on the other hand, the great costs of the current urban process are likely to reduce greatly these possibilities, "and may in the end totally eliminate them." Dr. Lithwick then enumerates ten likely consequences, namely:

(1) Land will continue to become so costly as to preclude all but extremely dense residential development within reasonable distance from the core.
(2) Families with children seeking single-family homes will have to commute for several hours per day.
(3) Downtown areas will be congested, polluted, and noisy.
(4) The drain on public funds to service the increasingly sprawled suburban areas and the increasingly intractable problems of the core will lead to higher taxes and yet higher land costs.
(5) Industries will flee to the suburbs leaving the poor without access to jobs, and the inner city without a tax base.
(6) Skilled workers will move increasingly to the suburbs with the jobs, reducing the quality of resident leadership in the core.
(7) The growing number of firms necessarily located in the core will require white-collar, technologically sophisticated service employees. Their space needs will squeeze the urban poor even further.
(8) The need to transport service workers to the core will add to the pressure on core space.
(9) The steady erosion of stable neighborhoods, the growing economic uncertainty facing core dwellers; and the deteriorating quality of their environment will create an increasingly explosive situation.
(10 The increased segregation of economic classes in the city because of land costs will serve to fragment the community at a time when divisiveness is of great concern to the nation.[134]

The benefits, presumably real incomes, are expected to rise at steady rate, but costs "will grow exponentially because of the interdependency of urban problems, and their sensitivity to growth pressures which we have forecast to be extremely great."[135] This is a fundamentally important conclusion derived largely from Dr. Lithwick's empirical studies. We have observed a similar situation occurring in the new metropolitan cities of Alberta, as will be discussed in Volume II. It is these fundamentally opposed trends — the benefits to producers of goods by increasing concentration on the one hand and, on the other, the escalation of costs particularly in the publicly supplied and financed sector — which make the very nub of future problems if they are allowed to continue. Dr. Lithwick expresses the issue in these terms:

> The approach (attacking by public policy the symptoms rather than the causes) will fail because the exponentiality inherent in the costs of growth will lead to a steadily increasing need for public assistance which in the extreme will eliminate the potential gains from urban development. Thus, the apparent welfare gains will be illusory, for real income will be watered down by the inflationary pressures latent in the accelerating costs of the urban system, and chopped into by the taxes required to deal with the growing problems.[136] (Parenthesis added.)

The ramifications of these opposed trends are enormous. Most significantly, Dr. Lithwick does not see market competition as reducing the conflict. Local urban dwellers experiencing a costly problem, and local urban manufacturing gaining benefits from its locality and tariff advantages, will not be obliged to reconcile their disparate situations by local means. Dr. Lithwick explains: "Because of the economic dominance of the largest centres, which of necessity also have the greatest urban problems, their high-level costs will be transmitted throughout the national economy."[137] Private manufacturing costs, as well as higher taxation to meet the public facilities considered necessary to alleviate growing urban costs, will together be passed on over the general range of Canadian citizens and company consumers. (Albertan farmers, for example, will become increasingly squeezed in the cost-return dilemma.) The strong monopoly position of firms in the Toronto-Montreal corridor, Dr. Lithwick argues, has made the Canadian economy far from competitive. "As a result, they do not have to adjust to rising costs, and indeed can easily pass them on. With further urban polarization, these monopolistic advantages will increase, so that the ability to impose the costs of urbanization on the rest of the nation will grow."[138] The prognosis under conditions of a continued unconstrained future, is "wasted resources and a growing oppressiveness of the urban system on individuals." From our more narrow perspective and enquiry we would support Dr. Lithwick's prognosis.

A National Urban Policy?

Too few years have elapsed since Dr. Lithwick's study to reveal the effectiveness of Mr. Andras's urban policy for Canada. Several of Mr. Andras's speeches seemed to suggest he was moving towards putting an urban policy into action, but the political scene did not appear to be favorable.

The first constitutional debate in the federal House was held in January, 1970 when the Prime Minister moved to set up a joint committee of the Senate and the House of Commons which would examine and report upon proposals made public by governments in Canada during the course of the constitutional review.[139] The review had been agreed upon at the federal-provincial conference of February, 1968.

Mr. Trudeau's opening remarks described a contradictory situation. All parties in the federal House had expressed interest in debating the process of constitutional review and of participating in the constitutional debate. At the same time, however, "there is a feeling in certain provincial quarters, and even in the country at large as expressed by members of provincial legislatures . . . that there is basically nothing wrong with the present constitution . . . "[140] The constitutional debate, in the Prime Minister's view, had started at the instigation of the provinces during the November, 1967, Confederation for Tomorrow Conference in Toronto, convened by the Prime Minister of Ontario, John Robarts. At that time the provinces had pressed the federal government to participate, but it had not done so and was sceptical of the urgency of the matter.[141] In its view a good deal of preparatory work had to be done, one aspect of which was a Canadian Bill of Rights.

Mr. Trudeau explained the attitude of provincial governments in terms of a changing power relationship at the provincial-federal level. Between 1954 and 1964 federal expenditures increased 56 percent, but provincial expenditures (including municipal expenditures) increased 204 percent. "The provinces realized in 1967 that new power relationships were being developed between the federal government and the provinces. It is perhaps natural that they wanted to insert these power relationships into a constitution which would be redefined."[142] What, then, was the Prime Minister's explanation for the alleged *volte-face* in the recent attitude of the provinces towards constitutional review?

After the period of euphoria, when the provincial governments recognized their increasing power, they came to realize that they had much to do under the existing constitution and that solutions to pressing problems could not wait. Industrialization and urbanization were increasing at a rapid rate. Mr. Trudeau remarked:

> And I think that urban growth has caused a great number of problems, particularly at the municipal level . . . I believe that after several years of debate on constitutional matters some provinces and municipalities realize that they really have much left to do and that all these problems must find a solution before the constitution is to be revamped. I think this is the reason why the provinces and municipalities very frequently suggest that the constitution is really of relative importance and that the federal government should not spend to much time considering it.[143]

The federal government, by contrast, was responsible for national unity, and the problems "that might lead to the disruption of Canada as a whole" were its particular concern.

What this parliamentary circumlocution really covers must be left to historians to reveal, but it is sufficient to illustrate the intense political competition existing among all levels of government in Canada. The proposals of the Canadian Federation of Mayors and Municipalities, discussed in our Introduction, bear witness to the competition present at the municipal-provincial level. This, we suggest, is the empirical political reality within which the urbanization process in Canada is occurring.[144]

National unity, as Mr. Trudeau saw it, was more than a matter of languages - " . . . disparities between regions and between the various classes of society can contribute to destroy national unity just as much as linguistic issues can."[145] DREE, tax sharing agreements, welfare, and other special allowances were set up precisely to contribute to maintaining a regular income for all Canadians. Transport, communications, and federal-provincial relations in non-constitutional fields remained now, as in the past, other important features of national unity. In the last analysis, it rested on the desire of people to share a consensus, a willingness of people to live together.[146] The existential paradox was expressed by the Prime Minister in these terms:

> The people have to be willing to recognize that the nation exists in order that it might continue to exist. This means, in reality, that all major groups, all important participants in a nation, have to feel that they are better within the nation than outside it.[147]

The continuation of this consensus was imperative — "It is this principle which guided federal action and, indeed, federal strategy in its whole approach to the constitutional question."[148]

The federal contribution to the maintenance of this state of mind required that the review be undertaken only "within a country which was fairly stable, and by that I mean at a time when the federal government and the provincial governments were both strong."[149] Although the whole of the constitution, rather than merely convenient parts, had to be reviewed, in the federal government's opinion there were two basic principles that had to be maintained. First, that Canada would continue as one federal country, i.e., that the federal form of government should be preserved. Second, that forms of special arrangements should not be entrenched whereby members of parliament from one part of the country would have less power than members from another part. He did not mean by this, such special arrangements as the federal government might wish to make over programs or activities with one or another part of the country, but political representation in the federal parliament. The central, essential powers of the country had to be maintained and the provincial parts be uniformly and fairly represented within its parliament. Mr. Trudeau considered it necessary:

> that Canadians realize that we are discussing all of the aspects which are of immediate concern to them, questions which have to do with responsibility for the cities, for poverty, for education, and for Indians. These precise questions are part of the constitutional review upon which we have now embarked."[150]

It is not our intention to review in detail the debate that followed. However, certain points are important. Robert Stanfield, Leader of the Opposition, urged the committee in its hearings across the country to attend in particular to a group of elected people so far too little heard from in constitutional conferences. He was referring to municipal councils. He remarked:

> It is my hope ... that the parliamentary committee will provide for the representatives of our cities, towns and counties precisely that forum and that public platform which as been denied to them through the past quarter century with regard to this matter.[151]

He suggested also that if some resource persons were to be provided to the committee, it would consider consulting the Canadian Federation of Mayors and Municipalities. He proceeded then to analyse the items over which the federal government had exerted pressure on the provinces, and those they had soft-pedalled in the previous conferences. Why had welfare been pressed, but pollution and urban affairs circumvented? "Why use welfare to seek an increase in federal authority rather than pollution? Is this the subconscious manifestation of the policy of confrontation?"[152]

Mr. Stanfield, after commenting on the apparent state of concern of the Liberal members at his remarks, commented:

> Certainly the federal government is engaged in a protracted struggle to preserve — not only preserve, but to increase — the federal authority in some fields. To date, however, it has been negligent in other areas where difficulties are arising as a result of technology and modern developments.[153]

These areas were those where most people would consider jurisdiction to be important. The committee therefore might consider a new area of thrust for the federal government.

There was a certain restraint in Mr. Stanfield's speech — he was anxious not to compromise the chances of success of a constitutional review, yet to indicate the critical nature of the issues that underlay it. On the other hand, David Lewis of the NDP was more blunt and explicit. He had wondered, as he had sat in on previous conferences, "whether I was present at an auction of power seekers to find the particular place where they can exercise more power without defining the purpose for which that power is to be used. It is a sense of competition between the federal government and the provinces. It is a sense of auctioning parts of Canada between the federal and provincial authorities."[154] He then said, quite bluntly, that it was not a question of the provinces having increased their powers under the constitution. "It is the development of the industrial urbanized society which has forced upon the provinces expenditures way beyond anything contemplated 100 years ago. That is the problem that faces Canada."[155] The increases in provincial (and municipal) expenditures vis-a-vis those of the federal government, which the Prime Minister had mentioned, were the product of the present constitution. He added:

> Everybody talks about urbanization and the effects of urbanization. The fact is that this is the source of the demand for a review of the constitution.[156]

In Mr. Lewis's view the urgent need was for "the kind of national approach which the present government has refused to take."[157] The prospect of the federal government moving out of the cost-shared programs, and of failing to assist the poorer provinces, made it impossible for provincial premiers to accept the prospect of a constitutional review with anything but alarm.

Both the major opposition parties supported strengthening the federal position on urban affairs. Mr. Trudeau had been severely attacked for upholding the constitutional position against the recommendations of the Hellyer Task Force. This enabled the opposition parties to attack the government as ineffective, impotent, and so forth. But neither opposition party undertook to analyze the forces and their structural connections, which were bringing about the log jam at the city level itself.

On February 2, 1970, Robert Andras announced his policy on the capital budget of CMHC for 1970. This budgetary item had, for the first time, been brought forward in the year in order to let lower levels of government have some idea of what they could expect from federal sources.[158] The budget raised CMHC's authorized loans under specified sections of the NHA to $854 million from $680 million the previous year. Of this amount some $570 million was to go towards various programs connected with low income families and persons. This aspect was largely a continuation of federal policy started in Mr. Nicholson's time, about 1963.

The point of major significance was the making of $265 million available to provincial housing authorities for the public housing program under section 35 of the NHA. The minister remarked: "In almost all cases, this matches provincial requests." The provincial housing authorities were therefore to be supported in this particular area of activity pretty well up to the maximum of their requests. Some $200 million was to be "reserved temporarily for new innovations and a balancing of distribution based on need."[159] The minister hoped that areas of acute poverty could be serviced by this provision, but in any event the sum would permit the construction of 35,000 housing units specifically for low income families if not used for special purposes. This alone was a considerable increase over previous construction in this area of need.[160] In addition the vote allowed for loans to assist sewage treatment plants and major trunk sewers up to $75 million — an increase over 1969's $50 million figure for this purpose. Other non-housing aspects of the NHA's provisions were not to be increased and urban renewal was to be left at the 1969 figure. In all, some $724 million was to go to housing and $130 million only to infrastructure programs. The minister concluded his remarks by saying:

> We, in co-operation with the provinces, are seeking to encourage and establish long-range budgeting for all NHA programs.[161]

It is apparent from this budget and remarks that a rather new and more co-operative approach was being adopted by the federal minister. Quebec had, since 1969, obtained agreement with the federal government over an annual "master agreement" covering certain NHA programs and was renewing it in 1970. But individual projects under the agreement "still required individual project approval by CMHC."[162] The new approach, therefore, was one involving annual planning, but each project was to be approved by CMHC. The federal government and

273

CMHC were still far away from giving the provinces the freedom over building standards and design which they might prefer to have. Mr. Andras's budget statement for CMHC had made no reference to guidelines on public housing — a policy statement expected since the previous summer.

During 1970 and 1971, Mr. Andras made several speeches in Canada and abroad.[163] These speeches, particularly the early ones, follow closely the ideas expressed by Dr. Lithwick in his *Urban Canada: Policies and Prospects*.

The February 27, 1970, speech to the Canadian Institute of Public Affairs, Toronto, was a resume of Dr. Lithwick's report. It dealt with the federal unawareness of its role in the cities; with the city as a complex and interdependent system most of whose problems were derived allegedly from intense competition for urban space and high rates of growth; with the interaction of public costs and private advantages; with the urban poor, transport, the national urban system; and with the goals and co-operation considered essential before a practical solution could be implemented.

On June 10, Mr. Andras addressed the 33rd Annual Convention of the Canadian Federation of Mayors and Municipalities in Halifax. Since he had spoken to them a year previously, he took that opportunity to identify the previous twelve months "as the year in which the Canadian people and their institutions have begun to accept the realities of *urban* Canada and all that goes with that altered conception of ourselves."[164] (Emphasis original.) This new self-conception had to become "the basis on which the political institutions of this country seek to provide leadership and response."[165] It was to be a leadership that recognized the role of knowledge and the widest possible level of understanding rather than "furious activity" and symbolic gestures of solution.

The minister had been deeply impressed by the unanticipated consequences of the benevolently intended solutions of the past - e.g., urban renewal which displaced the people it was intended to aid. The CFMM had itself contributed to the identification of the futility of "simple, straight line, linear kind of responses." The recent studies had identified the dimensions of the major urban problems and "have now been set out and early registered with all my colleagues in the federal Cabinet."[166] As a result the interconnectedness of federal acts to these problems and to the quality of urban life in Canada had become appreciated.

The minister was familiar with the difficulties of municipal finance — "The evidence of municipal finances does confirm a rapidly deteriorating fiscal position."[167] But the actual monetary supply was complicated by political considerations. In purely monetary terms, from 1951 to 1968, local government expenditures, except for Quebec, had increased from $721 million to $3.5 billion. Revenues had increased from $614 million to $3.3 billion. The direct tax source of local authorities, however, had increased by only three times while the transfers from higher levels of government - especially provincial *conditional* grants -

had increased eight times. The municipalities in consequence had been kept "in a state of controlled inability to respond."[168]

Mr. Andras then commented:

> One sometimes wonders if — in some cases — it is not a fear of municipal power in the political sense — that may be a factor.
>
> Is it by any chance the old fashioned male attitude toward the wife — 'keep them barefoot, pregnant and in the kitchen, so they won't bother us?'[169]

He did not elaborate further, but his remark led to applause as the wording of his speech shows.[170] Mayors had often argued they knew better than anyone what the problems were, all they needed was the money. But this was precisely the point to which the minister was opposed. The provinces in 1967 had adopted the same response to the federal proposals of that time.

The case against municipal rights to money, as outlined by Mr. Andras, rested on their inability alone to deal with the causes and consequences of urbanization. The causes, in many cases, lay beyond their jurisdiction.

> You — the cities — are the recipients of the effects (good and bad) of so many policies which clearly lie in other jurisdictions — and which transcend municipal and often provincial boundaries.[171] (Parenthesis original.)

Dealing only with "in-city" situations is far from simple. The high rates of increase in municipal expenditure resulted from higher standards of urban services and they were not "prone to productivity gains," as could be seen from housing. The costs had escalated in the public sector, but had not produced the tax revenues to the municipalities. Mr. Andras added: "those who want them must be made aware of the costs entailed."[172] He did not elaborate, but identified the following:

> Finally, and perhaps most important, these costs may be the result of a passive attitude to urban expansion or even, perhaps, an illogical worship of unplanned, uncontrolled fast rate of urban growth — a process which, when undertaken without foresight, leads to extremely rapid and inefficient urban development and hence inordinate pressures on the municipal treasury.[173]

This reasoning, though fascinating, is extraordinary.

Mr. Andras's perception appears to stop at the point of public expenditure, though he recognizes the urge, the illogical worship, of fast growth. Why did he not go on to recognize private investment and its relation to municipal expenditure? Why use circumlocutionary abstractions to explain a phenomenon capable of explicit identification? The illogical worship of fast growth is no mere state of mind. It is

275

the consequence of situational understanding. When a mayor has made a public investment whose funding is dependent upon the continued growth of user services, to avoid increasing the mill rate to pay for it he is in a situation which makes fast growth seem attractive. Similarly, private investment whose return is dependent on rapidly expanding local markets is in a situation which encourages favoring fast growth. There is no need for a minister, intent upon examining and understanding causes rather than symptoms, to leave his explanation at the level of abstractions.

Public transfers of money from senior governments can readily, as Mr. Andras recognized, lead to an exacerbation of wasteful urban expansion, and "to an even greater crisis in the future." He then added:

> We can see, therefore, why we have not responded to your demands for new resources with blind haste — we are unwilling to commit resources that not only will fail to solve your current problems, but will aggravate your future problems and demand an ever-increasing share of public resources.[174]

Simplistic solutions had been tried and failed — "it has created a crisis of public confidence in our ability as elected representatives to do anything about these growing problems." This was cold comfort to a conference of mayors! These were the very men in closest contact with the drive and demands of private investment and economic productivity, on the one hand, and with public poverty, public resentment, hostile tax payers, and the pressures of planners, on the other. The federal government was not to act hastily, it was to be knowledgeable, planned and decisive in its approach. Just because the federal authorities had not fully understood "the urban system" thus far, and were now gearing up "to deal with the urban totality — with the city as a complex system," the mayors were obliged to wait and cope as best they could. Mr. Andras did admit, however, "that within any one city — you the *municipal authorities* should have the dominant role — and the two other governments should be, in the main, supportive."[175] (Emphasis original.) The provinces too, it seemed, would now know what their role was likely to be. The answer Mr. Andras proposed was:

> a forum for Federal-Provincial-Municipal consultation on urban matters — all together — with the municipalities and the Federal government having a *legitimate, recognized* place at the table with the provinces — and to lay on that table all federal policies and actions that affect the cities — for discussion — for co-ordination with provincial-municipal needs.[176] (Emphasis original.)

This was to be recommended to the federal cabinet. The views of the provinces were to be sought as to whether they would be agreeable to some formal structure, "perhaps an urban council — in which political representatives and officials of all three levels of government could discuss urban policies regularly."

This was the basic instrument for attaining the national consensus on goals and policies that Dr. Lithwick's proposals rested upon. There was little doubt that the CFMM and the mayors would support it. They had already sought an explicit integral membership with the provinces and federal governments in any amended Canadian constitution. Mr. Andras then commented:

> I will assure the provinces — as I assure you — that this is not a federal takeover bid — it is not a federal unilateral intervention — it is a desire to get the key people together for the purposes of making a rational choice for a Canadian urban future.[177]

Mr. Andras concluded by stating that he rejected a big stick approach by the federal authorities. He would not advocate centralism in a federal system. On the other hand, he also rejected a balkanization of the approach to urban problems. Both concepts were myths. He believed "in decentralization of authority — after policy agreement between jurisdictions — to the lowest common denominator — the closest possible approach to the 'one-to-one' relationship with the people, we in government, in authority, are supposed to be serving."[178] Such an approach required the full participation of the municipal level. The only item which Mr. Andras forgot in this plea for collective action, was the jurisdiction ascribed to the provinces in 1867, and the provinces' recent appreciation of their significance within the reality of politics that the urban epitomizes.

In September, 1970 Mr. Andras was delighted "that provincial ministers responsible for urban affairs, at their Winnipeg meeting recently, took one absolutely vital step."[179] They had agreed to establish, first, clear-cut objectives and priorities, and only then to consider the allocation of resources. This was a conference to which municipal representatives had been invited. Mr. Andras saw it as a step towards a national urban policy — a turning point, an exciting opportunity. He had spent some time in thought — "to think out our own ideas on how structures might be set up to achieve policy co-ordination, to develop the federal government's own views on urban renewal, to come up with some real ideas on cost-sharing."[180] He was desperately anxious not to repeat 1967, "which was itself only a repeat of many such instances in the past." He was about to initiate discussion with the provinces about "ways in which we can reach a consensus on social objectives, on priorities and on allocation of resources." But, he added blithely, "Not — let me stress — with the objective of any level giving up any of its present powers."[181] Later in this speech he envisaged the federal role, after the structure of co-operation was agreed upon, as being one of progressively laying before those interested "all federal policies and plans for coordination — and modifications when need be — with provincial and municipal needs."[182] The federal government now had plans, and intended to implement them after modification by the junior levels of government.

These may be the techniques of political public-speaking, but they also suggest the thoughts of a person trying desperately to cope with impossible situations. There is ample evidence in *Hansard* and elsewhere to suggest that Messrs. Nicholson, Hellyer, and Andras were all most devout, hardworking, and sincere persons. Their political opponents were outspoken on this point. But the naivety of their respective approaches — with the possible exception of Mr. Hellyer's confrontation with the Prime Minister over the constitutional rights of the provinces — beguiles the difficulties of the reality within which they were operating. Mr. Andras's public speeches contain persistent reference, almost apologetically, to his use of motherhood pleas for co-operation, co-ordination, consensus, social objectives, etc. To him they "are vitally more than motherhood words. They articulate the only way we can approach the burgeoning problems of the cities today."[183] The desperation of tone implicit in these concepts was articulated by Mr. Andras in his comment at Penticton about how near Canada had come to the brink of the same disasters as had befallen cities elsewhere. The present, therefore, offered "an opportunity for greatness almost unique among affluent countries."[184]

The only new conclusion elucidated in the Penticton speech was that "Private investment, too, will have to be guided as never before (and I don't mean voluntary guidelines . . . we've had some experience with them), to achieve well-thought-out goals of urban design."[185] He did not elaborate, except to say that "some time-honoured beliefs are going to have to be challenged." But the examples of this he gave were to challenge the concept of growth for growth's sake, and the need to qualify the answer to the question, "Does it pay?" by reference to the social comfort and stimulation of the individual person. There was to be no "urban czar" at the federal level, no super-ministry; but the research was being done there, and there was also to be a rationalized, integrated approach as time went on.[186]

In the Speech from the Throne, of October 8, 1970, the federal government's position was expressed in these terms:

> To foster coordination of the activities of all levels of government, and to contribute to sound urban growth and development, the government proposes the re-organization of its urban activities under the direction of a Minister of State for Urban Affairs and Housing.[187]

The presently untapped and unco-ordinated scientific talent in Canada was to be better co-ordinated and used in the solution of common problems. One aspect of this covered the Senate Committee on Science Policy and the Science Council of Canada; another the development of expertise in the proposed Ministry of Urban Affairs and Housing. Dr. Lithwick had identified the need for co-ordinating existing urban expertise and the training of more in a high-powered research institute.

The same issue of co-ordination had been met in the handling of pollution control.

The Prime Minister's address on the Speech from the Throne contained reference to the reorganization of urban activities. This reorganization was "the result of detailed consultation and planning with other levels of government.[188] It was to be associated with a new concept of ministerial role "intended to permit government more effectively to deal with modern conditions."[189] The concept was described in these terms:

> The proposed legislation regarding governmental organization will contain provision for the creation by order in council of offices of ministers of state for designated purposes; they will have a status and a salary equal to a minister with a department. These ministers of state generally will be responsible for developing new and comprehensive federal policies in areas where the development of such policies is of particular urgency and importance. The mandates of these ministers will be of a temporary nature, of such a duration as to enable them to come to grips with the policy problems assigned to them. They will not generally have departments, but only relatively small secretariats with no program responsibilities. The new system will give to the Prime Minister more flexibility in assigning senior ministers to tackle important problems that require policy development.[190]

Previously, in 1968, the Cabinet had been reorganized by ordering its activities through four functional committees, each headed by a minister who held departmental responsibilities in addition. The Prime Minister co-ordinated these four Cabinet committees with the Treasury Board and the Department of Finance.

The Prime Minister appears to have been argued into accepting the concept of the ministries of state. Mr. Andras remarked:

> In our dialogue with the Prime Minister and other key actors about the federal role in urban affairs, the study led to a second step. For in my rejection of the traditional concept of a Department of Urban Affairs and Housing, with its policy making and massive program delivery apparatus, we argued that because of the interrelatedness and all inclusiveness of "urbanization", we preferred the establishment of a research, policy making and coordinative Ministry with no delivery system and no direct program responsibility.[191]

In the Prime Minister's view the mandates of these ministeries were of a temporary nature, "of such a duration as to enable them to come to grips with the policy problems assigned to them." Mr. Andras's research and policy instrument should, in these terms, be considered as having a limited purpose and duration. The urban study had been followed up by creating the new urban ministry "and our strong commitment is to maintain the organization of a highly expert and extremely small group whose primary function will be research, policy development and coordination within and between governments."[192] CMHC was to remain the primary program delivery institution.

The new urban ministry was to *co-ordinate* urban policies, *support* current and future urban programs, and *consult* the three levels of government. The new forum was to be its particular instrument for gaining "the broadest possible understanding (of) the process of urbanization and, thereby, initiating a consensus in the building of national policies and federal initiatives."[193] The minister, however, had "no illusions about the difficulties in seeking to coordinate the disparate urban activities of many levels of government."[194] Bureaucratic empires had a tendency to introspection and jealousy with which Mr. Andras was quite familiar.

Within this approach Mr. Andras emphasized the decentralization of federal power intended to guide his own policy studies. This was in line with his earlier public addresses. He identified in the House two principles which he considered as being the reasons for, and the guidelines implementable by, his own proposed ministry. These were "that the traditional decision-makers of power must move over a little so that choice devolves upon the greatest numbers of people . . . ," and secondly, that growth for growth's sake "must be increasingly tempered by consideration, by choices, which put growth at the service of the social comfort and stimulation of Canadians."[195] The choices included whether Canadians wanted to build new Chicagos or Tokyos, or wished for something different. It was a return to Dr. Lithwick's "unconstrained" and "constrained" futures as prognostic directions of choice.

Mr. Andras was adamant in the House that "it is within the present constitutional boundaries that we will work." The constitution did not "need to be bent, or broadened to implement an urban policy of choice." By research and co-operation among governments "We can begin to get decisions on whether we in fact want our cities to develop unconstrained . . ."[196] The new ministry would first be concerned with putting the federal urban input in order — with the 112 federal programs involved in financing one or other element of the urban process, 131 research programs applying to elements of the urban process, 27 departments and agencies with one or other kind of city influence; something should come from this alone.[197] The minister would himself influence Cabinet and its committees as well as having an overview capacity. The new secretariat to be headed by a deputy minister "will fully review the federal efforts in urban affairs and through consultation and agreement will carry further through the government systems the work of rationalizing, co-ordinating and planning."[198]

The secretariat was being put together in October, 1970. Dr. Lithwick's report, and the research monographs associated with it, were shortly to be published. The scarce human resources in urban skills were in the future to be drawn together "to plan and work out possible priorities and strategies. We will hope to attract the best minds now diffused through governments, industries and universities and to return them again to governments, universities and industry in a continuous and cross-fertilizing stream.[199] Presumably the best minds were to be put on the right track, given the plan to which all else was to be co-ordinated, and be returned to areas of urban Canada where ignorance was still bliss and the answers still unknown. The "more rational approach between governments and within the federal government" was seen by Mr. Andras as serving to protect the provincial jurisdiction — "helping to forestall past experiences when uncoordinated federal departmental programming inadvertently distorted provincial and municipal priorities."[200] CMHC would also report to the ministry and it too was being increasingly co-ordinated "into a more total urban effort." Its capital and expenditure budget was "a potent force" currently emphasizing low income housing, and aiming to achieve the one million new housing units planned for the period 1970-1974 inclusive. In 1970 CMHC committed about $1.1 billion in its capital budget.

But 1970 was a bad year for private mortgage activity. Mr. Andras had already met once with the approved lending institutions to set forth the capital requirements to meet the 1970-74 plan. He was to meet them again before the end of 1970 "to get their factual and realistic assessments of their participation.[201] He would then devise the necessary plan "to ensure mortgage flow." The leaders of prominent pension plans were also to meet with him for this purpose. They had become "extremely sizeable sources of capital."[202]

It is necessary to note at this point that Mr. Andras was not considering the question of why Canadians as individuals did not have the capital needed to house themselves. He was turning again to yet other sources of organized savings, pension funds, rather than seeking to encourage the individual to save and plan for his own housing. This remains the basic sociological research question; for it is an unusual society which is characterized by reliance on organized savings, beyond the control or influence of the individual person, to provide that individual with the elementary shelter and accommodation he requires as a member of it.[203] For all Mr. Andras's visions of an urban policy for Canada, the very persons whom he was anxious to participate in and to be concerned over its execution, were being left without a significant financial constituent in that involvement. The practical direction of his acts was towards greater and greater use of organization, co-ordinate planning, and abstractions such as "urban" in place of "housing." His only action in a contrary direction was his encouragement of "sweat equity housing," where a person is entitled to contribute his own labor to the construction of his house as his equity in it. The possibility of coupling this to new mortgage techniques was under review.

That Mr. Andras was obliged to adopt this course of action, as the very *sine qua non* of effectiveness, is also a sociological matter, but one we cannot become involved with here. An additional question for research is whether public participation in policy determination and implementation can be anything but political if the public have no financial stake in — if only a deposit of significant size on a house in which one lives and which one "owns" — the fixed property affected by such policy.

In his speech to the 66th Annual Conference of the Union of Nova Scotia Municipalities, he emphasized that "urban" included the "vital growth centres" of remote and rural regions. It was not just a metropolitan scheme. The rational development of growth centres meant both the most socially comfortable and pleasing and also the most cost-effective development. The *regions* of Canada had to be knit together co-operatively. Demographic and economic patterns of today had to be constrained and re-channelled to some degree, "Otherwise, they will *further* the dominance and powers of the urbanized, industrialised centres and the regions surrounding them."[204] (Emphasis original.) In April, 1971, federal, provincial, and municipal government representatives had committed themselves to starting a collective forum approach. A national tri-level consultation was to take place in future, as part of a continuing consultative process. But during his speech in Halifax, Mr. Andras emphasized that the Atlantic Provinces had been given particular privileges over CMHC's budget. CMHC had had "to institute a form of rationing, as it were, for the regions of Canada,"[205] but there was no rationing for the Atlantic Provinces. One can only wonder if such privilege had been agreed to at the April, 1971, tri-level conference the minister was so pleased about. DREE, CMHC, ADA, and other instruments were taking a particular interest in the Maritimes. The conditions necessary to attract such conspicuous federal support would, no doubt, shortly be determined by other provinces.

By June, 1971 the minister reported that "my own governmental colleagues and municipal and provincial governments in Canada are somewhat tentatively, maybe even dubiously, eyeing this apparently under-muscled but, we hope, supple and surprisingly lithe new creature."[206] The minister's speech, paradoxically, was directed at the need for the learned professions and politicians to learn to listen, hear and respond "to what people really want." They had been talking to and at each other long enough with too little regard for the masses they served. The Spadina Expressway in Toronto, for example, had recently been abandoned by the Ontario provincial government following the activities of vocal citizens banding together "in responsible ways and making responsible arguments and exerting pressure responsibly, against almost all odds."[207] Similarly, public housing tenants from across Canada had held a national conference in Ottawa to articulate and make responsible demands on federal authorities — "I can tell you that we are revamping, or trying to, our perhaps paternalistic approaches. The public housing tenants are forcing the pace."[208] There had been some resentment at their supposed impertinence, but in the minister's view their demands "often smacked of sense."

The paradox in the minister's speech appears between his having set up a small group of experts as a co-ordinating, supporting, and consulting instrument among governments, and his pleading for an ear to the wishes of the masses. Such a small group of experts, heavily weighted towards research, and intent upon generating a practical urban

282

policy for Canada, could only apply the latest techniques of research to come up with useful suggestions. Highly elaborate statistical analyses, using models of abstractions that require computer services to elucidate them, would without doubt be the means of deciding the appropriate policies for the future urban Canada. Yet Mr. Andras remarked:

> Because the time is passing fast when politicians or professional men can do very much *"for"* their countrymen . . . the man doesn't trust it, and he certainly has had enough talk over his head about it. Anything that's going to be done *"for"* him, he wants charge of. If there is to be talking, he is demanding to be part of that talk.[209]

There was, the minister felt, "a growing cynicism towards government and toward the liberal-professional establishment."[210] The only national urban policy likely to work was one "that is guided by the most responsively understood desires of the people of the nation."[211]

If this be the condition for the workability of the proposed urban policy for Canada, it requires the creation of more than the tri-level governmental forum the minister had initiated. It requires the introduction of plebiscitic mechanisms to cover every level of public decision from the local to the federal. The small group of experts in the ministry does not appear to be equipped in this direction. Yet this is precisely the area of conflict that governments at all levels are designed to obviate. In their administrative capacities governments must typically decide on proposals presented to them from either below them in the governmental hierarchy or from outside themselves, from private organized capital. The interest of lower governmental levels and of private capital are not necessarily those of the people. Elected representatives do not, and cannot, represent the views of the majority of electors on even a minority of the issues they become obliged to administer on the electors' behalf.

Because of its remoteness from the masses of Canadians, the federal level is perhaps the easiest of all to handle in the relation of "public" interest to administrative expediency, i.e., to get the job done but as the people would like it to be done. There is particularly little evidence available at present as to the nature of the working relationship currently established between, say, the urban ministry and CMHC.[212] But this relationship might be indicative of the feasibility of reconciling what appears to be irreconcilable, namely, an identified "public" interest and administrative expediency. It may be asked whether the small group of experts in the ministry or those responsible for the delivery system are the more capable of representing the public will. Or is the public will to be determined only by the political component in the trio? If a working relationship between experts and administrators cannot be achieved at that remote level from the conflicting pressures of masses of people, it surely cannot be done at the local city level where the mayors know full well the nature of local pressures and conflict. The way out envisaged by the minister is to obtain a national consensus about goals, or aims, or images of what the future urban Canada might be like. It would then be merely a matter of determining appropriate means to attain it and of regulating the subordinated authorities to do it. But privately organized capital, the very thing which benefits from being urban and which has largely created the urban of the past and of the present, has quite clearly stated and known goals of its own. These are not necessarily concerned with the consensus over urban images that the public's representatives in government may wish to ascribe to. In June, 1971 the minister was still optimistic that the nation would buy "a guided national urban policy."[213]

In his speech to the House on June 28, 1971, when the Proclamation establishing Canada's first Ministry of State for Urban Affairs was under discussion,[214] Mr. Andras emphasized the innovative nature of the attempt "to sharply split the twin functions of policy making and program administration." He said:

> It strongly argues against the concept that policy emerges only from those entrusted with its administration. It holds to the concept that objective policy development across a broad range of activities and authorities can emerge when unfettered by the vested interests that grow from administering programs.[215]

The minister's policy mandate was intentionally unrestricted and as wide as possible. This was, we assume, the essential condition for the "objective" input of research. The research findings had to be the outcome of including in the model as wide a range of influencing variables as technique permitted and the reality situation required. No one delivery system could encompass this reality situation, so the ministry had of necessity to go beyond it, and beyond many delivery systems and administrative instruments. Apart from the awkward question as to where the popular will might fit into the model, the sharp split raises important questions of power, of super- and sub-ordination, of influence and of prestige within the federal civil service itself.

Many provincial governments in Canada, including Alberta prior to August, 1971, had developed a cadre of bright young lads as assistants to ministers, but who were outside the regular departmental administrative system. Their function in Alberta, from our own observations, was to do very much what the new group of experts in the urban ministry were to do — but without the extensive emphasis on organized research that the federal ministry was intended to have. From our own observations, there appeared to be a latent hostility between these ministerial assistants and the senior departmental officials. We surmise that the relation of the experts in the ministry to the heads of administrative units at the federal level is likely to be little different from what we have observed at the provincial level. At the federal level, however, the difficulty is likely to be compounded in view of the fact that administrative units such as CMHC have long-established regional representatives in the provinces. These representatives, from long years of experience, have arrived at both a *modus operandi* and a *modus vivendi* with the provincial authorities. The experts in the ministry are largely dependent, therefore, on the administrative units for both their diagnosis and application of policy at the provincial level. Presumably, when the national consensus is achieved even this organizational complication will be smoothed out. But the system, for obvious reasons, is far from being a simple one.

In October, 1971, when addressing The Canadian Real Estate Association in Montreal, the minister regretted that at that time support for the objective of seeking methods to further intergovernmental co-operation and consultation "is limited both from governments and the general public."[216] Yet, this co-operation was the vital first step; in the minister's mind it was essential to "continue to question intuitive solutions." He argued that the proposed tax reforms would "go a lot further in redressing basic social inequities than any rehabilitation program."[217] Similarly, in urban affairs, when dollars are put behind a given project the result should not deceive us. The minister was forgetting, of course, that the tax reform program lay solely within federal jurisdiction. Urban affairs, however, are the product of multiple jurisdictions and therein lies both the opportunity and the difficulty.

The approach of the Prime Minister and the Minister of State for Urban Affairs at the First Ministers' Conference in mid-November, 1971, was largely an elaboration and clarification of the many issues discussed by Mr. Andras in his public speeches mentioned above.[218] This conference was, in effect, the crucial test of government policy and we regret we have not had the time to examine the available evidence from the provinces as to their reactions.[219] Some matters of elaboration and clarification may be drawn from these "Notes for Remarks" by the federal ministers, however.

The Prime Minister emphasized that although the federal government intended to consult among and co-ordinate the activities of federal departments in their approach to urban Canada, this did not mean:

> that Mr. Andras and his Ministry will become the only point of contact for provincial governments regarding existing and future federal programs relating to urban areas. On many specific programs or parts of programs, there will obviously be a continuing need for frequent and direct dealing with the appropriate federal department or agency. It will be our intention to ensure within the federal government that such specific programs will have been considered in the general urban context. In addition, where activities resulting from several federal programs concerning a number of federal departments are involved or when, taken together, such activities have a major impact on the urban environment, it will be the function of the Ministry to co-ordinate these activities. Needless to say, there is a requirement for wholehearted co-operation in this process and I am confident that such co-operation and support will be forthcoming and will be of lasting benefit to us all.[220]

The Prime Minister kept very close to the constitution on the subject of particpation by city governments. He remarked: "As to how this might be achieved is a question which must be left to you to decide. I would only say that I hope we can build on the progress that has already been made ... " He presumably had in mind the Winnipeg Conference of April, 1971, where the right of municipal involvement in conferences on urban affairs held by federal-provincial authorities had become a reality. Mr. Andras's "Remarks" added the significant point that each province "may have different ways of dealing with this matter. That is fine. We would like to see the principle, of accepting some kind of significant input from urban governments, adopted with the largest possible degree of unaminity."[221]

Consultation had, as a minimum, to involve the systematic exchange of information, opinions, and ideas about urban policies and programs. It could be carried further. Mr. Andras indentified "arriving at recommendations for mutually agreed policies and courses of action."[222] But he acknowledged that "it could obviously stop there. Governments and legislatures could reject or ratify, implement or shelve, any policy or program suggestion." This presumably included the federal government, which, in the past, had had precisely this power regarding provincially-supported requests for money from federal programs. On the other hand, his remark recognized the jurisdictional right of the provinces to reject a federal initiative. Whether this included the federal use of private lending institutions, as used since 1935, was not discussed.

Mr. Andras then elaborated the need to enhance the continuing consultations by using "some form of permanent, expert secretariat to build continuity and expanding knowledge into the process."[223] Quebec had already proposed such a step at a previous conference but it is not clear from Mr. Andras's remarks whether Quebec had proposed a provincial secretariat or the use of the federal instrument. The minister added: "The secretariat could be drawn from various sources. We have some suggestions but no fixed opinion on that."[224] This remark presumably referred to the research capacity already built into Mr. Andras's ministry; but Quebec appears, we may assume, to have preferred its own body of experts. This is only conjecture, but from the records of *Hansard,* Quebec appears to have had for many years an uncanny capacity to foresee federal manoeuvers on urban affairs and to get in ahead of the game. We see no reason to think Quebec might have acted differently on this occasion. Clearly, by monopolizing Canadian urban expertise within the urban ministry, the federal government would be putting itself into as prominent a position vis-a-vis the provincial governments as is a metropolitan centre to the struggling small towns within its own province. Within a common structural situation, knowledge is power. Apparently, power was precisely what the research and co-ordinatory capacity of the urban ministry was intent on obtaining through consultative techniques. Consensus on goals assumes the co-ordination of administrative instruments needed to achieve them. When only one party in a multi-party nexus has the "objective," the factual description, and the proof of how any given item works and affects other items, and when such "proof" is not subject to equivalent challenge from other parties, then seemingly "the facts speak for themselves." The relation among the parties becomes, theoretically, guided by the facts themselves rather than by the assumptions built-in unknowlingly into the models of those intent on acquiring "objective" information. The political stance of the federal government would be right in line with the findings of "objective" studies. There is, however, no way that science can replace the judgements of men nor avoid the political component inherent in all human relations.

As a token of its commitment to the process of consultation, the federal government was prepared to lay on the table at an early forthcoming conference "some federal urban-related policies for discussion."[225] There was no indication what these would be — whether, to take the most unlikely examples, CMHC was to be unscrambled and reassembled as part of the provincial instruments on housing and urban renewal, whether agreement could be reached on removing provincial incentives to the location of private industry, or whether, to take the most likely example, the federal inputs into "national urban" transport problems were to be outlined. But, but mid-November, 1971 the federal ministry *was* prepared to move. In Alberta, Peter Lougheed, the Premier, indicated that it was in the interests of municipalities and the provincial government "that tri-level consultation be a reality." The major municipalities, however, "should not expect to bypass the traditional provincial responsibility to municipalities."[226] The "elimination of the provinces as viable instruments within the constitutional framework cannot be allowed to happen." The relative inconsequence of provincial decision had not been removed by the new tri-level consultation machinery. The issue, then, is very much one of how Alberta's provincial government is placed to cope. The explicit battle around the consultation table has been joined. Provincial governments are in the unhappy position of being in between. We intend in Volume II of this study to examine some of the relevant issues within Alberta itself.

1. *House of Commons Debates,* 1968-69, 7:6894.
2. Ibid.
3. *House of Commons Debates,* 1968-69, 9:99199. Whereas overall housing costs rose by 80 percent between 1961 and 1968, the price of serviced land increased by 240 percent. Ibid. p. 9337.
4. Ibid., p. 9201.
5. Ibid.
6. Ibid.
7. Ibid.
8. Ibid.
9. *House of Commons Debates,* 1968-69, 10:10616.
10. Ibid., p. 10617. There was close contact and "persuasive discussions," between CMHC local officials and the officials of many local planning authorities. See Minutes of Proceedings and Evidence No. 39, Standing Committee on Health, Welfare, and Social Affairs, June 5, 1969, p. 1714.
11. *House of Commons Debates,* 1968-69, 10:10617.
12. Ibid., p. 10618.
13. See, for example, the discussion on the security required for loans by CMHC and the lending institutions respectively on pp. 1754-55 of the Minutes of Proceedings and Evidence No. 39, and the discussion of CMHC's role in introducing condominium type facilities: ". . . we would be encouraging the lenders to look at these seriously and indicating to them that there is nothing mysterious about them." Ibid. pp. 1707-8.
14. *House of Commons Debates,* 1968-69, 10:10618.
15. Minutes of Proceedings and Evidence No. 39, p. 1765.
16. *House of Commons Debates,* 1968-69, 10:10620.
17. Ibid.
18. Ibid.
19. Ibid., p. 10621.
20. Ibid.
21. Minutes of Proceedings and Evidence No. 39, p. 1706.
22. Ibid., p. 1705.
23. Ibid., pp. 1704-5.
24. *House of Commons Debates,* 1968-69, 10:10622.
25. Ibid., p. 10621.
26. Ibid., p. 10624.
27. Ibid.
28. Ibid., p. 10625.
29. Ibid., p. 10626.
30. Ibid., p. 10628.
31. Ibid.
32. Minutes of Proceedings and Evidence No. 39, p. 1765.
33. *House of Commons Debates,* 1968-69, 10:10844.
34. Ibid., p. 11222.
35. Ibid., p. 11691.
36. *House of Commons Debates,* 1969-70, 2:1700.

37. Ibid., p. 1703.
38. Ibid., p. 1367.
39. Ibid., p. 1705.
40. Ibid., p. 1709.
41. Ibid., p. 1728.
42. Ibid., p. 1729.
43. Ibid.
44. Ibid.
45. Ibid.
46. Ibid., p. 1729.
47. Ibid.
48. Ibid., pp. 1729-30.
49. Ibid., p. 1730.
50. Ibid.
51. See Chapter 2.
52. Hellyer, Paul T. *Agenda: A Plan for Action* (Scarborough, Ontario: 1971, Prentice-Hall of Canada Ltd.), p. 60.
53. *House of Commons Debates,* 1969-70, 2:2119.
54. Ibid.
55. Ibid., p. 2119.
56. Ibid., p. 2120.
57. Ibid., p. 2172.
58. Ibid., p. 1908.
59. The amendments to bill S-8 were referred to the Standing Committee on Finance, Trade and Economic Affairs. It has not been possible to consult this evidence to idenfify the likely consequences of the amendments on the lending institutions and related matters.
60. *House of Commons Debates,* 1969-70, 2:1908.
61. Ibid., p. 1910.
62. Address by the Honourable Robert Andras to the Conference on Cities, Indianapolis, Indiana. CMHC Press Release, May 26, 1971, p. 8.
63. Central Mortgage and Housing Corporation, Ottawa, December, 1970.
64. A series of six monographs was published in 1971.
65. Mr. Andras asserted that the purpose of the study was "to educate us at the federal level, the other levels of government, and the people of our country and bring us to a common basis for understanding urban problems and the basic alternatives for dealing with them." Press release, CMHC, May 26, 1971, p. 5.
66. Weber, M. "Science as a vocation," in Gerth H. H. and Mills C. W. (eds.) *From Max Weber* (London: 1947, Kegan, Paul, Trench, Trubner and Company Ltd.) p. 138. Our main fear is that we may have misunderstood or misinterpreted Dr. Lithwick's points or purposes in this very complex work. In that case, we ask only that our interpretation serve as a means of yet further analysis, and that it be speedily surpassed.
67. In the 6th Research Monograph, *A Survey of Alternative Urban Policies,* CMHC, January, 1971, L. D. Feldman and others have made comparative, international analyses of selected urban topics in their relation to governmental policy.
68. Lithwick, N. H. *Urban Canada: Problems and Prospects,* (Ottawa: 1970, CMHC) p. 169.
69. Ibid., p. 36.
70. Ibid., pp. 37-38.
71. Ibid., p. 38.
72. Ibid., p. 178.
73. Ibid., p. 38.
74. Ibid.
75. Ibid., pp. 38-39.
76. Ibid., p. 39.
77. Ibid.
78. Ibid., p. 178.
79. See Chapter 4, p. 142.

80. Bailey, F. G. *Stratagems and Spoils* (Toronto: 1969, Copp Clarke Co.).
81. Lithwick, *Urban Canada,* p. 36.
82. Ibid., p. 208.
83. Ibid., p. 40.
84. Ibid., p. 40. Though we would agree with Dr. Lithwick that there is a scarcity of urbanologists in Canada, the point currently is that the services of those available are dispersed because of the competitive general situation, and the need for each party, governmental and private, to defend itself through professional expertise. The absence of expertise in small towns and cities exposes them seriously to manipulation by well-served competitors.
85. Ibid., p. 178.
86. Ibid., p. 201.
87. Ibid.
88. Ibid., p. 38.
89. Ibid., p. 38.
90. Ibid., pp. 201-4.
91. Ibid., p. 204.
92. Ibid., p. 172.
93. We are aware that the Liberal Party from as early as 1960 was attempting to see the role of politics in Canada in rather a different way. We refer, however, more to the empirical reality than the intent insofar as urban affairs are concerned.
94. The ultimate in exemplifying the difficulties of this perspective is revealed in Research Monograph No. 4, *The Urban Public Economy* by W. I. Gillespie, pp. 91-92, where we are told *"that there exists virtually no body of positive theory that can be supported unambiguously by solid evidence."* (Emphasis original.) This study exemplifies the current difficulties of theoretical economics.
95. The next major section of this Chapter deals with the constitutional debate in the federal legislature where this point is clarified and developed.
96. Lithwick, *Urban Canada,* p. 172-73.
97. Ibid., pp. 213-36.
98. Ibid., p. 230.
99. Ibid., p. 225.
100. Ibid., p. 226.
100. Ibid., p. 226.
101. Ibid.
102. Ibid.
103. Ibid., p. 216.
104. Ibid., p. 215.
105. Ibid., p. 215-16.
106. Ibid., p. 216.
107. Ibid.
108. Ibid., p. 221.
109. It is referred to in Dr. Lithwick's report as "Policy Option U-1," see p. 217.
110. His Research Monograph No. 1 is on this subject.
111. Lithwick, *Urban Canada,* p. 217.
112. Ibid., p. 219.
113. Ibid.
114. Ibid.
115. Ibid., p. 220.
116. Ibid., p. 206.
117. Ibid., p. 220.
118. Ibid.
119. We suspect that the expansion of metropolitan centres, their ever-increasingly close connections with each other across national boundaries, and the ever-increasing concentration of manufacturing potential into the hands of fewer and fewer centres of decision, is related to a process of reducing the influence of national states and national governments. This is not, however, a topic we could take up here. We only note that provincial governments have in the past suffered a relative inconsequence of decision under the existing process.
120. Lithwick, *Urban Canada,* p. 221.
121. Ibid.

122. Ibid.
123. Ibid., p. 220.
124. Ibid., p. 227.
125. Ibid.
126. Ibid., p. 229.
127. Ibid., p. 230.
128. Dr. Lithwick specifically mentions the Vallingby-Stockholm model discussed fully in Research Monograph No. 6, *A Survey of Alternative Urban Policies* by L. D. Feldman and Associates.
129. Lithwick, *Urban Canada,* p. 233.
130. Ibid.
131. Ibid.
132. Ibid., p. 222.
133. Ibid., p. 233.
134. Ibid., p. 233.
135. Ibid.
136. Ibid., p. 224.
137. Ibid., p. 225.
138. Ibid.
139. For the full text see *House of Commons Debates,* 1969-70, 3:2811.
140. Ibid.
141. Ibid., p. 2812.
142. Ibid.
143. Ibid., p. 2813.
144. Later in his speech, Mr. Trudeau returned to this point by arguing that the existing constitution had to be rigorously respected right up to the point of adopting a new one by formal acts. This would forestall both the federal and provincial governments from usurping "whatever powers they wanted because this was the way they saw the new constitution in the future . . . " Ibid., p. 2816.
145. Ibid., p. 2813.
146. Ibid., p. 2814.
147. Ibid.
148. Ibid.
149. Ibid.
150. Ibid., p. 2815.
151. Ibid., p. 2819.
152. Ibid., p. 2822.
153. Ibid.
154. Ibid., p. 2825.
155. Ibid.
156. Ibid., p. 2826.
157. Ibid.
158. The Ontario government had been obliged to freeze its public housing program until the CMHC budget was tabled.
159. Ibid., p. 3061.
160. The construction of 62,000 units for low income families in 1969 and 1970 represented 75 percent of the previous 20 years' performance in this area.
161. Ibid., p. 3062.
162. Ibid., p. 3234.
163. We have been unable, due to time constraints, to continue the use of *Hansard* beyond February, 1970, for the analysis of federal trends. We have used, instead, this series of speeches.
164. Press release, CMHC, Ottawa, June 10, 1970, p. 1.
165. Ibid., p. 2.
166. Ibid., p. 5. The second of Dr. Lithwick's policy options, U-11, was being tried.
167. Ibid., p. 6.
168. Ibid., p. 7.
169. Ibid.
170. Ibid., p. 8.
171. Ibid.

172. Ibid., p. 9.
173. Ibid., p. 10.
174. Ibid.
175. Ibid., p. 12. But what, it may be asked, could the cities do until the federal national urban strategy and the provincial role were worked out and also agreed to? The assumption of working from the top down, when the action is at the bottom, is at best questionable.
176. Ibid., p. 15.
177. Ibid., p. 16.
178. Ibid.
179. Address to the Union of British Columbia Municipalities, September 17, 1970. CMHC, Ottawa, p. 2.
180. Ibid., p. 4.
181. Ibid.
182. Ibid., p. 17.
183. Ibid., p. 4.
184. Ibid., p. 7.
185. Ibid., p. 12. (Parenthesis original.)
186. Ibid., p. 18.
187. *House of Commons Debates,* 1970, 1:2.
188. Ibid., p. 36.
189. Ibid.
190. Ibid. The Ministry of State for Urban Affairs was formally set up in May, 1971.
191. Address by Mr. Andras to the "Conference on Cities," p. 8.
192. Ibid., p. 9.
193. Ibid., p. 10.
194. Ibid., p. 12.
195. *House of Commons Debates,* 1970, 1:466.
196. Ibid., p. 467.
197. Figures quoted in Ibid., p. 467.
198. Ibid.
199. Ibid.
200. Ibid. The same point was made in an address to the Canadian Real Estate Association in Montreal. CMHC press release, October 20, 1971, p. 8.
201. *House of Commons Debates,* 1970, 1:468.
202. Ibid.
203. Comparatively considered, this generality requires modifications, but in non-western societies the married man has a right, derived from membership in the kinship or village community, to accommodation or the means to erect it. In modern western society the right remains but the means are not assured.
204. Press release, CMHC, Ottawa, May 17, 1971, p.4.
205. Ibid., p. 9.
206. Address by the Honourable Robert Andras to the National Forum of the American Institute of Architects, Detroit, Michigan. CMHC press release, June 23, 1971, p. 10.
207. Ibid., p. 7.
208. Ibid., p. 8.
209. Ibid., p. 1.
210. Ibid., p. 2.
211. Ibid., That this might take the form of capital, particularly in the form of real estate, does not appear to have been considered. The return of capital to individuals, from whom savings and assets in one form or another have been removed — often by involuntary migration — is one of the forgotten means of assistance to the needy in western industrial society.
212. Mr. Hellyer's brief comment on the subject, mentioned earlier in this chapter, is indicative; but much more research is needed into the modes and mechanisms of intragovernmental co-operation.
213. Andras, Address to American Architects, Detroit, p.2.
214. Due to lack of time, we have consulted only the press release, CMHC, June 28, 1971.

215. Ibid., p. 3.
216. CMHC press release, October 20, 1971, p. 9.
217. Ibid.
218. The "Notes for remarks" by these ministers is contained in a CMHC press release and another from the Prime Minister's office dated November 15-17, 1971.
219. We have also not determined the nature of the evidence that might be available.
220. Page 2 of the Prime Minister's "Notes for remarks."
221. Pages 3-4 of Mr. Andras's "Notes for remarks."
222. Ibid., p. 3.
223. Ibid.
224. Ibid.
225. Ibid., p. 4.
226. *The Edmonton Journal,* November 17, 1971, p. 85.

Chapter 7
The federal direction 1935 to 1971
and some conclusions

To draw together the threads of federal urban policy since 1935 is no simple task. It must involve a selection of issues. Our criteria for this selection will be those matters that appear to have most relevance to the provincial government of Alberta — those matters it should keep in mind, those of which it should be wary, and also those which appear to offer opportunities. Such matters are different from those relevant to the perspectives of the federal government, of lending institutions, or of the major metropolitan areas within and outside Alberta.

Two threads have run consistently through federal policy on urban affairs since 1935: the reliance on and the pandering to the needs and wishes of lending institutions; and the use of urban construction in particular and urban affairs in general as instruments to meet demands for employment and other similar considerations. Dr. Lithwick's argument that there never has been a deliberate urban policy in Canada is correct in this sense. These two threads require analysis in many more areas than those we have been able to undertake, but some observations are possible.

The Federal-Lending Institution Relationship

The consistency of federal policy from 1935 onwards is evident. The depression obliged the federal government to use the resources of the lending institutions on the one hand to initiate urban construction and, on the other, to provide a safe and guaranteed investment for the savings of Canadians through, at that time, the life insurance companies; the federal government has relied on the resources of the lending institutions throughout the years since.

In 1935 the vagaries of the Canadian economy, dependent on world prices for primary products, made life an uncertain proposition for individuals in their daily circumstances, and the insurance and guarantee companies as well as the bond market, were favorites for the Canadian individual's investment.[1] While obliged to receive interest rates sufficient to meet their contractual obligations with their policy holders and creditors, the approved lending institutions were called upon to place their assets in the service of government policy concerning housing, urban development, and urban pathologies of a physical kind. Thereby they were most advantageously placed. But they were only encouraged by incentives to support government policy; moral persuasion and financial returns, rather than obligatory conditions, were the instruments used. The right afforded the controllers of organized private capital to use it in the interests which they adjudged to be their best has been scrupulously respected by all federal governments since 1935. From the federal point of view the "pump priming" quality implicit in the use of private money ensured the expanded effect of government incentive money towards the policy it was pursuing.

The relationship between the federal government and the lending institutions was not entirely that of equals offering a *quid pro quo* service to each other. There was an element of dependency by government on the lending institutions, rather than vice versa, which required one federal minister responsible for housing after another to seek information from organized lenders about the extent of their willingness to support government actions to further its policy. Though *prima facie* evidence cannot be provided, there were situations which suggested that lending institutions could have indicated the kind of amendment to the NHA they needed in order to bring their money back to the service of government policy. Equally there were institutions where the NHA was amended with the expectation that the new provisions would be used by lending institutions, and the expectation was not fulfilled. These observations should not be interpreted to mean that lending institutions dictated their terms, or that the federal government was their handmaiden. This is not the case; for the situational context within which the relationship was played out was not one that permitted any such clear-cut power to be exerted from either side. The relationship was far more subtle, more gentlemanly, essentially diplomatic, and decorous. It was a moral, proper, and respectable relationship in every way — but it was not necessarily a *quid pro quo.* Throughout the decades since 1935, the lending institutions were guaranteed their mortgage investments either by the federal government's personally coping with any losses which they might sustain on mortgages, and later by insurance provisions for which the mortgagor had to pay. Concurrently, the federal government was placed year after year in the dilemma of having to offer the lending institutions higher rates of interest to retain their willingness to invest in mortgages rather than elsewhere in the array of increasing opportunities open to them while, at the same time, trying to ensure that the lower income groups could house themselves within their restricted incomes. It has been an increasingly losing battle, and only since 1969, when interest rates approached or exceeded 9 percent, has the rate of building starts approached the minimum required to meet the rate of new family formation and to take some account of replacement of delapidated structures. This rate of construction, however, has been achieved increasingly by providing rental accommodation in company-owned multi-storied structures for the upper and middle income groups. The federal and provincial governments, through CMHC money, have been increasingly obliged to provide rental accommodation for lower income families. More recently still, the NHA mortgage interest rate was allowed to be fixed by open market forces, thereby removing the only justification government had for insuring the losses of mortgage investments, and removing its control of interest rates for NHA mortgages.

One has to ask why the federal government has stuck so tenaciously to the principles of the NHA, to the lending institutions and CMHC in the face of ever increasing and recurring difficulties with housing. Why should housing and its financing not be returned to provincial responsiblity, where jurisdictionally it appears to belong? Housing and the stimulation of urban construction was taken over by the federal government in the depression on the excuse that unemployment was a matter of national concern. This excuse has worn threadbare over the years, but the growth of a Canadian urban culture, in highly concentrated regions, has come now to evoke the national concern originally felt over housing. The federal government gained authority in 1935 and has so far held on to it, despite the change in emphasis from housing through urban redevelopment to a general urban policy. It has been the means whereby federal influence has been involved in changing the residential and domiciliary pattern of Canadians by moving them from rural and small town living to the metropolitan centres. The capital assets lost by these people when they moved to the centralized work opportunities in the cities had to be replaced by federal provisions for public housing, subsidized rentals, elaborate welfare and unemployment services and the like. Federal policy has been the means of ensuring that lending institutions were guaranteed their mortgage financing by both legal and practical means: by privileges in the administration of their loans, in capital appreciation and, above all, in the influence they would have in directing the process of urban expansion and development.

The circumvention of provincial governments in 1935-38, in the Dominion Housing Act, the Home Improvement Plan, 1937, and in the Municipal Improvements Assistance Act, 1938, was deliberate. The 1938 Act was the first of the series that required provincial government guarantee for and approval of a municipal loan by the federal government. Provincial governments were expected to legislate, if necessary, to allow their local authorities to make use of federal incentives; but the federal loan was made direct to the local authority. These financial and administrative measures were introduced on the grounds of expediency and equity. The non-discriminatory nature of federal provisions was ensured by using census returns. This principle verified the federal value of equal shares for all local authorities, and thereby obviated provincial government objections on the basis of favored treatment for particular provinces, but concurrently comprised the intent of the legislation as a measure of unemployment relief. Unemployment was not distributed equally across Canada, nor by city size. In this early measure, therefore, the relations of provinces to each other and to the federal government were paramount over the principle of relief for unemployment as such.

These Acts set the precedent for the federal use of lending institution money in addition to public money, to cope with social pathology — a trend which was later extended to sum clearance, urban

renewal, rental accommodation for the poor, and other tasks.[2] The
principle was extended, by means of tax incentives, to manufacturing
plants in the early 1960s in order to cope with excessive unemployment
in selected regions of Canada; and it was further expanded both
regionally and in its financial contribution by the 1969 DREE
reorganization and the enactment of the Regional Development
Incentives Act. Concurrently, from as early as the 1944 NHA, but
especially through the 1964 amendment to the 1954 NHA, the federal
government has stimulated investment by commerce in the downtown
multiple storied buildings. It was known in the 1950s as urban
redevelopment, rather than urban renewal, but it included commercial
and retailing investment as an integral part of the policy. Thus all
aspects of the private sector — agriculture, lending institutions and
banks, commerce and retailing, and most recently manufacturing —
have been invaded by the general policy of federal incentives to cope
with one or other pathological socio-economic situation.

The intensely political nature of the 1944 NHA, followed in
1945 by the setting up of CMHC, arose from two positions in radical
opposition to that established in legislation by the federal government
over the previous decade. The founding of the Bank of Canada in 1934,
the Sirois Commission on Federal-Provincial Relations, the centralization of fiscal control in federal hands as a war measure, and
the end of depressed economic conditions that the war achieved, were
the backdrop to the intense political conflict of 1944. The radical
positions were the socialistic policies of the CCF and of many returned
veterans, who saw their preferred future in terms of public ownership
and public development of facilities to meet personal needs such as
housing, health services and welfare services. The second position, a
corollary of the first in the thinking of the time, but in marked contrast
to the NDP's position over the constitutional issues of 1968-1970, was that
local public authorities would be the appropriate administrative
instrument to cope with housing and the local facilities of towns and
cities. Both of these positions conflicted with federal policy as it had
been since 1935 and especially at the close of the war when the
ideological choices affecting the preferred future were uppermost in the
public consciousness. The minister responsible for the 1944 NHA felt
that "several at least of the provincial governments would, I am sure,
not wish their municipalities to embark upon municipal housing
projects," and the federal government saw grave administrative
problems in the control of its money if the municipalities were given
their head.[3] Later in that debate the minister had to disparage the
provincial governments themselves in response to a suggestion that
they set up provincial authorities of their own — he had had "a pretty sad
experience in dealing with certain of the provinces so far as recovery (of
loans) is concerned."[4] There was, in the federal view, one way only to
handle loans, house construction, and the removal of urban slums. That
was by federal control; by the pump-priming quality of lending
institution money, and in 1945 by CMHC.

The records of *Hansard* do not refer to the point, and we have
not searched widely enough to procure what else may be available, but

we wonder what would have been the effects on the lending institutions of a government policy which recognized provincial housing authorities and local government responsibility for housing the needy after the war. Alberta at least had been in conflict with eastern lending and banking institutions for a decade. The lending institutions declined to make any loans in Alberta until the late 1940s, after the policy of the provincial government had become more moderate and the province's oil prospects looked encouraging. Each province might offer its own terms to lending institutions for becoming involved in the developmental urban process. As it was, the lending institutions had to be approved only by one authority — the federal minister — before they could be recognized for mortgaging services and other NHA privileges across Canada. Amendments to the NHA and other legislation had to be made to include an ever widening range of lending institutions, eventually to include the banks and later still, short-term money for long-term mortgage loans as the mortgage market through CMHC became more widely accepted and their liquidity improved.

Credit unions, the caise populaire, the British type of building society, and other essentially local means of saving were not approved. Thereby they were effectively denied NHA privileges. It was the larger institutions, whose head offices came increasingly to be centred in Toronto and Montreal, which got early approval. In 1969-1970, federal legislation facilitated the granting of federal recognition to previously provincially-registered institutions. It was not only convenient for the federal government to deal with large-scale, national lending institutions, but it suited the lending institutions themselves. The latter were enabled increasingly to centralize their administration and to have only one governmental level to handle. They had a national range of choice for lending and could watch what was happening to the money they lent, as well as being particularly and generally discerning about to whom they lent. The federal government was complicit, consciously, in fact — as the early involvement of CMHC in loans to small towns and rural areas, and the speeches of parliamentarians in the late 1930s demonstrate — in the process of urban centralization which characterized Canada in the 1950s and early 1960s. Only in 1969 through DREE — though also tentatively in the years before through tax holidays for selected industry and through ARDA and FRED — had the federal government eventually to pay the bill for its complicity in this process during the late 1940s and through the 1950s. The federal attitude towards centralization of administration has complicated its relation to the provinces who when faced with the costs of metropolitan development in the late 1960s turned to the politics of constitutional review as a means of coping both with local authority power and federal power. In consequence, the chances of obtaining an effective working relationship among all levels of government, to obtain the consensus essential to the national urban policy of 1970, were placed in jeopardy in fact though lip service has been paid to the idea.

DREE and its programs are coming to be increasingly criticized both by professional economists and civil servants. Politicians have so far been rather hesitant, for both the Conservatives and the

NDP have interests in the degraded areas of Canada and in the have-not provinces. The press to date also appears to be somewhat ambivalent on the matter, though finance-oriented newspapers by early 1972 were coming to take a critical stand.[5] In cold rational terms, DREE policy, not to mention its practice, does not make sense. The economic advantages to business accrue from concentration; it is only the individual person who has to give up any assets he may have on moving to the city to be an employee and user of high-cost consumer finance. There is already in prospect an incipient political conflict over DREE and its policies.

The 1944 legislation was significant in other regards. It elaborated the model nature of the NHA of 1938 to include six Parts. Increasing specialization of service — coupled to increasingly complex regulations — limited the terms and conditions of the participants in the facilities. The field of regulation ranged from the actual recipients of service such as mortgage borrowers or the poor in public housing, through a variety of organizational instruments such as limited-dividend and municipal organizations, to provincial and local government involvement in slum clearance and other public services. Each had carefully to be regulated for financial advantage, incentive to act at all, proper construction standards, constitutional jurisdictions, and so on. Action resulted not from a willing, interested state of mind desiring to get a worthwhile job done, but from administrative, financial, and picayune negotiations that wrung from each compromising situation a trivial item of momentary victory for one side or other. It was little wonder that specialists — both in the business side of government involvements with lending institutions and in building construction and town planning — had soon to be centred in a body like CMHC. It was little wonder, too, that CMHC was early obliged to set up regional offices in each of the provinces. In decentralizing its services it was doing again what the 1867 constitution envisaged as being done by three levels of government. Such regional emphasis, however, facilitated the centralizing of decision in Ottawa by one authority, ensured proper control and standards, and in consequence guaranteed the worthiness and uniformity of product standard represented in each and every loan assured under the NHA. The financiers could be assured of a reasonably uniform commodity which their money was commanding. To the federal ministers between 1935 and 1945, decentralization through lower levels of government was simply impracticable and undesirable. It offered no security adequate to the financial outlays involved. One had to rely on others rather than oneself.

The 1944 Act was also coercive over municipalities and provinces in the preparation of local plans. Advantageous loan provisions were awardable when proposals conformed to official plans. All three levels of government got involved in the planning process. The final act of approval was federal because without federal approval, a proposal had to be funded at lower levels. The federal government did not, in this way, prohibit a proposal; it did not jeopardize the freedom of action of lower governmental levels *if* they found the money. Concurrently, by using public money held at the federal level for increasing support for those activities of CMHC which lending institutions declined to undertake, the lower levels of government were denied the financial means of acting independently. In order to retain that right in effective terms, they had to raise their own funds by local taxation. Thus, while the federal government was demonstrating to the country its continued and sincere concern for the poorly housed, by expanding its grants to CMHC and ensuring the lenders and developers of adequate finance to expand construction, it was simultaneously handcuffing the provincial governments and limiting their effectiveness of independent action or remedial measures. Public funds were denied the latter. The price of businesslike rationality and support for lending institutions was the relative inconsequence of provincial decision. But constitutionally the provinces were responsible for planning. They were obliged to plan, however, without the effective means of implementing the plan. The developmental action was going on in the cities — at the point of location of building and manufacturing — and through being on the spot local governments had greater claim to make effective whatever planning could be done than had the provincial authorities. Such a process was bound to lead eventually to a confrontation between local authorities and provincial governments.

This was one aspect of a general attitude held by the federal government towards the lower levels of government. There was to be a business-like approach to all housing matters; only sound and proven policies were to be maintained. The means were to be the federal initiative, CMHC administration, and financing by lending institutions. Local and provincial governments were to fit in, to conform, to put their houses in order, and to work within the terms prescribed from on high. Even as early as the 1938 legislation the administrative structure for provincial involvement in low-rental housing was prescribed, but lending institutions were construed as being administratively self-regulating through the dictates of the market. Similarly, as early as 1938, incentives were introduced to speed up municipal action by paying municipal taxes on specified new construction started before 1940. This was the forerunner of timing incentives developed in the municipal sewage program of the early 1960s, the winter works program, the Municipal Development and Loan Board Act of 1963, and others. All were directly linked to the relief of unemployment in urban areas, especially winter unemployment. They were, nonetheless, direct intrusions into, and had immediate consequences for, the budgeting of local authority expenditures — matters normally the prerogative of provincial jurisdictions. Such measures were also expected to be funded by local commercial loans until the grant or loan was received by the local authority from one or other senior level of government.

This early legislation set the political stage on which the scenes of the following decades were to be played. The provinces moved towards their own housing instruments only in the mid-1960s, but these have undertaken only the peripheral aspects of the dynamic of urban development — the housing of the poor, rental and purchase accommodation for lower income groups, and a limited amount of urban renewal and land assembly. Provincial influence has reappeared since 1967, but at a level of political involvement which exceeds, though it is intimately associated with, urban affairs. The constitutional conferences bear witness to the scale of this influence. The main thrust of the urban dynamic, however, has remained with private commercial and industrial investors, and real estate and developer interests. This is complemented by municipal public investment, and by the helping hand of an ever more financially involved CMHC and federal government to meet an ever expanding range of urban facilities, from single family dwellings to public services, from downtown city core rehabilitation to the stimulation of growth centres, which the management of organized private money was reluctant to service or care about.

The National Advisory Housing Council first postulated by Mr. Nicholson and Mr. Pearson in late 1967, and later refined and developed by Mr. Andras and Dr. Lithwick in terms of a National Urban Council, does not significantly change this scene. The purpose of the council is to procure agreement among the three levels of government on the nature of the urban future and the means of bringing it about. Neither in 1967, nor in Dr. Lithwick's later study, was much attention given to the significant role which lending institutions have played in the urban dynamic for almost three decades. The federal initiative assumes that if government can only agree then the sources of private investment will move along with them. This assumption is not supported by historical evidence. The relation between the federal government and lending institutions has not been quite a *quid pro quo*. It has been rather one of support for government policy when it suited the lending institutions or if it paid them to go along. This relationship may well change, particularly if all levels of government, and all of the governments of Canada, are sincere in their unity and strength of purpose, for the security required by private investment whether in the form of lending institutions, industrial investment, or commerce might be adequately met if governmental policy was clear, continuous, and demonstrably sensible with regard to urban affairs. But the assumption of governmental unity over the long-term is not an easy one to rely on, particularly in a federal system and where the municipal-provincial relationship has already become attenuated.

Provincial governments will need to look very carefully, and continuously, at their peers and at the nature of the relations extant or proposed between the federal and provincial governments. Jealousies may easily disrupt the unity essential to the policy. Lending institutions would not readily take to the decentralization of their activities implied in the division of decision-making which the policy would entail.

The principal way of ensuring that lending institutions diversify their relation to governments, and that private investment generally comes to play a role in accord with the national urban policy, would be to replace the now centralized CMHC with the provincial housing and urban authorities intent upon affecting the issues which really determine urbanization. Currently the provincial instruments tend to be the regional arm of federal money for coping with matters pathological and peripheral to this process. Provincial planning authorities are hardly at the centre of action. Municipal instruments are

301

in much closer touch then provincial ones. DREE may be another federal institution requiring much greater decentralization if the degraded areas of the country are to be logically integrated into the national urban policy.

Such a prescription for success runs counter to the previous direction of federal policy since 1935. It requires that federal professional advisors recommend diametrically opposite to their natural, i.e., situational, inclinations. They need to understand the point that the effectiveness in application of any policy is dependent upon the willingly-given support of junior levels of people engaged in a common activity. The condition of this willingness is precisely that they are given responsibility — the freedom to make both mistakes and wise judgments. The means alone are not enough, as the events of the past three decades clearly show.

The effective direction of federal policy has been to centralize increasingly decision and control in Ottawa until it has reached the point of federal ministers — Mr. Hellyer and Mr. Andras in 1968-1970 — making on-site inspections of urban renewal and public housing applications. This was deemed necessary in order to stop abuse at the municipal level — the provincial governments, by implication, had neglected to do their duty; but this duty had, in empirical terms, become so attenuated as to absolve them from responsibility. Federal guidelines and advice to lower levels of government were just not enough; nor were they forthcoming. The district representatives of CMHC have for decades been the final arbiters of support for any local developmental proposal involving federal money, as the eloquent case put up by CMHC in 1956 for the Royal Commission on Canada's Economic Prospects, demonstrates.[6]

Dr. Lithwick correctly emphasized the inter-urban network of modern cities. This is not an aspect of Canadian urban affairs which can be dealt with provincially. Similarly, this network in Canada is related by means of private investment, most directly to the city network of the USA and less directly to those of Europe, Japan, and elsewhere. This is an obvious federal responsibility, and one likely to increase significantly if the ever-increasing importance of internationally-organized finance and corporations is recognized, and if Canada is sincere in its intent to have a genuinely Canadian national policy on urban development. The federal role of the future must be towards these influences, rather than towards the monopolistic control of its internal dynamic. To be successful in that role it must forsake its now petty concern over the politics of provincial-federal intrigue and leave the provinces with the responsibility and the means to do the job largely denied them since 1935.

This implies that the centralization of research expertise which Dr. Lithwick saw as essentially taking place in Ottawa, in order to further the evolution of a national urban policy for Canada, must be decentralized to the provinces, and in its place in Ottawa must be built up the expertise to cope with the new federal role of predominantly international responsibility. Dr. Lithwick's proposal might have been timely in 1967, when Mr. Pearson first proposed the idea along with the

302

National Advisory Housing Council, but it is outdated now. Among its terms of reference and also in the terms of reference of provincial centres of expertise, must be included the federal relation to private investment and particularly to lending institutions. This critical component seems presently to be forgotten in federal planning. It is partly remembered at the provincial level, and reappears very pronouncedly at the municipal and city level where the consequences of private locational decisions are born by local governments and local taxpayers.

The proposed provincial responsibilities should include urban renewal, new virgin city development, policies of decentralization and concentration in terms of functional criteria and the costs associated with them, as well as the provision of public services supporting these policies, and meeting the needs of private citizens. The present ambiguity over which level of government is responsible, over the terms offered by way of incentives to private investment by the three levels of government, and over the stringency or leniency of enforcing planning regulations, should be removed. A much clearer and decisive mode of relating government to private investment, and of understanding their joint contribution to urban affairs and to the economy in general is required. This cannot be achieved when all levels of government are involved in incentives of a variety of kinds; when the lower levels of government are involved in a competitive struggle with their peers to be awarded the favors of private investment, and when growing automation **of productive processes is increasingly threatening the employability of** very significant proportions of the Canadian work force, who happen also to be voters in the various levels of government.

The Vicarious Use of Urban Affairs

The second thread running consistently through federal policy since 1935, has been the vicarious use of urban affairs in the pursuit of broader national policies. The change in the economy of the nation from primary to industrial production has in Canada, as elsewhere, meant the growth of urban population and investment in concentrated centres. The evolutionary dynamic in technology, in the scale of organization of private investment, and in the scale of public investment in services required to meet the new concentrations and the technical devices of the age have thrown up problems unique to the recent situation. But there remain other problems endemic to Canadian administrators irrespective of the technical base and the organizational scale of units within the culture. How to integrate multi-national and linguistic communities brought in from outside, how to relate effectively to Quebec, how to make a federal system work to everyone's satisfaction, how to cope with embarrassing rates of unemployment, and how to provide services to the poor are among the problems of long-standing duration. Most of these issues are jurisdictionally federal matters, but even those which are not — for example, unemployment, poverty, and rights under the constitution — have tended to be dealt with federally, often as a matter of practical expediency.

303

The federal government has been coping with this twin set of problems — those of long standing and those derived from modern urbanization — in a predominantly pragmatic way. Until the early 1960s when the Liberal Party initiated several conferences, and a number of thoughtful books were written by people such as Walter Gordon, Maurice Lamontagne, and Pierre Trudeau, there were few attempts by persons or groups in power to relate the role of government to long-term national objectives in a systematic way.

During the war years and the post-war years when there were genuine housing shortages the government was obliged to be situationally oriented. It was only in the mid and late 1950s that federal policy on housing and urban affairs could have been anything but situational. This decade, however, was when the costs and consequences of suburban sprawl came home to local authorities with a vengeance. The urban dynamic was creating the wealth required to build the national infra-structure which industry, technology, and city concentrations required. Standards of living were rising and the NHA and the CMHC were coping with the demand for urban housing in a more or less satisfactory way. The demands of local authorities for a broader tax base, the demands of provinces to be provided with the money for their industrial and urban development, the demands of conscience to house the lower income groups, to provide equal opportunities for all Canadians, and to renovate or rejuvenate the slum environments of the cities, occupied the attention and generated the policies of the federal level of government.

Of these demands, none fell unambiguously into the jurisdiction of the federal government. Even the provision of equal opportunities for all Canadians involved provincial agreements over programs in what is now fashionably called "the delivery system." Federal policy inevitably meant bi- or tri-party agreements with other jurisdictions. By offering ever larger financial inducements, from the 75 percent federal, 25 percent provincial and municipal split of 1949 to help local authorities assemble and service land for public housing, to the recent 90 percent assistance to provincial housing authorities to do broadly the same thing, the federal government tried to generate the development and action it wished to bring about. Provincial and local governments were for decades desperately slow to respond. They had momentarily rewarding and "progressive" developments on which to spend their available money. If matters got sufficiently bad a yet greater incentive from federal authorities might confidently be anticipated. This was particularly so as the state of the economy moved from boom to depression and the rate of urban unemployment rose. Provincial governments had little reason to feel responsible for matters that had so decisively been assumed by the federal level. Having been denied the responsibility by federal circumvention of them through lending institutions and CMHC they were, humanly, disinterested in developments which affected their welfare only indirectly.

To expand its range of means of coping with urban degradation the federal government, step by step, brought private investment into what was ostensibly a matter of public concern.

Ministerial speeches in the federal House show a persistent reticence at taking this step. There were very rarely out and out accusations against provincial governments for doing nothing effective in slum clearance or in the provision of housing for the poor. It was a process of step-by-step inclusion of opportunities for private investment to move in and do the job formally identified as a public responsibility. Times of economic crisis, high unemployment, municipal debt, financial crisis and inability to provide the public services the NHA supported housing developers required, were typically those which induced federal amendments to the NHA in the direction of private capital involvement.

The suburban boom of the 1950s taxed the capacity of local authorities to service land. They looked to provincial governments to help them out, but with no clear financial aid in sight. Yet the population kept streaming to the cities roughly in proportion as the opportunities for employment became centralized there and denied elsewhere. By 1956, the dilemma of local authorities had to be resolved. The amendment to the NHA of that year was aimed deliberately at relieving urban costs in suburban sprawl by rejuvenating city cores. Urban redevelopment was at that stage to be primarily a housing instrument. Housing, rather than urban affairs in general, was then the major federal intrusion into provincial jurisdiction. It may have been on that account that the housing emphasis in city centres was politically necessary. But the principle introduced concurrently was that of the use of downtown land for its "highest and best use." This not only ensured a maximum of return to the city by way of taxes; but seemed an obvious and rational thing to do with expensive core land for which interests other than the displaced slum dwellers had plans. At first it was to be only governmental use of such cleared land. The redevelopment also had to be sufficiently large in scale to facilitate proper planning, but this very scale limited the type of institution that could capitalize the development. The official community plan was again, as it had been in 1944, the condition of federal assistance. Such a plan was seen as being essential to forestalling the re-introduction of urban blight in the same area and to forestalling the development of blight in adjacent areas tending to this condition. Federal policy was conditional on the local authority deliberately planning to arrange its affairs with the control of incipient physical pathology in mind. But local authorities were in no financial position to forego chances of immediately remunerative taxable investments. The provinces were either relying on municipal authorities responsibly to handle their own affairs — as for example, in the hands-off attitude of Alberta's provincial government — or were unwilling to supply the additional money needed by local authorities to build the city beautiful by foregoing immediately remunerative taxable investments. The opportunities for developers, lending institutions, and large-scale retailers, to move into the situation were excellent.

During 1952-56, the conventional lending of finance houses was leading the way in the construction of multiple-storey family dwellings. The 1956 NHA amendment opened up federal money for this purpose which hitherto had been devoted to the conventional suburban home. Concurrently, with the initiative for urban planning remaining with local authorities, CMHC rather than provincial planning authorities was to conduct the necessary studies, or to have them financed, to facilitate this planning. Provincial approval for the plan and for its minority financial contribution had to be obtained, but it was the working relationship between the local authority and the federal CMHC which formed the critical point of contact. Thus, CMHC rather than provincial planning authorities, was placed in the centre of downtown core renewal programs. CMHC already knew the developers and the investors; it had established construction guidelines and standards; and it had a body of experienced regional officers adept at handling all three levels of government as well as private interests. From this perspective, the decision was sensible; but, by way of unanticipated consequence, it would be difficult to argue in 1972 that the provinces were responsible for building up the high cost urban concentrations across the country. CMHC had moved into city core financing and administrative control of planning and standards at a time of urgent municipal financial embarrassment. The provinces were either unable or unwilling to prevent this trend.

The federal ministers felt that sufficient money could be raised through local authority debentures on the open market. Any form of subsidy to local authorities by way of interest rates would merely divert the tax payers' dollars to uneconomic proposals. That "economic" was determined by the rate of interest in the private financial market had its consequences both for the poorly paid citizen and for the cities in general. The so-called "quality of life" was conveniently forgotten only to reappear a decade later. Alberta instituted the revolving-fund principle for municipal borrowing and later expanded it to the Municipal Financing Corporation. Oil revenues were giving Alberta an advantage, but its Social Credit philosophy was also demonstrated as a principle of universal application if only the federal government would use the Bank of Canada instead of the lending institutions to service public development. Federal expenditures on the St. Lawrence Seaway, national highways, airports, and the North, were claiming large amounts of federal revenue and borrowing capacity. Problems of degradation in the Maritimes came to the fore in 1955. The mayors were invited to the 1956 federal-provincial conference as observers to note the financial arrangements agreed upon between the two senior levels of government. The funding of urban development was being played out "in the open," amidst the vicarious pressures of policies elsewhere in the nation. Conditional federal grants to the provinces greatly increased provincial expenditure, but only in terms of the policies for which the grant was awarded. The straight-jacket to the provincial right of decision was not removed.

The boom of the mid '50s put the traditional lending institutions largely out of the NHA mortgaging business. The banks by 1956 were the main source of funds. Consumer credit by way of instalment buying was booming. During 1957 and 1958, the authorized funds of CMHC for direct mortgage lending were boosted from $250 million to $750 million, and had reached a billion dollars by 1959. It was the start of the ever-increasing weight of federal direct funding into the cities. The central aim of this funding has been to house the lower income groups. A second aim was, by means of the construction industry, to rejuvenate the economy when it faltered, to give employment, and to ensure continued growth of the metropolitan centres. The capital already invested there had to pay off even if the price of ensuring it was the investment of yet further sums of public money. Public investment in any part of the country fed back money to manufacturers based overwhelmingly in the metropolitan centres. The cities had to be maintained as growing, vital instruments in order to stave off a serious slump. There was more building going on in Toronto for instance, in the slump of 1958 than in any other part of Canada.

By 1958 the Liberal opposition was pressing for a national development program. National development was the largest scale of program that could be devised. The scale of private organization, and of public investment already achieved, required that the scale of future development planning be commensurate with this technical and organizational scale. Technical and organizational scale is only economic when it is used to its potential. The nation's affairs were thought to require it in any event, if Canada was to remain comparable in its achievements to other industrial nations. This was the type of thinking that led in 1967 to the first National Advisory Housing Council proposal and in 1969 to the national urban policy, though the latter proposals originated from more direct and immediate political problems of men in office rather than in opposition. It meant, however, that "things got done" rather than being merely proposed or compromised as they passed on down the levels of government to the reality of the on-site situation.

The Conservative government at the turn of the decade moved more cautiously in its scale proposal, but with careful insight into the measures adopted. The winter works program provided relief for unemployment at the same time as permitting local authorities considerable discretion over the work they undertook. The sewage proposals of 1960 involved direct federal involvement in local authority services. It was argued for on the basis of being an anti-pollution measure. But having to do largely with main trunk sewers it was expanding the zones of land being opened up by developers. Land prices were expected to fall as the supply increased. Septic tanks were to be discouraged. But the unanticipated consequence was that the individual home owner was to have his choice of residence location limited to "the sewage system." His choice had hitherto been polluting the land and causing him unnecessary costs when the mains caught up with him. Industrial pollution, large scale municipal dumping of raw sewage into rivers was to be tackled only much later. The Liberals saw the sewage proposals as not going far enough in the direction of federal involvement in municipal service needs. Provincial health authorities had had to approve the proposals but the provincial governments were not to be "the middleman" in the sewage proposals. CMHC officials were to have "informal discussions" with provincial governments. Building construction in the smaller centres was encouraged by CMHC information circulars and by officials visiting the towns to inform them

307

of the services available. But the minister finally admitted the demand in small towns was not what he had anticipated. Industry was to be encouraged by tax holidays to locate in selected depressed areas of the country as a means of providing employment and "take off" conditions. This was not the direct involvement of the federal government in provincial industrial matters which was to come in 1963 when the Department of Industry was established. It was still just a remedy for seriously pathological conditions.

In the cities, urban renewal studies had shown by 1959 that several habitable houses and apartments were being torn down in the interests of clearing sites for future development. In 1968 Mr. Hellyer made the same discovery and also met the opposition of tenants in public housing. But at the turn of the decade the government moved to permit public ownership of marginal housing in order to facilitate its rental to the poor. It was to be a federal-provincial joint ownership of slum-prone property, but would have the effect of stopping local authorities from letting "total blight" invade an area planned for renewal. Property maintenance regulations had also to be properly enforced. In fact, little but planning had so far been done in urban renewal by 1960. It was only between 1960 and 1964 that large developers and lending institutions turned their attention to the large-scale high-rise development typical of the decade. Their interest previously had been in general national development, in government bonds, and in other non-directly urban matters. CMHC had been carrying much of the urban responsibilities.

Owner's equity in new housing was running at about 18 percent in 1964. Lending institutions, governments, etc., were supplying about 82 percent. Lending institutions were powerfully placed to influence the efficacy of government housing policy if they chose not to co-operate. The meaning of the words "rental accommodation" changed. It had previously referred to accommodation which the man with a job on frequent transfer, or the man unable to raise the downpayment for a house he wanted to own, was obliged to occupy. It came now to mean the accommodation put up by organized private money for the new, propertyless class of urban middle and upper income groups to live in. Urban sprawl, at four houses to the acre, or eight if hard pressed, had proven unsuitable for the type of urban living that city concentration required. The interest of lending institutions in easily administered and large-scale apartment blocks increased rapidly. Interest rates were raised again in 1963, this time as the economy picked up.

Amidst this change in the view of the urban itself and in the interests of lending institutions, the first call was heard in the federal House for a Department of Urban Affairs. The Canadian Federation of Mayors and Municipalities (CFMM) had proposed it. They felt they were becoming far too dependent on provincial authorities. Developments south of the border led planners to think of massive urban regions rather than cities. Such urban development presupposed the ready crossing of all political boundaries, and only the federal government was capable of action on this scale. It was first mentioned in the House in 1962, as a

308

measure to ensure to city local authorities the financial means of doing what needed to be done. In the same year a private bill to set up a federal department of federal-provincial affairs was talked out in the House. Too much power was being given to boards, to CMHC, and too little influence remained with elected members.

The return of the Liberals to power in 1963 heralded the new approach to national planning. An extended program of rural redevelopment was initiated at the same time as the interests of lending institutions had turned powerfully to downtown city cores. The Economic Council of Canada was to be the means of integrating through a "broad consensus," government policies, the interests of individual Canadians and of companies. Togetherness and agreement on the objectives and methods of economic policy were to permit the application of more rational techniques to the country's problems. Especially close contact was to be kept between private industry and government. It was the direct forerunner of Mr. Andras's consensus on the goals of urban policy of 1969; but in 1963 the same approach was to apply to economic planning in general, and particularly in the relation of organized private money to federal policy — a matter that did not seem important in 1969.

Concurrently the new Department of Industry was to have on staff a select group of industrialists to help it get started in practical terms on its service capacity to Canadian industry. Exports and secondary industry were to be of particular concern. Manufacturing was to be the means of encouraging immigration to Canada. The new department was to be the focus for clarity and direction of government action to encourage industrial development.

The 1963-64 re-organization had to contend with the hitherto provincial influence over industrial location. The new department was ostensibly "to look after the industrial problem at the national level," and was envisaged as assisting the provinces in their particular and promotional problems. The way the bill was handled in the House led to bitter opposition remarks as it had not been first referred to provincial governments for their comments. Provincial incentives to attract industry to their provinces and metropolitan centres — to assist the former with tax rights and the latter with local government revenues — were already well established. Federal incentives to direct industry in terms of national policies were likely only to complicate matters. The provinces with little industry were likely to welcome federal initiative, but those with much industry would oppose it. A "broad consensus" about objectives and methods of economic policy was still, however, to be the philosophy within which practical politics was to be played out. The Area Development Agency (ADA), which was made part of the Department of Industry, was envisaged as a specialized, small group in Ottawa to plan for the co-ordination of federal policy and action in selected, pathological regions of the country. It was co-ordinatory, not executive, just as was the policy branch in the Ministry of Urban Affairs in 1971.

Federal departmental reorganization in both 1963 and 1969 took place to gear up federal initiative in areas that were previously provincial responsibilities. Each occurred within the context of a philosophy of national need that required deliberate research and planning facilities. Each was carried out without prior negotiation with provincial governments, though the 1969 re-organization had been preceded by federal-provincial discussions on the constitution and on non-constitutional fiscal arrangements. These had behind them the ever-present problem of urban affairs and of the political aspirations of city governments. Lastly, each reorganization was undertaken to be the answer to morbid situations — the first to remedy the degraded rural regions of Canada, and latter to cope with the consequences of urbanization of an "unconstrained" kind. The federal government was again moving to cope with the present or incipient pathological situations which the provincial level of organization was apparently unable to handle.

This federal thrust was reproduced in the cities by way of the Municipal Development and Loan Board Act, 1963. Unemployment was the excuse; but the Act was intended, though never achieved due to Quebec's provincial intrusion, to link up directly by loans the federal government with the provision of city public services. The CFMM had long seen the need for this step. The outcome of the federal-provincial conference, which discussed the bill, was to increase greatly the influence of provincial governments over local authority public expenditures supportable by federal funds, if the provincial governments opted to take this initiative. Alberta was among the provinces which declined this option. The local autonomy of urban centres was seen as being inviolate in Alberta, and the services of CMHC were seen as adequate to guide the local authorities. Equal distribution of resources on a per capita basis among local authorities was seen as the only fair means in theory to allocate funds.

The 1963 Act was the third of a series of steps which increased federal involvement — the 1960 sewage program and the 1962 technical training and building scheme were the others. All, in one way or another, were unemployment measures. All involved approval by the provincial governments, but as observers rather than as initiators or active participants. To obviate the jealousies of provinces federal money was distributed on a per capita basis, "the only fair way," thus meeting equally the claims of provinces suffering from excess urban concentration as well as those suffering from too little. The final distribution of money among provinces came to emphasize neither relief for rural degradation nor relief for urban deficiencies in services, though it provided jobs for the unemployed of both situations. It was hardly an auspicious beginning to the federal attempt at national planning. It was foiled by the awareness by the Quebec provincial government of what was involved, and opposed again at the July, 1963, federal-provincial conference. Intergovernmental politics brought down the effectiveness of the initiative in principle and in detail, save as it represented a make-work measure.

The 1964 amendments to the NHA were seen by the minister as representing "a completely fresh approach" to housing problems. It was to be done by increasing the powers of CMHC and by boosting its authorized funds from two to two and one-half billion dollars. Low-income housing on the one hand and urban renewal on the other were to be the means. The former never really got off the ground, but the lending institutions and city governments were now ready to go with the latter. The case for low-income housing rested on the minister's opinion that 90 percent of the entire housing output under the NHA over the years 1953-1963 had "been provided for the middle income and upper income classes."[7] He admitted that federal aid had been heavily committed to the interests of the private market. Housing the poor had represented "the greatest single area of failure" of federal housing policy. The provinces were expected to initiate low-income housing, to "designate" the municipalities to work with CMHC; and the municipalities were now entitled to ownership, after provincial approval, of public housing projects. Governments, it appeared, were really to be brought into the initiative. The bill had been discussed with the provinces and their agreement indicated. Provincial sincerity was demonstrated by the provinces in the various moves initiated to set up provincial housing and urban renewal instrumentalities from this time on. But by 1965, the minister was touring the provinces to bring home to local officials the widely extended powers of the Act. He introduced education programs to ensure that local authorities, especially in country districts, knew what was now available to them to help the poor and lower income groups. CMHC again had its funding increased in order to cope with the anticipated response in low-income provisions.

By removing the residential-use clause over land cleared through federally assisted urban renewal plans, the door was opened to the high-rise, commercial use of cleared urban renewal land. The federal government, through CMHC, was now entitled to get into the urban renewal program at its inception, not at the point of assistance for clearing already done. The excuse was "the development of fine cities in Canada." But city core development by private finance was being undertaken after public money had been used to buy up the high-priced original slum — high-priced because of its speculative component and the potential its location offered for the next step towards increased concentration — to clear it, to determine its future use, and to provide needed amenities. The terms for the co-operation of private investment were very advantageous. Because of the public support provided to initiate its development, the city core became the area in which to do business economically. The concentration of lending institutions in such areas is less explained by the ease of the face-to-face management contact it offers — which in an age of telephonic communication is questionable at best — than by the ease with which the institutions are able to locate on the land itself and to watch the projects in which their money is invested.

While the door had been opened to city core redevelopment in 1964, the federal government continued in 1965-66 to examine the nature of the political hindrances to effective rationalization of the economy. The budget speech of 1965 made clear reference to the handicap which government represented to private initiative. The scale of organization was now so large that it had narrowed the time interval between the need to initiate one set of major national developmental projects and the next. The speed, the need for, and the urgency of "growth" were mounting. The handicap of government was envisaged as being overcome in 1965 through "the use of the whole range of policies available to us and to provincial government and local authorities."[8] A co-ordination of policies and plans seemed essential — even if only because, by this time, the lower levels of government were spending much more than the federal level. This was the situation that gave rise to the idea of tri-level consensus among governments. It was first perceived as an instrument of economic development, and only in 1967-1971 as an instrument of urban development. Speeches in the federal House openly recommended a department of housing, with a full-time minister, to co-ordinate urban activities, to give comprehensive planning at all levels, to conduct research and train the urban administrators of the future. The minister, however, emphasized the need for local initiative. If only action would originate there, and the provinces be behind it, the battery of federal legislation and funding was ample to cope with it. Somewhere or other even the governmental initiative, apparently at the local level, was lacking.

In this regard Mr. Nicholson's approach was diametrically different from the two ministers who followed him — Mr. Hellyer and Mr. Andras. Mr. Nicholson appeared to accept the fundamental orientation to the division of authority implied in the constitution — a position Mr. Trudeau was later to hold to tenaciously. Mr. Hellyer's resignation in 1969 on a matter of principle over how to get the urban job done, was typical of the thoroughly political component of urban affairs which typified the end of the 1960s. At the grass roots level, individuals and ethnic minorities were strongly objecting to urban renewal and to the class of person coming to occupy the new developments, to the remoteness of the centre of decision-making, and to "buck-passing." Quebec was outspokenly unsympathetic towards the federal government, and minority parties emerged calling for a free Quebec. Ontario followed British Columbia in adopting an increasingly independent attitude towards both financial and political matters. The idea of a one prairie province rose significantly. The Maritimes were thinking of a political unity. Urban rioting south of the border raised doubts about the wisdom of city life in general, though the ethnic component of that rioting gave solace to the hope that it would not happen in Canada.

The Federal Drive for Unity

The threat of political fragmentation occurred in association with the rise of interest rates. People were caught in the paradox of a seemingly bustling and opportunistic economy with governments appearing impotent to cope with it either by taming or by directing it. There was a boom in house and high-rise construction in 1965. Consumer credit balances rose yearly more than 15 percent. Government general expenditures on universities, and similar items conspicuous to an individual's opportunities and ambitions, were rising. Inflation threatened, and interest rates started to rise more rapidly. The minister's defence was to clamp down on NHA mortgages. Home builders would in future have to get finance from conventional lenders. NHA resources, though increased, would serve the needs of the lower-income groups, students, and the aged. Conventional lenders had bigger interests than single-family dwellings, and the smaller-scale builder was in distress.

The metropolitan centres were booming for the same reasons as they had in earlier booms — a major proportion of investment anywhere eventually found its way back to them. The demographic requirements derived from Canada's post-war birth rate, coupled to a high rate of international immigration and of movement of population from rural and degraded areas of Canada, made the metropolitan housing crisis serious. Toronto's claims to increased construction as a result of long waiting lists for public housing were pressed. The cities were in trouble. The CFMM was preparing its case for "partnership" with the provinces in a revised constitution. The federal link with municipalities to service their needs, as expressed in the original idea behind the Municipal Development and Loan Board Act of 1963, had been attenuated by the provincial governments. In 1966 the minister agreed to continue NHA assistance to municipalities for urban renewal and public facilities.

In the federal House political pressure came from the contradiction between higher interest rates and higher land costs, on the one hand, and NHA responsibility for the needs of lower- and middle-income groups, on the other. One attempt after another to introduce emergency housing debates was thwarted. To try to encourage the lending institutions back to the NHA the maximum interest rate on NHA mortgages was fixed at 1½ percent above the long-term federal bond rate, to be adjusted quarterly. Flexibility of the NHA rate was expected to attract mortgage lenders, and it dropped the interest rate slightly for one quarter. Later it was found necessary to raise the ceiling to 2¼ percent above the bond rate, and later still to free the NHA rate to be fixed in terms of the market. An amendment to the Bank Act in 1966 brought the banks back into mortgages at interest rates over 6 percent. They had been lost to the field since 1959 due to this restriction. The unexpected drop in housing starts in 1967, after several added incentives had been given the lending institutions, exacerbated the political situation by enabling the opposition to question the entire housing policy in its relation to lending institutions, adequacy of construction, and financial advantage by way of return on capital at the rates of interest being charged. In the midst of this situation the minister remarked, "if you're going to live in a city you're going to have to live in an apartment." The urban dynamic, generated by the technical and organizational scale of private investment in the metropolitan centres, had put the federal government and its housing policy against the wall. The Prime Minister, over Easter 1967, undertook to review the entire housing policy.

It could be seen as being an unfortunate coincidence of events that led to this political embarrassment; but from almost every situation the independence of action and decision held sacred to private investors lay behind the difficulties. High government expenditure added to the opportunities. The federal incentives to redirect private decisions seemed only to be cumulative, yet still ineffective. Lending institution response was half-hearted. Lending institution leaders when meeting with the minister, had asked him frankly if he preferred their money to go into bonds or into mortgages. Yet the demand for housing was insatiable in the growth-prone metropolitan centres. The opposition rubbed it in. An election was due in 1968. Additional money for selected purposes was forthcoming through CMHC and the 15 percent increase in house starts of 1967 was due largely to federal money. But it did not have the impact that it had had in 1957-59. By October, 1968, NHA interest rates were at 8¾ percent, and exceeded 10 percent in January, 1970. The Prime Minister's review of 1967 did nothing to influence the main contributor to the housing contradiction — interest rates and land costs versus an inability to afford new housing.

The minister, J. R. Nicholson, identified the difficulty as resting in the rate of growth of metropolitan centres. As was the case in 1952, even if more housing could be built per year than the 160,000 odd starts currently, the city authorities were in no position to service the land required. Toronto's and other cities' by-laws, were hindering the federal initiative in housing. It was obvious to him that the only solution lay in much closer co-operation among the three levels of government in order to generate long-range planning of services and facilities to cope with this growth. The necessity for co-operation did not derive from housing *per se,* but from public investment in the regional infra-structure associated with urban concentrations and through a planned approach to suburban developments and provisions for the poor. He had suggested to the Prime Minister that some form of federal-provincial discussion take place. The BNA Act had been identified for some years as the major stumbling block to effective federal action. Regional planning, arterial highways, coping with the poor etc., all seemed to require an adequate inter-governmental mode of co-ordination. It was, therefore, at a time of genuine difficulty and political embarrassment that the federal government took the first step, in 1967, to co-operate with their elected counterparts in the provinces. Co-operation at the level of officials, of those of CMHC, the provinces, and municipalities, had been extensive for decades before. Mr. Nicholson had himself been involved in another education campaign of local officials to advise them of the provisions of the NHA. In 1967 it was a matter of moving at the political level.

The handling of that December conference by the federal government seems to have corresponded with its attitude towards the provinces since 1935. The ethos of equality among negotiators, which was abroad among the radical revolutionary minorities of the time, had not reached Ottawa. Mr. Andras, as late as 1970, had not forgotten the approach taken by the federal government, and was using the lesson to good effect that year in his own provincial discussions. But though the federal attitude was of the "take it or leave it" kind, the position it was in left little choice. Its housing policies were failing, the lending institutions were neglecting its incentives, the economy had to be reigned in, and above all, the inherent difficulty of federal-provincial relations remained. When a province was in trouble, or even a number of them were, the federal government did and would help, as several pieces of legislation affecting both have and have-not provinces, urban and rural areas, well demonstrate. But if the federal government was in trouble, as it was over a housing and urban affairs policy, would the provinces reciprocate? It was clear, following the Conference on Confederation held in Toronto in 1967 that they smelt new opportunities for power. The only possible response of the federal government was that of people with their backs to the wall, and attack was the best means of defence. They offered generous future financial support if the provinces would co-operate on larger scale planning and executive (delivery system) functions. But such co-operation could be interpreted only as the continuation of federal intrusion into the affairs over which provinces were coming increasingly to seek control.

It was not coincidental that a review of the constitution was sought by the provinces in 1967. Ontario initiated the conference on "Confederation for Tomorrow" in 1967. The federal government cold-shouldered it on the ground of there being need to do much more preparatory work. The mood of Quebec was increasingly secessionist. The CFMM was making its political position felt. Pressures in the House to establish a department of housing, or of urban affairs, were mounting. The government remained hesitant. The subject was politically sensitive in view of the initiative underway at both the lower levels of government. In Mr. Trudeau's view, with the advantage of hindsight, "The provinces realized in 1967 that new power relationships were being developed between the federal government and the provinces."[9] Mr. Pearson's proposed National Advisory Housing Council was not warmly received, nor were other aspects of his proposals, despite the federal undertaking to increase its monetary support, when it was later in a position to do so, if the province took it up. Even on the part of provincial governments, monetary incentives were proving inadequate to re-direct the thrust of urban affairs. Lester Pearson considered that the provinces required more time to consider his proposals. Urban affairs were thoroughly subservient to the interests in profit and security of the lending institutions and to the interests in political possibilities of the provinces during the last half of the 1960s.

It was in the midst of this political intrigue that Paul Hellyer accepted responsibility for housing. He was already Minister of Transport. The Treasury had agreed to commit yet more funds to CMHC for 1968, but the areas of greatest need were then identified as being regional planning, land assembly, suburban area development, and homes for moderate income families. The transport-cost item was only to emerge later, but already suburban sprawl was re-emerging in the focus of interest. Condominium housing, as one means of relieving the greater risk involved in high-rise apartments, was slow to catch on. Members of the House were pressing for a re-assessment of the traditional Canadian preference for a single-family dwelling. Provincial housing instruments were accepting responsibility for land assembly, sewage treatment plants, and public housing, under CMHC financing. To distribute better the proportion of single-family to multiple-storey, and therefore rental accommodation, CMHC was awarded special funds to boost the former. This placed CMHC in the residual role of supporting the single-family dwelling when the lending institutions were disinterested. This virtually brought full circle the involvement of the federal government in the support of family dwellings. This involvement had started in 1935 through assistance to lending institutions for the construction of this type of dwelling. By 1970 the federal government had itself become the direct provider of finance while lending institutions were leaving the field for bigger and better things. There was now no area with which CMHC was not directly involved.

The cancellation of the winter works program, and its replacement by stepped-up vocational training at federal expense to train the unemployed rather than hire them, hit the municipalities very hard. They were deprived of a useful source of winter funds which allowed them some discretion over its use. The blow of 1968 was the need once again to depress the economy to curb inflation. The federal government had also reasserted its intention to get out of some of the shared-cost programs which it had initiated with the provinces. Provincial governments had ample cause for concern. This was the context in which the Hellyer Task Force was announced in August, 1968. This "genuine search for the facts" received a very mixed reception both inside and outside the House. Its reception by the provinces was not improved by the interim freezing of urban renewal and public housing. The task force was itself rather cold to provincial participation. The federal government was seen as intruding at the level of the minister himself into the details of municipal and provincial planning at the level of the building site. It was not too bad when CMHC officials were there; but not a politician. The minister's cancellation of projects reflected badly on the local authorities. Some 16 of the recommendations were concerned with matters which the provinces liked to feel were within their jurisdiction. The task force reiterated the need for a department of housing and urban affairs.

By 1969, the federal government had warmed to the constitutional revision initiated by the provinces in 1967. Its revision was coming to be seen increasingly as the instrument to accomplish the handling of a number of national issues including pollution and urban affairs. Mr. Trudeau recognized the present constitution as "either silent or vague about the level of government which has the legal competence to tackle them."[10] The constitution needed to be brought into the 20th century. But the Prime Minister recognized the continued need for inter-governmental agreement over the *modus operandi* to do the job. The opposition parties urged that the federal government behave as it had since 1935 and get on with the jobs that needed to be done. Mr. Hellyer was similarly disposed. The rift in government ranks was apparent in the House by March, 1969. The CFMM was pressing for the recognition of official representation at the forthcoming federal-provincial constitutional review conference in June. Mr. Trudeau felt it was a matter for the provinces to decide, and that the federal government had to remain outside the decision. Mr. Hellyer's resignation became effect on April 30, 1969. It was a time of fundamental political crisis with urban affairs as its centre. No longer was it a problem only of housing.

The relation of all three levels of government to each other and to the urban in general was at stake.

The thread of Mr. Andras's thought has been much more subtle. To proceed from an initial uncertainty and groping with an unfamiliar field to a clear-cut plan of action to cope with urbanism on a national scale, and involving co-ordinated federal policy as a deliberate act, is his achievement. The achievement has turned what might be construed as a last-ditch stand of the federal government over its long-standing authority over housing, urban pathological proneness, and related matters, to one of potential initiative. The form of this initiative, however, differs from that existing since 1935.

The federal government is now searching for a unitary governmental approach to urban affairs. It is having to do so within the terms of the existing constitution, though it has not formally given up the prospect of a new constitution. That these two issues of urban affairs and constitutional revision are irrevocably linked has been clear for many years. Whether both issues can be accomplished together through a unitary perspective remains to be seen.

The Provincial Role in the Urban Policy for Canada

The units of political significance with which provincial governments are structurally bound to relate may be identified as being: their citizenry and electors; their local authorities of immensely varied size and political significance; the lending institutions and privately organized capital active in their metropolitan centres, but many of whose head offices are located elsewhere and who are in close touch with federal authorities; the professional opinion and contemporary fashion of their intelligentsia whether in the civil services or in consulting capacities; the trade union movement, whose influence on urban affairs we suspect to be significant but have been unable to determine in this study; the other provinces of Canada; and, lastly, the federal authorities in their diverse kinds. This is a formidable array. Each in turn has its own structural arrangement, social process, and dynamic.

The national urban policy, as outlined so far by federal authorities, has concerned itself largely with obtaining consensus about the future nature of the urban in Canada. Once goals are agreed upon, then rational methods of allocating responsibility, resources, decisions, etc., can be worked out. The straight-jacketing of people, and of people's relation to things, and of things to things, is made so very much simpler if this can be done. Politics and jurisdictional rights of decision can be put aside in the interests of achieving the end already agreed upon. The end comes to justify the means. The guarantor of success is the acquisition of and the sensibly-directed use of "perfect knowledge" about everything involved. Reality is reduced to the conditions of the laboratory and the computer. This concern over goals, so far as our evidence suggests, has also been limited largely to public institutions. The tri-levels of government must reach a consensus. Very little has been said or written so far about the other very influential components of the structural nexus in which provincial governments have to operate.

The reasons for this are obscure. Perhaps the naive belief was held that the relation between governments and privately organized capital is in its reality one of direction — that if necessary the federal government could get the co-operation of lending institutions, manufacturers, and so forth, with its policies. The history of the influence of companies on urban affairs suggests the opposite to be the case, whether inside NHA provisions or not. Privately organized capital remains the critical component in the success of any policy for Canada. As such, the relation that any and all levels of government established with it will affect, in the long-term, the success or failure of any agreed upon consensus to which governments may arrive. Similarly, the relation of the governments to each other will be influenced in marked degree by the relation which any level of government establishes with privately organized capital. In the past, this latter relation has been established overwhelmingly in terms of the tax dollar, its distribution over the levels of government, and the intent behind its expenditure. If an urban policy is to have any practical hope of success, the relation must come increasingly to apply at the point of locating privately organized investment, rather than coping with situations emerging after that investment has occurred.

This swing of influence to that point in time prior to making private investment is already increasing in extent and influence. The incentives offered to manufacturing throughout the 1960s to locate in degraded regions and especially under DREE, illustrate the point. The free reign given the lending institutions since 1935 to decide the location of the investments they were making under NHA incentives has been one of the major lacunae in government influence. Similarly, the slum clearance, urban redevelopment, and urban renewal measures, especially in the 1960s, have been governmentally-induced directives as to the location of particular kinds of public and private investment. The required influence is not new in Canada, despite the sacredness afforded the right of location to private investment. Governments and companies have always been aware of the influence of public investment on private investment. What is needed for the effectiveness of an urban policy is to regulate more efficaciously the relation of private investment to governmental policy. This Dr. Lithwick certainly had in mind in the discrimination of a "constrained future" from an "unconstrained future." What he did not consider was the way the instruments of government should be related to private investment.

The municipalities, rather than the federal government, should be the level at which governmental planning and private enterprise relate together in the interests of a national urban policy. Approaches to problem-solving too often assume that because the apex of decision is at the top in Ottawa, affairs should be put in order there first. Federal responsibility since 1935 has given urban affairs the appearance that effective action is possible only through the top. This responsibility has similarly been the excuse for retaining public funds at that level and thereby emasculating the efficacy of lower governmental levels. The reason for the municipality being an appropriate level at which governmental planning and private enterprise relate together in the interests of a national urban policy is because it is the site on which money capital is transformed into physical capital. The nature of capital is thereby transformed from a flexible state which may cross political boundaries, into a fixed asset. The municipality is also the point at which public investment relates to the productive process whether in physical matter or human terms. As such it is the point at which public control may be exercised over privately organized capital, and the concept of an urban policy made effective.

The difficulties of tri-level governmental co-ordination with centralized decision-making arise from three interlocked processes. First, the time taken to apply a fundamental re-orientation of policy inhibits and complicates the decisions essential to the administration of day-to-day matters at the point of real, i.e., enduring, action. The handling of urban renewal and public housing guidelines since 1969 illustrates the point. The time taken to get effective agreement on policy, not to mention the *modus operandi,* is similarly stultifying, as the lengthy discussions since 1969 between federal and provincial governments and their ministers clearly show. Frustrations, prejudices, and mistrust build up. Second, the discipline imposed on lower levels by the application of superiorly conceived plans of action, even within the terms of an agreed upon policy, tends to be resented. It is a discipline not always understood, and tends to be understood as political control rather than as a sensible means to acceptable ends. Third, centralization of decision comes inevitably to be associated with the urgent requirement of "perfect knowledge" at the top to ensure the accuracy and efficacy of decisions themselves. Mr. Andras's awareness of the extreme complexity of the urban, and of the frequent unanticipated consequences that resulted from benevolently-intended federal acts, bear witness to this trend. The fact is that "perfect knowledge" is unattainable in social matters, for people carry their own consciousness around in their own heads. In a society that permits, in fact even encourages, the expression of that consciousness both in verbal forms and in acts and contracts, it is ridiculous to expect that that consciousness continuously conforms to the requirements derived from a mythical state of "perfect knowledge." The frequency with which grandiose corrective or developmental schemes at the top come to pieces on the rocks of reality and end up being the data of historians, bears witness to this fact.

The relating of the municipal level to privately organized capital takes place within provincial jurisdiction under the present constitution. On the assumption that this is not amended, then the legal power of the provincial legislature and the limited boundaries (and hence limited jurisdiction) of municipal governments are the two chief instruments for reasserting a consequence to provincial decision. A third possible instrument is the funds for public investment held at the provincial level. In the past, however, far too much reliance has been placed on the power of holding the purse strings whether at the federal or provincial level of government. This is the convenient way of exercising authority when it is important to retain the myth of independence of subordinate governmental levels. But it is fundamentally dishonest, obscures the policies which senior levels are implementing, and denies that attribute of democracy which concerns public involvement, public awareness of the issues, and public concern over the handling of public affairs by elected representatives. An administration which is prepared to say "No," to state its reasons for so saying, and to expect its subordinates to respect both its rights of decision and the merits of its case, is far more likely to make work a national urban policy for Canada than one which hides this unpleasant duty under the mirage of bureaucratic manoeuvres and financial excuses.

More than that, however, such clear-cut demonstration of both policy and authority would oblige lending institutions in the exercise of their right to lend capital to developmental proposals put to them, to consider and negotiate with lower levels of government over that investment. Privately organized capital in general would have much clearer terms laid out by governments within which their actions and choices could be made effective. Currently, the grey area of ifs and buts, of manoeuvre, pressure, intrigue, pay offs, and other bargaining, is so wide in its relation to governmental authorities that only the management of that company is fully aware of the whole range of possibilities it has obtained. In consequence it is immensely powerfully placed in its relation to any urban policy.

Business enterprises, indeed, are organizing in this grey area of uncertainty. In the December 18, 1971, edition of the *Financial Post* an editorial feature by Philip Mathias describes the activities of a still small number of companies whose specialty is to assist lower levels of government, or companies, intending to benefit from some public incentive. The president of one company is reported to have remarked:

> More and more provinces are discovering you need an expert in Ottawa to work out just what a company is entitled to from the federal government.[11]

A carefully cultivated and very extensive network of contacts, who are already working in the business of industrial promotion, is said to be the "lifeblood" of this company. The president then explained:

> Our direct mail programs generate industrial prospects for our client communities and provinces, but also enable us to provide lists of expansion-minded industrialists to the business development offices of Canadian banks here and abroad, the railways, engineering companies and anyone in the business of industrial development. They in turn provide us with the names of prospects that might be of value in the regions we are servings.[12]

This service to both lower levels of government and to companies in search of developmental locations is the consequence of the growing contribution of public incentives to the direction of industrial investment. It is a prime example of the competitive nature of subordinate levels of government with each other to cope, on the one hand, with federal incentives and on the other, with private capital.

The struggle for growth, as was argued earlier, is associated with the scale of modern organization and technological effectiveness. It is associated too with the pay-off on large investments already made. Mayors, no less than company management, are involved in it. Company management is always under the pressure of threats of being taken over, of losing out in the race for control of markets or of primary materials. Mayors are relieved of this in some measure, though the importance of population data, of companies established in their midst, and of access to water, electricity and a means of disposing of effluent, are genuine concerns. The threat to mayors tends to come from an inability to negotiate successfully with the superior levels of government, the public utilities, public governmental but administrative boards, and with companies considering the prospect of locating in their jurisdiction. This problem of the mayoral office reflects the competitive relation of municipalities. The struggle is the essence of the regulatory process which permits and facilitates metropolitan concentration. The influence of the provincial government over its subordinate local governments must be exerted over this struggle.

Looking at urban affairs from this perspective differs markedly from approaches which see the constitutional rights of provinces as hindrances to the evolution of a federally initiated national urban policy, or which seek the gaining of consensus over goals without clearly specifying the roles and responsibilities of the lower levels of government. This perspective differs too from the emphasis given the nexus of urban interlocking relations among metropolitan centres of Canada, a nexus that can and must remain only a federal responsibility. It permits a much clearer definition of duties and therefore of relations among the three levels of government.

In Volume 2 we deal specifically with the Alberta scene. But in its more general application, the regulation of metropolitan concentration requires provincial governmental decision. It cannot be left to the decision of companies, with governments at all levels merely struggling to cope with the consequences that follow. Each province will need to bear in mind the consequences of its policy towards both concentration and decentralization. Only very recently have the costs in terms of public investment required to meet either the development of growing city infrastructures or the redevelopment of degraded rural regions been brought to consciousness. In the struggle to compete in world markets, to raise Canadian incomes and standards, to provide the services manufacturing claimed it needed, and to meet the consequences of urban living for Canadian individuals, the costs of concentration and attrition have been forgotten. When these costs are brought home to provincial governments, when it becomes their responsibility to enforce some of the obvious answers to these costs, they will become increasingly inclined to play a constructive role in the implementation of a national urban policy in Canada. At the present time their relative inconsequence of decision obliges them to play the political rather than the developmental and constructively administrative game.

Provincial governments have power to determine the boundaries, responsibilities, and privileges of local authorities. They also have rights of taxation. It is already within their power to influence the location of private investment through differential taxation mechanisms and publicly provided incentives affecting location. Thus, if the wishes of a company to locate in an area poorly served with effluent treatment facilities are to be coped with, the decision must be taken not by the local authority but by the province. If the public, through municipal and provincial tax revenue, has already financed in a nearby town the development of sewage facilities sufficient to meet the effluent of the intended investment, the company could be advised and told also that no differential taxation would be imposed on it were it to locate there. If the company wished to locate where costly services would have to follow from that decision then it would have the choice of either providing them to given standards itself, or of paying a business tax sufficient to amortize the public expenditure which would be involved. The business tax could be amended pro rata as other companies became users of the service. This is but the principle of user taxation applied broadly. It is the principle required in a much wider sphere. It is currently unpopular among influential sections because it is so convenient to companies when public subsidies might be arranged, and it is relatively easy to have it forgiven when there is every opportunity of playing off one local authority against another over the right to locate.

The implication of this proposal is that provincial governments must generate greater co-operation among their own departments, among the senior governmental instruments affecting development, and among municipalities and provincial authorities. The province as a unit needs to be seen in terms of its totality. Regional development in so far as it means the relating of a region to a given urban centre within it, is conceptually abortive. It is derived from concepts of planning that expand from the city outwards. These are often convenient in that they conform to the "reality" of the forces involved; but it is precisely this "reality" that needs questioning through a provincial and a national dimension of control and co-ordination. Regional development, in so far as it means the identification of economic assets and human rights in particular parts of a provincial administration, is a necessary part of a province's responsibilities. If a population is already present, as in the degraded regions, and is in possession of useful personal assets such as housing and town facilities, then that region should be identified as warranting particular incentives to locate industry suitable to its economic assets. Industrial location may then be placed in the service of people rather than people's migration and loss of personal assets put in the service of industrial location. By the governmental provision of adequate housing in an identified area, to accommodate workers already employed by local industry in difficulties over labor because of the absence of accommodation; by arranging adequate heavy-duty road standards, or a low business tax, a

322

diversity of non-metropolitan locations come within the ambit of possibility of location for private investment.

This principle, of course, lies at the base of the current federal DREE program. In principle it is nothing new, but the method of making the principle effective is at stake. One has to ask why it was necessary to build into the department federal legislative provision for the supply of needed public service infra-structure to support a new industry when this is a provincial responsibility. Why should federal-provincial agreements be necessary to develop the public services to support incentive directed manufacturing? It is also questionable whether public money should be given to a private company by way of incentive grant merely as the inducement for it to locate in degraded areas. There are other techniques available, but they are unpopular to the power centres of metropolitan cities and to private capital already located there. The federal initiative is in this sense the easy way out. It typifies the subordinate role of government to established centres of power and thereby brings into question the principle upon which Dr. Lithwick's "constrained future" and the urban policy for Canada has a practical reality.

Correspondingly, however, the principle of a user tax, at the rate of the cost of the service, should be practised increasingly in the metropolitan centres. This principle merely applies the same principle to companies and people as they expect of others, namely, that a program, organization, or person pay his way. At present, larger and larger subsidies for bigger and bigger projects are anticipated by local authorities from the senior levels of government, and therefore ultimately from the taxpayer. The scale of organization and technology requires this scale of enterpise and expenditure, but only governments and the public are expected to fund it. The ideas of negative incentive and of pay-your-own-way are far from new or alien to Canadian culture, but it is a matter of to whom they should be made to apply.

The apparent "failure" of present schemes of regional development apart from the hostility of "rationalists" — is due to the split at the federal level between DREE and the Ministry of Urban Affairs. The split seems such good sense in view of the different geographic localities of the respective problem areas. But both are coping with the same problem, namely, the right of private investment to locate at its discretion and the expectation that public money will assist it to carry out its intentions under conditions where it can ignore the socio-economic consequence of its decision. The condition for the success of DREE is that the growth of Toronto, Montreal, and other large cities, be restricted to a rate and to a type with which these centres can economically cope. Currently the success of the urban ministry is that more and more of the public's money must be devoted to making the urban centres rationally provided for, rationally structured, and habitable. There is a contradiction inherent in these intents. The taxpayer is expected to reconcile it.

Both agencies are seen as federal responsibilities, as meeting a national need, and immediately become compromised in constitutional entanglements with provincial jurisdictions. Agreements and contracts covering specific issues become necessary to protect the rights of provinces, the execution of a program, and the delineation of responsibilities. The making of such agreements is a cumbersome and expensive procedure brought about by the compromised administrative capacity of both levels of senior government. A change in the constitution to smooth out the problem is one alternative, but the only change which could be effective would be one that provided a clear-cut federal initiative. The present constitution gives this clear-cut initiative to the provinces. But the provincial initiative is crippled by its relative inconsequence of decision with regard to both the federal and local government levels. If provincial governments themselves, however, were responsible for seeing urban concentration and regional degradation as two halves of one process — not as separate but interacting processes, but as one process, with a common denominator in the right of private capital to locate and the public to pay for the consequences — then their attitude to the issues and responsibilities would change.

Should provincial governments take on the responsibility for guiding urban development, the urgent need for province-wide plans and regional developmental mechanisms would emerge. These are currently within the range of civil servants' and elected members' consciousness; but they are subordinate to other, momentarily more significant issues. The study and research centres would be decentralized to the provinces in sympathy with the change in importance that their new role would require. The federal research emphasis could also have clear terms of reference instead of its currently compromised national, intra-national, and international interests. The need for mythical states of "perfect knowledge" on all relevant things at the centre of decision would evaporate. Research might then come to take up more realistic and rewarding problems.

The metropolitan growth mania and the degraded region phobia would become part of the one administrative concept. Similarly, the motive that has guided federal initiative in urban affairs since 1935 — one or other state of human or physical morbidity — would change to a more genuinely constructive emphasis. Over the past three and a half decades federal urban initiative in every form it has taken has been aimed to cope with existing or developing pathology. This is no basis on which to build national urban policy. The prerequisite for changing to a more constructive federal initiative is the freeing of the federal government from its entanglement with provincial governments over their respective constitutional jurisdictions in the interests of "doing something" for the poor, the degraded regions, the blighted slums, the aged and so forth.

The provinces are not in any particularly good shape at present to handle constructively the responsibilities which such a re-arrangement would involve. Though there are provincial research institutions, and provincial departments carry out research enquiries of diverse kinds, there are no institutions like the one established within the Ministry of Urban Affairs and Housing. Similarly, some excellent research branches exist in the local authorities of metropolitan centres.

Their concern, however, is the furtherance of metropolitan interests, not of the interests of the province collectively considered. It is at the provincial level that the research and planning capacity needs to be considerably strengthened.

1. In the western prairies this tendency was modified until as recently as the past two decades, perhaps, by the belief that savings put into a small piece of land and a house was the ultimate in investment security. Elderly people in Alberta today still argue in these terms despite the evidence to the contrary, i.e. they themselves hold or seek jobs in neighboring urban centres.

2. We refer only to urban and regional degradation, not to the use of private companies for other public purposes such as railways, etc. It is their use to cope with the pathological aspects of the social, rather than as instruments of national construction and development which concerns us.

3. See quotation, Chapter 2, p. 87.

4. See Chapter 2, p. 87.

5. The criticisms of DREE and its programs are a rewarding research area in their own right. How private capital — in the form of manufacturing, agricultural interests, commerce and lending institutions — reacts and adjusts to this federal initiative is important for several reasons. If a policy of urban decentralization is adopted, some lessons from the DREE initiative could usefully be learnt ahead of such a policy decision, such as the degree of importance of the support of lending institutions.

6. *Housing and Urban Growth in Canada,* CMHC, 1956, Chapter VII.

7. See Chapter 4, pp. 154.

8. See Chapter 4, pp. 162.

9. Quoted in Chapter 6, p. 270.

10. Quoted in Chapter 5, p. 208.

11. *Financial Post,* December 18, 1971.

12. Ibid.

The purpose of this bibliography is to list in one place the sources for the material quoted and the statements made in the text of both volumes in this study. The items in the bibliography are grouped according to kind of source and to status of publication. Generally, they move from published material fairly easily accessible to unpublished material not so easily accessible.

I. Non-Governmental Sources

A: Books

Alonso, W., "Planning as a Profession," in H. Wentworth Eldredge (ed.), *Taming Megalopolis,* New York, Praeger, 1967.
Bailey, F. G., *Strategems and Spoils,* Toronto, Copp Clark Co., 1969.
Berton, Pierre, *The National Dream: The Great Railway 1871-1881,* Toronto/Montreal, McClelland Stewart Ltd., 1970.
— *The Last Spike: The Great Railway 1881-1885,* Toronto/Montreal, McClelland and Stewart Ltd., 1971.
Blue, John, *Alberta: Past and Present,* Volume One, Chicago, Pioneer Historical Publishing House, 1924.
Blumenfeld, Hans, *The Modern Metropolis,* Cambridge, MIT Press, 1967.
Brewis, T. N., *Regional Economic Policies in Canada,* Toronto, Macmillan, 1967.
Gershaw, F. W., *Saamis: The Medicine Hat,* Medicine Hat, Val Marshall Printing Ltd., n.d.
Gerth, H. H., and Mills, C. W., (eds.), *From Max Weber,* London, Kegan Paul, Trench, Trubner and Company Ltd., 1947.
Gertler, Leonard, O., "Some Economic and Social Influences on Regional Planning in Alberta," in Gertler (ed.), *Planning the Canadian Environment,* Montreal, Harvest House, 1968.
Hanson, Eric J., *Local Government in Alberta,* Toronto, McClelland and Stewart Ltd., 1956.
Hellyer, Paul T., *Agenda: A Plan for Action,* Scarborough (Ont.), Prentice-Hall of Canada Ltd., 1971.
Irving, John A., *The Social Credit Movement in Alberta,* University of Toronto Press, 1959, paperback ed., 1968.

Johnson, L. P. V., and MacNutt, Ola J., *Aberhart of Alberta,* Edmonton, Co-op Press Ltd. for the Institute of Applied Art, 1970.

Kellough, W. R., and Beaton, W., "Anatomy of the Housing Shortage," in R. Matsushita (ed.), *Issues for the Seventies: Housing,* Toronto, McGraw-Hill, 1971.

Kenward, John K., "Contemporary Administrative Problems," in Dr. F. Jankunis (ed.), *Southern Alberta: A Regional Perspective,* Department of Geography, University of Lethbridge, Lethbridge, Alberta, 1971.

Kindleberger, Charles (ed.), *The International Corporation, Cambridge. MIT Press, 1970.*

MacGregor, J. G., *Edmonton: A History,* Edmonton, M. G. Hurtig Publishers, 1967.

MacPherson, C. B., *Democracy in Alberta: Social Credit and the Party System,* University of Toronto Press, second edition, 1962.

Moore, A. M., Perry, J. H. and Beach, D. I., *The Financing of Canadian Federation, the First Hundred Years,* Toronto, Canadian Tax Foundation, 1966.

Myrdal, Gunnar, *Rich Lands and Poor,* New York, Harpers, 1957

Nowland, D. and N., *The Bad Trip,* New Press/House of Anansi, 1970.

Thomas, L. G., *The Liberal Party in Alberta,* University of Toronto Press, 1959.

Turner, Louis, *Invisible Empires,* New York, Harcourt, 1971.

B: Journal Articles

Boumol, W., "Macroeconomics of Unbalanced Growth: The Anatomy of Urban Crisis," *American Economic Review,* 58 (1967), 415-426.

Gibson, John, "The Impact of the Railroad on Urban Patterns . . . An Alberta Example," *The Albertan Geographer* (Department of Geography, University of Alberta, Edmonton), 1 (1964-65), 41-6.

Hanson. E. J., "Provincial Grants in Alberta," *The Canadian Tax Journal,* (Sept.-Oct., 1953).

Laux, F. A., "The Zoning Game: Alberta Style," *Alberta Law Review,* 9 (1971), 268-308.

— "The Zoning Game — Alberta Style: Part II, Development Control," *Alberta Law Review,* 10 (1972), 1-37.

"Regional Potpurri," *TPIC News* (Town Planning Institute of Canada), August 1971 and August 1972.

C: Newspapers

The Albertan, October 30, 1970; January 5, January 7, February 1, April 26, May 5, 1972.

The Calgary Herald, February 29, 1970; February 20, August 14, November 27, December 17, 1971; January 3, 4, 5, 12, 13, 17, 26, February 4, 9, 10, 12, 15, 23, 24, 25, 29, March 1, 2, 10, 16, 24, 27, 28, April 18-22, 24-27, May 6, 8, 9, 13, 18, 24, June 17, 1972.

Canadian Homes section, *The Canadian Magazine and The Canadian Magazine Star Weekly.* October 1971.

Edmonton Journal, March 26, December 30, 1968; November 17, 1971.

The Financial Post, December 14, 1957; January 16, December 18, 1971.
Lethbridge Herald, April 2, 3, 6, August 6, 1970.
Rocky View News and Market Examiner, November 30, 1971.

D: Theses

Anderson, James, "Change in a Central Place System: Trade Centres and Rural Service in Central Alberta." Unpublished MA Thesis, Department of Geography, University of Alberta, 1967.
Bussard, Lawrence H., "Early History of Calgary." Unpublished MA Thesis, Department of History, University of Alberta, 1935.
Chan, Wah May Winnie, "The Impact of the Technical Planning Board on the Morphology of Edmonton." Unpublished MA Thesis, Department of Geography, University of Alberta, 1969.
Dale, Edmund H., "The Role of Successive Town and City Councils in the Evolution of Edmonton, Alberta, 1892 to 1966." Unpublished PhD Thesis, Department of Geography, University of Alberta, Edmonton, 1969.
Kenward, J. K., "Political Manipulation and Rewards in The Crowsnest Pass, Southern Alberta." Unpublished MA Thesis, Department of Political Science, Sociology and Anthropology, Simon Fraser University, Burbaby, B.C., 1971.

E: Reports, Briefs, Unpublished Manuscripts

Bowness Community Association, Planning and Development Committee, Report to the Mayor, February 18, 1972 (Calgary).
Canadian Chemcell Company Ltd., Submission to the Local Authorities Board, May 30, 1963 (Edmonton).
Canadian Industries Ltd., Submission to the Local Authorities Board, May, 1963 (Edmonton).
Dant, Noel, "A Brief History of the Planning Statutes in Alberta," unpublished paper.
Hickling-Johnson Ltd., Management Consultants, *Economic Study: Town of Fort Saskatchewan,* June 1970.
The Immorality of the Motor Car, An Information Project of The University Practicum in Community Analysis, Community Resources Division, The Department of Extension, The University of Alberta, Winter Session 1970-71.
Seymour, Horace L., "Town Planning Progress in Alberta up to December 31st, 1931," manuscript in Provincial Archives, Edmonton.
Social Planning Council of Calgary, *Housing in Calgary,* January 1968.
Society for Pollution and Environmental Control, Brief to the Public Hearing, February 22, 1972, Concerning City of Calgary Transportation System Bylaw No. 8500.
Urban Development Institute, Calgary Chapter, Charter.
Urban Research Group, *Decision Making in Plant Site Location,* Saskatoon, Saskatchewan, September 1970.

II: Governmental Sources

A: *Federal*

Canada Year Book, 1911 to 1967, but especially 1936, 1938, 1946, and
1967.

1. *House of Commons:*

House of Commons Debates, 1935 to 1970.
House of Commons, Special Committee on Housing, *Report,* Ottawa,
Government Printer, 1935.
House of Commons, Standing Committee on Health, Welfare, and Social
Affairs, *Minutes of Proceedings and Evidence,* No. 39, June 5, 1969.
House of Commons, Standing Committee on Regional Development,
Minutes of Proceedings and Evidence, No. 15, June 11, 1969, and
No. 16, June 16, 1969.

2. *Senate:*

Senate of Canada, *Report of the Special Committee on Land Use in
Canada,* Ottawa, Queens Printer, 1964.

3. *Royal Commissions and Task Forces:*

Graver, A. E., *Housing, a Study Prepared for the Royal Commission
on Dominion-Provincial Relations,* Ottawa, 1939.
Mackintosh, W. A., *The Economic Background of Dominion-Provincial
Relations,* being Appendix 3 to the *Report of the Royal Commission on
Dominion-Provincial Relations,* Ottawa, 1939.
1964 Report of the Royal Commission on Banking and Finance,
Ottawa, Queen's Printer, 1965.
Report of the Task Force on Housing and Urban Development, Ottawa,
Queen's Printer, 1969.

4. *Various Government Departments, Councils, and Bureaus:*

Federal Services for Businessmen, Department of Industry, Trade and
Commerce, Ottawa, Queen's Printer, 1970.
McCrorie, James N., *A.R.D.A.: An Experiment in Development
Planning,* Special Study No. 2, Canadian Council on Rural
Development, Ottawa, Queen's Printer, 1969.
Monthly Reports, Department of Regional Economic Expansion,
Ottawa, 1970.
Stone, L. O., *Urban Development in Canada,* 1961 Census Monograph,
Dominion Bureau of Statistics, Ottawa, 1967.

5. *Economic Council of Canada:*

Anderson, Isobel B., *Internal Migration in Canada, — 1921-61,* Economic
Council of Canada, Staff Study 13, Ottawa, 1966.
Buckley, Helen, and Tihanyi, Eva, *Canadian Policies for Rural
Adjustment,* Economic Council of Canada, Special Study No. 7,
Ottawa, Queen's Printer, 1967.
Economic Council of Canada, *Fourth Annual Review: The Canadian
Economy from the 1960's to the 1970's,* Ottawa, 1967.

Illing, Wolfgang M., *Housing Demand to 1970,* Economic Council of Canada, Staff Study 4, Ottawa, 1965.

Illing, Wolfgang M., Kasahaia, Yoshiko, Denton, F. T., and George, M. W., *Population, Family, Household, and Labour Force Growth to 1980,* Economic Council of Canada, Staff Study 19, Ottawa, 1967.

6. Central Mortgage and Housing Corporation:

Andras, Robert (federal minister responsible for housing), "An Address to the Canadian Institute of Public Affairs," Toronto, February 27, 1970.

— Press Release, CMHC, Ottawa, June 10, 1970.

— "Address to the Union of British Columbia Municipalities," Press Release, CMHC, Ottawa, September 17, 1970.

— "Address to the 66th Annual Conference of the Union of Nova Scotia Municipalities," Press Release, CMHC, Ottawa, May 17, 1971.

— "Address to the Conference on Cities, Indianapolis, Indiana," Press Release, CMHC, Ottawa, May 26, 1971.

— "Address to the National Forum of the American Institute of Architects, Detroit, Michigan," Press Release, CMHC, Ottawa, June 23, 1971.

— "Federal Minister Responsible for Housing, Remarks by," Press Release, CMHC, Ottawa, June 28, 1971.

— "Address to The Canadian Real Estate Association, Montreal," Press Release, CMHC, Ottawa, October 20, 1971.

Canadian Housing Statistics, CMHC, Ottawa, 1960, 4th quarter 1960, 4th quarter 1965, 1967, 1970, March 1971.

CMHC Report — Land Values (for year 1971).

Feldman, L. D., *et al., A Survey of Alternative Urban Policies,* Research Monograph 6, CMHC, Ottawa, 1971.

Gillespie, W. L., *The Urban Public Economy,* Research Monograph 4, CMHC, Ottawa.

Housing and Urban Growth in Canada, CMHC, Ottawa, 1956.

Lithwick, N. H., *Urban Canada: Problems and Prospects. A Report Prepared for the Hon. R. K. Andras, Minister for Housing,* CMHC, Ottawa, 1970.

Press Releases, CMHC, Ottawa, November 15 and 17, 1971.

7. Other:

Press Releases, Office of the Prime Minister, Ottawa, November 15-17, 1971.

B: Inter-Provincial Organizations

Atlantic Development Council, *A Strategy for the Economic Development of the Atlantic Region, 1971-1981,* Fredericton (N.B.), 1971.

Canadian Federation of Mayors and Municipalities, *Brief to the Prime Minister of Canada, Ottawa,* April 26, 1971.

The Municipality in the Canadian Federation, Position Paper prepared by the Joint Municipal Committee on Intergovernmental Relations, Canadian Federation of Mayors and Municipalities, August 1970.

C: Provincial (Alberta)

1. Laws and Orders:

Statues of Alberta, 1906 to 1970.
Revised Statutes of Alberta, 1922 to 1970.
Order-in-Council No. 969-53, *The Alberta Gazette,* July 15, 1953, 1126.
(Order dated July 6, 1953).
Provincial Planning Board Order 286-M-68, October 16, 1968.
Provincial Planning Board Order, October 27, 1971.
Local Authorities Board Order No. 1234, March 31, 1964, *The Alberta
Gazette,* April 30, 1964, 959-997.
— No. 3981, *The Alberta Gazette.* January 15, 1969, 114-120
— No. 4192, *The Alberta Gazette.* May 31, 1969, 1227-1233.
— No. 4804, *The Alberta Gazette.* August 15, 1970, 1582-1589.
— No. 5008, *The Alberta Gazette,* January 15, 1971, 207-222.
— No. 5010, *The Alberta Gazette,* January 15, 1971, 226-231.
— No. 5505, *The Alberta Gazette,* November 15, 1971, 2831-2837.

2. Government of Alberta — Policy Speeches and Statements:

Budget Speeches to the Legislature, 1950, 1952, 1953, 1954, 1955, 1957,
1958, 1962, 1963, 1966, 1967, 1969, 1970, 1971, Edmonton, Queen's
Printer.
Government of the Province of Alberta, *The Case for Alberta 1938,*
Edmonton, 1938.
Manning, the Hon. E. C., *A White Paper on Human Resources
Development,* presented to the Alberta Legislature, March 1967.
— Speech to the Legislature, March 5, 1951, Edmonton, Queen's
Printer.
Strom, the Hon. Harry E., "Address to the Town Planning Institute
of Canada, 1970 Conference, Edmonton, on July 21, 1970," Press
Release, Office of the Premier, July 21, 1970.
— Premier of Alberta, *"A Position Paper* to the Federal-Provincial
Constitutional Conference in Ottawa, September, 1970," Edmonton,
Queen's Printer, 1970.
— "Address to the Alberta Urban Municipalities Association," Press
Release, Office of the Premier, Edmonton, October 30, 1970.

3. Royal Commissions, Special Committees, Task Forces:

The Interim First Report of the Co-Terminous Boundary Commission,
Edmonton, Government of the Province of Alberta, 1953.
*Report of the Public Expenditure and Revenue Study Committee,
Province of Alberta,* Edmonton, March 1966.
"Report of the Royal Commission on Taxation," *Sessional Paper* No. 71,
1948, Government of the Province of Alberta, Edmonton, February 12,
1948.
*Report of the Royal Commission on the Metropolitan Development of
Calgary and Edmonton,* Edmonton, Queen's Printer, 1956. (McNally
Commission Report.)
*Report of the Special Committee Appointed by the Government of
Alberta to Study Assessment and Taxation,* Edmonton, March, 1970.

Task Force on Urbanization and the Future, *The Role of Regional Planning*, Edmonton, November 1971.

4. Government Departments; Bureaus, and Corporations:

Alberta Bureau of Statistics, *Alberta Industry and Resources*, Edmonton, 1970.

Alberta Housing and Urban Renewal Corporation, *Alberta Housing Profile*, September 10, 1968.

— *A Satellite Community Study for the Edmonton and Calgary Areas*, October 1969.

Alberta Housing Corporation, "Public Housing," Pamphlet, Alberta Housing Corporation Public Relations Department, n.d.

Department of Education, *Thirty-Third Annual Report*, 1938.

Department of Education, *Forty-Third Annual Report*, 1948.

Department of Municipal Affairs, *The Alberta Planning Fund: To Provide Equitable Financing For: Regional Planning, Provincial Planning*, March 1971. (Later draft of *A Proposal* etc., below).

— *Municipal Statistics including Improvement Districts in Special Areas for the year ended December 31, 1969.*

— *A Proposal: To Provide Equitable Financing: City Planning, Regional Planning, Provincial Planning*, August 1970. (Earlier draft of *The Alberta Planning Fund*, above.)

— "The Story of the Industrial Tax Proposal," Unpublished Brief, n.d. (*circa* 1961).

Minister of Municipal Affairs, Statement, January 5, 1972.

Municipal Development and Loan Board, *Annual Report*, March 31, 1968.

Public Accounts of the Province of Alberta, 1939-1941.

The Treasury Department Ledger, Edmonton.

5. Local Authorities Board (LAB) (Alberta):

LAB, Application for Annexation, March 9, 1971. (Concerns the MacEwan Glens application, Calgary.)

— hearings re: Annexation of Jasper Place and other lands to the City of Edmonton, 1963.

— Transcript of Annexation Hearings re: R. Bolster Property (Lot A), March 3, 1969.

Transcript of proceedings, Annexation No. C-20-A, City of Edmonton, re: Alldritt Construction Ltd., held in Edmonton Court House, room 9, March 4, 1970.

Transcript of proceedings of hearings before the Local Authorities Board in regard to the Proposed BACM Annexation of Land, May 19, 20, 21, 1970.

Transcript of public hearings, Annexation C-20-A4, City of Edmonton South-East Development Area, held at Edmonton Court House, room 9, November 24, 1970.

D: Intermediate and Regional Organizations (Alberta)

Calgary Regional Planning Commission, "Guide Sheet as to replies and suggested action resulting from referral of the Preliminary Regional Plan," February 1, 1971.

— *Minutes,* April 14, May 7, 1971.
— *Preliminary Regional Plan,* July 29, 1963, and *Amendments,* May 1, 1964, and October 1, 1965.
Edmonton District (now Regional) Planning Commission, "The Edmonton District Water Supply: A Preliminary Study," 1960.
— *Annual Reports,* 1961-1970.
— Meeting, October 7, 1970, Item XIV.
Edmonton Regional Planning Commission staff, re: *Spruce Grove Development Plan,* August 24, 1970.
Urban Crisis: Alberta Municipal Finance Study, prepared by the Cities of Alberta, The Alberta Urban Municipalities Association, and the Public and Separate School Boards in each city, January 8, 1968.
The Urban Fiscal Problem — Piecemeal or Aggregate Solutions? Position Paper, The Alberta Urban Municipalities Association, 64th Annual Convention, 1970.

E: Municipal (Alberta)

1. Edmonton:

Adams, T. E., Commissioner of Economic Affairs, City of Edmonton, *1972 Current Budget Overview,* January 17, 1972.
Bargen, P., Chief Commissioner, *A Review of Provincial Involvement in the Land Assembly Program,* September 8, 1969.
Gillespie, W. E., Roadway Design Engineer, City of Edmonton, "Progress Report on Edmonton's Roadway Program," presented to the Edmonton Chamber of Commerce Council Meeting, September 16, 1970.
Hanson, E. J., *The Potential Unification of the Edmonton Metropolitan Area,* a Report prepared for the City of Edmonton, 1968.
The City of Edmonton, *City Boundaries and a Unitary Form of Government, A Proposal,* Brief submitted to the Metropolitan Affairs Committee of the Provincial Government, March 1972.
— *Estimates of Capital Expenditures for the Years 1971-1980,* Summary.
— *The General Plan,* Bylaw 3279, adopted May 18, 1971.
— "Capital Estimates — Source of Funds, Summary," 1970.
City Commissioners; Report to City Council, November 3, 1959.
City Commission Board Report No. 8, February 17, 1969.
— March 10, 1969.
City Commissioners' Report No. 4 to the Aldermen of the City of Edmonton, "1971 Current Budget," January 22, 1971.
City Council, *Minutes,* May 27, August 20, 1957; June 26, 1958; May 6, 24, November 28, 1960; February 13, March 13, May 5, 1961; February 19, June 25, July 3, 1962; April 6, 1964; November 14, 1967; February 12, March 25, May 27, 1968; February 2, April 29, October 23, 1969; April 26, 1971.
City Council, Annotated Agenda, July 19, 1971.
— Financing and Budgeting Committee, Report No. 7, April 1, 1969.
— Report of the Public Expenditure and Revenue Study Committee, March 1966.

City Planning Department, "Appendix II," *Amendments to the City of Edmonton General Plan,* May 1971.
— *BACM Proposal,* October 1969.
— *General Plan.*
— memorandum, May 1969.
— *A New Area for Residential Growth for the City,* January 30, 1969.
— Research Branch, *Records of Supply of Vacant Serviced Lots in Developing Residential Areas,* n.d.
— Report to City Council, February 1, 1971.
— *Residential Land Use Staging 1967-1981* June 1967.
— *Residential Land Use Study 1967-1971,* June 1967.
— *Revisions to the General Plan suggested at the Council Meeting held November 16, 1970, February 1, 1971.*
— Submission by the City of Edmonton at the Public Hearing, November 1970.
Edmonton Public School Board, "Accommodation Report and Building Program, 1971."
Re: Staging of Residential Development, Joint Brief by the Public and Separate School Boards presented to City Council, April 16, 1970.
Minutes of meeting with Mr. R. Orysiuk, Alberta Housing Corporation, Mr. P. Ellwood, City Planning Department and P. Bargen, Chief Commissioner, City of Edmonton, July 28, 1969.
Minutes of meeting of Alberta Housing Corporation and City representatives re land assembly, August 26, 1969.

2. Calgary:

City of Calgary, *Annual Report,* 1970.
— Current Budget 1972 Estimates.
— Evidence given before the Hellyer Task Force, November, 1968.
— *The Municipal Manual,* 1920.
— *The Municipal Manual,* 1970.
— Transportation System Bylaw No. 8500, Supplementary Information.
City of Calgary's Board of Commissioners, Submission to Calgary Regional Planning Commission, January 26, 1971.
City Commissioners' Report re MacEwan Glens, June 2, 1971.
City Commissioner's Report to the City Council's Operations and Development Committee, April 10, 1972.
Citizens' Budget Commission, *Report on 1971 Capital Budget,* Part 1, February 22, 1971.
Citizens' Budget Advisory Committee, "Summary of Observations by Citizens' Budget Advisory Committee Regarding City of Calgary 1972 Capital Budget."
Industrial Expansion Committee of the City of Calgary, *Minutes,* February 15, June 17, 1971.
Liaison Committee to Meet With Council Committee of the Municipal District of Rocky View, *Minutes,* April 8, 1971.
Planning Advisory Committee, *Minutes,* November 24, 1971.
Special Co-ordinating Committee on Housing, *Minutes,* November 16, 1971.

Standing Policy Committee on Finance and Budget, *Minutes,* December 22, 1971.

Technical Co-ordinating Committee for Land Use and Transportation Planning, *Minutes,* February 9, 1972.

City Planning Department, *The Calgary Plan: A General Plan prepared on behalf of the civic administration,* March 1970, and *Addendum,* April 1971.

— Director of Planning, *The Proposed Preliminary Regional Plan — 1970,* report submitted to Calgary Regional Planning Commission, January 26, 1971.

— Report (on proposed MacEwan Glens annexation), March 30, 1971.

Director of Planning, Report to Calgary City Council, June 1, 1971.

Calgary School District No. 19, "Submission to the Local Authorities Board . . . ," n.d. *((circa* May 1971).

Separate Comments of Joseph Yanchula as a Member of Citizens' Budget Advisory Committee Regarding City of Calgary 1972 Capital Budget, January 1972.

(A City Alderman) Report to Calgary City Council "Re: MacEwan Glens Annexation and Development," February 24, 1972.

1972 Residential Development Agreement between the City of Calgary and the Urban Development Institute, draft.

3. Other Municipalities:

Municipal District of Foothills, *Minutes* of Council Meeting, January 1971.

Municipal District of Kneehill, *Minutes* of Council Meeting, January 18, 1971.

Municipal District of Kneehill, Submission to Calgary Regional Planning Commission, January 18, 1971.

Municipal District of Rocky View, *Minutes* of Council Meeting, August 11, 1970.

— Reply to Regional Planning Commission, January 26, 1971.

— "A Brief on Appeal to the Provincial Planning Board Regarding the Calgary Preliminary Regional Plan 1971," June 3, 1971.

"Regional Planning as Designed and Practised in the Southern Portion of the Province of Alberta with Particular Reference to the Region Surrounding the City of Calgary," A Brief by a Representative of the MD of Rocky View. Office files of Municipal District of Rocky View.

Town of High River, *Minutes* of Council meeting, January 13, 1971.

Town of Okotoks, *Minutes* of Council meeting, January 18, 1971.

Town of Spruce Grove, "Brief to the Department of Municipal Affairs: Regarding Finance Borrowing Requirements," prepared during 1971.

Village of Cockrane, *Minutes* of Council meeting, January 1971.

III: Letters

Calgary Assistant Deputy Director of Planning to the City's legal department, December 19, 1971.

Calgary Assistant Deputy Director of Planning to the City Commissioner of Operations and Development, December 28, 1971.

Calgary Commissioner of Operations and Development to Assistant Deputy Director of Planning, January 3, 1972.

Calgary Director of Planning to the City Engineer, re MacEwan Glens, February 1, 1971.

Calgary Director of Planning to Commissioner of Operations and Development, May 31, 1971.

(Memorandum from) Calgary Director of Planning to a member of his staff, December 10, 1971.

Calgary Property Taxpayers Association; letter received by Special Co-ordinating Committee on Housing, November 16, 1971.

Chairman of the Board of Trustees, Calgary School District No. 19, to Minister of Education, April 23, 1971.

Colborne, the Hon. F., Minister of Municipal Affairs, to His Worship, Dr. I. G. Dent, Mayor, City of Edmonton, July 11, 1969.

Dent, I. G., Mayor, City of Edmonton, to the Hon. F. Colborne, Minister of Municipal Affairs, July 16, 1969.

Director of Field Services, Department of Education, to Mr. Cote of Underwood, McClellan and Associates Ltd., January 25, 1972.

Director of the National and Historic Branch, Department of Indian Affairs and Northern Development, to Calgary Regional Planning Commission, December 29, 1970.

Frigon, Charles H., President of Edmonton Home Builders' Association, to the Mayor and Council, City of Edmonton, December 16, 1965.

Edmonton Home Builders' Association to the Mayor and Council, City of Edmonton, October 31, 1967.

Edmonton Home Builders' Association to the Mayor and Council, City of Edmonton, December 13, 1967.

Edmonton Home Builders' Association (signed by the President of EHBA) to Edmonton City Council, January 20, 1969.

Hamilton, J. W., of Imperial Oil Ltd., to Mr. Anthony Adamson, April 26, 1963.

Local Authorities Board to Calgary City Council, May 5, 1971.

Minister of Education to Chairman of the Board of Trustees, Calgary School District No. 19, June 9, 1971.

Minister of Highways and Transport to Calgary Regional Planning Commission, January 27, 1971.

Minister of Lands and Forests to the Calgary Regional Planning Commission, January 25, 1971.

Minister of Municipal Affairs to the Mayors of Edmonton and Calgary, July 11, 1969.

A Representative of Carma Developers to a City of Calgary Commissioner, re MacEwan Glens, March 9, 1971.

A Representative of the County of Strathcona to the City Solicitor, October 19, 1970.

Three Edmonton Councillors on the Edmonton Regional Planning Board to the Executive Secretary of the Alberta Urban Municipalities Association, undated (written sometime before January 29, 1971).